W9-CFQ-265

SCOTT FORESMAN

SOCIAL STUDIES

ILLINOIS

PEARSON

Scott
Foresman

Editorial Offices: Glenview, Illinois • Parsippany, New Jersey • New York, New York
Sales Offices: Boston, Massachusetts • Duluth, Georgia • Glenview, Illinois •
Coppell, Texas • Sacramento, California • Mesa, Arizona

www.sfsocialstudies.com

TEACHER REVIEWERS

Peggy L. Beauchamp
4th Grade Teacher
Turner School District #33
West Chicago, Illinois

Bernice Bellamy
4th Grade Teacher
Judge Billy Jones Elementary School
East St. Louis, Illinois

Lois M. Hickey
Forest View Elementary School, District 59
Arlington Heights, Illinois

ISBN: 0-328-24106-7

Copyright © 2008, Pearson Education, Inc.

4 5 6 7 8 9 10 V057 12 11 10 09

Contents

Unit 1 The Land Called Illinois

"A rolling plain spread before us, the farther side bounded by timber, while the prairie itself was free from tree or brush. . . ."

—Dr. Robert Ridgeway describing Richland County, 1871

Unit 1 Continued

Unit 2 The Early People of Illinois

"We obtained all the Information that we could . . . the names of the peoples and of the places . . . [and] the Course of the great River. . . ."

—Father Jacques Marquette's diary (May 17, 1673)

Unit 3 The Great State of Illinois

> "Old America seems to be breaking up and moving westward."
>
> —Morris Birkbeck, a settler from Britain, describing migration to Illinois Territory, 1817

Unit 4 A Country in Conflict

"With malice toward none, with charity for all, with firmness in the right . . . to do all which may achieve and cherish a just and lasting peace . . ."

—Abraham Lincoln,
March 4, 1865

Unit 5 Illinois Grows

"We are moving forward to greater freedom, to greater security for the average man than he has ever known before in the history of America."

—Franklin D. Roosevelt, from a "Fireside Chat," 1934

Unit 6 Into the Twenty-first Century

"As an American I
believe in generosity,
in liberty, in the rights
of man. These are
social and political
faiths that are part . . .
of all of us."

—Adlai E. Stevenson

Reference Guide

★ BIOGRAPHY ★

Maps

Skills

Reading Social Studies

Map and Globe Skills

Thinking Skills

Research and Writing Skills

Chart and Graph Skills

Fact File

Citizen Heroes

Issues and Viewpoints

Then and Now

Here and There

Literature and Social Studies

Charts, Graphs, Tables, Diagrams, Time Lines

Let the Discovery Begin

Your world can turn upside-down on a roller coaster—like this one that has six loops and rolls. Many people experience thrills and chills every year on hundreds of roller coasters in the United States.

Make an exciting discovery of your own: Find a cool coaster in your state. Hyper coasters have at least one drop over 200 feet. Inverted coasters, in which the train travels under the tracks, may have several loops. There are many different types of roller coasters in the parks in Springfield, East Dundee and Gurnee. Let's go!

Building Citizenship Skills

There are six ways to show good citizenship: through respect, fairness, caring, responsibility, courage, and honesty. In your textbook, you will learn about people who used these ways to help their community, state, and country.

Respect
Treat others as you would want to be treated. Welcome differences among people.

Fairness
Take turns and follow the rules. Listen to what other people have to say.

Caring
Think about what someone else needs.

Responsibility
Do what you are supposed to do and think before you act.

Courage
Do what is right even when the task is hard.

Honesty
Tell the truth and do what you say you will do.

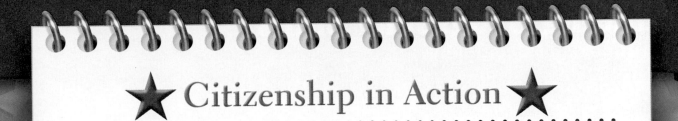

★ Citizenship in Action ★

Good citizens make careful decisions. They solve problems in a logical way. How will these students handle each situation as good citizens?

Decision Making

The students are choosing a pet for their classroom. The following steps will help them make a decision.

1. **Identify a situation that requires a solution.**
2. **Gather information.**
3. **Identify options.**
4. **Predict consequences.**
5. **Make your decision.**
6. **Take action to implement a decision.**

Problem Solving

Sometimes students argue at recess over whose turn it is to have a ball. Fourth graders can use the following steps to help them solve the problem.

1. **Identify a problem.**
2. **Gather information.**
3. **List and consider options.**
4. **Consider advantages and disadvantages.**
5. **Choose and implement a solution.**
6. **Evaluate the effectiveness of the solution.**

Building Geography Skills

Five Themes of Geography

Geography is the study of Earth. This study can be divided into five themes that help you understand why the Earth has such a wide variety of places. Each theme reveals something different about a spot, as the following example of the Shawnee National Forest shows.

Location

Where can something be found?
The Shawnee National Forest is in the southern tip of Illinois.

Place

How is this area different from others?
The Shawnee National Forest has canyons and forests.

Human/Environment Interaction

How have people changed this place?
People have made changes to better use Illinois's natural resources.

Movement

How has movement changed the region? People have left artifacts of their settlement.

Region

What is special about the Southern Forests and Hills Region?
Many waterways, hills, canyons, and forests cover the region.

Building Geography Skills
Map and Globe Skills Review

What Does a Globe Show?

This is an image of Earth. It lets you clearly see some of Earth's large landforms (continents) and bodies of water (oceans).

The image below shows Earth as it actually is.

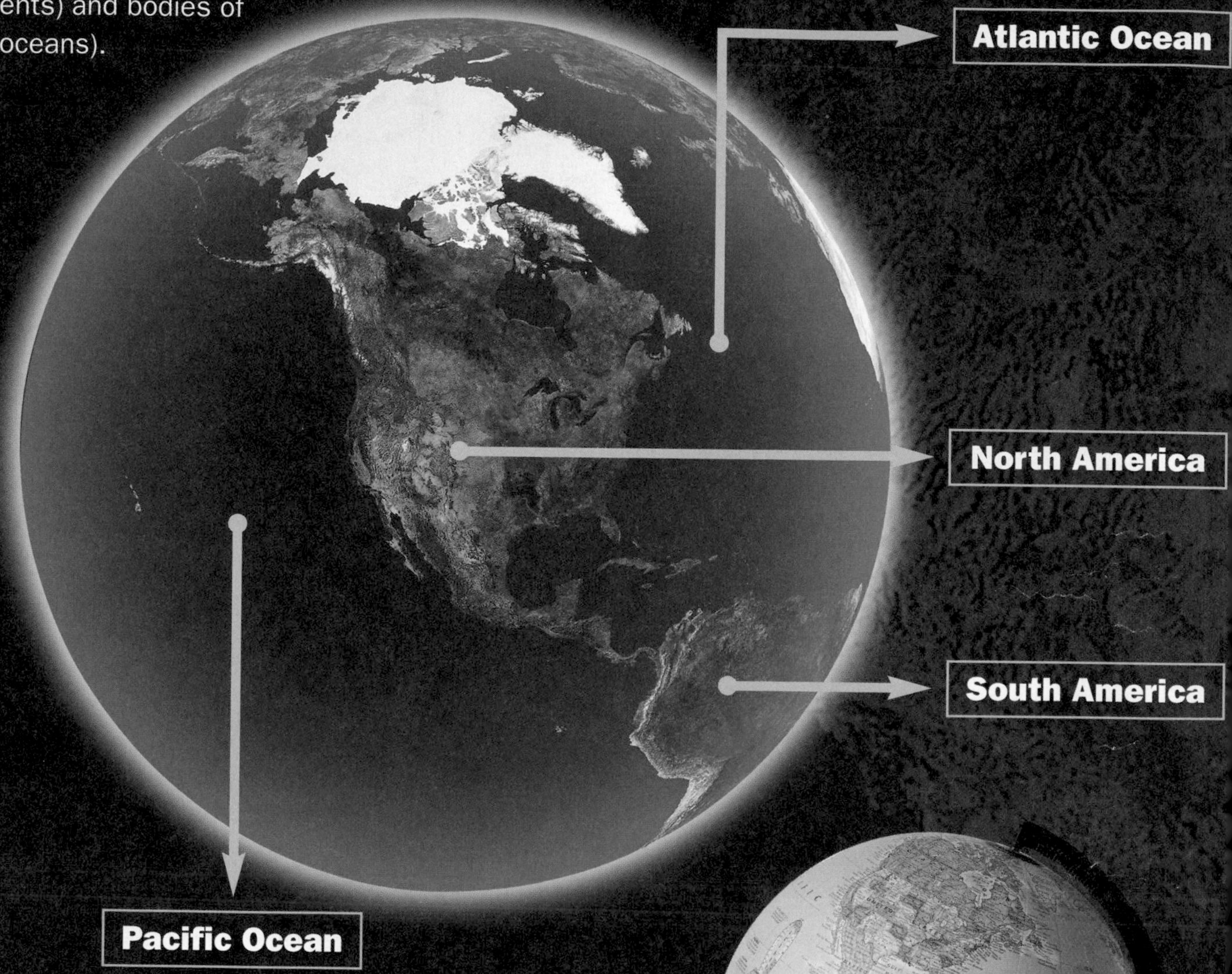

Atlantic Ocean
North America
South America
Pacific Ocean

NORTH
ATLANTIC
OCEAN

At the right is a **globe,** a small copy of Earth you can hold in your hands. It has drawings of Earth's seven continents and four oceans. Can you name the continents and oceans not shown here?

Also, a globe shows the two imaginary lines that divide Earth into halves—the **equator** and the **prime meridian.**

Hemispheres: Northern and Southern

Like any kind of a ball, you can see only half of Earth and a globe at a time. Half views of Earth have names—**hemispheres**—and the illustration at left below shows Earth separated into these views at the equator line. The **Northern Hemisphere** is the half north of the equator, which circles Earth halfway between the poles. However, there is only one way to see the Northern Hemisphere all at once. You have to turn a globe until you are looking down directly at the North Pole. The top picture below shows that view. What are the only continents not found, at least in part, in the Northern Hemisphere?

The **Southern Hemisphere** is the half of Earth south of the equator. The bottom picture below turns the globe until you are looking down directly at the South Pole. You see all of the Southern Hemisphere. Which hemisphere—Northern or Southern—contains more land?

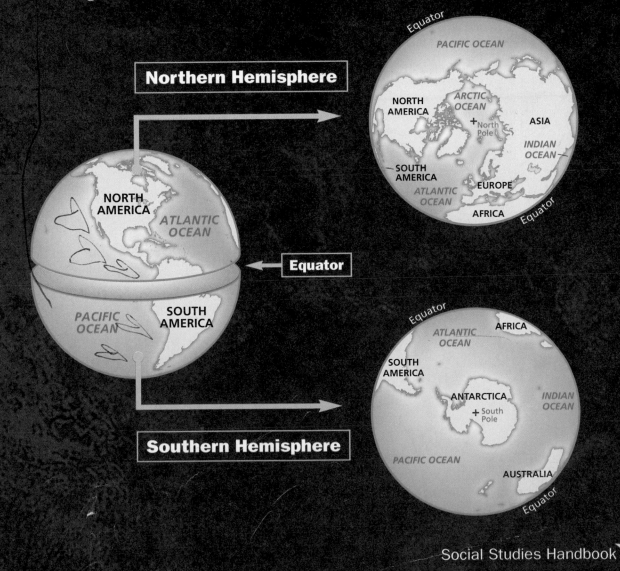

Building Geography Skills
Map and Globe Skills Review

Hemispheres: Western and Eastern

Earth has two other hemispheres. They are formed by dividing Earth into halves a different way, along the prime meridian. The prime meridian is an imaginary line that runs from the North Pole to the South Pole. It passes through Greenwich, England, an area of London. The **Eastern Hemisphere** is the half east of the prime meridian. The prime meridian passes through which continents?

The **Western Hemisphere** is the half of Earth west of the prime meridian. Which two continents are found entirely within this hemisphere? Which of the four oceans is not found in this hemisphere? In which two hemispheres is the United States found?

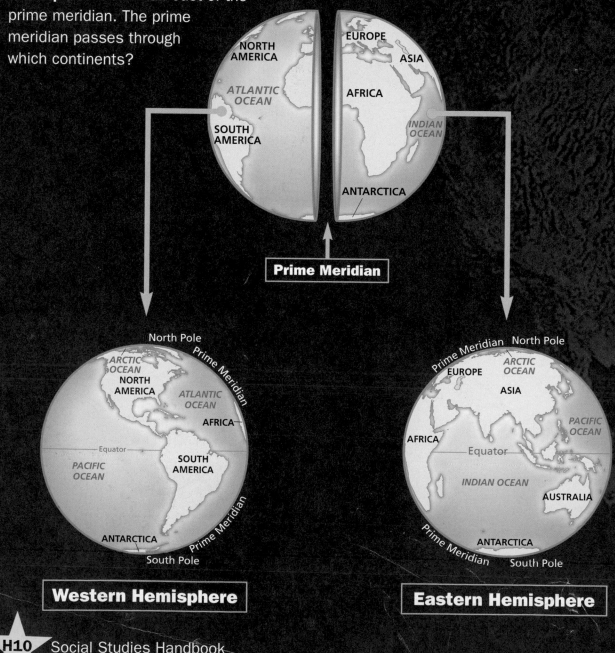

Prime Meridian

Western Hemisphere

Eastern Hemisphere

Understand Latitude and Longitude

Mapmakers created a system for noting the exact location of places on Earth. The system uses two sets of imaginary circles crossing Earth. They are numbered in units called **degrees.**

Lines of **latitude** are the set of circles that go east and west. The equator is 0 degrees (0°) latitude. From there, the parallel circles go north and south. They get smaller and smaller until they end in dots at the North Pole (90°N) and the South Pole (90°S). The globe below at the left is tilted to show latitude lines 15° apart up to the North Pole. Most of the United States falls between which degrees of latitude?

Lines of **longitude** are the set of circles that go north and south. They are all the same size. The prime meridian is 0° longitude. However, from there, the degrees fan out between the North and South Poles. They are not parallel and go east and west for 180°, not just 90°. The globe below at the right shows longitude lines 15° apart. They meet at 180° on the other side of Earth directly behind the prime meridian. Most of Africa falls between which degrees of longitude?

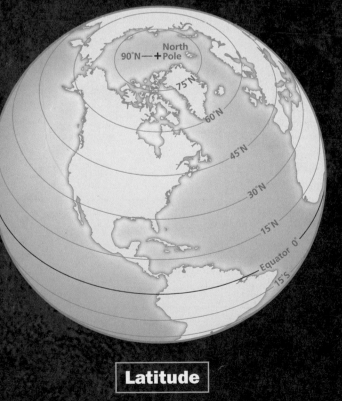

Latitude

Longitude

Building Geography Skills

Map and Globe Skills Review

Use Map Features to Help Read Maps

A **title** tells what a map is about. What is the title of the map at right?

A **political map** shows the location of cities, states, and countries. A **physical map** shows landforms such as mountains and rivers. What kind of map is on this page?

A **compass rose** is a decorative pointer that shows the four major directions, or **cardinal directions.** On the compass roses in this textbook, **north** is straight up and is marked with an *N.* **East** is to the right, **south** is straight down, and **west** is to the left. This compass rose also shows **intermediate directions,** which are pointers halfway between cardinal directions. Intermediate directions are **northeast, southeast, southwest,** and **northwest.** What direction would you travel to go from Chicago to Peoria?

Many maps have **symbols** in a **key** or legend. A symbol is a mark, a drawing, or a color that stands for something else. What mark at right shows cities with more than 500,000 people?

Some maps have a **locator,** a small globe or map found in a corner. It shows where the main map is located within a larger area of Earth. Describe what you see in the locator.

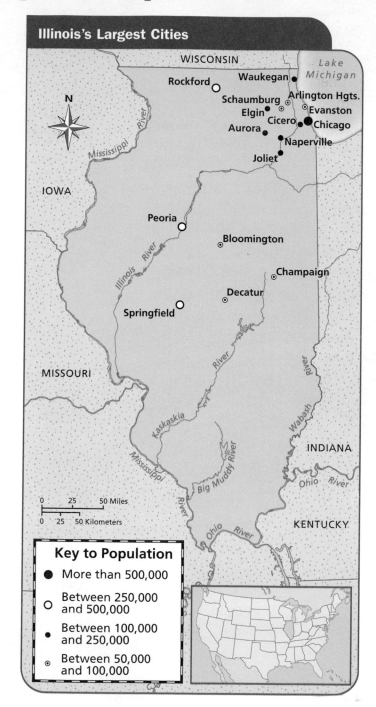

Illinois's Largest Cities

Key to Population
- More than 500,000
- Between 250,000 and 500,000
- Between 100,000 and 250,000
- Between 50,000 and 100,000

Use a Map Scale

A **scale** will help you figure out how far it is in real miles or kilometers from one point on a map to another. It can be found in a nearly empty spot to make it easier to read. Starting at 0, a scale marks off tens, hundreds, or even thousands of miles. The measurement chosen depends on the size of the area shown. One way to use the scale is to hold the edge of a scrap of paper under the scale and copy the scale onto it. Then you can place your copy directly on the map and measure the distance between two points. Use the scale on the map to help you find out about how far it is in miles from the Carl Sandburg Home to the Grant Home. Then find out about how far it is in miles from the Elijah Lovejoy Monument to Fort Kaskaskia.

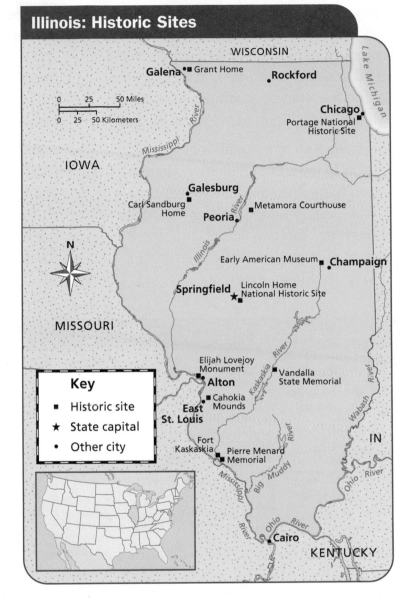

Illinois: Historic Sites

Building Geography Skills
Map and Globe Skills Review

Use a Grid

A city map shows the streets of a city. It might also show some points of interest to visitors or natural features such as rivers and lakes. What natural features do you see on the map of downtown Chicago below? Point to and name a street.

This map also has a **grid.** A grid is a system of rows of imaginary squares on the map. The rows of squares are numbered and lettered along the edges of the map. You can find places where rows of numbers and letters cross. All you need is an index.

An **index** is an alphabetical listing of places you are likely to be searching for. The letter-number combination attached to each then tells you where the two rows cross. In this square, you can find the place you are looking for.

Suppose you want to find where City Hall is. Look for "City Hall" in the index. You'll see that it is located in B2. Find the B row on the map and move your finger to where the 2 row crosses it. Now find the Sears Tower the same way.

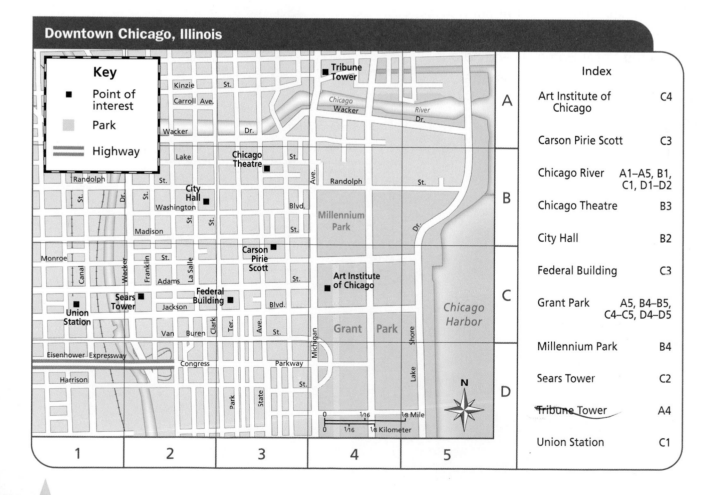

Downtown Chicago, Illinois

Use Latitude and Longitude for Exact Location

Lines of latitude and longitude act similarly to city-map grid rows. Think of latitude as the east-west rows of letters on the grid map on the opposite page. Think of longitude as the north-south rows of numbers. The point where latitude and longitude cross is an exact location. If a city or place is found at or nearly at where latitude and longitude lines cross, the city or place takes those two numbers as its exact location.

Look at the map of Illinois. The location of the Lincoln Home National Historic Site is about 40°N, 89°W. The Portage National Historic Site is about 42°N, 88°W. What lake is about 38°N, 89°W?

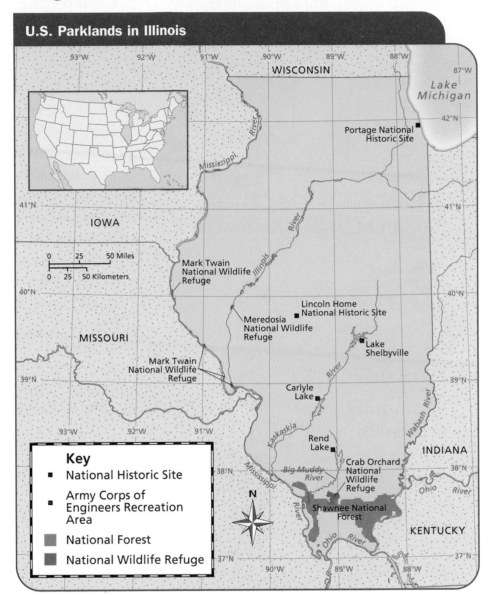

U.S. Parklands in Illinois

Key
- National Historic Site
- Army Corps of Engineers Recreation Area
- National Forest
- National Wildlife Refuge

Building Research Skills
Gather and Report Information

When you need to find information for a report or a project, you can use three main resources:

Technology
Resources

Print
Resources

Community
Resources

The information you find can be from either primary or secondary sources. **Primary sources** are documents that were recorded by people who were at an event and saw it or who lived at that time. Journals, diaries, letters, and photographs are all primary sources. When you write an entry in your journal, you are creating a primary source. Items from an event such as a program or a store receipt are also primary sources.

Secondary sources are descriptions of an event written by people who have researched the event. These people tell what they learned from reading about the event and looking at primary sources, but they were not there.

Look for both kinds of sources when you do research. This section of Building Research Skills will help you find information and report what you have found.

Technology Resources

There are many kinds of technology resources that you can use when you look for information. You can use the Internet, CD-ROMs, software such as databases, television programs, and radio programs.

The Internet is a system of linked computers that can store information for others to find and use. The World Wide Web, which is part of the Internet, has a great deal of information.

It is important to know who put the information on the Web. Check your information by finding at least three reliable sources that give similar information.

On the computer, you can mark the sites you want to look at again. Click BOOKMARKS at the top of your screen and choose ADD BOOKMARK.

Search Engines

Before you turn on your computer, you need to plan your research. If you want to do research on the Illinois River, write down some words that you can use to search the World Wide Web. The name of the river would be a good search term. The name of a town through which it passes might also be a good search term. If you have not used the Internet before, you might want to ask a librarian, teacher, or parent for help.

Search by Subject To find the search engines, click on SEARCH or NET SEARCH at the top of your screen. Type one of your subject words into the search engine field. Then click SEARCH or GO.

If you can't find what you need, try a different search engine. It might be connected to a different site with more information.

Search by Address World Wide Web sites have Uniform Resource Locators, or URLs. A URL is like an address. If you already know the address of a site that might have the information you need, type it in the LOCATION/GO TO box in the upper left corner of the screen. Here is an example of a URL: *www.sfsocialstudies.com*

Print Resources

There are many reference tools that you can use to find information. A reference tool is any source of information.

Books are reference tools. Libraries often have reference shelves with books such as atlases and almanacs, as well as dictionaries and encyclopedias. Usually, reference materials in a library cannot be checked out, but you can use them to look up information while you are at the library.

Encyclopedia

An encyclopedia is a collection of articles, listed alphabetically, on various topics. When you need information quickly, an encyclopedia is a good choice. Electronic encyclopedias, available on the Internet or CD-ROM, have sound and video clips in addition to words.

Dictionary

A dictionary is a collection of words, their spellings, their meanings, and their pronunciations. Words in a dictionary are arranged in alphabetical order. If you find a word you don't understand, you can look it up in a dictionary. Many dictionaries also include abbreviations, names, and explanations of well-known people and places.

Atlas

An atlas is a collection of maps. Some atlases have one particular kind of map. Others have a variety of maps showing elevation, crops, population, natural resources, languages spoken, or historical developments. Teachers and librarians can help you find the type of atlas that would be best for your search.

Almanac

An almanac is a book or computer resource that lists many facts about a variety of topics. Almanacs are usually organized in sections by topic. Much information is given in charts, tables, and lists. Almanacs are usually updated every year, so they have the latest statistics on populations, sports records, political events, weather, and other interesting topics.

Nonfiction Books

A nonfiction book is a book on a particular topic that was researched and written by someone who knows about that topic. Nonfiction books can be a valuable reference tool.

In a library, all nonfiction books are numbered and placed in order on the shelves. Books on the same subject are grouped together. Whether your library has a computer catalog or a card catalog, you can search for a book by title, subject, or author.

Once you find information on a book that looks interesting, look for the call number of the book. That number will guide you to the area of the library where you will find the book. A librarian can help you.

974.73
H27
   ILLINOIS
   Heinrichs, Ann
      Illinois (This Land Is Your Land)
   [by] Ann Heinrichs
   Compass Point Books: Mankato, MN, 2002
     48 p. ill (some col.)

   I. ILLINOIS (THIS LAND IS YOUR LAND)
   I. Title

Subject

974.73
H27
   ILLINOIS (THIS LAND IS YOUR LAND)
   Heinrichs, Ann
     Illinois (This Land Is Your Land)
   [by] Ann Heinrichs
   Compass Point Books: Mankato, MN, 2002
     48 p. ill (some col.)

   I. ILLINOIS (THIS LAND IS YOUR LAND)
   I. Title

Title

974.73
H27
      Illinois (This Land Is Your Land)

     48 p.

   I. ILLINOIS (THIS LAND IS YOUR LAND)

Author

Periodicals

A periodical, such as a newspaper or a magazine, is published on a regular basis, usually daily, weekly, or monthly. Most libraries have a special periodicals section. Many magazines and newspapers also have their own Web sites where you can read all or part of the publication online.

Libraries have guides that list magazine articles by subject. The *Children's Magazine Guide* and the *Readers' Guide to Periodical Literature* are the most frequently used guides. These guides list information by title, subject, and author. Each entry in the guide lists the title of the article or story, the author, the name and date of the magazine, and the page number on which the article appears. If your library has the magazine, you can find it and read the article.

Ridgeville Public Library Catalog

HOME   SEARCH

Author: Heinrichs, Ann
Title: Illinois (This Land Is Your Land)
Published: Compass Point Books: Mankato, MN, 2002
Local Call No: 974.73 H27

Community Resources

In addition to the Internet and reference tools, the people in your community are good sources of information. If you are studying the owls at the Shawnee National Forest, you can talk to people at government agencies, such as the Division of Wildlife Resources. Or try a local college, university, or a nearby natural history museum for information. Perhaps you know someone who has visited the forest often for many years. You might want to interview that person for more information.

Interviews

An interview is a good way to find out what people in your community know. This means asking them questions about the topic you are studying. Follow these steps:

Plan Ahead

- List the people you want to interview.
- Call or write to ask if you can interview them. Let the person know who you are and why you need information.
- Agree on a time and place for the interview.
- Find out about the topic that you want to discuss.
- Write down questions that you want to ask at the interview.

Ask/Listen/Record

- Ask questions clearly.
- Listen carefully. Be polite. Do not interrupt.
- Write notes so that you will remember what was said. Write down the person's actual words. If possible, use a tape recorder to help you remember.

Wrap-up

- Thank the person when you are finished with the interview.
- Send a thank-you note.

Use a Survey

Another way to find information in your community is to conduct a survey. A survey is a list of questions that you ask people, recording everyone's answers. This gives you an idea about what the people in your community know, think, or feel about a subject. You can use yes/no questions or short-answer questions. To record the things you find out, you will want to make a tally sheet with a column for each question. If you were doing research about a river that is near your town, your survey sheet might look like this:

The following steps will help you plan a survey:

- Write down a list of questions.
- Where do you want to conduct the survey? How many people do you want to ask?
- Use a tally sheet when conducting the survey so that you can record people's answers.
- After the survey, look through the responses and write what you found out.

Write for Information

Another way to get information from people or organizations in your community is to e-mail or write a letter asking for information. Use these steps:

- Plan what you want to say before you write.
- Be neat and careful about spelling and punctuation.
- Tell who you are and why you are writing.
- Thank the person.

Our River

	How long have you lived in our community?	How often do you visit the river?	How has the river changed since you have been coming here?	What do you like about the river?
Person 1	30 years	Not very often—I haven't been there for years.	It seems dirtier. I hear that there are fewer fish because it's so polluted.	It's peaceful there.
Person 2	Two years	Every day	There used to be more ducks and a few geese. Now there are more geese.	I like fishing. I throw everything back, but it's relaxing to fish.

Writing a Research Report

Prewrite

- Decide on a topic for your report. Your teacher may tell you what kind of report to research and write and how long it should be.
- Write down questions that you want to find out about the topic.
- Use different sources to find information and answer your questions. Be sure to write down all your sources. This list of sources is called a bibliography.
- Take notes from your sources.
- Review the notes you have taken from all your sources.
- Write down the main ideas that you want to write about. Two or three ideas are enough for most reports.
- Make an outline, listing each main idea and some details about each main idea.

Write a First Draft

- Using your outline, write what you have learned, using sentences and paragraphs. Each paragraph should be about a new idea.
- When you use exact words from your sources, write down the source from which you got the information. This list will become part of your bibliography.

Revise

- Read over your rough draft. Does it make sense? Do you need more information about any main idea?
- Change any sentences or paragraphs that do not make sense. Add anything that will make your ideas clear.
- Check your quotations to make sure they are accurate.

Edit

- Proofread your report. Correct any errors in spelling, grammar, capitalization, sentence structure, and punctuation.

Publish

- Add pictures, maps, or other graphics that will help make your report interesting.
- Write or type a final copy as neatly as possible.

The Illinois River

The Land Called Illinois

Begin with a Primary Source

"A rolling plain spread before us, the farther side bounded by timber, while the prairie itself was free from tree or brush. . . ."

—Dr. Robert Ridgway describing an 1871 visit to Fox Prairie in Richland County

Robert Marshall Root painted **Shelbyville on the Kaskaskia** in 1918.

Meet the People

John Deere

1804–1886

Birthplace: Rutland, Vermont

Inventor, manufacturer

- Designed and manufactured plows that worked well in sticky prairie soil
- Moved from Grand Detour to Moline and started a successful manufacturing company
- Served as president of Deere & Company until his death

John Muir

1838–1914

Birthplace: Dunbar, Scotland

Naturalist

- Noticed the shrinking oak and hickory forests in Illinois
- Urged the federal government to protect the national forests
- Wrote about conservation and convinced many people of its importance

Joy Morton

1855–1934

Birthplace: Nebraska City, Nebraska

Businessman, conservationist

- Owned the Morton Salt Company in Chicago
- Turned his home in Lisle, Illinois, into the Morton Arboretum in 1922
- Encouraged the planting and conservation of trees and other plants from all parts of the world

Florence Fifer Bohrer

1877–1960

Birthplace: Bloomington, Illinois

Illinois state senator

- Early supporter of women's rights
- First woman to serve as Illinois state senator (1924 to 1932)
- Supported laws that helped protect children, women, the poor, and prisoners

1800	1850	1900

1804 • John Deere 1886

1838 • John Muir 1914

1855 • Joy Morton 1934

1877 • Florence Fifer Bohrer

Students can research the lives of significant people by clicking on *Meet the People* at **www.sfsocialstudies.com**.

Jim Edgar

b. 1946

Birthplace: Charleston, Illinois

Governor of Illinois

- Served as governor from 1991 to 1999
- Helped the state add 38,000 acres of land for recreation
- Signed legislation creating the Illinois Conservation Foundation

Tom Skilling

b. 1952

Birthplace: Aurora, Illinois

Broadcast meteorologist

- Took his first job in broadcasting at age 14
- Uses up-to-date technology to make and deliver weather forecasts
- Won Emmy Award and other awards for his television reports and specials on weather topics

1950   2000   2050

1960

b. 1946 • Jim Edgar

b. 1952 • Tom Skilling

The Land Called Illinois

Main Idea and Details

Knowing how to recognize the main idea and supporting details will help you understand what you read.

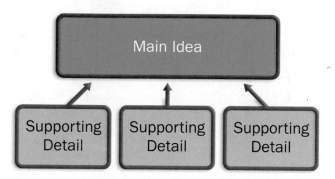

- A main idea is the most important idea in a paragraph or longer passage.

- The supporting details give more information about the main idea.

- A main idea can be stated or unstated. When it is unstated, the reader must use the important details to figure out the main idea.

> Read the paragraph. The **main idea** and **supporting details** have been highlighted.

In Chapter 1, you will read about the land called Illinois. Illinois is an exciting place to live. You can visit the state capital and historical sites. You can watch lake freighters unload at the port of Chicago. You can even see frozen waterfalls at Starved Rock State Park.

A Varied Land

How would you describe Illinois to someone who has never been here? You might say that Illinois is a varied land.

The geography of Illinois changes as you go from north to south. The northern part of the state has a mix of cities and farms. Although most of this area is flat, some hills rise above the plains. The highest point in the state is in the north. The central part of the state has many farms, and most of them are located on flat plains that are good for growing food. In the southern part of Illinois are hills, canyons, and forests.

Even the weather of Illinois is varied. Our state reaches so far from north to south that our weather often varies from one area of the state to another. Also, in any specific area of the state, the weather can be very different from one day to another.

Illinois also has a variety of natural features and resources. Our state's rich farmlands and other natural resources such as coal and minerals have long benefited Illinoisans. The rivers, lakes, streams, and canals of Illinois serve both as cargo routes and as places to enjoy nature. Our forests provide homes for wild animals like owls, coyotes, and badgers. They also provide recreation for hikers, canoists, and birdwatchers.

Apply it!

Use the reading strategy of identifying the main idea and details to answer these questions.

1 Which sentence states the main idea of the passage?

2 Identify a detail that supports the main idea that the weather of Illinois is varied.

3 What is the main idea of the last paragraph?

CHAPTER 1

The Geography of Illinois

Lesson 1

Chicago
The third largest city in the nation, Chicago is a center for travel and trade.

1

Lesson 2

Pearl
Illinois is a land of natural wonders and, from time to time, natural hazards as well.

2

CANADA

NORTH
AMERICA

2

1

UNITED STATES

Chicago

ILLINOIS

Pearl

PACIFIC OCEAN

ATLANTIC OCEAN

Gulf of Mexico

MEXICO

Why We Remember

Illinois is the place we call home. Yet how many of us have visited every part of Illinois? Who can describe all the different places, people, and events that make our state great? For hundreds of years, people have celebrated Illinois by writing books, painting pictures, and taking photographs. And today we still enjoy the things that make Illinois special—its rivers and prairies, its forests and rolling hills, and its people. You probably know a lot about our state already. Now you can learn even more!

Chicago

A Bird's Eye View of Illinois

PREVIEW

Focus on the Main Idea
Illinois is a large state located near the middle of North America.

PLACES
Illinois
Midwest
Lake Michigan
Chicago
Mississippi River
Wabash River
Ohio River
Illinois River

PEOPLE
Florence Fifer Bohrer

VOCABULARY
continent
glacier
landform
prairie
hub
waterway

You Are There As the plane lifts off the ground, you look out the window. The earth falls away below you. You see the highways, factories, and office towers of the city. Soon you are soaring over neat farms and straight roads arranged in patterns, like the squares on a quilt. As the plane climbs higher, you realize that the river below connects one city to another one nearby. Barges and cargo ships look tiny, floating in the sunshine. A freight train crawls along its tracks by the river. Interstate highways cross the countryside. "Wow!" you say. "That's Illinois!"

▶ Chicago's O'Hare Airport is one of the busiest in the nation.

EAST
190
Chicago
NEXT RIGHT

WEST
190
O'Hare ↗

Main Idea and Details As you read, look for main ideas and details about Illinois's location and geography.

Target Skill

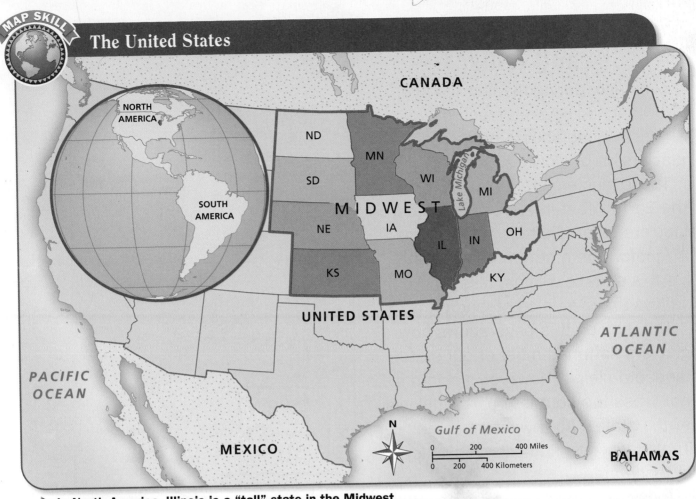

▶ In North America, Illinois is a "tall" state in the Midwest.

MAP SKILL Location *Describe the location of Illinois in the United States.*

Finding Illinois

On a globe, you can see that the surface of Earth is covered with water and land. The largest bodies of water are the world's oceans. The seven large areas of land are called **continents.** Earth's continents are Africa, Antarctica, Asia, Australia, Europe, North America, and South America. The United States of America is on the North American continent.

Look at the map of the United States. You will find the state of **Illinois** near the center of our country. Illinois is part of an area of the United States that we call the **Midwest** region.

On the map, you can see that Illinois borders several other states in the Midwest. Wisconsin lies to the north. To the west are Iowa and Missouri. At the southern tip is Kentucky, and Indiana is to the east.

On the map, you will also see that Illinois is bordered by **Lake Michigan** on the northeast corner. Because Lake Michigan is one of the Great Lakes, Illinois is sometimes called a Great Lake state.

REVIEW In what region of the United States is Illinois located?
⟳ **Main Idea and Details**

11

Prairies, Forests, and Hills

Long ago, during the last Ice Age, snow and ice covered much of North America. Huge sheets of ice called **glaciers** crept slowly southward.

These glaciers gradually changed the Earth's features. In other words, glaciers created different landforms. A **landform** is a natural feature on Earth's surface. Plains, hills, and valleys are examples of landforms.

The map on this page shows how glaciers flattened most of our state's land into plains. However, glaciers did not cross the southern part of Illinois or the state's northwestern corner. That is why you find hills and valleys in those areas.

Today the land in Illinois is mostly flat. Much of the state is covered with prairies. A **prairie** is a large area of flat or rolling grassland with few or no trees. The soil in this land is especially good for growing crops and plants.

The geography of northern Illinois includes prairies, hills, and the shore of Lake Michigan. Many cities are found in northern Illinois, including **Chicago**, the third largest city in the nation.

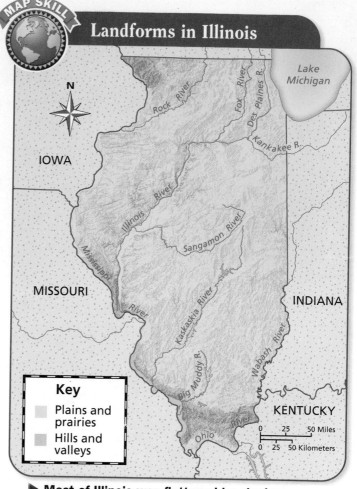

MAP SKILL Landforms in Illinois

Key
- Plains and prairies
- Hills and valleys

▶ Most of Illinois was flattened by glaciers.

MAP SKILL Use a Landform Map *What types of landforms can you find in southern Illinois?*

▶ Prairies are the most common landform in Illinois.

12

▶ The Shawnee National Forest is in the southern tip of Illinois.

The middle part of Illinois has many prairies. Like northern Illinois, this area supports many farms.

In the southern part of Illinois, the prairie ends. You see not only hills and valleys but also canyons and forests.

The beautiful scenery of Illinois has inspired many artists, writers, and musicians. In 1925 State Senator **Florence Fifer Bohrer** helped pass a law making "Illinois" the state song, celebrating the state's varied landscape.

REVIEW What kinds of landforms do you find in Illinois?

⟳ **Main Idea and Details**

Literature and Social Studies

Illinois

Archibald Johnston wrote music and C. H. Chamberlain wrote words for a song called "Illinois." Below is the first verse of the song.

By thy rivers gently flowing,
  Illinois, Illinois,
O'er thy prairies verdant growing,
  Illinois, Illinois,
Comes an echo on the breeze.
Rustling through the leafy trees,
  and its mellow tones are these,
  Illinois, Illinois,
And its mellow tones are these,
  Illinois.

Map Adventure

Illinois, the Nation's Transportation Hub

You will remember that Illinois is almost in the middle of the nation. The state's central location means that many people and goods travel into, out of, or through Illinois.

This map shows some of the roads, rivers, railroads, and airports that serve Illinois. Look at the map and follow these steps.

1. Put your finger on the city of Cairo.

2. With your finger, trace the path that you would take to Peoria if you were traveling by boat.

3. From Peoria, trace the path you would travel to Chicago if you were traveling by airplane.

4. From Chicago, figure out how many ways there are to travel back to Cairo.

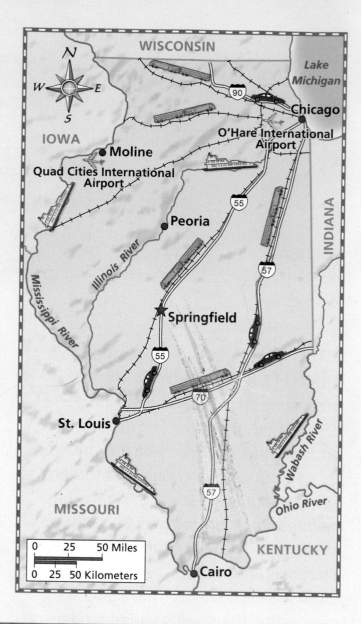

The Middle of Everything

The map above shows how our state connects to other parts of the nation—and to the world. Because of its location, Illinois has developed into a transportation **hub**, or center, for the United States.

From the earliest history of Illinois, people have traveled by water. As you can see on the map, Illinois is almost surrounded by water. Lake Michigan serves as the northeastern border, and the **Mississippi River** forms the entire western border of the state. The southeastern border of Illinois is formed by the **Wabash River** and the **Ohio River**. One of our state's most important rivers is the **Illinois River**. It is 273 miles long and stretches across the central part of the state. Illinois has more than 1,118 miles of **waterways**, or rivers and canals on which goods and people can travel.

Major highways connect cities in Illinois. For example, Interstate Highway 57 links Chicago with other cities such as Champaign, Urbana, and Cairo. Likewise, Interstate 55 links Chicago to such cities as Springfield and East St. Louis.

In addition, railroads from all over the nation lead to Illinois. The city of Chicago serves as a hub for air travel as well. Chicago's O'Hare International Airport is one of the world's busiest airports.

Because Illinois seems to be in the middle of everything, many people see Illinois as a great place for companies to do business. The people of Illinois know that the products they produce, like grain and machinery, are used all over the country and even around the world.

Because of its location, Illinois is a great place for sharing ideas—ideas that travel all over the world through telephones, computer lines, and radio and television signals. This makes Illinois an exciting place to live.

REVIEW What are the important rivers that flow through or along Illinois? ⊙ **Main Idea and Details**

Summarize the Lesson

- **Illinois is located on the North American continent in the Midwest region of the United States.**
- **Five states and Lake Michigan border Illinois.**
- **Illinois has a variety of landforms.**
- **Illinois is an important trade and transportation hub.**

LESSON 1 ⟩ REVIEW

Check Facts and Main Ideas

1. Main Idea and Details On a separate sheet of paper, write details to support the following main idea.

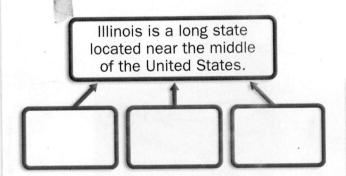

Illinois is a long state located near the middle of the United States.

2. On what continent are the United States and Illinois located?

3. How do northern and central Illinois differ from the southern part of the state?

4. What forms of transportation are important in Illinois?

5. **Critical Thinking: Apply Information** How does the location of Illinois make it an important center of trade and transportation?

Link to ⟶∞∞⟵ Language Arts

Where Did Our Rivers Get Their Names? The names for the Wabash, Ohio, and Mississippi Rivers come from Native American names. Use the Internet, reference books, and other resources to look up the meanings of these three names.

Glaciation

During the last Ice Age, glaciers covered the area of the world that later became the state of Illinois. Deep ice also covered many other parts of the world. Glaciers are thought to have shaped the landscape of Illinois and the world. Glaciers still exist in the world's high mountain ranges. Over the last 2 million years, glacier buildup has happened each time a cold glacial period follows a warmer interglacial period. Today, Earth is thought to be in an interglacial period of glacier melting. When a glacier melts, it leaves bouldery gravel mounds. The gravel heaps are known as the terminal moraine of the glacier.

Pacific Ocean   *Pack ice*

Satellite Snowscape
This satellite photo of Alaska's coast shows how ocean water freezes into pack ice.

Continental Ice Sheet
Most of Greenland and Antarctica are covered with ice sheets thousands of feet thick. The ice thins near the ocean. Near the northwest Greenland coast, valley glaciers cut through surrounding mountains. The glacial ice pushes and carries rocks along its path.

Ice sheet

Terminal moraine

Valley glacier

Crevasse (kreh VAS), a deep crack

From Snow to Ice

Snow is made of fluffy flakes that trap air in the new snow layer. As new snow melts in the day and refreezes at night, it gets more compact. This mature snow is called *névé* (nay vay). It soon packs into hard ice.

Freshly fallen snow

New snow

Névé

Glacier ice

Air squeezed out

Impermeable ice (ice that fluids cannot pass through)

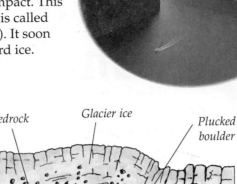

Creating Fjords

When Ice Age glaciers melted, seas rose and flooded valleys carved by glaciers in mountainous coasts. In Norway, these deep inlets are called fjords (FEE ords). Fjords also cut into the New Zealand, Antarctic, and Canadian coasts.

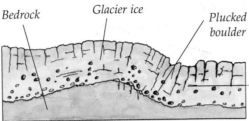

Bedrock *Glacier ice* *Plucked boulder*

Meltwater seeps into cracks

Plucked Rock

Glaciers "pluck" rocks and carry them in the moving ice. Water seeps into cracks in rock formations, freezes, and lifts fragments off the valley floor into the ice as it passes.

Boulder clay cemented with lime

Scratch marks made by rock fragments trapped in glacier

Glacial fragments in rock

Glacier Grater

Rock fragments trapped in the flowing glacier polish the floor of the glacial valley. The smooth stone face (left) shows glacial scratches. Glaciers carry loads of boulders, stones, fragments, and rock powder. When a glacier melts, it dumps this material in great heaps, which harden into boulder clay (right).

Limestone rock from Switzerland

Chalky boulder clay

17

Pearl

Illinois's Physical Environment

PREVIEW

Focus on the Main Idea
Illinois is the home of a variety of ecosystems.

PLACE
Pearl

PEOPLE
Tom Skilling
Joy Morton
Jim Edgar

VOCABULARY
climate
temperate climate
precipitation
growing season
natural hazard
meteorologist
ecosystem
environment
conservation
arboretum

▶ Hailstones

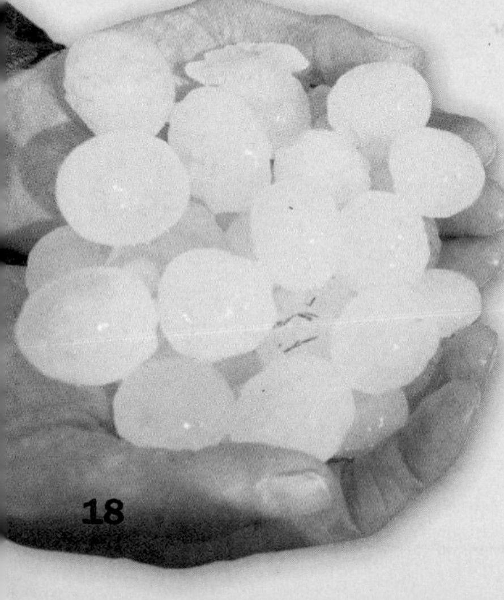

You Are There "I just heard a weather alert on the radio," your mother warns. "We need to go downstairs right away." For a few minutes, you read your book quietly in the basement. Then something starts hitting the house. It sounds like rain, only louder. Soon the noise is so loud that you think it is raining rocks.

After the racket stops, you both go upstairs and look out the window. The sun has come out, but your yard is full of little balls of ice! You run outside with a bucket to collect some of them. To the west, a sunset stretches over the plains. To the east is a rainbow, shining against the dark clouds as they move away.

 Main Idea and Details As you read, look for main ideas and details about Illinois's climate, weather, and ecosystems.

Illinois Climate

City	Average temperature	Average precipitation	Average growing season
Galena	47°F	34"	155 days
Springfield	53°F	37"	180 days
Cairo	58°F	48"	205 days

Source: Illinois State Water Survey

▶ **Location causes variations in climate within Illinois.**

The Climate of Illinois

If a person from another country asked you to describe today's weather in your part of Illinois, you would be able to answer easily. What if that person asked about our state's climate? **Climate** is the pattern of weather in a region over time.

Describing the climate of Illinois can be complicated. Illinois has a **temperate climate,** meaning that it has cool winters and warm summers.

Landforms and bodies of water also affect climate. For instance, Lake Michigan affects the temperature and **precipitation,** or rain and snow, of the northeastern part of the state.

Both temperature and precipitation affect the length of the **growing season,** the number of days in which it is warm enough to grow most crops. The growing season in southern Illinois averages 50 days longer than the growing season in northern Illinois.

REVIEW What kind of climate does Illinois have?
⟳ **Main Idea and Details**

Natural Weather Hazards

Because of its midwestern location and its climate, Illinois gets its share of bad weather, or weather hazards. A **natural hazard** exists when weather or some other force poses a danger to people or property. Illinoisans face tornadoes, floods, blizzards, and lightning storms—not to mention cold and heat waves. One such weather hazard happened when the community of **Pearl,** in Pike County, was hit by the Great Flood of 1993.

Tom Skilling, an Illinois meteorologist, tries to warn people about weather hazards before they happen. A **meteorologist** (mee tee uh ROL uh jist) is a scientist who studies climate and weather. Skilling gives details on what to do if rivers rise to flood level or if conditions are right for a tornado.

REVIEW What types of dangerous weather occur in Illinois? **Summarize**

▶ **In the summer of 1993, the Illinois River flooded tiny Pearl, Illinois.**

19

Illinois Ecosystems

An **ecosystem** is a group of plants and animals that live together in a natural environment. For example, the wild prairie of Illinois is home to milkweed, prairie cordgrass, and black-eyed Susans, as well as pocket gophers, coyotes, bobolinks, and badgers. Floodplains support river birch and slippery elm trees, as well as many snakes and insects. In our forests, you find white pine, tamarack, walnut, and cypress trees, in addition to owls, bobcats, and salamanders.

Prairie

Black-Eyed Susans

Pocket Gopher

Prairie Chicken

Cotton Tail Rabbit

Bobolink

Coyote

Prairie Cordgrass

Prairie Milkweed

Floodplains

Slippery Elm

Mallards

Great Egret

Blue Gill

Cattails

Dragon Fly

Forest

Pileated Wood Pecker

Bobcat

Deer Mouse

Soft Pine

Salamander

Horned Owl

White-Tailed Deer

Preserving Illinois

As you probably know, people's actions sometimes can damage the **environment,** or natural surroundings. For example, many of our state's forests have been chopped down for lumber and to make room for crops. Plowing prairies into farmland also has destroyed habitats.

Conservation is the protection of important resources. In the 1920s, for example, a Chicago businessman named **Joy Morton** turned his home and the lands he owned into an arboretum. An **arboretum** is a place that encourages conservation of trees and other plants. Conservation also can mean using fewer resources or reusing materials like glass and aluminum.

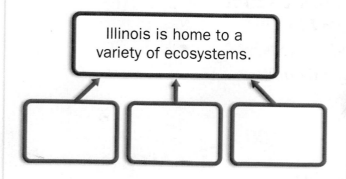

▶ Recycling keeps useful materials from being wasted.

In 1994 Governor **Jim Edgar** signed legislation creating the Illinois Conservation Foundation. The foundation provides money to groups to clean up lakes, replant forests, and teach children how to help the environment.

REVIEW Why is conservation important for the environment? **Draw Conclusions**

Summarize the Lesson

- Illinois has a temperate climate.
- Illinois faces natural hazards such as flooding, tornadoes, and heat and cold waves.
- Illinois is home to a variety of ecosystems.
- Through planning and conservation, Illinois can conserve and protect important resources.

LESSON 2 ⟩ REVIEW

Check Facts and Main Ideas

1. ◉ **Main Idea and Details** On a separate sheet of paper, write details to support the following main idea.

> Illinois is home to a variety of ecosystems.

```
┌──────┐  ┌──────┐  ┌──────┐
│      │  │      │  │      │
└──────┘  └──────┘  └──────┘
```

2. What two factors have an effect on the climate in Illinois?

3. How did human beings disturb the wild prairie ecosystem?

4. What are three weather hazards that can occur in Illinois?

5. **Critical Thinking:** *Cause and Effect* Explain how temperature and precipitation affect the growing season of an area.

Link to ━◁○○▷━ **Art**

Picture a Weather Event Read a description of a tornado, a flood, or another example of dangerous weather. Then create a drawing, painting, or collage that shows how the weather looks or feels.

Tom Skilling
b. 1952

As a child in Aurora, Illinois, Tom Skilling became interested in weather and broadcasting. When he was only fourteen years old, Tom took his first job at a local radio station. In college Skilling studied science and news writing, and at the same time he continued to work in radio and television. Skilling decided he wanted to be a meteorologist. He has been a meteorologist in Chicago since 1978.

Tom Skilling reports on weather in newspapers and on television. He has also made videos about unusual weather subjects. For instance, "It Sounded Like a Freight Train," examines tornadoes. Many schools use "When Lightning Strikes" to teach children about the causes and effects of lightning.

Have you ever wondered why weather forecasters are called *meteorologists*, even though they don't study meteors? Tom Skilling explains:

> *"The use of the term* meteorology *dates back to early Greece. In Aristotle's time, anything that was suspended in or fell from the sky was called a* meteor, *including rain, snow, hail, rainbows, and meteoroids."*

BIOFACT

In the 1990s Skilling was host of "The Cosmic Challenge," a television program in which children answered questions about space.

Learn from Biographies

Name some of the weather hazards about which Tom Skilling has produced videos.

Students can research the lives of significant people by clicking on *Meet the People* at **www.sfsocialstudies.com.**

Use an Elevation Map

What? An **elevation map** shows you how high the land is. Elevation is height above sea level. A place that is at sea level is at the same height as the surface of the ocean's waters. Elevation is usually measured in feet or meters above sea level. At sea level, elevation is 0 feet or 0 meters.

Elevation maps often use color to show ranges of elevation. The map on page 25 shows the average height of the land in Illinois. You have read that Illinois has a variety of landforms, including prairies, valleys, and hills. The map will help you understand the elevations of landforms in Illinois.

Why? An elevation map helps you see the different heights of landforms. It can also show the direction in which a river flows because rivers flow from higher to lower elevations.

How? To use an elevation map, first scan the map. Then read the map key. Finally, compare the information in the key with the areas shown on the map.

Look at the map on the next page. Notice that there are number ranges next to each color on the map key. They show the range of elevation that each color represents. You can see that dark green is used to show the lowest elevations. The range for dark green is between 0 and 400 feet above sea level.

▶ **The lowest elevation in Illinois is along the banks of the Mississippi River.**

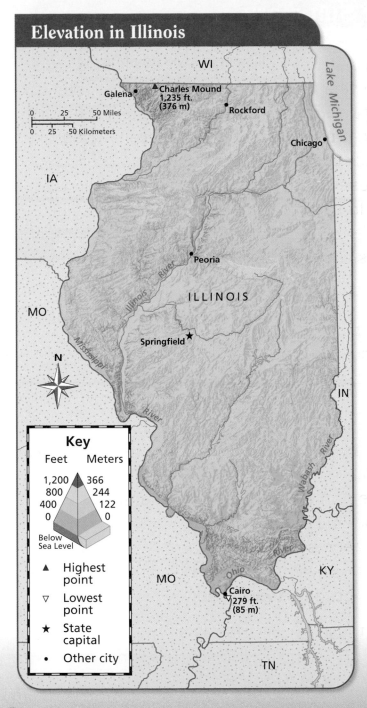

Elevation in Illinois

WI

Galena

▲ Charles Mound
1,235 ft.
(376 m)

Rockford

Lake Michigan

0   25   50 Miles
0   25   50 Kilometers

IA

Chicago

MO

Peoria

ILLINOIS

Illinois River

Springfield ★

N

Mississippi River

IN

Key

Feet   Meters

1,200   366
800   244
400   122
0   0

Below
Sea Level

▲ Highest
   point
▽ Lowest
   point
★ State
   capital
• Other city

Wabash River

MO

Ohio River

Cairo
279 ft.
(85 m)

KY

TN

Now look in the northwest corner of the map to find Charles Mound. At about 1,235 feet above sea level, this is the highest point in Illinois. With your finger, follow the Mississippi River down toward the southern tip of the state. Cairo, Illinois, is only 279 feet above sea level.

Think and Apply

❶ What elevation range does light green represent on the map?

❷ Calculate the difference in feet between the highest and the lowest points in Illinois.

❸ Is most of Illinois closer to the highest or the lowest point in elevation?

For more information, go online to the *Atlas* at **www.sfsocialstudies.com**.

Chapter Summary

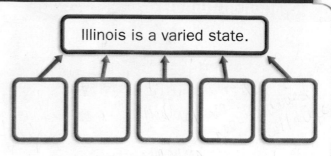

Main Idea and Details

On a separate sheet of paper, write details to support the main idea.

Illinois is a varied state.

Vocabulary

Match each word with the correct definition or description.

1. **continent** (p. 11)

2. **prairie** (p. 12)

3. **hub** (p. 14)

4. **climate** (p. 19)

5. **ecosystem** (p. 20)

6. **conservation** (p. 22)

a. the pattern of weather in a region over time

b. a large area of land on Earth

c. a group of plants and animals that live together in a natural environment

d. center

e. large area of flat or rolling grassland with few or no trees

f. the protection of important resources

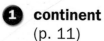

People and Places

Write a sentence about each of the following people and places. You may use two or more of the items in a single sentence.

1. **Midwest** (p. 11)

2. **Lake Michigan** (p. 11)

3. **Chicago** (p. 12)

4. **Florence Fifer Bohrer** (p. 13)

5. **Mississippi River** (p. 14)

6. **Illinois River** (p. 14)

7. **Tom Skilling** (pp. 19, 23)

8. **Pearl** (p. 19)

9. **Jim Edgar** (p. 22)

Internet Activity

To get help with vocabulary, people, and places, select the dictionary or encyclopedia from *Social Studies Library* at **www.sfsocialstudies.com**.

Facts and Main Ideas

1 What three rivers lie along the borders of Illinois?

2 Where in Illinois are canyons and forests found?

3 What is a temperate climate?

4 **Main Idea** In what ways is Illinois "in the middle of everything"?

5 **Main Idea** What are some of the hazardous weather events that occur in Illinois?

6 **Main Idea** What are some plants and animals that live in Illinois?

7 **Critical Thinking:** *Cause and Effect* What sort of effects did glaciers have on the land we call Illinois?

Write About Geography

1 **Write a postcard** to a friend or relative who has never visited Illinois. Include a description of interesting landforms or waterways.

2 **Write a poem** in which you describe two or three of the plants or animals that live in the natural environments of Illinois.

3 **Write a 24-hour weather forecast** for Illinois. Imagine that the forecast will be printed in the newspaper. Include information about temperature, winds, precipitation, and storm activity that might affect any part of the state.

Apply Skills

Use an Elevation Map

Look at the elevation map below. Then answer the questions.

1 How do you know that the map below is an elevation map?

2 What features of the map help you see the different heights of places in Illinois?

3 What conclusion can you draw about the physical geography of Illinois from looking at an elevation map?

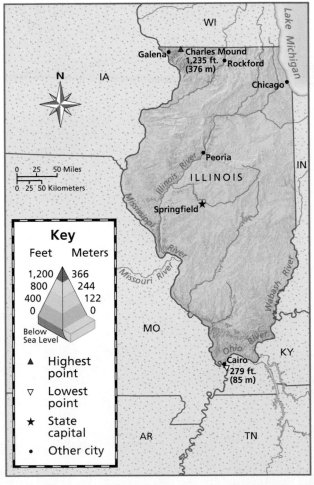

CHAPTER 2

The Natural Regions of Illinois

Lesson 1

Northern and Central Plains

A section of wild prairie shows how the Northern and Central Plains may have looked 200 years ago.

1

Lesson 2

Southern Forests and Hills

Forests still cover the southern part of Illinois.

2

Why We Remember

How often have you stepped outdoors and suddenly noticed something special about the place where you live? Perhaps it is the particular song of a bird, the damp smell of trees, or the way a river curls through one section of a city. Each region of Illinois has its own special qualities. Over the years these qualities have attracted people to live and work in Illinois. Farmers recognized the value of the rich prairie soil. Land developers saw ways that they might profit from the mineral deposits. Adventuresome people settled near rivers and other waterways.

Northern
and
Central
Plains

The Northern and Central Plains

PREVIEW

Focus on the Main Idea
The Northern Plains region is largely an industrial area, while farming is key in the Central Plains.

PLACES
Northern Plains
Central Plains
Charles Mound
Apple River Canyon State Park
Starved Rock State Park
Illinois Beach State Park

PEOPLE
John Deere

VOCABULARY
moraine
tributary
erosion

TERMS
urban
metropolitan area

▶ Wildflowers adorn the natural prairies of Illinois.

You Are There

As you look around you, the prairie stretches out as far as the eye can see. The grasses and wildflowers are almost as tall as you are! You and your family have decided to stop near this field to have a picnic and rest for a while before continuing on your driving tour of Illinois.

Your sister opens the picnic basket, and the sight of sandwiches and fruit makes your stomach growl. Maybe you should eat before exploring this wide, open land.

Walking through the field, you notice the different kinds of plants and flowers that cover the ground. Your neighborhood in Chicago looks so different. It's hard to believe that long ago, much of Illinois looked just like this!

Main Idea and Details As you read, look for main ideas and details about the Northern and Central Plains of Illinois.

Glaciers

As you learned in Chapter 1, glaciers once crossed most of the land we now call Illinois. In fact, ice sheets covered the area several times. Over hundreds of thousands of years, the climate shifted between cold and warm periods. What happened during these periods? During cold periods glaciers formed and began to drift across the land. In warm periods the glaciers melted.

Although glaciers disappeared from the Midwest about 10,000 years ago, you can still observe their effects. In Illinois glaciers flattened hills and valleys and left behind the rich prairie soil of the Northern and Central Plains region. The only parts of the region that glaciers did not reach were areas near Jo Daviess, Carroll, and Calhoun Counties.

REVIEW What caused the forming, melting, and reforming of glaciers in what is now Illinois? **Cause and Effect**

▶ Glaciers created landforms in Illinois.

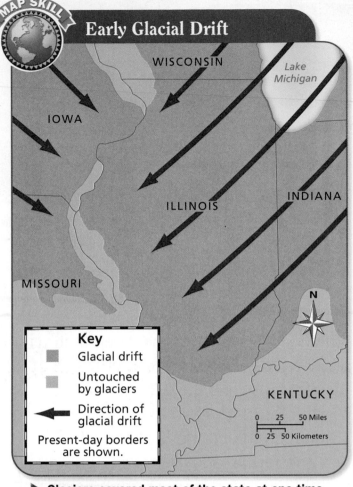

MAP SKILL Early Glacial Drift

Key
- ■ Glacial drift
- ■ Untouched by glaciers
- ◀ Direction of glacial drift

Present-day borders are shown.

0 25 50 Miles
0 25 50 Kilometers

▶ Glaciers covered most of the state at one time.

MAP SKILL Trace Movements on Maps *From which direction did glaciers travel across the area we now call Illinois?*

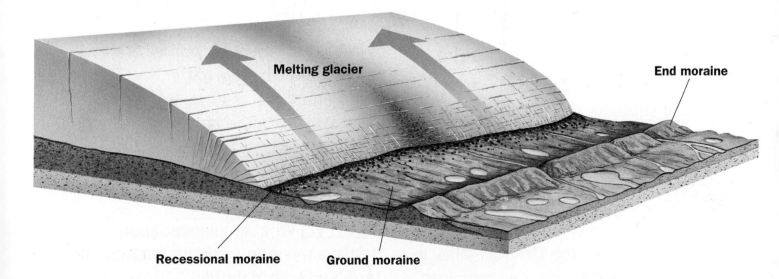

Melting glacier

End moraine

Recessional moraine

Ground moraine

▶ The rich soil of the Illinois prairies attracted many farmers.

From Lake to Rolling Hills

If you had traveled to the **Northern Plains** in the early days of Illinois statehood, you would have seen that prairies, or grasslands, covered much of the region. During the 1800s settlers came to build farms in this area.

Although the prairie is made up of rich and fertile land, its tough sod was a problem for farmers. Over and over they had to scrape thick sod from their plow blades.

How was this problem solved? **John Deere,** a settler in Grand Detour, Illinois, developed a curved plow blade on which soil did not stick. Deere's invention made farming in the Northern Plains easier and more productive.

As more people settled in Illinois, the Northern Plains changed. Today the area still supports many farms, but it is becoming more **urban.** It is best known for its cities and industries. Cities such as Moline and Kankakee are centers of manufacturing, often of machines and farming equipment.

Further south are the **Central Plains.** In some places glaciers created **moraines,** or ridges of dirt and rocks that were carried and deposited by a glacier. Like the Northern plains, flat prairie once covered most of the Central Plains.

Farming is very important in this region because of the rich soil left by glacial drifts. Three of Illinois's major rivers flow through the Central Plains. The Sangamon River is a tributary of the Illinois River. A **tributary** is a river that flows into a larger waterway. The Sangamon River joins the Illinois River near Beardstown, Illinois. The Illinois River itself is a tributary of the Mississippi River. The Kaskaskia River, another tributary of the Mississippi River, also runs through the Central Plains.

In the northwestern corner of Illinois, the flat land of the Northern and Central Plains gives way to rolling hills. Why does the landscape change here? Glaciers did not reach this area. Small towns, such as Galena, dot these hills.

REVIEW What challenge faced settlers trying to plow the prairies into farmland? ⟳ **Main Idea and Details**

Landmarks and Sights

If you were taking a trip to some of Illinois's landmarks, you could start at the summit, or highest point, in the state, **Charles Mound.** Located in Jo Daviess County, less than one-half mile from the Wisconsin border, this site stands 1,235 feet above sea level. The gentle, rolling land is covered with pastures and grazing cows.

Your trip might take you to nearby **Apple River Canyon State Park** in northern Illinois. There the Apple River slices through hilly, rocky ground. Centuries of erosion have left deep canyons in the rocks. **Erosion** occurs

▶ Starved Rock State Park has year-round beauty.

▶ Sand dunes are a common feature at Illinois Beach State Park.

when water or wind wears away soil or stone. You might be lucky enough to see deer and rabbits wandering through the park. Meanwhile, if you look up, you could see some eagles or hawks soaring overhead. Amid these natural wonders, people picnic, hike, and camp.

At **Illinois Beach State Park,** along the sandy shores of Lake Michigan, a very different landscape appears. Sand dunes contain more than 650 species of plants, including prickly pear cactus, cattails, and bluejoint grass, growing in or near the water.

In Illinois's north-central area, on the Illinois River, **Starved Rock State Park** is home to 18 sandstone canyons. When snow and ice melt in the spring, thrilling waterfalls appear in each canyon. Near the Illinois River grow forests of oak, cedar, and pine trees. Elsewhere, hickory trees tower over witch hazel and black huckleberry plants. Wildflowers bring color to the prairie soil.

REVIEW How has erosion shaped the canyons of Apple River Canyon State Park? ⊙ **Main Idea and Details**

Major Cities in Illinois

▶ Decatur's Milliken University (above) and the Lincoln Home National Historic Site in Springfield (below)

▶ The Tinker Swiss Cottage Museum in Rockford (above) and Chicago's Buckingham Fountain (right)

Major Cities			
City	Population	Major Industry	Culture
Rockford	150,115	Machine tools, furniture, farm implements	Tinker Swiss Cottage Museum
Chicago	2,896,016	Steel, food production, printing	Art Institute of Chicago, Buckingham Fountain
Peoria	112,936	Heavy machinery, trailers	Lakeview Museum of Arts and Sciences
Champaign	67,518	Light manufacturing	Krannert Art Museum and Kinkead Pavilion
Decatur	81,860	Tractors, tires, communications	Milliken University
Springfield	111,454	Tractors, electronics, paint	Lincoln Home National Historic Site

Population Source: Illinois Census 2000

Urban and Metropolitan Areas

Chicago is the heart of northeastern Illinois as well as the state's largest urban center. This famous city is home to nearly 3 million people. Many other people live in Chicago's **metropolitan area**, or a city and its surrounding areas.

As pointed out in Chapter 1, Chicago is a transportation hub. Materials are carried to Chicago, and products made there are shipped to other places. The city supports industries such as steel, food production, and printing.

▶ **The Sears Tower stands 1,450 feet high. It is the tallest building in North America.**

Many people visit Chicago for its culture. Perhaps you have attended plays, concerts, or festivals, such as the Viva! Chicago Latin Music Festival. Or you may have explored the city's many museums, such as the Museum of Science and Industry, the Art Institute of Chicago, or the Du Sable Museum of African American History.

REVIEW What important industries are found in Chicago?
⊙ Main Idea and Details

Summarize the Lesson

- **The Northern Plains have changed from prairies to a mix of cities and farmland.**
- **The Northern and Central Plains are home to many natural landmarks.**
- **Chicago is a center of population, industry, and culture.**

LESSON 1 REVIEW

Check Facts and Main Ideas

1. ⊙ **Main Idea and Details** On a separate sheet of paper, copy the chart below and write details supporting the following main idea.

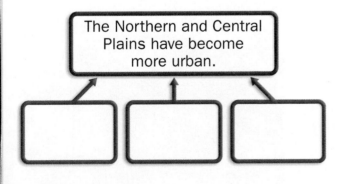

The Northern and Central Plains have become more urban.

2. How did glaciers shape the land of the Northern and Central Plains?
3. What are some of the natural landmarks of the Northern and Central Plains?
4. How are the cities of the Northern and Central Plains similar?
5. **Critical Thinking:** *Cause and Effect* How has being a transportation hub affected the culture of Chicago?

Link to ⚬⚬ Mathematics

Make a List Use a recent reference book or the Internet to learn the populations of ten cities in the Northern and Central Plains. Present the cities in order of population from largest to smallest.

John Deere
1804–1886

As a young boy growing up in Middlebury, Vermont, John Deere learned the skills of a blacksmith. A blacksmith is a craftsperson who makes and repairs metal items such as horseshoes and tools for working in the fields.

BIOFACT

In 1846 Deere sold about one thousand plows. By the mid-1850s, he was selling more than 13,000 plows each year.

Deere moved to Illinois in 1836. Farmers were always bringing in their iron plows for sharpening. They complained that the thick clay soil stuck in the plow's blade and made it dull. They could not plow more than a few feet at a time before they had to stop and clean the blade. That gave Deere an idea. He used a broken steel saw to make the blade for a new plow. It worked much better than the old iron plow blades. John Deere was soon in the plow-making business. His new plow helped farmers work larger spreads of land.

John Deere once said,

> *"I will never put my name on a plow that does not have in it the best that is in me."*

Learn from Biographies

How did John Deere use problem-solving skills to improve the plow?

Students can research the lives of significant people by clicking on *Meet the People* at **www.sfsocialstudies.com**.

Illinois and Thailand
Crops and Water

Farms in Illinois and farms in Thailand, in Southeast Asia, raise important food crops. However, while corn is grown on many Illinois farms, rice is the most important crop on Thai farms. Corn is grown in soil that is moist, but not wet. Rice is planted in flooded fields called rice paddies.

Illinois

THAILAND

▶ Heavy rains in Thailand (below) allow farmers to grow rice in well-watered fields. On the other hand, Illinois farmers (right) often have to water their crops.

37

Use Inset Maps

What? An **inset map** shows a small area of a main map in greater detail. The area is outlined on the main map; then it is enlarged and reproduced near the main map. Each map has its own scale. **Scale** is a unit of measure that is used to represent an actual distance on Earth. Because the inset map shows a much smaller area, it uses a different scale. Notice that on the main map on page 39, half an inch represents 50 miles. On the inset map, half an inch represents 6 miles.

Why? Maps can give you different kinds of information. The main map provides information about the region including Illinois and the states that surround it. The inset map gives you more detailed information about Chicago and its metropolitan area. The amount of detail in a map is related to the amount of area it shows. A map covering a large area, such as the main regional map, shows fewer details. A map of a smaller area, such as the urban and metropolitan inset, gives more detailed information.

How? Look at the main map and the inset map on page 39. Notice that the main map shows midwestern cities. Now look at the inset map of the metropolitan area of Chicago. What information can you find on the inset map that you cannot find on the main map? The kind of map you use depends on the kind of information you need. What if you needed to find a particular highway in Chicago? You should use the inset map of metropolitan Chicago.

▶ **Downtown Chicago, as seen from Lake Michigan**

Midwestern Cities

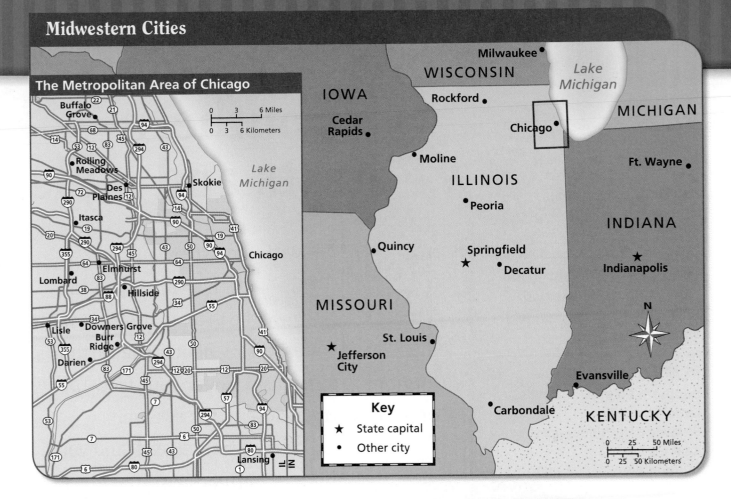

The Metropolitan Area of Chicago

Key
★ State capital
• Other city

The map of the midwestern cities will not show enough details to help you. If you want a map that shows the distance between Chicago and Indianapolis, the map of midwestern cities will contain the information you need.

For more information, go online to *Atlas* at **www.sfsocialstudies.com**.

Think and Apply

1. What does an inset map show?

2. Which of the two maps shown here would be better for determining the distance across the state of Illinois?

3. Which of the two maps helps you choose a route between Skokie and Chicago?

Southern
Forests
and Hills

Southern Forests and Hills

PREVIEW

Focus on the Main Idea
The Southern Forests and Hills region has rich soil and small towns.

PLACES
Southern Forests and Hills
Little Egypt
Shawnee National Forest
East St. Louis
Carbondale
Cairo

PEOPLE
John Muir
James Piggott

VOCABULARY
delta

▶ **Blue heron**

You Are There
With each step you take through the woods, you can *hear* the ground growing wetter. Luckily, you are wearing boots. The earth is beginning to "squish" under your feet. You must be getting close to the swamp.

You see tall cypress trees ahead, and you hear the sounds of warblers and tree frogs. After you come over the crest of a hill, you see the swamp—a huge pool of water covered with a blanket of bright green. The tour guide says that this green film is a plant called duckweed. Trees poke up from the water, their roots hidden below.

"Shhh!" whispers the guide, pointing to a bird at the swamp's edge. Your eyes widen. It's the first time you've ever seen a great blue heron.

Main Idea and Details As you read, look for main ideas and details that tell you about the Southern Forests and Hills.

Untouched by Glaciers

As glaciers drifted across land, they changed the landforms of Earth. As you learned in Chapter 1, landforms are natural features, such as plains, hills, and valleys, on the Earth's surface. During the Ice Age, glaciers affected all of Illinois except northern Jo Daviess and Carroll Counties, western Calhoun County, and the **Southern Forests and Hills** region. In the southern counties of Illinois, you find rolling hills, valleys, and canyons.

The Southern Forests and Hills region is bordered on the east by the Wabash River, on the south by the Ohio River, and on the west by the Mississippi River. Its northern border traces a line roughly across the state from East St. Louis through towns such as Mount Vernon and Carmi. How does this region differ from the Northern and Central Plains? You will find different landforms, trees and plants, and mineral resources in the Southern Forests and Hills region. The state's mining and oil industries are centered in the southern counties.

Several rivers serve as tributaries to the three large rivers that lie along the state's borders. The Embarrass and the Little Wabash Rivers empty into the

Glaciers in Illinois

▶ Glaciers did not reach the southernmost tip of the Southern Forests and Hills region.

MAP SKILL Place *In addition to the southernmost tip of the state, list the two places in the state that were untouched by glaciers.*

▶ Cypress trees are common in the swamps of the Southern Forests and Hills region of Illinois.

Wabash River. The Saline River feeds the Ohio River. And the Big Muddy and the Kaskaskia Rivers drain into the Mississippi River.

At the southern tip of Illinois is a region sometimes called **Little Egypt.** The region may have earned this unusual name because of the region's similar appearance to Egypt's Nile River valley.

REVIEW How does the Southern Forests and Hills region differ from the Northern and Central Plains regions? **Compare and Contrast**

41

Oak and Hickory Woods

To learn what Southern Forest and Hills was like hundreds of years ago, just look at the thick forests of oak and hickory trees in the region today. Much of this region is covered by the **Shawnee National Forest.** The only national forest in the state, Shawnee includes part of ten Illinois counties.

As shown in the photo on this page, these woods are a natural treasure. In the late 1800s, however, many people thought trees would always be around. **John Muir** made people realize that forests in Illinois needed to be protected. Today, these forests support many species of animals and plants.

If you visit the Southern Forests and Hills region to understand old Illinois landscapes, you can also see some of

Shawnee National Forest

▶ **Shawnee National Forest (above) is the largest wilderness area in Illinois.**

MAP SKILL Use a Map *What river borders more of the Shawnee National Forest?*

the state's most exciting landmarks. For example, the Trail of Tears State Forest, in western Union County, features some of the most rugged landscapes in Illinois. Fort de Chartres and Fort Kaskaskia, built by French explorers during the mid-1700s, show that the southern part of Illinois was the first area settled by European explorers.

REVIEW Parts of how many counties are covered by the Shawnee National Forest? ⟳ **Main Idea and Details**

42

Natural Landmarks

Shawnee National Forest is home to many of southern Illinois's natural landmarks. One of the forest's most famous sites is the Garden of the Gods. Here you can see sandstone cliffs and rock formations caused by erosion and temperature changes. Because of their shapes, some rock formations have gained interesting names, such as Camel Rock. The Pomona Natural Bridge is another landmark found in the Shawnee National Forest.

Many different types of forest grow within the Southern Forests and Hills region. For instance, dense forests of bald cypress or tupelo gum trees grow in the region's swamps.

To the north and east of the forests, the region features open, rolling hills and valleys. However, at the southernmost tip of the state, you will find a very different landform called a delta. A **delta** is a low-lying plain made up of soil left behind by rivers.

REVIEW What types of landforms are found in southern Illinois? **Summarize**

Pomona Natural Bridge

Millions of years ago, this sandstone bridge was a hard, solid cliff. Small cracks in the sandstone grew wider as the climate changed from freezing to warm and back to freezing. Waterfalls flowed over and through the cliff, and erosion slowly ate away at the stone. Today the stone bridge is 90 feet long, from 6 to 12 feet wide, and about 9 feet thick.

▶ Over many years, the solid stone cliff (far left) was transformed into the Pomona Natural Bridge.

Small Towns

The Southern Forests and Hills region is home to many small towns. In the late 1700s, Captain **James Piggott** operated a ferry service that crossed the Mississippi River from what is now **East St. Louis,** Illinois, to St. Louis, Missouri. Today bridges for automobiles and commuter and freight trains link the two cities.

Carbondale is located at the northern edge of Shawnee National

▶ **This 15-foot statue of Superman stands in the small town of Metropolis, Illinois. The Illinois state government officially named Metropolis as the Hometown of Superman in 1972.**

Forest. The city was settled when the Illinois Central Railroad reached the area in 1852. Today Carbondale is the center of a mining and agriculture area.

The Ohio and Mississippi Rivers meet at the small city of **Cairo,** in an area known as Little Egypt. The city serves as an important cargo port for southern Illinois.

REVIEW How are Cairo and East St. Louis similar? **Compare and Contrast**

Summarize the Lesson

• **The Southern Forests and Hills region was left untouched by glaciers.**

• **The region features forests, hills and valleys, and a delta.**

• **The Southern Forests and Hills region contains small cities.**

LESSON 2 ⟩ REVIEW

Check Facts and Main Ideas

1. **Main Idea and Details** On a separate sheet of paper, copy the chart below and write details to support the following main idea.

```
The Southern Forests and
Hills region contains varied
landforms.
```

2. Why is Shawnee National Forest so important to Illinois?

3. What caused the cliffs and rock formations in the Garden of the Gods?

4. What Illinois city is located where the Mississippi and Ohio Rivers meet?

5. **Critical Thinking: Make Inferences** How might southern Illinois be different if it had once been covered by glaciers?

Link to ⟛ Science

Make a Poster Use reference books and the Internet to compare and contrast the two types of swamps found in Illinois—scrub swamps and true swamps. Make a two-column poster that presents information on each type of swamp.

BUILDING CITIZENSHIP

Caring

⭐ Respect

Responsibility

Fairness

Honesty

Courage

Protecting the Planet

Our natural world must be respected and protected. Read about John Muir, a naturalist who has been called the "Father of our National Parks."

As a young man, John Muir took long walking journeys in Illinois and other states as well as in Canada. The purpose of these trips was to study the natural world.

During John Muir's lifetime, little was being done to protect natural resources. In Illinois the state's forests were shrinking. He wrote many articles that convinced people of the need to conserve wooded areas. He said,

▶ **President Theodore Roosevelt meets with John Muir (right) at Yosemite National Park.**

"Thousands of tired, nerve-shaken, over-civilized people are beginning to find out . . . that wilderness is a necessity."

Muir explained that the government must respect both its land and its citizens. Some government officials agreed, and Sequoia National Park and Yosemite National Park were established in 1890.

In 1903 Muir invited President Theodore Roosevelt to visit Yosemite. During this trip Muir convinced the President that the government must protect other forests, rivers, and parks all over the country. In the years that followed, President Roosevelt started new programs to conserve our environment.

Respect in Action

Research a person or group who is trying to protect the environment. How does that person's action show respect for the environment?

Chapter Summary

 Main Idea and Details

On a separate sheet of paper, write details to support the main idea.

> The regions of Illinois contain a variety of landforms and economic activities.

[ ]   [ ]

Vocabulary

Match each word with the correct definition or description.

1. **moraine** (p. 32)
2. **tributary** (p. 32)
3. **erosion** (p. 33)
4. **delta** (p. 43)

a. a ridge of dirt and rocks carried and deposited by a glacier

b. a river that flows into a larger waterway

c. a low-lying plain made up of soil left behind by rivers

d. a process that occurs when water or wind wears away soil or stone

People and Places

Write a sentence about each of the following people and places. You may use two or more of the names in a single sentence.

1. **John Deere** (pp. 32, 36)
2. **Apple River Canyon State Park** (p. 33)
3. **Illinois Beach State Park** (p. 33)
4. **Shawnee National Forest** (p. 42)
5. **John Muir** (pp. 42, 45)
6. **James Piggott** (p. 44)
7. **East St. Louis** (p. 44)
8. **Carbondale** (p. 44)

Facts and Main Ideas

1 How did glaciers shape the Northern and Central Plains regions?

2 Describe the landscape of Illinois Beach State Park.

3 Why is the southernmost part of Illinois sometimes called Little Egypt?

4 **Main Idea** What cultural attractions are found in Chicago?

5 **Main Idea** What natural resource helped the Central Plains of Illinois become an important farming region?

6 **Main Idea** What are two important natural landmarks of the Southern Forests and Hills region?

7 **Critical Thinking:** *Make Inferences* How does the Shawnee National Forest link Illinois's past with its present?

Write About Geography

1 **Write a list of ten words** that describe the form, movement, or effects of a glacier.

2 **Write the words to a song** about a favorite landscape or natural feature of Illinois.

3 **Write a newspaper editorial** about the importance of conserving forests and other natural areas in Illinois.

Apply Skills

Use Inset Maps

Look at the map and inset map on page 39. Then answer the questions.

1 Which of the two maps is an inset map?

2 What does the inset map help you learn?

3 What lake borders the metropolitan area of Chicago?

Internet Activity

To get help with vocabulary, people, and places, select the dictionary or encyclopedia from *Social Studies Library* at **www.sfsocialstudies.com**.

Laughing Corn

by Carl Sandburg

Carl Sandburg wrote hundreds of poems about the land and people of Illinois. In 1918 he published a book called Cornhuskers, *which contained the poem "Laughing Corn."*

In this poem Sandburg describes parts of nature as if they were living human beings. For instance, Sandburg gives the corn, wind, rain, and sun the ability to speak and listen to one another. In this way the poet helps readers imagine that an Illinois cornfield is truly alive.

There was a high majestic fooling
Day before yesterday in the yellow corn.

And day after to-morrow in the yellow corn
There will be high majestic fooling.

The ears ripen in late summer
And come on with a conquering laughter,
Come on with a high and conquering laughter.

The long-tailed blackbirds are hoarse.
One of the smaller blackbirds chitters on a stalk
And a spot of red is on its shoulder
And I never heard its name in my life.

Some of the ears are bursting.
A white juice works inside.
Cornsilk creeps in the end and dangles in the wind.
Always—I never knew it any other way—
The wind and the corn talk things over together.
And the rain and the corn and the sun and the corn
Talk things over together.

Over the road is the farmhouse.
The siding is white and a green blind is slung loose.
It will not be fixed till the corn is husked.
The farmer and his wife talk things over together.

Main Ideas and Vocabulary

TEST PREP

Read the passage below and use it to answer the questions that follow.

Illinois is a large state near the middle of the United States. It borders several other states: Wisconsin, Iowa, Missouri, Kentucky, and Indiana.

Illinois is almost surrounded by rivers. Those rivers and Lake Michigan have long helped people and goods travel to, from, and through our state. Today railroads and major highways crisscross Illinois. Railroads link the state with its five neighboring states and with the rest of the nation. Together with our waterways, the highways and railroads make it possible for goods that are grown or manufactured in Illinois to reach people all over the world. This is why Illinois is called a transportation <u>hub</u> for the United States. The city of Chicago serves as a hub for air travel as well.

Northern Illinois is made up of low plains where you find cities, factories, and farms. It contains several <u>metropolitan areas</u>. The northeastern corner of Illinois borders on Lake Michigan. Here you find the city of Chicago, a center for shipping and manufacturing. Chicago is the third largest city in the United States.

Central Illinois is mostly plains and farmland, with three major rivers. The most important river is the Illinois River. It starts in northeastern Illinois and flows across the state to join the Mississippi River. The Illinois River is a tributary of the Mississippi River. A tributary is a river that flows into a larger waterway.

Much of southern Illinois is covered by Shawnee National Forest. Spreading over nearly 300,000 acres, this forest includes part of ten Illinois counties. Two of the forest's most famous sites are the Pomona Natural Bridge and the sandstone rock formations at the Garden of the Gods.

1 According to this passage, how many states border Illinois?
A three
B four
C five
D six

2 In this passage <u>hub</u> means
A center.
B station.
C a river that flows into a larger river.
D training ground.

3 A <u>metropolitan area</u> is
A a floodplain.
B a center for shipping and manufacturing.
C a city and the surrounding area.
D a flat prairie good for farming.

4 Where is Pomona Natural Bridge?
A in northwestern Illinois
B near Lake Michigan
C near the Illinois River
D in Shawnee National Forest

Vocabulary

Match each vocabulary word to its definition.

1 **conservation** (p. 22)

2 **tributary** (p. 32)

3 **erosion** (p. 33)

4 **delta** (p. 43)

a. water or wind wearing away soil or stone

b. a river that flows into a larger waterway

c. a low-lying plain made up of soil left behind by rivers

d. protecting natural resources

Write and Share

Make a Booklet Form four groups, one for each lesson in Unit 1. Within your group, choose different topics from the lesson. Then write a one-page composition on your topic. Take time to illustrate the information you provide. Then, combine each group's information with the material from the other groups. You can make a class booklet called "Here's Illinois!" or "What's So Special About Illinois?" You might wish to donate the booklet to the school library.

Apply Skills

Use an Elevation Map to Describe a Trip
Study the elevation map of Illinois on page 25. Choose one town, city, or natural landmark to visit in each region. Trace the route while you describe the elevation changes you would pass through as you travel from one place to the other.

Read on Your Own

Look for these books in the library.

Discovery CHANNEL SCHOOL

UNIT 1 Project

Eye on Our Region

Take visitors on a video tour of your part of Illinois. Show what's great about it.

1 Form a group. Choose an interesting topic about your part of Illinois.

2 Make a map of your part of Illinois.

3 Make a list of facts about your topic. Draw pictures that illustrate your facts. Write a sentence or two to describe each picture.

4 Put your group's pictures together in the sequence in which you will show them. Use your map as an introduction. This is your video tour to share with the class.

Internet Activity

For more information and activities, go to **www.sfsocialstudies.com.**

52

The Early People of Illinois

Why do you think people might want to go to a new land?

Begin with a Primary Source

13,000 years ago

1400

About 12,000 years ago
New groups of Native Americans begin to settle in what is now Illinois.

500 years ago
Mississippians disappear from the area we call Illinois.

> **"We obtained all the Information that we could . . . the names of the peoples and of the places . . . [and] the Course of the great River. . . ."**
>
> — Father Jacques Marquette's diary (May 17, 1673)

French explorer Jacques Marquette and others traveled down the Mississippi River in 1673.

1600

1800

1673
Marquette and Jolliet explore the Mississippi.

1680
La Salle builds Fort de Crèvecoeur.

1754
The French and Indian War begins.

1775
The first battles of the American Revolution are fought.

Meet the People

Father Jacques Marquette

1637–1675

Birthplace: Laon, France

French missionary, explorer

- One of the first Europeans to visit Illinois
- Explored the Mississippi River
- Established a mission at Kaskaskia

René-Robert Cavelier Sieur de La Salle

1643–1687

Birthplace: Rouen, France

Explorer

- Claimed the Mississippi River and surrounding land for France
- Built Fort de Crèvecoeur and Fort St. Louis
- Made contact and began trading with several Native American peoples

Pontiac

c. 1720–1769

Birthplace: near present-day Detroit, Michigan

Ottawa chief

- Rebelled against British rule in the Great Lakes region
- Organized thousands of Native Americans for an attack against the British
- Signed peace treaty with the British to end the rebellion

Françoise Outelas

c. 1730–1801

Birthplace: near Kaskaskia

Businessperson, homemaker

- Married Antoine Drouet de Richerville at Kaskaskia
- Was widowed young and raised three children
- Ran the family trading post business after her husband's death

---

1630   **1705**   **1780**

1637 • Jacques Marquette 1675

1643 • La Salle 1687

c. 1720 • Pontiac 1769

c. 1730 • Françoise Outelas 1801

c. 1745 • Jean-Baptiste-Point du Sable 1818

1752 • George Rogers Clark 1818

Students can research the lives of significant people by clicking on *Meet the People* at **www.sfsocialstudies.com**.

Jean-Baptiste-Point du Sable

c. 1745–1818

Birthplace: San Marc, Haiti

Trader, businessperson, diplomat

- Traded in New Orleans, Louisiana, and Peoria, Illinois
- Helped maintain peaceful relationships between Native Americans and colonists
- Founded the city of Chicago

George Rogers Clark

1752–1818

Birthplace: near Charlottesville, Virginia

Surveyor, frontiersman, military leader

- Surveyed land west of the Appalachian mountains
- Led the campaign against the British in the Ohio Valley
- Captured forts at Kaskaskia and Cahokia

John Froman

b. 1961

Birthplace: Miami, Oklahoma

Peoria chief

- Became the youngest elected chief of the Peoria people in modern times
- Descendant of the great Miami chief Little Turtle
- Currently serves on the Oklahoma Indian Affairs Commission

1855   1930   2005

b. 1961 • John Froman

Early People of Illinois

Compare and Contrast

To compare is to tell how two or more things are alike. To contrast is to tell how two or more things are different.

Compare	Contrast
How things are alike	How things are different

- Clue words such as *like, as,* and *also* often show comparisons.

- Clue words such as *unlike, different,* and *but* often show contrasts.

- Writers do not always use clue words. Readers may have to find comparisons and contrasts themselves.

Read the paragraph at the right. The sentences that include **comparisons** and **contrasts** have been highlighted.

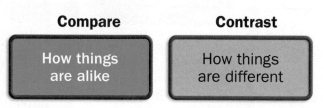

In Unit 1 you read about the natural regions of Illinois. The Northern Plains region has mostly flat land. The huge Central Plains region also has flat land. This region is known for its rich soil. The Southern Forests and Hills region is different from the other two regions because it has hills, canyons, and forests.

Who Came to Illinois Long Ago?

The first people who came to the land now called Illinois lived thousands of years ago during the Ice Age. They were hunters of large animals such as woolly mammoths. They moved from place to place, following the herds of animals.

When the Ice Age ended, some of the large animals died out. People had to live in a different way. They now hunted smaller forest animals, fished in lakes and streams, and gathered nuts and berries from the forests.

These foods became a more important part of people's diets than they had been in the past.

Eventually people learned to grow their own food. Although they still hunted, they no longer had to follow the herds of animals. Groups of people settled in villages and traded with other groups. They made pottery and decorated it. Later the people lived in larger towns that were surrounded by small farming villages. They grew corn and stored it for use during the winter.

Apply it!

Use the reading strategy of comparing and contrasting to answer these questions.

1. In what ways were the lives of the people of Illinois during the Ice Age and after the Ice Age alike?

2. In what ways were the lives of the people of Illinois during and after the Ice Age different?

3. What clue words in the passage help you notice comparisons and contrasts?

The First People of Illinois

Lesson 1

**About 1,000 years ago
Cahokia Site**
The Mississippians construct earthen mounds.

1

Lesson 2

**1600s
Grand Village of the Kaskaskia**
The lives of the Illini people change with the seasons.

2

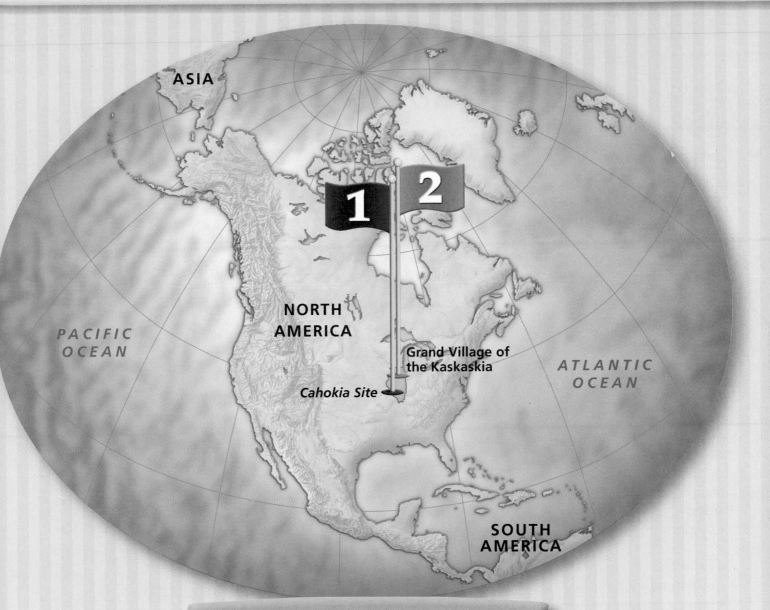

ASIA

NORTH
AMERICA

PACIFIC
OCEAN

Grand Village of
the Kaskaskia

ATLANTIC
OCEAN

Cahokia Site

SOUTH
AMERICA

Why We Remember

After the Ice Age, ancient people hunted large animals in what is now Illinois. As the weather grew warmer, people began farming. Some groups of people built cities with many large buildings.

These early Illinoisans developed their own languages, governments, arts, and traditions. They also traded goods with other peoples from far away, a tradition that is important to Illinois to this day.

14,000 years ago   400 years ago

About 12,000 years ago
The first people arrive in the area we call Illinois.

3,000 years ago
Woodland Indians begin to grow their own food.

500 years ago
Mississippians disappear from the Cahokia Site.

Cahokia Site

PREVIEW

Focus on the Main Idea
The first people to live in what is now Illinois were hunters.

PLACES
Bering Strait
Cahokia Site
Monks Mound

VOCABULARY
migrate
archaeologist
culture
artifact
adapt
mound
trade
government

TERMS
prehistoric
hunter-gatherer
cultural group

▶ Giant woolly mammoths once roamed the area we call Illinois.

Humans Arrive

You Are There
It is still dark, but it is time to get up. You and the others must find the herd of woolly mammoths you spotted only two days ago. The families in your group are almost out of meat, and the nuts, roots, and berries gathered by the women will not last.

You join the men and follow the trail left by the mammoths. Soon you catch up with them. You hold your breath and creep toward the huge animals.

That evening all of the families feast. Everyone eats as much as possible. The leftover meat will be dried. The women will clean the hides and make clothing from them. The animals' bones will make good tools.

 Compare and Contrast Look for ways that the lives of the earliest people differ from your life.

Target Skill

Earliest People of Illinois

When did the first people arrive in North America? One theory is that people have always been here. But many scientists think that the first people probably came from Asia during the Ice Age many thousands of years ago.

On the map, find the **Bering Strait,** the waterway that separates Asia and North America. Many scientists believe that during the Ice Age, the water level of the strait dropped, which allowed animals and people to cross from Asia to North America.

These first people may have **migrated,** or moved from one place to another, south through the American continents.

How did the earliest people live? They depended on wild animals for food, clothing, and shelter, so they followed the animals' movements.

We learn about these early people from **archaeologists** (ar kee AHL uh jists), or scientists who study the cultures of people who lived long ago. **Culture** includes the ways of life, beliefs, traditions, and languages of a group or people. Some archaeologists study **prehistoric** times, or the times before history was recorded. Archaeologists look for pottery, weapons, and other objects that tell them about early cultures. An object made by humans is an **artifact** (AR tuh fakt).

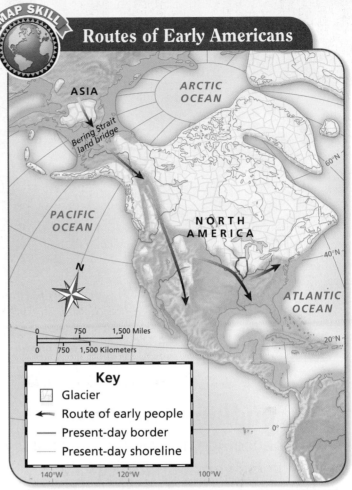

MAP SKILL · **Routes of Early Americans**

▶ The earliest Native Americans may have followed these routes.

MAP SKILL Trace Movement on Maps *In which direction did people travel from Asia to North America?*

The first known people in what is now Illinois are called Paleo-Indians. They lived here between 10,000 and 12,000 years ago, during the end of the Ice Age. They had to **adapt,** or change their way of life, to survive the harsh conditions. They were **hunter-gatherers,** which means that they got their food by hunting animals and gathering plants.

REVIEW How does the way an archeologist learns about the culture of early people differ from the way you would learn about a culture today?
➲ **Compare and Contrast**

▶ Woodland Indians lived in villages like the one shown.

▶ Woodland Indian artifact

Woodland Indians

After the Ice Age, the climate of what is now Illinois grew warmer. How do you think this affected the lives of the early Americans? Between 2,000 and 3,000 years ago, Native Americans in Illinois began to rely not only on hunting and gathering but also on growing their own food. The main crops they grew were corn, beans and squash. As a result, these early farmers, whom we call the Woodland Indians, began to settle in permanent villages. Farming also gave people more time for other activities.

What did they do? The Woodland Indians were the first people of Illinois to be potters, or people who make clay pottery. The pottery containers were used to store food.

They had time to build too. The Woodland Indians built log buildings and **mounds,** or piles of earth that were used for religious ceremonies or for other purposes such as making a lookout point. In fact, the Woodland Indians are so well known for their mounds that they are sometimes called "Mound Builders."

The Woodland Indians had a system of **trade,** or exchange of goods and services, that may have covered much of North America. In some of their mounds, scientists have found items that came from areas far from Illinois.

About 1,000 years ago, the Woodland Indians' culture was slowly replaced by the culture of the Mississippians. However, many of their mounds and artifacts remain.

REVIEW How were the lives of the Woodland Indians similar to and different from the lives of earlier peoples? ⟳ **Compare and Contrast**

Mississippian People

The Mississippian people lived throughout Illinois about a thousand years ago. Their culture was different from that of the peoples who came before them. If you had been a Mississippian, you probably would have lived in a large town, perhaps with several thousand people. You would have had a **government,** or a system for making rules and decisions, and an organized religion. You would have been part of a **cultural group,** or a group of people who shared a common language, religion, and customs.

You might have helped farm the rich soil along the Mississippi River. Mississippians grew crops such as corn, squash, and beans in small villages that surrounded their towns.

Like the Woodland Indians, the Mississippians traded with other groups and made pottery. Their pottery was thinner and lighter than Woodland Indian pottery and was often decorated with symbols.

You might have helped build mounds. Mississippians built their mounds as platforms for important buildings. These buildings were usually rectangular, with walls made of wooden stakes and twigs covered with mud. Today, although the wooden buildings have disappeared, the mounds remind you of an important part of your state's past.

REVIEW How was the culture of the Mississippians like that of the Woodland Indians? How was it different? ↺ **Compare and Contrast**

▶ **Mississippians lived in villages like this one.**

Mississippian Culture

Mississippians were such good mound builders that some of their mounds still exist. In fact, in Collinsville, Illinois, you can see the **Cahokia** (cuh HOH kee uh) **Site.** It was one of the largest Native American cities in North America.

The city was home to between 5,000 and 20,000 people. Inside the city Mississippians built homes in rows around open plazas. They grew crops in fields outside the city.

▶ **The Cahokia Site was a regional center for Mississippian politics and trade.**

The Mississippians built more than 120 mounds at the Cahokia Site. They created these mounds by carrying about 50 million cubic feet of earth in small woven baskets. To move that much earth would probably take 100 people, working eight hours each day, more than 100 years! **Monks Mound** stands as the largest of these mounds. Its base stretches 1,000 feet long and almost 800 feet wide. Monks Mound rises a little more than 100 feet from the ground, about as high as a seven-story building. A very large wooden building probably sat on the top, making the Monks Mound site something like an early skyscraper.

▶ **Monks Mound shows that the Mississippian people had excellent construction skills.**

The thriving community at the Cahokia Site lasted about 400 years. By 1500 the city was completely abandoned. What might have happened to this once successful city and its people? Archaeologists suggest several reasons for the disappearance. Over the years, the people might have used up many of the natural resources that they needed for survival. In addition, a climate change may have slowed crop production. As a result, the Mississippians would not have had enough food. The city might also have been affected by war, disease, or conflicts among its people.

REVIEW Both the Woodland Indians and the Mississippian people built mounds. How were the mounds different from each other?

 **Compare and Contrast**

Summarize the Lesson

12,000 years ago The first people arrived in the area we call Illinois.

3,000 years ago Woodland Indians began to grow their own food and build settlements.

500 years ago Mississippians disappeared from the Cahokia Site.

LESSON 1 REVIEW

Check Facts and Main Ideas

1.  **Compare and Contrast** On a separate sheet of paper, contrast the lives of people in Illinois during the Ice Age with the lives of people in Illinois two thousand years ago.

Ice Age	2000 Years Ago

2. How do many scientists think the first people probably came to North America?

3. Why might prehistoric people have followed herds of animals?

4. What were some important traits of Mississippian culture?

5. **Critical Thinking: Analyze** How did farming allow Mississippians to stay in one place for longer periods of time?

Link to ━━ **Science**

Other Theories A theory is an idea that is supported by many pieces of information. The idea that people came to the Americas over a land bridge is a theory. However, some scientists think that people came to the Americas by different routes. Archaeologists are making new discoveries at sites in North and South America. Research this topic. Find out what other theories are being developed.

Make Generalizations

What? A **generalization** is a broad statement or rule that applies to many examples. Clue words such as *all, most, many, some, sometimes, usually, seldom, few,* and *generally* often tell you that a generalization is being made. Readers can make generalizations on the basis of main ideas, details, and their own knowledge.

Why? In this chapter you read about the early people of Illinois. Making generalizations can help you remember the facts in the lesson. Generalizations also help you see similarities between ideas and facts that may seem unrelated.

How? To make a generalization, you must first gather and compare information about a topic. Then bring this information together to make a general statement. In some cases you may add your own knowledge to the information.

Suppose that you want to make a generalization about geography and the settlement patterns of early peoples in present-day Illinois.

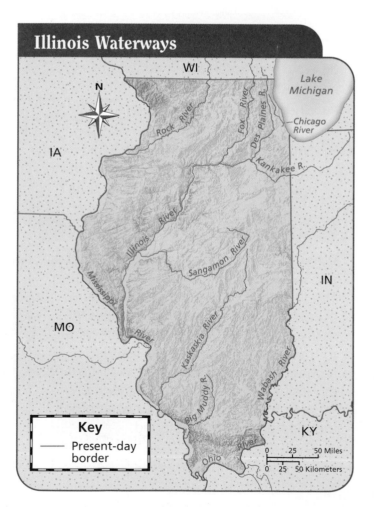

Illinois Waterways

▶ **Many Woodland Indian settlements were located near water.**

Mississippian Settlements in Illinois

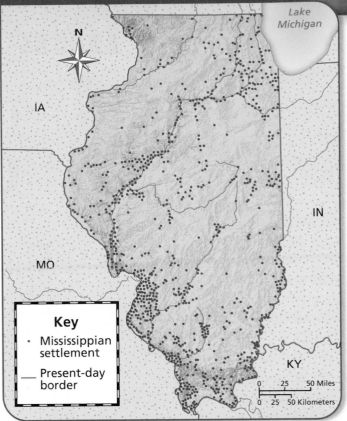

Key
- Mississippian settlement
- — Present-day border

First, examine the map of Illinois waterways on page 68.

Then, look at the maps on this page. In what ways are they similar? In what ways are they different? When you find similarities, you have the beginnings of a generalization. Before you make your generalization, make sure that you have enough facts or examples to support it. Otherwise, your generalization could be faulty.

Woodland Indian Settlements in Illinois

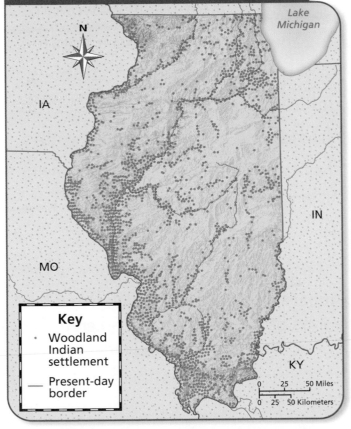

Key
- Woodland Indian settlement
- — Present-day border

Think and Apply

1. Make a generalization about how geography affected the location of early settlements.

2. What generalization can you make about the number of Woodland Indian settlements compared with the number of Mississippian settlements?

3. Tell whether the following generalization is valid or faulty: *Mississippians built most of their villages in eastern Illinois because that is where most of the rivers are located.* Explain your answer.

1600   1700   1800

1600s
New groups of Native Americans begin to arrive in the area we now call Illinois.

1673
Illiniwek Confederacy includes 12 to 13 different groups.

1770
Kickapoo establish settlements in central Illinois.

Grand Village of the Kaskaskia

PREVIEW

Focus on the Main Idea
After 1600 new groups of Native Americans migrated to and settled in what is now Illinois.

PLACES
Central Mississippi River valley
Grand Village of the Kaskaskia

VOCABULARY
wigwam
longhouse
maize
cultivate

▶ Native Americans attached animal bones to sticks and used them as hoes.

The Illiniwek Confederacy

You Are There

The spring sun is hot as you bend over to plant squash seeds. This new land that your family has moved to is good for farming. Many other people have moved into the area too.

You can hardly wait for the day's work to end. During the winter you live in a hunting camp with your family. When spring comes, all the families move back to the village. You see your friends and tell stories about your winter adventures. Some people might even come to visit for a few days and share their stories.

Compare and Contrast Think about how the lives of the Native American groups that you study are alike and different.

70

▶ *Pah-me-cow-ee-tah,* or **Man Who Tracks,** a Peoria Illinois Chief

The Illini Arrive

By the 1600s new groups of Native Americans settled in the area that is now the state of Illinois. The Illiniwek (IL i ni wek) Confederacy, or Illini, was the largest of these groups. By 1673 the confederacy, which had between 6,500 and 12,000 members, consisted of 12 to 13 allied groups of Native Americans. The five main groups were the Cahokia, Kaskaskia (kas KAS kee uh), Michigamea (mich i GAH mee uh), Peoria, and Tamaroa (tam ah ROW ah).

Many Illini built villages throughout the **Central Mississippi River valley,** which includes most of the western border of present-day Illinois. One of the largest villages was the **Grand Village of the Kaskaskia,** located on the Illinois River near present-day Starved Rock. Because the Illini settled along the rivers that later explorers traveled, many places in Illinois have names that come from their language,

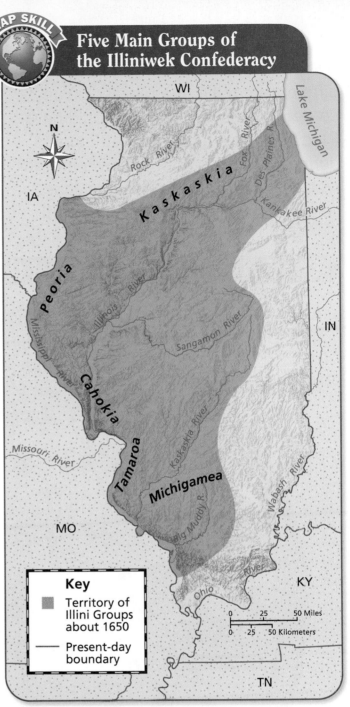

▶ **In the 1600s many different Native American groups lived in the area that is now Illinois.**

MAP SKILL Location *In what part of Illinois did the Peoria people live?*

including Peoria and the Kaskaskia and Illinois Rivers.

REVIEW Who were the five main groups of the Illiniwek Confederacy? **Main Idea and Details**

Illini Settlements

Life in an Illini settlement was very different from life in a Mississippian settlement. As an Illini you would have lived in different kinds of settlements during the year. You would have moved with the change of seasons. In June, July, and the winter months, the Illini divided into small family groups and lived in hunting camps on the prairie. Their homes, called wigwams, housed one or two families. **Wigwams** are dome-shaped structures made with bent-pole frames. The Illini covered these frames with tree bark or reed mats.

The Seasonal Movements of the Illini People

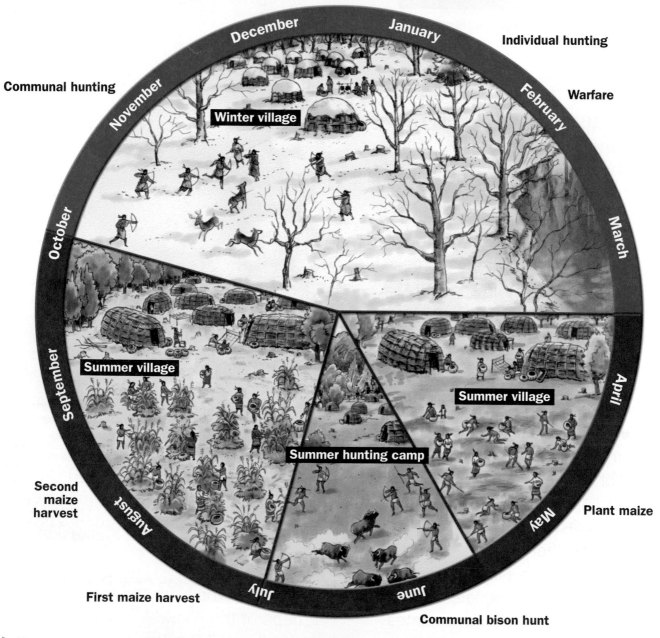

▶ The graph shows the annual movement of Illini settlements.

A Native American Longhouse

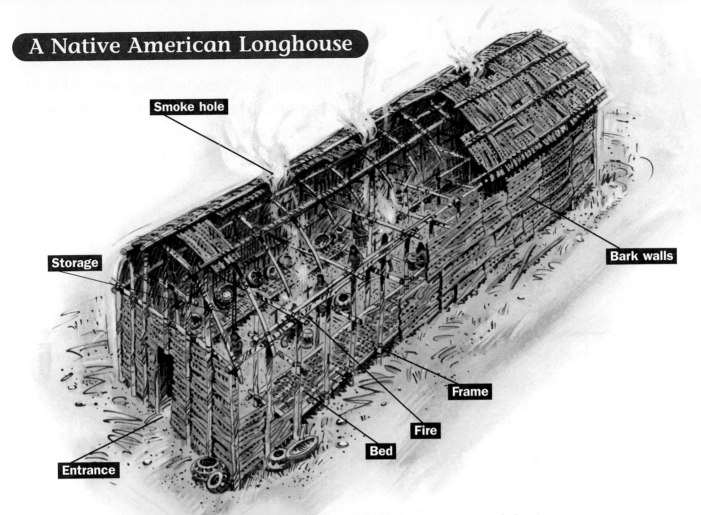

Smoke hole

Storage

Bark walls

Frame

Fire

Bed

Entrance

▶ Space inside a longhouse was divided into separate living quarters for each of about ten families. Several fires burned in a row down the center of the longhouse.

For much of the spring and some of the summer, the Illini settled along riverbanks in large villages. Some villages had as many as 350 homes. These homes were large rectangular lodges called **longhouses.** About ten families lived in each longhouse.

What was daily life like in an Illini village? In April and May, women planted squash, beans, and **maize,** a type of corn. From mid-July through mid-October, they harvested the maize and beans. By the end of October, they had harvested the squash as well.

Most of the Illini clothing was very simple. They made their winter robes from buffalo hides. The rest of their clothing was made from deerskin. Both men and women wore moccasins.

Illini men hunted and conducted warfare. With bows and arrows, as well as clubs, they hunted buffalo, deer, bear, elk, and small animals.

Women did much of the work in Illini villages throughout the year. They built homes, collected firewood, gathered plants to eat, tended gardens, and made clothing.

REVIEW Describe how wigwams are different than longhouses.
⟳ **Compare and Contrast**

The Kickapoo

At the beginning of the 1700s, a different group of Native Americans, the Kickapoo (KIK uh poo), began moving into northern Illinois from

▶ **A Kickapoo Native American**

Michigan. By 1770 they had established themselves in central Illinois, near Peoria. They were skilled farmers. Like the Illini they **cultivated,** or grew, corn, squash, and beans. They also practiced hunting and gathering.

REVIEW How did the Kickapoo meet their need for food after moving to Illinois? **Summarize**

Summarize the Lesson

1600s New groups of Native Americans moved into the area that is now Illinois.

1673 The Illiniwek Confederacy consisted of 12 to 13 different groups.

1770 The Kickapoo established settlements near Peoria.

LESSON 2 ◗ REVIEW

Check Facts and Main Ideas

1. ◗ **Compare and Contrast** On a separate sheet of paper, fill in the ways in which the Illini and Kickapoo cultures were alike and different.

Alike	Different

2. In what kinds of different homes did the Illini live, depending on the season of the year?

3. Where did the Illini build the Grand Village of the Kaskaskia?

4. Where did the Kickapoo first settle when they moved into Illinois?

5. **Critical Thinking:** *Analyze* How did the Illini and Kickapoo use their environment to meet their needs for food, clothing, and shelter?

Link to ⬗⬗ **Art**

Draw a Picture Draw a picture of daily life in an Illini settlement. Include wigwams or longhouses, people working, and other important details of Illini culture.

John Froman
b. 1961

John Froman was born and raised in Miami, Oklahoma. He is a member of the Peoria people. When John was a young boy, his grandfather, Guy Froman, was serving as the chief of the Peoria people. His grandfather taught him that service to your community was important. As a young boy, one of John's weekly responsibilities was to trim the grass in the tribal cemetery.

BIOFACT

As chief of the Peoria people, Chief John Froman is the official representative for more than 2,900 Peoria.

In 2002 John Froman was elected chief of the Peoria people, a four-year term that he is currently serving. Chief Froman works to improve the living conditions of the Peoria people by increasing their educational and economic opportunities. He is in charge of all tribal meetings. He is also responsible for dealing with state and federal government officials. Chief Froman stated,

"It takes a certain kind of person to be a public servant."

Learn from Biographies

Who had a great influence on the life of Chief John Froman?

Students can research the lives of significant people by clicking on *Meet the People* at **www.sfsocialstudies.com**.

Illinois and Oklahoma

THE PEORIA PEOPLE

During the 1600s the Peoria people were an important group in the Illiniwek Confederacy. The city and county of Peoria are named for this group of Native Americans. By the 1700s the Peoria population had drastically declined. By 1850 war with the Iroquois and the arrival of French settlers had completely forced the Peoria off their lands in Illinois. At first, they moved west to Missouri, then to Kansas, and finally, in 1867, to Oklahoma, where many Peoria people live today.

▶ **A Peoria Native American greets a European trader.**

Key

▨ Territory of Native Americans in Illinois

— Present-day border

1650

1750

▶ **By 1850 no Native Americans lived in Illinois.**

ILLINOIS

OKLAHOMA

1850

76

▶ The official symbol of the Peoria people today (above)

▶ Each spring the Peoria people in Oklahoma host a pow wow. This is one way that this group works to preserve its culture.

▶ Many different Native American people live next to the Peoria in Oklahoma.

Peoria

Ottawa | Quapaw

Eastern Shawnee

Wyandotte

Modoc

Miami

Seneca-Cayuga

Oklahoma

N

Digging Up the Past

We owe our knowledge about ancient Illinois cultures to archaeologists. They study everything about people from the past—their tools, houses, and even garbage! Archaeologists work in the outdoors, as well as in laboratories, schools, and museums. After they have dug up—or excavated—artifacts, archaeologists clean them and then try to put broken pieces back together. Finally they work as historians. They try to figure out what these objects can tell us about how early people lived and what they believed. What are some places you can visit in Illinois where archaeologists have worked?

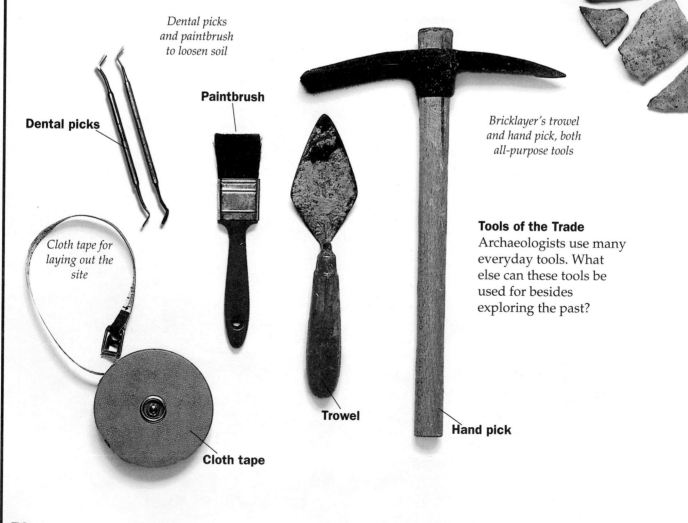

Dental picks and paintbrush to loosen soil

Paintbrush

Dental picks

Cloth tape for laying out the site

Bricklayer's trowel and hand pick, both all-purpose tools

Tools of the Trade
Archaeologists use many everyday tools. What else can these tools be used for besides exploring the past?

Trowel

Hand pick

Cloth tape

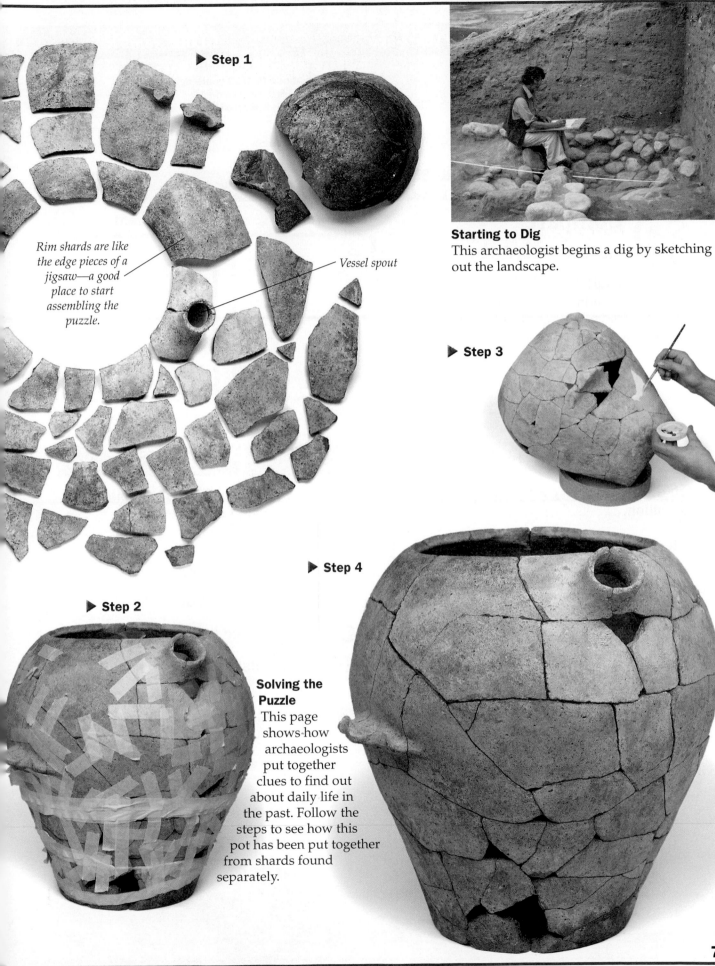

▶ **Step 1**

Rim shards are like the edge pieces of a jigsaw—a good place to start assembling the puzzle.

Vessel spout

Starting to Dig
This archaeologist begins a dig by sketching out the landscape.

▶ **Step 3**

▶ **Step 4**

▶ **Step 2**

Solving the Puzzle
This page shows how archaeologists put together clues to find out about daily life in the past. Follow the steps to see how this pot has been put together from shards found separately.

79

CHAPTER 3 REVIEW

15,000 years ago   10,000 years ago

About 12,000 years ago
The first people arrived in what is now called Illinois.

Chapter Summary

Compare and Contrast

Target Skill

Copy the chart on a separate sheet of paper, and fill in the ways that the Illini and the Mississippian people were alike and different.

Alike	Different

Vocabulary

Match each vocabulary word with its definition.

1. **archaeologist** (p. 63)
2. **culture** (p. 63)
3. **artifact** (p. 63)
4. **mound** (p. 64)
5. **wigwam** (p. 72)
6. **longhouse** (p. 73)
7. **maize** (p. 73)

a. an object made by humans

b. ways of life

c. a type of corn

d. a large rectangular lodge

e. a scientist who studies the cultures of people who lived long ago

f. a pile of earth

g. a dome-shaped structure covered with bark or mats

Places

Write a sentence for each of the places listed below, using details you have learned in this chapter.

1. **Bering Strait** (p. 63)
2. **Cahokia Site** (p. 66)
3. **Monks Mound** (p. 66)
4. **Central Mississippi River valley** (p. 71)
5. **Grand Village of the Kaskaskia** (p. 71)

3,000 years ago Woodland Indians farmed and built permanent structures.

1,000 years ago Mississippians built mounds and cities.

400 years ago New groups of Native Americans came to Illinois.

300 years ago Kickapoo and other groups started moving to area.

Facts and Main Ideas

1 How do many scientists think people came to North America during the Ice Age?

2 How did the end of the Ice Age affect the people living in what is now Illinois?

3 Which group of Native Americans built the mounds at Cahokia?

4 In what parts of present-day Illinois did the Illini and Kickapoo settle?

5 **Time Line** When did the Woodland Indians begin building permanent structures and farming?

6 **Main Idea** How did the change of seasons affect the lifestyle of the Illini?

7 **Main Idea** What responsibilities did men in the Illiniwek Confederacy have? What responsibilities did women have?

8 **Critical Thinking:** *Make Inferences* Why do you think many of the Native American groups that lived in Illinois were so similar?

Internet Activity

To get help with vocabulary and places, select the dictionary or encyclopedia from *Social Studies Library* at **www.sfsocialstudies.com.**

Apply Skills

Make Generalizations

Use the maps on pages 68–69 to help you answer the questions below.

1 What generalizations can you make about the Woodland Indian and Mississippian settlements along the Mississippi River?

2 In what parts of present-day Illinois did the Woodland Indians and the Mississippians build the fewest settlements? State your answer as a generalization.

3 Write a fact that would prove the following generalization is faulty: *The Woodland Indians and the Mississippians built most of their settlements near rivers that flowed east and west.*

Write About History

1 **Write a paragraph** about a day in the life of an Illini man or woman.

2 **Write a set of instructions** that tell how to make a model of Monks Mound.

3 **Write an essay** describing the group of Native Americans with whom you would most like to have lived in Illinois. Explain why you chose that group.

CHAPTER 4

The Europeans Arrive

Lesson 1

**1600s
New France**
France establishes New France in North America.

1

Lesson 2

**1763
Fort Detroit**
Pontiac rebels against the British.

2

Lesson 3

**1776
Philadelphia**
American colonists declare their independence from Great Britain.

3

Locating Time and Place

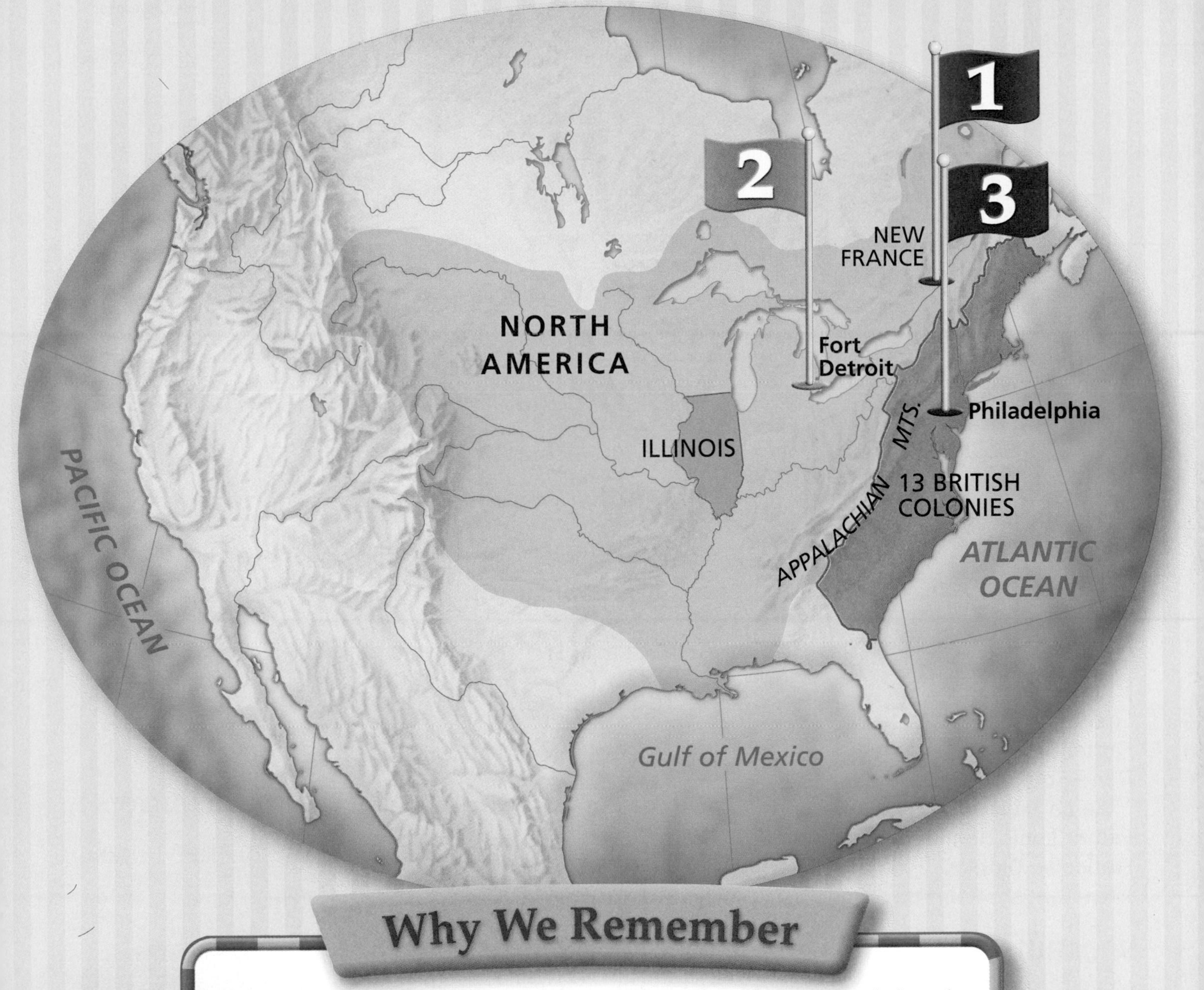
1
2
3
NEW FRANCE
NORTH AMERICA
Fort Detroit
Philadelphia
ILLINOIS
APPALACHIAN MTS.
13 BRITISH COLONIES
PACIFIC OCEAN
ATLANTIC OCEAN
Gulf of Mexico

Why We Remember

About 400 years ago explorers and traders began arriving in North America. Though many were looking for riches, they also valued the land itself, and they set up colonies. Soon Great Britain and France fought a war over control of this land. The British won, but peace did not last. In 1775 the colonies rebelled against Great Britain. Native Americans fought against the takeover of their lands as well. Before long the war reached the territory that is now Illinois. In this chapter you will learn what caused these wars and how the American colonies gained their independence.

1600	1650	1700

1608 Samuel de Champlain creates a settlement in Quebec.

1673 Marquette and Jolliet explore the Mississippi.

1680 La Salle builds Fort de Crèvecoeur.

NEW FRANCE

PREVIEW

Focus on the Main Idea
The first Europeans to arrive in Illinois were French traders and fur trappers who lived peacefully among the Native Americans.

PLACES
New France
Fort de Crèvecoeur
Peoria
Fort St. Louis
Fort de Chartres

PEOPLE
Louis Jolliet
Father Jacques Marquette
René-Robert Cavelier Sieur de La Salle
Father Louis Hennepin
Françoise Outelas
Jean-Baptiste-Point du Sable

VOCABULARY
colony
missionary
voyageur

The French

You Are There
You and your family live in New France. Your father is a French trader who trades beads, knives, silver pins, and other European goods for furs that the Native Americans bring to him.

You live in a log home that many people come to visit. Sometimes you see other French traders. Sometimes you see Native Americans from different places.

Today you and your mother will walk to your grandmother's home in a small village several miles away. You take beads, rings, and mirrors to share with your cousins. Your mother takes spices and metal cooking pots for your aunts. You can't wait to get to the village and play with your cousins!

Summarize As you read the lesson, summarize information about the French in North America in the 1600s.

▶ French explorers used pots such as this one.

84

▶ **The French arrival in the St. Lawrence River area**

The French in North America

During the 1500s and 1600s, Europeans began arriving in North America. Many were English, French, Spanish, and Dutch. Why did they leave their homes for an unknown land? Some were looking for a new trade route to Asia through North America. Others heard tales of great wealth and journeyed across the ocean hoping to become rich. Some left their homes seeking religious freedom.

In 1608 Samuel de Champlain helped a small group of French people form a settlement in Quebec. They claimed large areas of land and set up colonies around the St. Lawrence River. A **colony** is an area claimed, settled, and governed by another country. The French colonists called their land **New France.** French explorers, missionaries, and traders set off to explore the Great

Literature and Social Studies

Voyages

In 1604, as Samuel de Champlain explored North America, he wrote:

"So many voyages and discoveries without result, and attended with so much hardship and expense, have caused us French in late years to attempt a permanent settlement in those lands which we call New France, in the hope of thus realizing more easily this object; since the voyage in search of the desired passage commences on the other side of the ocean, and is made along the coast of this region."

Lakes, the Mississippi River, and as far south as the Gulf of Mexico.

The French traders brought European goods to trade for furs in Illinois. They traded with the Illinois people and other Native American groups.

REVIEW What are some of the reasons that Europeans came to North America in the 1500s and 1600s?
Main Idea and Details

The French in Illinois

In 1673 **Louis Jolliet,** a French fur trader, and **Father Jacques Marquette,** a French missionary, left New France to explore the Mississippi River. A **missionary** is a person who travels to tell other people about his or her religion. Jolliet and Marquette paddled down the Mississippi River in birchbark canoes. They visited villages of the Kaskaskia and other Illinois peoples.

Back in New France, **René-Robert Cavelier Sieur de La Salle** heard about Marquette and Jolliet's journey. In 1679 La Salle and his men traveled down the Kankakee and Illinois Rivers. When La Salle returned north for supplies, three of his companions, including **Father Louis Hennepin,** went on to explore the upper Mississippi.

During the 1700s French men—and women—established trade with many of the peoples they met. **Françoise Outelas** helped run her husband's business in the frontier town of Vincennes, in the area we now call Indiana. In the late 1700s **Jean-Baptiste-Point du Sable** was one of the first people, other than Native Americans, to settle in the area of modern-day Chicago.

REVIEW Describe the events leading to La Salle's exploration. **Sequence**

Then and Now

Excavation of La Salle's Ship

In 1682 La Salle claimed the area along the Mississippi River for France in the name of King Louis XIV. In 1686 La Salle's ship, the *Belle,* sank in the Gulf of Mexico. Today the Texas Historical Commission works to recover the wreckage.

▶ La Salle's ship was similar to the image above.

▶ Researchers discovered the remains of La Salle's ship off the coast of Texas.

▶ Researchers reconstruct the hull, or the bottom, of La Salle's ship.

▶ A bronze cannon

Photos, Texas Historical Commission

Map Adventure

French Forts

Step back in time, and visit some early North American forts. The French built forts in the 1600s and 1700s in what is now Illinois.

1. Fort de Crèvecoeur was built near which river?

2. Fort de Chartres was used by the French and their trading partners. The fort was built near which Native American group?

3. Which fort on the map was built first? Which fort was built last?

4. What two things do Fort de Chartres, Fort Kaskaskia, and Fort Tamarans have in common?

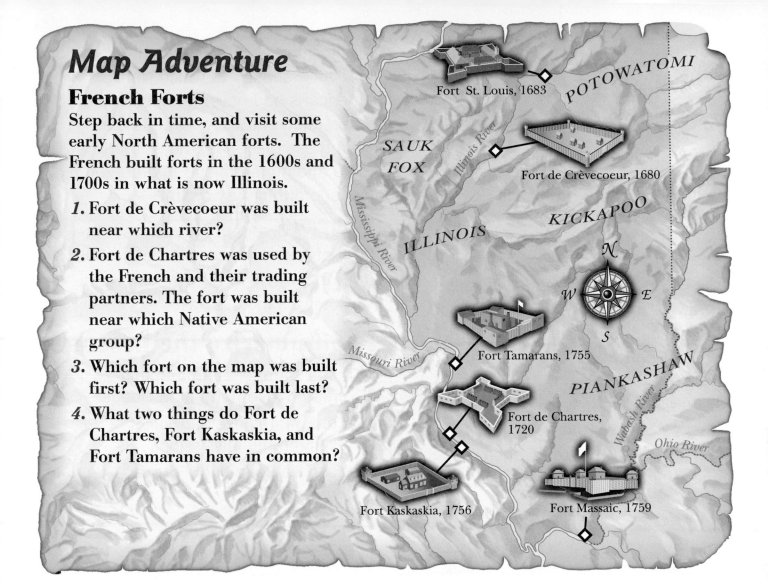

Fort St. Louis, 1683
POTOWATOMI
SAUK FOX
Illinois River
Fort de Crèvecoeur, 1680
KICKAPOO
Mississippi River
ILLINOIS
Missouri River
Fort Tamarans, 1755
PIANKASHAW
Fort de Chartres, 1720
Wabash River
Ohio River
Fort Kaskaskia, 1756
Fort Massaic, 1759

The French Frontier

As the French used rivers to explore, they also built forts along them. That way the forts were near food and water, and the French could see anyone who was traveling along the river.

In 1680 La Salle and his men built **Fort de Crèvecoeur** near present-day **Peoria** as a base for their explorations. This fort was the first public building in Illinois, but it was soon abandoned.

Three years later, La Salle's men built **Fort St. Louis.** The fort was used by the French and by the Kaskaskia for protection against other peoples, such as the Iroquois. However, both groups abandoned Fort St. Louis in 1691. In the early 1700s the Peoria started using the fort.

Fort de Chartres was built three times—in 1720, 1725, and 1754. The fort was damaged twice when the Mississippi River flooded but was rebuilt both times. For more than 40 years, Fort de Chartres was the center of French government for the surrounding area.

REVIEW What caused so many French forts to be built near Illinois rivers? **Cause and Effect**

The French and the Native Americans

Although the French generally respected the Native Americans and their culture, contact with the French changed the lives and culture of Native Americans in many ways.

Initially, French **voyageurs**, or traders, came to trade with the Native Americans living in Illinois. Because furs were in great demand in Europe, the French traded European goods for furs that the Native Americans brought them.

Life also changed for some Native Americans when they adopted the Catholic religion of the French missionaries.

Unfortunately, the French also brought diseases to which Native Americans had never been exposed. When many Native Americans died from these diseases, they found it more and more difficult to defend their lands and their way of life.

REVIEW Compare and contrast the lives of Native Americans before and after the arrival of the French.

➔ Compare and Contrast

Summarize the Lesson

1608 Samuel de Champlain created a settlement in Quebec.

1673 Marquette and Jolliet explored the Mississippi.

1680 La Salle built Fort de Crèvecoeur.

LESSON 1   REVIEW

Check Facts and Main Ideas

1. Summarize On a separate sheet of paper, write down information to support the summary given.

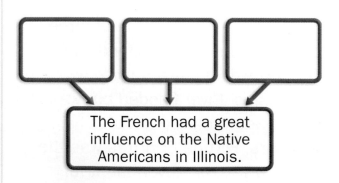

The French had a great influence on the Native Americans in Illinois.

2. Which European countries sent colonists and explorers to North America?

3. What did La Salle accomplish in 1680?

4. Fort St. Louis protected French settlers and traders from which group of Native Americans?

5. Critical Thinking: *Draw Conclusions* Why were the French able to get along as well as they did with most of the Native American peoples in Illinois?

Link to   Art

Trading Poster Make a poster illustrating the goods that the French and Native Americans traded with one another. When possible, use a different object to represent each trade item. For example, use beads to represent jewelry.

Jean-Baptiste-Point du Sable

c. 1745–1818

Jean-Baptiste-Point du Sable (zhahn bah TEEST pwahnt DOO SAH bluh) was a black pioneer who has been called the founder of Chicago. Born in Haiti, du Sable attended school in France. In the 1760s, he joined a French trading firm and sailed to New Orleans. After working his way up the Mississippi to what is now Peoria, he moved again. He settled at the mouth of the Chicago River in the late 1770s.

Du Sable set up a trading post that soon grew to be the largest in the Midwest. It had a mill, bakehouse, dairy, smokehouse, workshop, poultry house, stable, and barn. Du Sable sold items to trappers, and he sent food, furs, and other goods to trading posts in Detroit and Canada. Soon Chicago became an important trading post for people living in the areas now known as Wisconsin and Michigan.

BIOFACT

In 1800 du Sable sold his post and moved away. Soon Fort Dearborn was built in the area.

Learn from Biographies

Chicago is located on Lake Michigan and along the Chicago River. Why did du Sable choose to build his trading post there?

Students can research the lives of significant people by clicking on *Meet the People* at **www.sfsocialstudies.com**.

1600	1700	1800

1607
The English settle in Jamestown.

1754
The French and British fight the French and Indian War.

1763
The French and British sign the Treaty of Paris.

1763
Pontiac leads a rebellion against the British.

BRITISH COLONIES

PREVIEW

Focus on the Main Idea
Both the French and the British (as the English were known after 1707) wanted to control the land and resources of Illinois, as well as the surrounding area.

PLACES
Roanoke Island
Jamestown
Fort Detroit

PEOPLE
Pontiac

VOCABULARY
ally
rebellion
proclamation

EVENTS
French and Indian War
Treaty of Paris of 1763
Pontiac's War
Proclamation of 1763

▶ Craftspeople who made barrels were known as coopers.

The British

You Are There
You're busy making barrels in your father's shop in London. You have to pay attention and do a careful job. These barrels will carry food and supplies across the ocean to North America.

It seems that everyone in London is talking about the voyage. A hundred people will be sailing next month. No one really knows what they will find. They must be very brave. You can't even imagine leaving England!

Now you hear your father talking to some sailors who have just come into the shop. You can make out words like "gold" and "treasure." But your father pokes his head in when he hears your hammer stop and tells you to get back to work.

 Compare and Contrast As you read, compare and contrast how the British and the French treated the Native Americans.

The English in North America

England realized that colonies in North America would provide resources for England and opportunities for its people. In 1585 Sir Walter Raleigh sent English settlers to **Roanoke Island,** off the coast of present-day North Carolina. The colonists suffered many hardships, and the survivors returned to England a year later.

The full story of the second Roanoke Island colony is a true mystery. English settlers tried to form another colony in the same place. Led by Governor John White, more than 100 people landed on Roanoke Island in July of 1587. In August, White sailed back to England for supplies. However, England's war with Spain delayed his return for three years. When he returned to North America in 1590, the Roanoke colony had disappeared. What happened to the colonists has remained a mystery.

In 1607 England finally settled its first successful, permanent colony.

▶ The word *croatoan*, the name of a Native American group that lived near by, was the only clue that John White found at Roanoke in 1590.

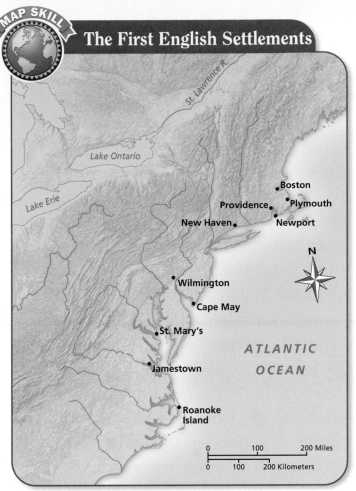

MAP SKILL **The First English Settlements**

▶ The English established colonies along the Atlantic coast in the late 1500s and early 1600s.

MAP SKILL Location *Why did the English colonists build their settlements along the coast?*

It was located in **Jamestown,** in present-day Virginia.

Some of those who left England for the new colony hoped to find quick wealth. Others who settled in different parts of North America sought religious freedom. Over time, these colonists moved west. They wanted to own land themselves and be more independent. By the 1700s the English were exploring and settling in the Illinois area.

REVIEW How were the French and the English colonies similar? How were they different? ⟳ **Compare and Contrast**

The French and Native Americans Fight the British

Some people study history because they like to read about exciting battles. Some of those battles were fought by the French and the British, who waged war with each other for years in order to control land and resources around the world. In North America the French took action when they saw their hold over the fur trade slipping away. War broke out in 1754. Many Native American groups did not trust the British because of bad experiences. These groups became allies with the French. An **ally** is a partner or supporter. This struggle over North America lasted nine years and was called the **French and Indian War.**

► **British forces battled the French for control of the Ohio River Valley.**

In the first four years of the war, the French and their Native American allies won many victories. But by 1757 France was running out of money and supplies.

The British won the war when both sides signed the **Treaty of Paris of 1763.** France lost most of its claims in North America—all of Canada and all lands east of the Mississippi River.

REVIEW What caused many Native Americans to join forces with the French against the British? **Cause and Effect**

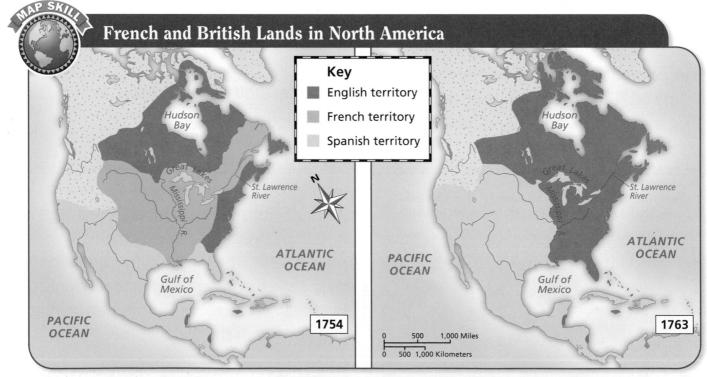

MAP SKILL

French and British Lands in North America

Key
- English territory
- French territory
- Spanish territory

Hudson Bay

Great Lakes

Mississippi R.

St. Lawrence River

N

ATLANTIC OCEAN

Gulf of Mexico

PACIFIC OCEAN

1754

Hudson Bay

Great Lakes

Mississippi R.

St. Lawrence River

PACIFIC OCEAN

ATLANTIC OCEAN

Gulf of Mexico

0   500   1,000 Miles
0   500 1,000 Kilometers

1763

► **The maps show European claims in North America before and after the French and Indian War.**

MAP SKILL Observe Change Through Maps *What important change happened in North America in 1763?*

92

Pontiac's War

Unlike the French, the British were not interested in becoming partners with the Native Americans. Instead, the British wanted to take Native American land for their own settlements. Native Americans were angry about this treatment. At first the British were not able to occupy the area of Illinois because of problems with **Pontiac** (PAHN tee ak), an Ottawa chief, who was angry that the French had lost the war.

In 1763 Pontiac led a **rebellion**, or a fight against a government or other authority. He attacked **Fort Detroit**, in what is now Michigan. Within a few months, however, Pontiac lost what was called **Pontiac's War.** In order to prevent other conflicts over land, the British issued a **proclamation**, or an official announcement. The **Proclamation of 1763** was supposed to close lands west of the Appalachian Mountains to British settlements. Many settlers ignored this law and crossed the Appalachians, forcing out the Native Americans.

REVIEW How did Great Britain react to Pontiac's attack on Fort Detroit? **Cause and Effect**

Summarize the Lesson

- **1607** The English colonists settled in Jamestown.
- **1754** The French and British fought for control of North America.
- **1763** Pontiac led a rebellion against British forces.

LESSON 2 REVIEW

Check Facts and Main Ideas

1. **Compare and Contrast** On a separate sheet of paper, write a sentence in each box contrasting how the French and the British treated Native Americans.

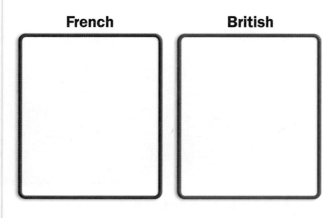

French	British

2. Why did English colonists come to North America?

3. What was one cause of the French and Indian War?

4. Tell one reason that the British were able to defeat the French and the Native Americans.

5. **Critical Thinking:** *Draw Conclusions* Why did Pontiac lead a war against the British?

Link to ⛓ Writing

Write a Paragraph Work in small groups. Use library resources to find information about how the British tried to colonize lands west of the Appalachians. Then, with your group, write a paragraph explaining the British point of view. Why did they think they had the right to claim the land?

Chart and Graph Skills

Read a Time Line

What? A **time line** is a tool you can use to organize events. It is a straight line that is divided into time periods. The time line below is divided into periods of ten years. Other time lines may be divided into longer or shorter periods of time.

Why? Time lines can help you keep track of when events took place. Time lines can be historical or personal. Looking at a time line is an easy way to remind yourself of facts, such as that the French and Indian War began before the British and French signed the Treaty of Paris.

1700 1710 1720 1730 1740 1750 1760 1770 1780 1790 1800

1720
French build first Fort de Chartres.

1754
The French and Indian War begins.

1763
The French and British sign the Treaty of Paris.

1763
Pontiac leads attack on Fort Detroit.

▶ A battle scene from the French and Indian War

▶ The attack on Fort Detroit

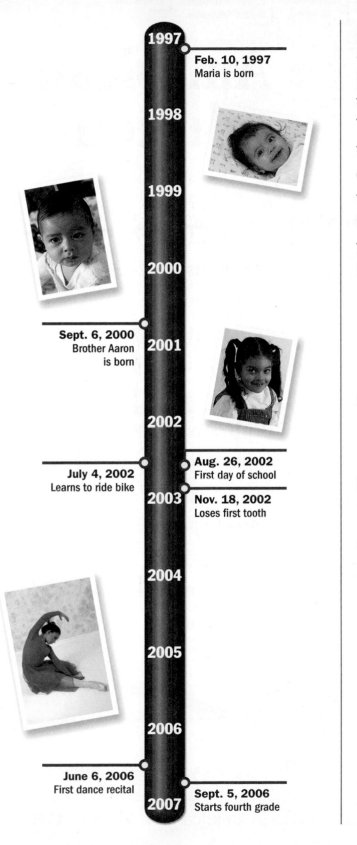

1997

Feb. 10, 1997
Maria is born

1998

1999

2000

Sept. 6, 2000
Brother Aaron
is born

2001

2002

Aug. 26, 2002
First day of school

July 4, 2002
Learns to ride bike

2003

Nov. 18, 2002
Loses first tooth

2004

2005

2006

June 6, 2006
First dance recital

Sept. 5, 2006
Starts fourth grade

2007

How? Events on a time line are arranged according to when they happened. Always read a time line from left to right or from top to bottom. The earliest events are placed at the far left or at the top. As events move closer to the present, they move farther right or farther toward the bottom. The event on the far right or the bottom of the time line, therefore, is the most recent event.

Think and Apply

① On the time line of events in Illinois in the 1700s, what event took place in 1754?

② What are the two events that took place in 1763?

③ On the time line of events in Maria's life, what event happened in 2000?

1775   1780   1785

1776
The Declaration of Independence is approved.

1778
George Rogers Clark forces the British to surrender at Fort Kaskaskia.

1781
Cornwallis surrenders at Yorktown.

The American Revolution

PREVIEW

Focus on the Main Idea
The American Revolution affected all of the British-controlled lands in North America, including that which became Illinois.

PLACES
Philadelphia
Lexington
Concord
Kaskaskia
Cahokia
Yorktown

PEOPLE
George Washington
Thomas Jefferson
Benjamin Franklin
John Adams
George Rogers Clark

VOCABULARY
repeal
revolution

TERMS
Stamp Act
Quartering Act
Townshend Acts
Declaration of Independence

EVENTS
Treaty of Paris of 1783

PA
Philadelphia

You Are There

July 4, 1778

Our victory over the British was amazing! And it all happened without one shot being fired. It was the most exciting day of my life!

I was one of many soldiers who left Kentucky with George Rogers Clark. We traveled to Fort Kaskaskia, along the Mississippi River, which was controlled by the British. Following Clark's clever plan, we dressed as Native Americans. Clark was able to persuade the French settlers who were living at the fort to help us. When the British realized we were inside the fort and ready to fight, they surrendered immediately.

► A musket

Sequence As you read, note the sequence of major events that occurred in North America from 1763 to 1783.

FACT FILE

Events Leading to the American Revolution

What	Year	Why	Impact
Proclamation Act	1763	Kept colonists from settling in lands west of the Appalachian Mountains	Many colonists ignored the act and moved into the western lands.
Stamp Act	1765	Taxed almost all printed materials	Colonists protested and boycotted. The act was repealed in 1766.
Quartering Act	1765	Forced colonists to provide food, housing, and supplies for British soldiers	Colonists protested.
Townshend Acts	1767	Tax on glass, paint, oil, paper, and tea	Colonists stopped buying imported goods.

► Tea was a popular drink among the colonists.

► Colonists had to buy stamps for legal documents and even for newspapers.

► British troops could live in colonists' homes.

Causes of the American Revolution

Before 1763 the British had given the North American colonists much control over their government. However, the French and Indian War had cost Great Britain a great deal of money, so the British government began passing laws that would bring in money from the colonies. The **Stamp Act** was a tax on legal papers, licenses, and newspapers. The **Quartering Act** said that British soldiers must be allowed to stay in colonists' homes and that the colonists must provide the troops with food and supplies. The **Townshend Acts** made the colonists pay taxes on many items, including tea.

Many colonists did not want to pay all of these extra taxes. They were upset that they had to pay even though they had no representatives in the British government.

In an effort to tell the British rulers how they felt, the colonists protested against the new taxes. By 1770 Great Britain had **repealed,** or canceled, the most unpopular taxes.

REVIEW How did Great Britain's attitude toward the North American colonists change after 1763?

⮂ Compare and Contrast

Revolution Begins

In 1773 the colonists became angry about another British tax on tea. A group of Boston citizens dressed as Native Americans and crept onto the British ships in Boston Harbor. They threw more than 300 boxes of British tea into the water. This event became known as the Boston Tea Party. The British government reacted quickly, closing Boston's port and outlawing meetings. They sent more troops to the city. A British military commander became the governor of Massachusetts.

These actions angered more and more colonists. Some thought that they should be independent from Great Britain.

In 1774 the First Continental Congress, a meeting of leaders from 12 colonies, met in **Philadelphia,** Pennsylvania. They discussed the issues each colony had against Great Britain.

In the meantime, tensions between the British soldiers and the colonists grew. The first battles of the American Revolution were fought at **Lexington** and at **Concord,** near Boston, Massachusetts, in April 1775.

▶ Thomas Jefferson (right) wrote the Declaration of Independence with the help of Benjamin Franklin (left) and John Adams (center).

The Second Continental Congress met in May of 1775 to discuss independence. Some of these men believed that it would take a **revolution,** or a complete overthrow of the existing political system, to win such independence. They discussed who should be the commander in chief of the Continental Army. John Adams, a member of the Congress, recommended **George Washington,** who accepted the job on June 15. He spent the next few months training his troops.

On July 4, 1776, members of the Second Continental Congress approved the **Declaration of Independence,** written largely by **Thomas Jefferson,** with the help of **Benjamin Franklin** and **John Adams.** This document declared the American colonies to be "free and independent states." The signers of the Declaration knew that they had to unite all 13 colonies if they were to succeed in the fight against the British. John Adams wrote that uniting the colonies was "a singular example in the history of mankind. Thirteen clocks were made to strike together."

In March 1776, George Washington's troops had forced British troops out of Boston. Then Washington tried to defend New York City. However, he was forced to retreat. By the end of the year, Washington found that he had few men left and that he was short on supplies. The British successfully took

▶ **General George Washington became commander in chief of the Continental Army. A special flag (above left) was created for his forces.**

over New York City. The members of Congress feared that Philadelphia would be next, so they fled that city.

After serving in the Continental Congress in 1776, Benjamin Franklin sailed to France to serve as America's first ambassador to that country. He was able to persuade the French government to help the Americans. In 1778 the tide began to turn in favor of the Americans, largely because of Franklin's efforts in gaining French support.

The French loaned the colonists money and troops to support the war effort. Later, Franklin helped work out a peace plan between the French, the Americans, and the British.

REVIEW Why was it necessary for all 13 colonies to approve the Declaration of Independence? **Main Idea and Details**

The Revolution Spreads Westward

In the West, **George Rogers Clark** led the fight against the British. In 1778 Clark's men captured the forts at **Kaskaskia** and **Cahokia**, in present-day Illinois, without any fighting.

Then, in 1779, Clark's men braved snow and freezing rain as they walked 180 miles to Fort Sackville at Vincennes, in present-day Indiana. Clark surprised the British and easily took the fort.

▶ The Kaskaskia bell became known as the "Liberty Bell of the West" after George Rogers Clark captured Fort Kaskaskia.

Within two years Lord Cornwallis, the general in charge of the British troops, surrendered to George Washington at **Yorktown,** Virginia. The new American government signed the **Treaty of Paris of 1783**, which formally ended the war.

REVIEW Which event happened first, the fall of Fort Kaskaskia or Cornwallis's surrender at Yorktown? **Sequence**

Summarize the Lesson

1776 The Declaration of Independence was approved.

1779 George Rogers Clark's campaign forced the British to surrender at Fort Kaskaskia.

1781 Cornwallis surrendered at Yorktown.

LESSON 3 REVIEW

Check Facts and Main Ideas

1. **Sequence** On a separate sheet of paper, write the sequence of events in the conflict between the British and the American colonists after 1763.

   Great Britain issues the Stamp Act.
   ↓
   [ ]
   ↓
   [ ]
   ↓
   [ ]

2. How did Great Britain respond to the Boston Tea Party?

3. What was the purpose of the Declaration of Independence?

4. Where did British troops surrender to George Washington in 1783?

5. **Critical Thinking: Compare and Contrast** Compare George Washington's efforts against the British in Boston to his efforts in New York City.

Link to ∞ **Writing**

Write a Letter Suppose that you are writing a letter to a cousin in Virginia. Explain how you feel about George Rogers Clark's victories against the British in 1778.

CITIZEN HEROES

BUILDING CITIZENSHIP

Caring
Respect
Responsibility
Fairness
Honesty
★ Courage

Against the Odds

Sometimes people risk their lives for what they think is right. George Rogers Clark faced overwhelming odds when he set out to fight the British in the West.

George Rogers Clark was born on November 19, 1752. As a boy, he dreamed of traveling west. When Clark was 19, he set off on a surveying trip to the West. To *survey* means to measure and mark land. Over the next four years, Clark claimed land in Kentucky for himself and his family. At that time, Kentucky was part of Virginia.

During the Revolutionary War, George Rogers Clark asked the Virginia government to help the settlers protect their land. The new American government gave Clark the job of protecting the settlers.

Clark marched against the British and their allies with fewer than 200 men. He showed great courage. Arriving at Fort Sackville in February 1779, he said

> *"[O]ur cause is just. . . . [O]ur country will be grateful."*

Clark's victory at Fort Sackville helped the new American government claim land in the West after the American Revolution. When Clark died in 1818, he was called "the mighty oak of the forest" and "the father of the western country."

Courage in Action

Research the story of a young person or a group of people who are working courageously for a cause they believe in.

CHAPTER REVIEW

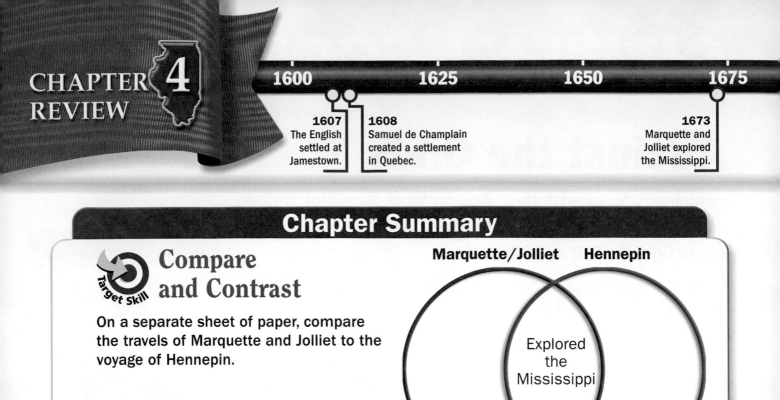

1600   1625   1650   1675

1607
The English settled at Jamestown.

1608
Samuel de Champlain created a settlement in Quebec.

1673
Marquette and Jolliet explored the Mississippi.

Chapter Summary

Compare and Contrast

Target Skill

On a separate sheet of paper, compare the travels of Marquette and Jolliet to the voyage of Hennepin.

Marquette/Jolliet   Hennepin

Explored the Mississippi

Vocabulary

Match each word to its definition.

1 colony (p. 85)

2 voyageur (p. 88)

3 ally (p. 92)

4 rebellion (p. 93)

5 proclamation (p. 93)

6 repeal (p. 97)

a. cancel

b. a fight against a government or other authority

c. an official announcement

d. an area claimed, settled, and governed by another country

e. French trader

f. a partner or supporter

People and Places

List two important things about each of the following places and people.

1 New France (p. 85)

2 Father Jacques Marquette (p. 86)

3 René-Robert Cavelier Sieur de La Salle (p. 86)

4 Jamestown (p. 91)

5 Pontiac (p. 93)

6 George Washington (p. 99)

7 George Rogers Clark (pp. 100, 101)

8 Kaskaskia (p. 100)

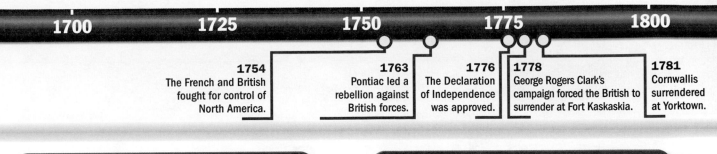

1700	1725	1750	1775	1800

1754
The French and British fought for control of North America.

1763
Pontiac led a rebellion against British forces.

1776
The Declaration of Independence was approved.

1778
George Rogers Clark's campaign forced the British to surrender at Fort Kaskaskia.

1781
Cornwallis surrendered at Yorktown.

Facts and Main Ideas

1. Why was the fur trade so important to Europeans in North America?

2. Who was inspired by Marquette and Jolliet to explore the Mississippi River?

3. How was George Rogers Clark able to defeat the British at Fort Sackville?

4. **Time Line** How many years passed between the approval of the Declaration of Independence and Cornwallis's surrender?

5. **Main Idea** What was the main purpose of French settlement in North America?

6. **Main Idea** Why did the French and British fight the French and Indian War?

7. **Main Idea** What did the American colonists want to gain in declaring independence from the British?

8. **Critical Thinking:** *Draw Conclusions* Why were rivers like the Mississippi and the Illinois so important to European explorers and colonists?

Apply Skills

Read a Time Line

Use the time line at the top of pages 102 and 103 to answer the questions.

1. What happened in 1673?

2. How many years passed between the beginning of the French and Indian War and the year when Pontiac led a rebellion against British forces?

3. Which event occurred in 1776?

Write About History

1. **Write a letter** to a friend as a member of George Rogers Clark's force. Describe your experiences.

2. **Write a comparison** of what you think life was like for Native Americans both before and after they started trading with the French.

3. **Write an essay** explaining why Native Americans should or should not be trading with the British during the 1740s.

Internet Activity

To get help with vocabulary, people, and places, select the dictionary or encyclopedia from *Social Studies Library* at **www.sfsocialstudies.com**.

Toliver's Secret

by Esther Wood Brady

Even before the American Revolution reached Illinois, young people in the East were learning what it meant to be at war. In December of 1776, ten-year-old Ellen Toliver overhears her grandfather and her mother as they place a secret message inside a loaf of bread. The message is for General George Washington. Grandfather's plan for delivering the message is ruined when he sprains his ankle. Who can deliver the message without causing suspicion? Could the timid Ellen find the courage to be a hero?

Ellen could see that Grandfather was very serious about the need to send his message. She, too, had been worried about all the news of lost battles and retreats, especially since Ezra [her brother] was with that army. She remembered how joyous everyone had been last July when they heard about the Declaration of Independence. There had been bonfires on the village green and singing and dancing in the streets. And then the British army came to New York and there had been three months of defeat.

"If you understand how important it is to take the message, Ellen, I'll tell you how it can be done. And then you are to decide."

Ellen listened and didn't say a word.

"You walk down to the docks near the Market-house and get on a farmer's boat—or an oysterman's. They come over early every morning and they go back to Elizabeth-town at eleven o'clock. Elizabeth-town is a very small town. When you get off the boat, you'll find the Jolly Fox Tavern without any trouble. My good friend Mr. Shannon runs the tavern, and you give the loaf of bread to him. That's all there is for you to do, Ellen. The Shannons will welcome you and take good care of you."

Sailing across the bay didn't seem so hard. It was finding a boat here in New York and asking a stranger for a ride that worried her.

"How could I find the right boat to take me?" she asked. She didn't intend to go, but she thought she'd ask anyway.

"The docks are right near Front Street where we walked on Sunday afternoon. The farmers and the oystermen tie up their boats near the Market-house. They are friendly people and they often take passengers back to Elizabeth-town since the ferryboat stopped running. I'll give you money to pay."

"And how would I get home again—if I should decide to go?" she said in a very low voice.

"Oh, the Shannons will put you on a boat early in the morning. You'll be back here by ten o'clock."

"Does Mr. Shannon take the bread to General Washington?" she asked.

"No, he takes it to a courier who will ride part of the way. Then he'll give it to another courier who will ride through the night with it. And finally a third man will carry it to the General in Pennsylvania."

Review

Main Ideas and Vocabulary

TEST PREP

Read the passage below, and use it to answer the questions that follow.

Many scientists think that people arrived in North America thousands of years ago. These hunters learned to grow their own food and settled in villages.

Some descendants of these people came to the land we now call Illinois. The Illiniwek Confederacy was the largest <u>cultural group</u>.

During the 1500s and 1600s, Europeans arrived in North America. France claimed land in Canada. England settled colonies along the Atlantic Ocean.

French explorers traveled down the Mississippi River. French traders lived among the Native Americans, whose lives were forever changed.

The French and British both wanted to control trade and land in North America. In the mid-1700s they fought the French and Indian War. France lost, and the Native Americans were unhappy under the British. Pontiac, leader of the Ottawa, led a rebellion. However, he was defeated by the British army.

The British tried to raise money to pay for the French and Indian War by taxing the American colonies. The <u>colonists</u> rebelled, and the American Revolution began in 1775. In the West, George Rogers Clark led the fight against the British and captured three forts. The colonists eventually won their independence.

1 Some early Americans settled in one place after
   A learning to hunt bison.
   B developing their own culture.
   C learning to fish.
   D learning to grow their own food.

2 In this passage, <u>cultural group</u> means people who
   A move from place to place following herds of animals.
   B live in the same village.
   C share the same language, religion, and customs.
   D grow their own food.

3 The French and British fought over
   A control of North America.
   B who could tax the colonists.
   C Spanish land in Florida.
   D problems between the colonists and Native Americans.

4 In this passage, <u>colonists</u> means people who
   A win freedom.
   B settle a new country.
   C support the government.
   D sign a peace treaty.

Vocabulary

Match each term with its definition.

1 archaeologist (p. 63)

2 adapt (p. 63)

3 mound (p. 64)

4 voyageur (p. 88)

5 ally (p. 92)

6 rebellion (p. 93)

a. French trader

b. pile of earth

c. a fight against a government or other authority

d. change way of life

e. a scientist who studies the cultures of people who lived long ago

f. a partner or supporter

Apply Skills

Use a Time Line Pick a time line in Unit 2. On a sheet of paper, write three questions about information presented on the time line. On a separate sheet of paper, write the answers to your questions. Exchange questions with another student. Answer your partner's questions. Then check each other's answers.

Write and Share

Present a Documentary Your class has been asked to produce a TV documentary about the people of Illinois from prehistoric times until 1700. Form three groups. Each group should do one of these tasks: **1.** Write a brief script about the people. **2.** Write a description of important events. **3.** Create visuals—pictures, drawings, posters, and charts. Then combine your information, and present your documentary as a class.

Read on Your Own

Look for these books in the library.

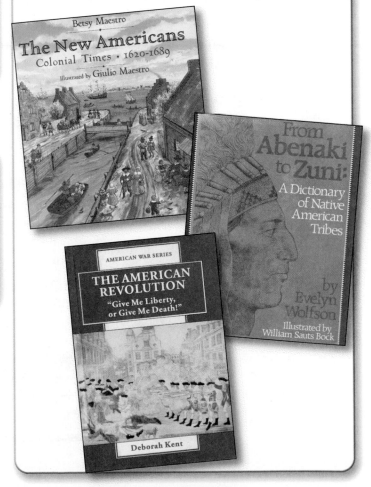

Discovery Channel School

Unit 2 Project

On the Spot

Life was often challenging for early European settlers, as well as for Native American groups who had lived in Illinois for hundreds of years. Make a documentary about their experiences.

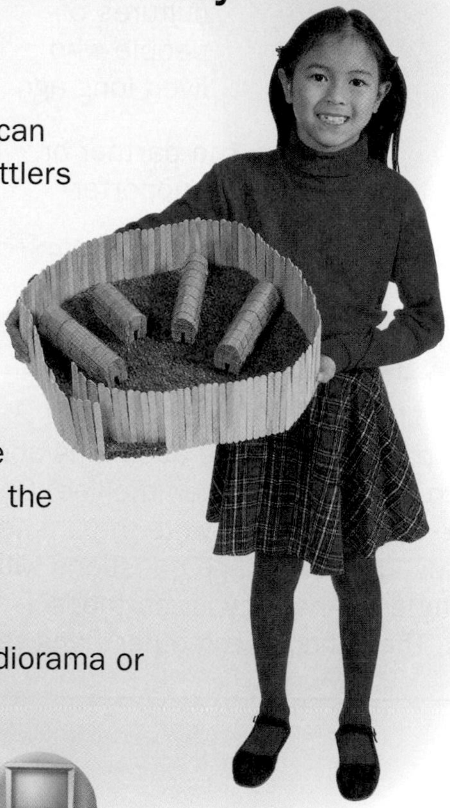

1 **Form** a group. Choose a Native American group or a group of early European settlers who settled in Illinois.

2 **Write** sentences about the group's experiences and observations. Include a variety of topics.

3 **Make** a diorama or model to show the environment and settlements. Include the group's dwellings, other buildings, and the physical setting.

4 **Present** your documentary. Show the diorama or model to the class.

Internet Activity

For more information and activities, go to **www.sfsocialstudies.com.**

The Great State of Illinois

What makes Illinois a great state?

Begin with a Primary Source

1785   1795   1805   1815

1787
The Northwest Ordinance forbids slavery in the western lands.

1809
Illinois becomes a territory.

1818
Illinois becomes the twenty-first state of the Union.

"Old America seems to be breaking up and moving westward."

—Morris Birkbeck, a settler from Britain, describing migration to Illinois Territory, 1817

J. Jeffrey Grant painted **Harvest Time —Barney's Orchard** around 1925.

1825

1835

1845

1855

1832
U.S. Army defeats Sauk and Fox Native Americans in the Black Hawk War.

1837
John Deere designs a new steel plow.

1848
Illinois and Michigan Canal is completed.

Meet the People

Black Hawk
1767–1838

Birthplace: Sauk Sautenuk (Virginia Colony)

Sauk and Fox leader

- Joined British soldiers in attacking U.S. forces in the War of 1812
- Refused orders from the U.S. government to leave lands near the Rock River
- Led Sauk and Fox warriors against Illinois militia in the Black Hawk War

Ninian Edwards
1775–1833

Birthplace: Montgomery County, Maryland

Governor, senator, judge

- Served as the first governor of Illinois Territory
- Helped organize Illinois's first state government
- Served from 1818 to 1824 as senator from Illinois in the U.S. Congress

Nathaniel Pope
1784–1850

Birthplace: Louisville, Kentucky

Judge, territorial representative to the U.S. Congress

- Served as secretary of Illinois Territory
- Helped pass bill for Illinois statehood in the U.S. Congress
- Helped expand Illinois's borders

Edward Coles
1786–1868

Birthplace: Abermarle County, Virginia

Assistant to President Madison, governor

- Urged Thomas Jefferson to abolish slavery in the early 1800s
- Freed slaves from his Virginia plantation and invited them to join him in Illinois as free citizens
- Worked as governor to outlaw slavery in Illinois

1760	1785	1810

1767 • Black Hawk

1775 • Ninian Edwards

1784 • Nathaniel Pope

1786 • Edward Coles

1794 • Daniel Pope Cook 1827

1806 • Juliette Magill Kinzie

1809 • Cyrus McCormick

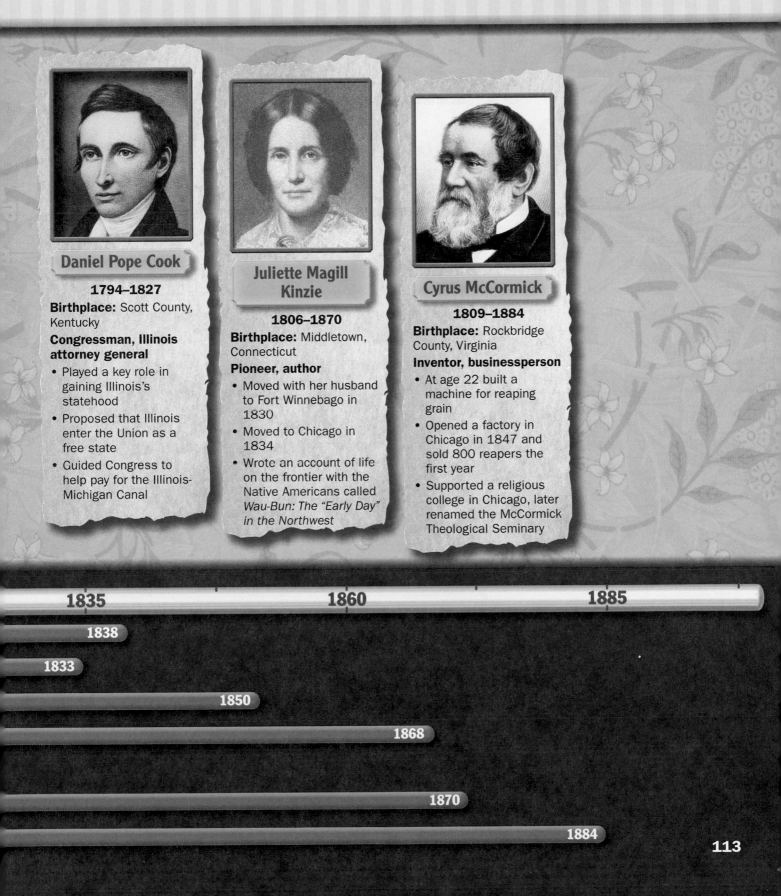

Students can research the lives of significant people by clicking on *Meet the People* at **www.sfsocialstudies.com.**

Daniel Pope Cook

1794–1827

Birthplace: Scott County, Kentucky

Congressman, Illinois attorney general

- Played a key role in gaining Illinois's statehood
- Proposed that Illinois enter the Union as a free state
- Guided Congress to help pay for the Illinois-Michigan Canal

Juliette Magill Kinzie

1806–1870

Birthplace: Middletown, Connecticut

Pioneer, author

- Moved with her husband to Fort Winnebago in 1830
- Moved to Chicago in 1834
- Wrote an account of life on the frontier with the Native Americans called *Wau-Bun: The "Early Day" in the Northwest*

Cyrus McCormick

1809–1884

Birthplace: Rockbridge County, Virginia

Inventor, businessperson

- At age 22 built a machine for reaping grain
- Opened a factory in Chicago in 1847 and sold 800 reapers the first year
- Supported a religious college in Chicago, later renamed the McCormick Theological Seminary

1835   1860   1885

1838

1833

1850

1868

1870

1884

113

The Great State of Illinois

 Sequence

Sequence means the order in which things happen. Most historical writing is organized in sequence, or time order.

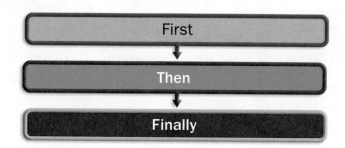

- Clue words such as *first, then, next,* and *finally* can help you figure out the sequence of events.

- Clue words are not always used. Other helpful clues are dates, times of day, and times of year.

Read the paragraph at the right. The clue words that show what came **first, then,** and **finally** have been highlighted.

In Chapter 5 you will read **first** about how the Confederation Congress formed the Northwest Territory in 1787. **Then,** as more and more settlers moved westward, the Illinois Territory was formed in 1809. **Finally,** through the hard work of men such as Nathaniel Pope, Illinois became the twenty-first state of the Union in 1818.

Changes in Illinois

The land we call Illinois changed in many ways from the end of the American Revolution to 1860. Right after the Revolution, the land had few European settlers. Then Congress passed the Northwest Ordinance. This law set up a government and protected the rights of people living there. After the law was passed, more settlers began to arrive.

In 1800 Illinois became part of Indiana Territory. Then in 1803 the United States bought from France a huge area of land called the Louisiana Purchase. Even more settlers headed westward. Illinois was no longer the western border of the nation.

Six years later the government formed the Illinois Territory, and Illinois had its own government for the first time. Finally, in 1818, Illinois joined the United States as the twenty-first state.

After statehood was granted, land offices, banks, and schools were started. Towns and cities began to grow. Canals and railroads were built to connect different parts of the state to one another. In just over 20 years, Illinois's population grew from about 55,000 to nearly half a million! Now more and more people were living in cities. By 1860 the population of Illinois climbed to more than 1,700,000 people.

Use the reading strategy of sequence to answer these questions.

1 How did Congress encourge settlement of western lands?

2 When did land offices, banks, and schools begin to open?

3 After statehood what events caused the population to grow a great deal?

CHAPTER 5

From Territory to State

Lesson 1

1809
Northwest Territory

After the Illinois Territory was formed in 1809, the territorial legislature met in this building (right) in Kaskaskia.

1

Lesson 2

1812
Fort Dearborn

The United States and Britain battle in the War of 1812.

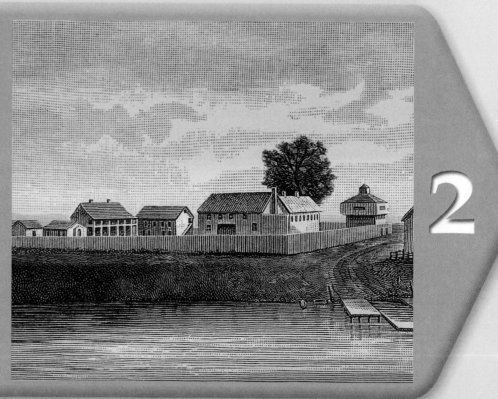

2

CANADA

1

2

LOUISIANA
PURCHASE

Fort Dearborn

NORTHWEST
TERRITORY

UNITED
STATES

MEXICO

PACIFIC OCEAN

ATLANTIC
OCEAN

Gulf of Mexico

Why We Remember

In the years following the Revolutionary War, great changes took place in Illinois. Different groups and states claimed the land we call home. The state of Virginia claimed Illinois, as did Native Americans who had lived on the land longer than anyone else. But with settlers arriving in Illinois, life here changed forever. More and more, lands that once had few people living on them became increasingly populated. Soon the land of Illinois would become a territory, and eventually a state.

NORTHWEST TERRITORY

1780   1790   1800   1810

1787
Confederation Congress passes the Northwest Ordinance.

1803
United States completes the Louisiana Purchase.

1809
Illinois becomes a territory.

The Changing West

PREVIEW

Focus on the Main Idea
The organization of the Northwest Territory attracted people to the western lands, including the area that became Illinois.

PLACES
Northwest Territory
Indiana Territory
Illinois Territory

PEOPLE
Arthur St. Clair
Ninian Edwards
Meriwether Lewis
William Clark

VOCABULARY
ordinance
district
constitution
expedition

TERMS
Confederation Congress
Northwest Ordinance
Louisiana Purchase

You Are There

You sit quietly next to the warm fire in your kitchen as you listen to your parents talk. They are discussing the idea of leaving Virginia for land in the West. "The land there is rich," your father says. "We could farm much more land than we now have."

"There's no law out there," your mother replies. "We could claim some land, but it wouldn't be a legal claim. I don't want to move until I know the land is truly ours. Then no one can take it away."

You wonder what will happen next. Saying good-bye to all your friends would be hard. At the same time, you can't help but think how exciting it might be to live in a new land.

Sequence Look for words that show the sequence, or order, of western settlement in the United States and Illinois in the early 1800s.

The Northwest Territory

After the end of the Revolutionary War in 1783, western lands, including the land we call Illinois, were claimed by several states. Then in 1784 the new United States government, called the **Confederation Congress,** claimed these lands.

The Confederation Congress passed the **Northwest Ordinance** in 1787. This **ordinance,** or law, formed the **Northwest Territory.** As you can see on the map, the Northwest Territory stretched northwest from the Ohio River to the Mississippi River. **Arthur St. Clair** became the first governor of the Northwest Territory, in Marietta, Ohio.

The Northwest Ordinance made rules for governing western lands and forming new states. It said that a

The Northwest Ordinance, 1787

- Established rules for governing the Northwest Territory
- Explained the steps a territory would take toward statehood
- Banned slavery in the Northwest Territory
- Provided western settlers with freedom of religion and other basic rights
- Promised fairness to the region's Native Americans

▶ **The Northwest Ordinance of 1787 formed the Northwest Territory.**

district, or section, of the territory could become a state when its population reached 60,000. The Northwest Ordinance also included a bill of rights. It provided citizens with certain basic rights, such as freedom of religion.

In September 1787, leaders such as George Washington and Benjamin Franklin helped ratify, or approve, the United States Constitution. A **constitution** is a written plan for how a government should be organized. An important part of the Constitution is the Bill of Rights. Some of the same ideas that were included in the Northwest Ordinance, such as freedom of religion, are also included in the Bill of Rights.

REVIEW What happened three years after the Confederation Congress claimed the western lands? ⟳ Sequence

▶ **The map shows the Northwest Territory as it appeared in 1787.**

Illinois Becomes a Territory

Life in Illinois changed with the passage of the Northwest Ordinance. In particular, Governor St. Clair brought order to an area that was formally ungoverned. Through St. Clair's visits in 1790 to places such as Kaskaskia and Cahokia, settlers sensed that they were no longer free to make their own rules. Instead, settlers would live by rules made and upheld by the territorial government of Illinois—a government St. Clair soon began forming. In so doing he established the first county, which he named for himself.

In 1795 a treaty with a Potawatomi group gave the United States control of much of the land in what is now Illinois. In Chapter 4 you learned that as Native Americans were pressured to leave this area, settlers began to arrive.

Hundreds of miles separated the territorial capital of Marietta, Ohio, from places such as Cahokia and Kaskaskia. The settlers in the West felt cut off from the officials in Marietta. As a result, in 1800 the United States government formed the **Indiana Territory** and set the new capital at Vincennes, in the area we now call Indiana.

However, people in western Illinois still were not satisfied. They wanted "Illinois Country" to become its own territory. Finally, in 1809 the United States government formed the **Illinois Territory.** The first territorial governor was **Ninian Edwards.**

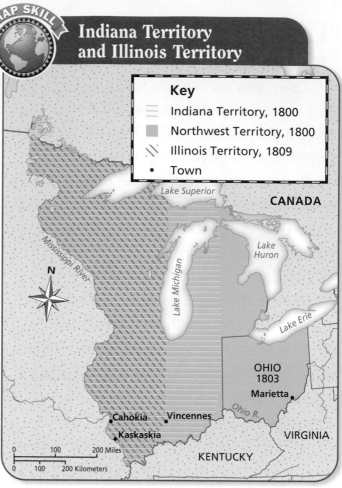

MAP SKILL — Indiana Territory and Illinois Territory

Key
≡ Indiana Territory, 1800
▨ Northwest Territory, 1800
⟍ Illinois Territory, 1809
• Town

Lake Superior

CANADA

Lake Huron

Lake Michigan

Mississippi River

N

Lake Erie

OHIO 1803

Marietta

Cahokia   Vincennes

Kaskaskia

Ohio R.

VIRGINIA

KENTUCKY

0   100   200 Miles
0   100   200 Kilometers

▶ The present-day states of Minnesota, Wisconsin, Michigan, and Illinois were once part of the Illinois Territory.

MAP SKILL Use Map Symbols *In what year was the Indiana Territory larger—1800 or 1809?*

REVIEW Which territory was formed first, the Indiana Territory or the Illinois Territory? ⟳ Sequence

▶ Pioneer families settled in the Illinois Territory in the early 1800s.

Westward Expansion

For years the westward movement of American settlers stopped at the Mississippi River. Then in 1803 President Jefferson guided the United States government to make the **Louisiana Purchase.** The United States agreed to pay France $15 million for 828,000 square miles of land stretching from the Gulf of Mexico to present-day Canada, and from the Mississippi River to the Rocky Mountains. The United States doubled its size.

▶ **Thomas Jefferson won the government's support for the Louisiana Purchase.**

The United States government sent two army officers, **Meriwether Lewis** and **William Clark,** to lead an expedition. Throughout their **expedition,** or journey, Lewis and Clark kept a record of their observations. As more western lands came under the control of the United States, more people were encouraged to move out west.

REVIEW What western expedition was begun after the Louisiana Purchase? ⟳ Sequence

Summarize the Lesson

1787 The Confederation Congress passed the Northwest Ordinance.

1803 The Louisiana Purchase encouraged westward expansion.

1809 Illinois became a territory.

LESSON 1   REVIEW

Check Facts and Main Ideas

1. ⟳ **Sequence** On a separate sheet of paper, list in order four events that led to westward expansion across the Mississippi River.

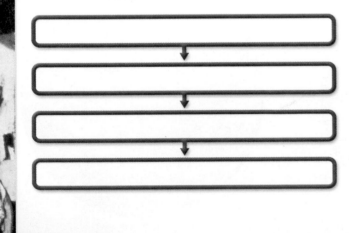

2. Name three ideas included in the Northwest Ordinance.

3. Why were some citizens of Illinois upset about the location of the territorial capital at Marietta and then Vincennes?

4. How did the Louisiana Purchase encourage settlers to move west?

5. **Critical Thinking:** *Express Ideas* In your opinion what was the most important feature of the Northwest Ordinance?

Link to ⬦⬦⬦⬦ Geography

Make a Large-Scale Map Using a ruler and the map on page 120, design a wall map of the Illinois Territory. Include on your map a compass rose, map key, and scale bar.

Find Latitude and Longitude

What? Latitude and longitude are lines that mapmakers draw on maps and globes. Each latitude line and each longitude line is numbered. These lines give an "address," or location, to cities, towns, and other places on Earth.

Look at the globes below. On the globe at the left, the lines extending from east to west are lines of **latitude.** We also call them **parallels.** The **equator** is a parallel that lies halfway between the North and South Poles. This parallel is numbered 0°. Lines of latitude north of the equator are labeled *N.* Lines of latitude to the south are labeled *S.*

Lines of **longitude** are shown at the right. These lines extend from the North Pole to the South Pole. We also call these lines **meridians.** The **prime meridian,** like the equator, is numbered 0°. Lines of longitude west of the prime meridian are labeled *W.* Lines of longitude to the east are labeled *E.*

Notice that the lines are labeled with numbers and with the symbol °. This symbol stands for the word *degree.* A **degree** is a unit of measure. On these globes, the lines of latitude and longitude are 20° apart.

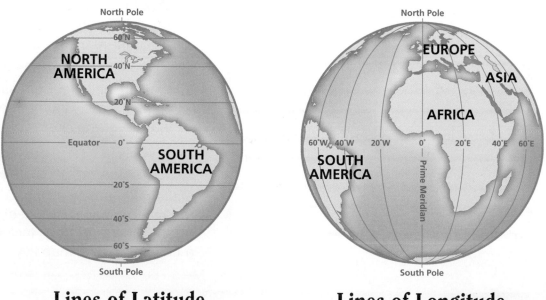

Lines of Latitude   **Lines of Longitude**

The Northwest Territory

How? Lines of latitude and lines of longitude cross each other to form a grid. A grid is a set of crossing lines. Now study the grid on the map of the Northwest Territory on this page. Can you identify the latitude and longitude of Kaskaskia? Find the line of latitude closest to this settlement. Write down the number. Then find the line of longitude closest to Kaskaskia. Write down that number. Be sure to include direction labels for both latitude and longitude.

Why? Lines of latitude and longitude help you find the exact location of a place, such as a city or a river. This is important to people such as ship captains. Suppose that you are far out on Lake Michigan in a boat. Knowing your latitude and longitude would tell you where you are. You could use this information to steer your ship in the direction you wish to go.

① How many degrees apart are the lines of latitude and the lines of longitude on the map of the Northwest Territory?

② Which line of latitude is closest to Vincennes? Which line of longitude is closest?

③ Which settlement shown on the map of the Northwest Territory has an "address" that is very close to 42°N, 88°W?

For more information, go online to *Atlas* at **www.sfsocialstudies.com**.

123

1810   1815   1820

1812
United States declares war on Britain in the War of 1812.

1818
Illinois becomes the twenty-first state.

Fort Dearborn

PREVIEW

Focus on the Main Idea
In 1818 Illinois became the twenty-first state in the Union.

PLACES
Fort Dearborn
Kaskaskia

PEOPLE
William Henry Harrison
Daniel Pope Cook
Nathaniel Pope
Elias Kent Kane
Shadrach Bond
Edward Coles

VOCABULARY
legislative branch
executive branch
judicial branch

EVENT
War of 1812

▶ Cannons such as this one once defended the Illinois frontier.

Forming a State

You Are There You are standing as straight and tall as possible. You have held this position for almost 20 minutes! Several men have given speeches from the steps of the old territorial government building in Kaskaskia. Over and over, speakers talk about how Illinois is no longer a territory. The territorial capitol is now a state capitol. Illinois is now the twenty-first state of the United States!

Two American soldiers light the fuse of a large cannon. Quickly you plug your ears with your fingers. The cannon fires, and people cheer! Again and again you hear the booming cannon and voices shouting in triumph.

Along with the others, you begin to shout, "Illinois! Illinois!"

 Sequence As you read the lesson, look for words that show the sequence of events related to Illinois's statehood.

The War of 1812

In the early 1800s settlers in Illinois faced challenges from Native Americans as well as from British soldiers who remained in the Northwest Territory after the American Revolution. The United States government wanted Native Americans to leave the area so that settlers could live, work, and trade without fear of attack. In 1809 **William Henry Harrison,** governor of the Indiana Territory, signed treaties with the Potawatomi, the Kickapoo, and other groups, opening parts of the Illinois Territory to white settlers.

British soldiers urged those Native Americans who remained in Illinois to hold on to their land. As the years passed, relations between the new settlers and the British and their Native American allies grew worse. To protect settlers U.S. soldiers built forts at key locations in the Northwest, such as **Fort Dearborn,** in present-day Chicago.

In 1812 tensions between the settlers and the British boiled over. Once again, the United States was at war with Great Britain. The conflict was called the **War of 1812**. Then, on a hot August day, a group of Potawatomi attacked and destroyed Fort Dearborn. U.S. troops responded by attacking many Native American villages. When the United States won the war in 1814, the British left the Northwest.

REVIEW What happened in the Northwest after the War of 1812 ended? ⟳ **Sequence**

Fort Dearborn and Chicago

Fort Dearborn (below) was built in 1803 near the mouth of the Chicago River. After being destroyed in 1812, the fort was rebuilt in 1816. The fort was abandoned in 1836. Most of the structures were destroyed in the late 1850s. Those buildings that still stood were destroyed in the Great Chicago Fire of 1871. Today the site of Fort Dearborn is home to the modern buildings of the Chicago skyline.

▶ The circled area in the photo of downtown Chicago (right) shows the former site of Fort Dearborn (below).

Our First Constitution

In 1817 **Daniel Pope Cook**, a newspaper editor who later was elected to Congress, suggested that Illinois join the Union. **Nathaniel Pope**, Illinois's representative in Washington, guided the plan through Congress. On December 3, 1818, Illinois became the twenty-first U.S. state.

Elias Kent Kane, a judge from Randolph County, helped write the first state constitution. The Illinois constitution divided government into three branches: the **legislative branch** to make the laws; the **executive branch** to carry out these laws; and the **judicial branch** to determine whether laws are fair and to see that laws are carried out fairly.

The Illinois constitution set the capital at **Kaskaskia.** For the next several years, lawmakers in Illinois would argue whether slavery should be legal. The first constitution provided that no new slaves could come to Illinois. However, slaves were still used in parts of the state. Illinois's first governor, **Shadrach Bond**, supported slavery. However, after **Edward Coles** became governor in 1822, he finally defeated the efforts of lawmakers to make slavery legal. Illinois would remain a free state.

REVIEW What happened in 1818, one year after Daniel Pope Cook suggested that Illinois join the Union?
⟳ Sequence

Summarize the Lesson

- **1812** The United States declared war on Britain.
- **1818** Illinois became the twenty-first state.

LESSON 2 ⟩ REVIEW

Check Facts and Main Ideas

1. ⟳ Sequence On a separate sheet of paper, list in order three events that led to Illinois's statehood.

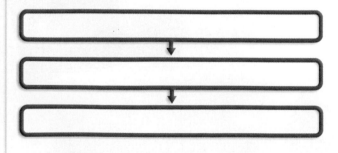

2. Explain the sequence of events in Illinois that led to the War of 1812.

3. List the three branches of government provided for by the first state constitution.

4. Which difficult political issue was addressed by the Illinois constitution?

5. Critical Thinking: *Point of View* Why might the U.S. Congress have been eager to admit new states?

Link to 〰 Writing

Make a Chart Show the structure of Illinois's first state government in a chart. Include the names of the three branches of government as well the responsibility of each branch.

Nathaniel Pope
1784–1850

At age 25, Nathaniel Pope served as secretary of Illinois Territory—and as governor for six months when Governor Edwards was absent. However, Pope did his most important work when he served as Illinois's territorial representative in Washington.

In 1818 Pope guided the plan for Illinois statehood through Congress. Pope urged lawmakers to approve a plan that extended the northern border of Illinois from near the southern end of Lake Michigan to a line 41 miles farther north. The plan was approved, and Illinois entered the Union in 1818.

BIOFACT

Pope was the cousin of Illinois Governor Ninian Edwards (top) and the uncle of Illinois Congressman Daniel Pope Cook (bottom).

By giving Illinois a longer coastline, Pope shaped the state's history. This area now includes Chicago.

Pope also suggested ways to promote education. He knew that Illinois could earn money by selling land. Pope suggested a law that said that three percent of this money should be used

". . . for the encouragement of learning, of which one-sixth part . . . [should] be exclusively bestowed upon a college or university."

Learn from Biographies

What important work did Nathaniel Pope perform in Washington?

Students can research the lives of significant people by clicking on *Meet the People* at **www.sfsocialstudies.com.**

Standing Up for Freedom

Governor Edward Coles believed that slavery was unfair and wrong. When he worked to make slavery against the law in Illinois, he was acting responsibly.

Edward Coles grew up in the state of Virginia, where slavery was legal. He was friends with many of Virginia's government officials. Many of his relatives and friends owned plantations and slaves. In fact, 21-year-old Edward Coles was given a plantation and all of its enslaved workers. Even though he accepted the gift, he remained troubled by it. He came to believe that it was unfair for one person to own another person.

Coles worked for six years as the private secretary to President Madison in the White House. During this time he urged leaders to make a plan to free enslaved people in the western territories. Finally, Coles quit his job in Washington, D.C., and made his own plan to move to the Illinois Territory.

In the spring of 1819, Coles sold his land in Virginia. Then he traveled west with the enslaved African Americans who had worked on his plantation. As the group floated on a flatboat down the Ohio River, Coles announced that every one of the group was now a free person. Furthermore, any and all were free to join him in Illinois. There he would provide them with farms and pay them to work.

In 1822 Coles became the second governor of Illinois. He held office until 1826, working hard to end slavery within the state. However, most of the leaders of Illinois's legislature were trying to make slavery legal. In 1824 Coles gave a speech that helped defeat a call for a constitutional convention to consider legalizing slavery. Coles said that Illinois's people must choose

> *"whether all [of Illinois's] inhabitants shall live in simple and happy freedom, or one half of them shall be reduced to . . . cruel servitude to support . . . the other half."*

Responsibility in Action

Research a story of a person or a group of people who are working to make their communities stronger. How does their work show their sense of responsibility?

129

Chapter Summary

 **Sequence**

On a separate sheet of paper, make a chart like this one. Fill in the events in the order they happened.

- Illinois became the 21st state.
- Northwest Territory was formed.
- Illinois Territory was formed.
- Indiana Territory was formed.

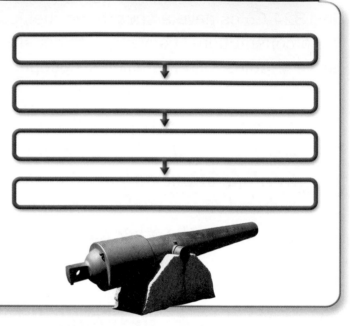

Vocabulary

Match each word with the correct definition or description.

1 **ordinance** (p. 119)

2 **district** (p. 119)

3 **expedition** (p. 121)

4 **legislative branch** (p. 126)

5 **executive branch** (p. 126)

a. a journey

b. section

c. the part of government that makes laws

d. the part of government that carries out laws

e. a law

People and Places

Write a sentence explaining why each of the following people or places was important in Illinois. You may use two or more in a single sentence.

1 **Northwest Territory** (p. 119)

2 **Indiana Territory** (p. 120)

3 **Illinois Territory** (p. 120)

4 **Ninian Edwards** (p. 120)

5 **Fort Dearborn** (p. 125)

6 **Nathaniel Pope** (pp. 126, 127)

7 **Kaskaskia** (p. 126)

8 **Shadrach Bond** (p. 126)

1809
Illinois Territory
was created.

1812
The United States
declared war
on Britain.

1812
Potawatomi
attacked
Fort Dearborn.

1818
Illinois became the
twenty-first state.

Facts and Main Ideas

1 How did the Northwest Ordinance change life in Illinois?

2 How did the Louisiana Purchase change the geography of the United States?

3 **Time Line** How many years passed from the passage of the Northwest Ordinance until the formation of the Illinois Territory?

4 **Main Idea** What were some of the features of Illinois' first Constitution?

5 **Main Idea** How did Nathaniel Pope help Illinois gain statehood in 1818?

6 **Critical Thinking:** *Compare and Contrast* How was slavery handled in the Northwest Ordinance and in the first constitution of Illinois?

Write About History

1 **Write a letter** to a friend or relative explaining your parents' decision to move to the Northwest Territory in the late 1700s. What draws them to the region?

2 **Write a composition** explaining why people in western Illinois were unhappy with territorial capitals in Marietta and Vincennes.

3 **Write a "What If" story** describing what might have happened if Nathaniel Pope had failed to extend the state's northern border.

Apply Skills

Find Latitude and Longitude

Look at the map, and answer the questions below.

1 What line of longitude is closest to the intersection of the Mississippi and Missouri Rivers?

2 Which city is closest to 38°N latitude and 90°W longitude?

3 The southern tip of Lake Michigan is nearest what latitude? What longitude?

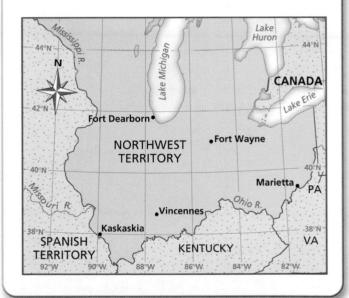

Internet Activity

To get help with vocabulary, people, and places, select the dictionary or encyclopedia from *Social Studies Library* at **www.sfsocialstudies.com**.

131

CHAPTER 6

Growth and Change in Illinois

Lesson 1

Bad Axe River 1832
Native Americans are defeated during the Black Hawk War.

1

Lesson 2

Chicago 1860
Chicago becomes one of the busiest cities in the Midwest.

2

Why We Remember

Between 1830 and 1860, new ideas for farming and new ways to transport goods and people helped increase settlement and improve life in Illinois. For example, state leaders made plans to link the Illinois River with the Great Lakes. Railroad tracks soon crisscrossed the state. As a result, cities grew across the former prairie. Factories produced goods that previously had been made only by hand. These changes became the building blocks for the Illinois we know today.

1800	1825	1850

1804
The first land office opens at Kaskaskia.

1832
Sauk and Fox forces are defeated by U.S. military troops in Black Hawk War.

1833
The Treaty of Chicago opens northern Illinois to settlers.

1844
Abraham Lincoln buys a house in Springfield.

MICHIGAN TERRITORY
Bad Axe River

PREVIEW

Focus on the Main Idea
In the first years of statehood, settlers in Illinois began building a frontier society.

PLACES
Springfield
Shawneetown
Vandalia
Rock Spring Seminary
Michigan Territory
Bad Axe River
Cumberland, Maryland
Erie Canal

PEOPLE
Juliette Magill Kinzie
Abraham Lincoln
John Mason Peck
Keokuk
Black Hawk

VOCABULARY
institution

TERM
National Road

EVENTS
Black Hawk War
Battle of Bad Axe
Treaty of Chicago

The People and the Land

You Are There You awaken to the sound of freezing rain tapping the roof. In a flash you pull on your clothes and head downstairs to greet your mother. She smiles as she stands at the fireplace, stirring a pot of oatmeal.

Although the ice and rain burn your face, bitter cold weather doesn't stop you from completing your morning chores. First you go to the well and fill a bucket with water for the livestock in the barn. You give each cow and horse a generous drink of water. Now it's time for you to eat. As you head back to the house, you begin thinking about the day ahead.

▶ **A frontier home**

Sequence As you read, look for words that show the sequence of events in our state's growth into a frontier society.

Daily Life on the Illinois Frontier

In the early 1800s, life on the Illinois frontier was challenging. As a result, all members of a family, including young children, worked together to do chores in and around the home. Men worked in the fields to raise crops for food. They used tools, simple plows, and animals to plant seeds, turn the sod, and harvest crops. Farmers used axes to split logs for use as fuel or for building furniture.

While men raised and hunted food, women on the frontier kept the family's home running. Before dawn each day, women built fires to heat the house. They also baked bread, cooked, cleaned the house, and tended to the garden. Children helped with light chores. They might have helped their mothers by collecting eggs from chickens and by milking the cows.

Juliette Magill Kinzie was one such pioneer woman who moved to Chicago in 1833. Later in her life, she wrote about her memories of what life was like on the frontier. Another Illinoisan was a young man named **Abraham Lincoln.** Lincoln was born near Hodgenville, Kentucky. His family moved to Indiana when he was seven and then to Illinois. Lincoln bought his house in **Springfield** in 1844. He would later become the first President from Illinois.

Most pioneers had a firm sense of independence, or freedom. Yet families helped one another in times of need.

Literature and Social Studies

Frontier Newspapers

Newspapers were printed in larger towns and cities in Illinois. Many of these newspapers featured poems about life on the prairie. For example, the *Sangamo Journal,* a newspaper in Sangamon County, printed these lines in 1832 by a woman named Mrs. Sigourney.

And see our rugged prairie men:
O, who more free than they;—
They're tall, they're stout—they
never give out;
Who dares them to the fray?
But free as the wild winds that
sweep
Along our boundless plains,
Are we, and still the boon we'll keep,
While earth—while heav'n remains.

They worked together to clear fields, raise barns, and build fences. Although life on the frontier was hard, it was not all work. To relax, people went visiting, attended dances and weddings, wrestled, and held foot races. Pioneers were known for their lively sense of humor and their fondness for tall tales. Some people could read, and they kept a few books in the house for relaxing by the fire.

REVIEW How did daily life differ for men and women?
Compare and Contrast

Building a Society

In its early years of statehood, Illinois had few institutions. An **institution** is a place or an organization that serves the public. The first institutions in the area were land offices, created by the U.S. Congress to sell land to settlers. In 1804 the town of Kaskaskia opened such a land office. Another early land office opened in **Shawneetown,** on the banks of the Wabash River. In 1816 Shawneetown became home to the first bank in Illinois. By 1821 banks were helping people save money and making loans in **Vandalia** and Edwardsville. Such institutions also provided a place for settlers to get news from other parts of the country.

During the 1820s and 1830s, schools and colleges began to open in Illinois. Many of the earliest schools in Illinois were opened by church leaders. For instance, in 1827, **John Mason Peck** opened the first college in Illinois, called **Rock Spring Seminary.** In 1834 the first public school opened in Chicago. Over the next few years, public schools opened in other cities such as Alton, Springfield, and Jacksonville.

REVIEW What were the purposes of Illinois's first institutions?
Summarize

FACT FILE

Famous Firsts in Illinois History

What	Where	When
Coal mine	Jackson County	1811
Newspaper	Kaskaskia	1814
State prison	Alton	1830
Educational institution for women	Jacksonville	1835

▶ Schools and newspapers were important to frontier Illinois.

▶ State prisons kept order in Illinois.

▶ Coal mines were a good source of jobs in southern Illinois.

▶ During the Battle of Bad Axe Native American women and children were forced to flee.

Taking More Land

As settlers created new communities in the western lands, efforts were made to remove Native Americans from the area. Representatives from the Sauk and Fox people signed a treaty with the United States government that transferred 50 million acres of Sauk and Fox land.

A few years later, in 1819, Kickapoo leaders in northern Illinois signed over nearly all Kickapoo land in Illinois. Then the Kickapoo moved west into Missouri.

These land treaties with the United States angered some Native Americans. Yet some Native Americans, such as the Sauk leader **Keokuk,**

thought that they had no choice but to give up their land. Because Keokuk signed many of these treaties, he became a rival and enemy of another Sauk leader, **Black Hawk.** Black Hawk thought that resisting settlers and the United States government was the proper course of action. So, in 1832, Black Hawk led Sauk warriors into battle against Illinois soldiers. The **Black Hawk War** had begun.

After months of fighting, the United States troops joined the Illinois militia. They trapped Black Hawk and his men in the part of the **Michigan Territory** that we now call Wisconsin. This final battle took place near the **Bad Axe River** and the Mississippi River. Many people died in what is now called the **Battle of Bad Axe.**

REVIEW How did Keokuk and Black Hawk differ in their views about land treaties with the United States? **Compare and Contrast**

▶ Black Hawk encouraged Native Americans to resist giving up their land to settlers.

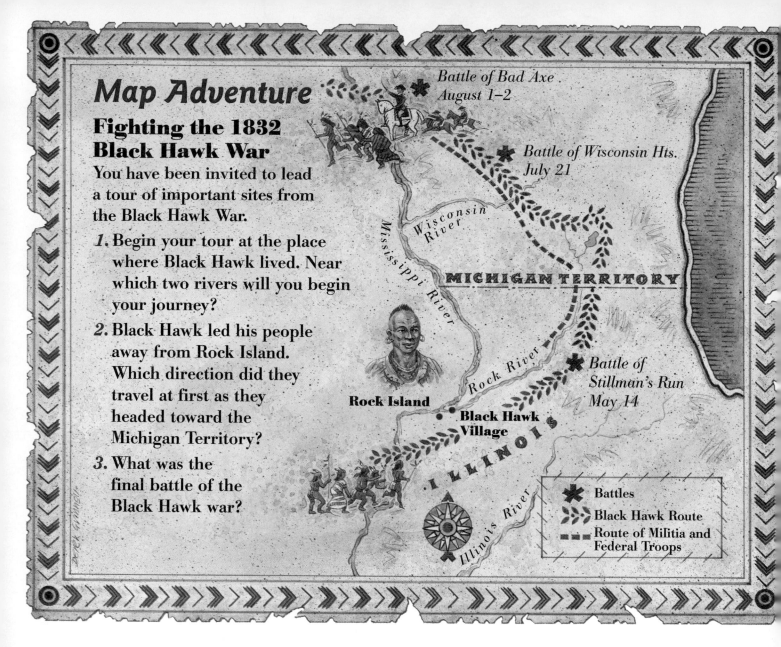

Map Adventure

Fighting the 1832 Black Hawk War

You have been invited to lead a tour of important sites from the Black Hawk War.

1. Begin your tour at the place where Black Hawk lived. Near which two rivers will you begin your journey?

2. Black Hawk led his people away from Rock Island. Which direction did they travel at first as they headed toward the Michigan Territory?

3. What was the final battle of the Black Hawk war?

Battle of Bad Axe
August 1–2

Battle of Wisconsin Hts.
July 21

Wisconsin River

Mississippi River

MICHIGAN TERRITORY

Rock River

Rock Island

Black Hawk Village

Battle of Stillman's Run
May 14

ILLINOIS

Illinois River

✳	**Battles**
🌿	**Black Hawk Route**
– –	**Route of Militia and Federal Troops**

The War Ends

The Black Hawk War greatly affected Native Americans in Illinois. United States troops had forced most of the Sauk and Fox people out of Illinois. Those Native Americans who remained from other groups faced difficulties with the white settlers. Soon, most left for the far west.

In 1833 leaders of 77 Native American groups met with United States officials in Chicago. The two sides signed the **Treaty of Chicago**, in which the Native Americans traded their remaining lands in Illinois to the United States for money and supplies. As a result of the treaty, the United States government controlled the land of northern Illinois, as well as areas to the north and west. A large area of Illinois now was open to settlers, who took advantage of the newly available land.

People came to northern Illinois in great numbers, mostly from eastern states. Some people came by way of the **National Road**, which stretched from **Cumberland, Maryland,** to Illinois by 1838. Many others traveled along the new **Erie Canal,** opened in 1825, and then on steamboats across the Great Lakes. The backgrounds of these people differed from those of earlier settlers in southern and western Illinois.

Some of the thousands of new settlers were soldiers who had battled Native Americans in the Black Hawk War. Many of these veterans were granted plots of land in the northwestern part of the state.

REVIEW How did Illinois change as a result of the Treaty of Chicago?
Cause and Effect

Summarize the Lesson

1804 The first land office opened at Kaskaskia.

1832 Sauk and Fox forces were defeated by U.S. troops in the Black Hawk War.

1833 The Treaty of Chicago opened up northern Illinois to settlers.

1844 Abraham Lincoln bought a house in Springfield.

▶ **After the Black Hawk War ended, many settlers came to Illinois.**

LESSON 1   REVIEW

Check Facts and Main Ideas

1. ⊙ **Sequence** On a separate sheet of paper, list in order three events that led to the settlement of northern Illinois.

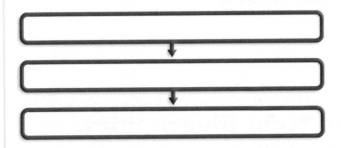

2. What tools were important to early Illinois settlers?

3. What was the first institution to open in early settlements?

4. How much land was transferred by the Sauk and Fox people to the U.S. government?

5. **Critical Thinking:** *Point of View* Why did Black Hawk lead his Sauk warriors against United States forces in 1832?

Link to ⊶∞⊷ **Art**

Make a Mural Use reference sources and other books in the library to research the construction of the National Road. Then make a mural showing how this construction project changed the lives of people in Illinois.

Juliette Magill Kinzie
1806–1870

Juliette Magill was born on September 11, 1806, in Middletown, Connecticut. As a child she loved to read letters her uncle sent to her family from Chicago. In 1830 Juliette married John H. Kinzie and they moved to Fort Winnebago in the Michigan Territory. John worked with the Winnebago people at the fort. In 1833, one year after the Black Hawk War ended, John and Juliette moved to Chicago.

BIOFACT *Juliette Kinzie's* Wau-Bun *is the earliest account of life on the Northern Illinois frontier.*

In 1856 Juliette published the book *Wau-Bun* about her life at the fort and a visit she made to Chicago in 1831. *Wau-Bun* means "early day" in Winnebago. This included stories about the Black Hawk War. The preface of her book states why she wrote *Wau-Bun*.

". . . a comparison of the present times with those that are past, would enable our young people, emigrating [moving] from . . . 'the East,' to bear . . . the slight . . . hardships they are at this day called to meet with."

You can still find the book in many libraries today.

Learn from Biographies
Why did Juliette Kinzie write *Wau-Bun?*

Students can research the lives of significant people by clicking on *Meet the People* at **www.sfsocialstudies.com.**

HERE AND THERE

Hodgenville, Kentucky, and Springfield, Illinois
Lincoln's First and Last Homes

Our state's most famous resident, Abraham Lincoln, was born in a small log cabin three miles south of Hodgenville, Kentucky. That home no longer exists. But you can see a model of Lincoln's boyhood home in Hodgenville, where he spent the early years of his life.

Later Lincoln lived in southwest Indiana and then in two places in Illinois before moving to Springfield in 1837. Lincoln bought his first and only house, a two-story building in Springfield, in 1844. Lincoln lived in that house until he moved to Washington, D.C., 17 years later to become President.

Today you can find a memorial to Lincoln's first home in Hodgenville. You can also take a tour of Lincoln's Springfield house, now run by the National Park Service.

▶ **A model of Lincoln's boyhood home in Hodgenville, Kentucky**

▶ **Lincoln made many speeches at the capitol in Springfield.**

▶ **Lincoln's home in Springfield**

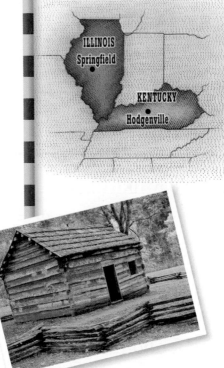

1830   1845   1860

1837
John Deere designs a new steel plow.

1848
Illinois and Michigan Canal is completed.

1856
Construction is completed on Illinois Central Railroad.

Chicago

PREVIEW

Focus on the Main Idea
People in Illinois developed new ways to farm, to travel, and to transport goods.

PLACE
Chicago

PEOPLE
Cyrus McCormick
John Deere

VOCABULARY
reaper
canal
immigrant

TERMS
Illinois and Michigan Canal
Northern Cross Railroad
Illinois Central Railroad

▶ In the early 1800s, farmers used scythes to cut wheat by hand.

Growth and Technology

You Are There

Dear Cousins,

Today was a day like many others on our farm. Father took the horses and wagon into the fields. First he used a long blade to cut stalks of wheat. Then he carried each armful of wheat and dumped it into the wagon. I helped too, but both of us were exhausted after such hard work. Father's workdays may be different very soon!

Tomorrow he will go to the workshop of a man named Mr. McCormick. Father wants to buy a new machine called a reaper, which can cut wheat and dump it into a wagon all by itself! Father says that the reaper will help us harvest more wheat so that we can sell some in town. He is very excited. I can hardly believe such a machine exists!

Sequence Look for words that show the sequence of changes in farming, transportation, and the growth of cities.

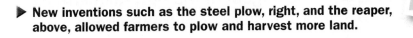

▶ New inventions such as the steel plow, right, and the reaper, above, allowed farmers to plow and harvest more land.

New Methods for Farmers

As you learned in Lesson 1 of this chapter, the early pioneers raised crops for their families. Then new machines and new ideas let farmers harvest more crops from their land. Because farmers could work more land in less time, they were able to sell crops to others.

The first of these new machines was a reaper built by **Cyrus McCormick** in Virginia in the early 1830s. A **reaper** is a machine that cuts and gathers grain. Using this reaper, a farmer could cut ten acres of wheat in a day. That is more than three times as much as could be cut by hand! During the next few dozen years, McCormick kept improving this reaper in many ways.

McCormick had a keen eye for business. He knew that he could sell more reapers in the Midwest than anywhere else in the United States. Therefore he moved from Virginia and opened a factory in Chicago in 1847. Then McCormick traveled around the state, talking to farmers and filling hundreds of orders for reapers.

As you read in Chapter 2, in 1837, **John Deere** designed new steel plow blades that let sod fall directly to the ground. This kept the plow blades free of sticky sod and saved farmers time, since they did not have to stop plowing to clean the blade with their hands. Deere manufactured plows in his factory in Grand Detour, Illinois. In 1848 he opened a new factory in Moline.

REVIEW Was the reaper invented before or after the steel plow was invented? ⟳ **Sequence**

Illinois Railroads, 1856

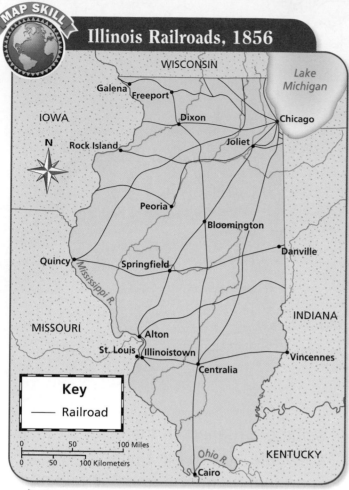

WISCONSIN

Lake Michigan

IOWA

Galena
Freeport
Dixon
Chicago
Joliet
Rock Island
N
Peoria
Bloomington
Quincy
Springfield
Danville
Mississippi R.
INDIANA
MISSOURI
Alton
St. Louis
Illinoistown
Vincennes
Centralia
KENTUCKY
Ohio R.
Cairo

Key

—— Railroad

0   50   100 Miles
0   50   100 Kilometers

▶ **Early rail lines crossed Illinois from east to west, as well as from north to south.**

MAP SKILL Location *Name a city in the center of Illinois that was served by two early train lines.*

New Ways to Travel

As farmers began to produce more crops than they needed to survive, they needed ways to carry extra crops to market. For this reason, Illinois planned a transportation system of canals and railroads. A **canal** is a waterway dug across land to connect two bodies of water.

In 1836 work started on a canal that would connect the Illinois River and Lake Michigan. When it was finally finished in 1848, it was named the **Illinois and Michigan Canal.**

In addition, road construction also opened up the Illinois frontier to new settlers and economic opportunities. The National Road finally reached Vandalia in 1839. The project would continue westward, linking Vandalia to cities such as St. Louis, Missouri.

In 1838 the first railroad in Illinois, the **Northern Cross Railroad**, began running from Meredosia to Morgan City—only 12 miles. When the line was completed years later, it linked the cities of Quincy, Springfield, and Danville.

The largest of the new railroads was the **Illinois Central Railroad,** started in 1851. The line was built to connect with others crossing Illinois from east to west. When the railroad was finished in 1856, it stretched from Galena to Cairo and was the world's longest railroad. This railroad system provided a new and faster way to transport people and goods within Illinois.

REVIEW How did a transportation system affect the lives of Illinois farmers? **Cause and Effect**

Changing Cities in Illinois

The improvements in farming and in transportation encouraged more people to move to Illinois. Many immigrants came to live and work in Illinois in the 1840s and 1850s. An **immigrant** is someone who travels to another country to live. Many people came from Germany, Ireland, and Sweden to help build the Illinois and Michigan Canal and then remained in Illinois. At the same time, people migrated from the eastern United States to Illinois.

Illinois experienced tremendous growth in these years. Settlements appeared near new roads and railroads, and towns swelled into cities. In 1818 Illinois had a population of just over 40,000. By the time the U.S. Census was taken in 1830, the population had grown to 157,445. By 1850 more than 850,000 people lived in the state.

By 1860 Chicago was the state's largest city, with a population of 112,172. The growth in population in places such as Chicago, Peoria, Springfield, Galena, and Alton led to another important change. People soon demanded that the capital be moved to a central location. As you remember from Chapter 5, Kaskaskia had served as the first capital of Illinois. However, after just two years, the capital was moved to Vandalia, where it remained from 1820 until 1839. In that year the capital was moved again, to Springfield, where it remains today.

REVIEW What led to the growth of many Illinois cities? **Cause and Effect**

▶ Railroads made it easier to move goods and people across the state.

Illinois in 1860

Between 1850 and 1860, the population of Illinois doubled to more than 1,700,000 people. Industry was making its mark on the state, especially in the north. Railroads and canals quickly made **Chicago** the center of trade and business in the Midwest. For instance, Chicago was the leading market for livestock in the United States.

Progress touched towns and cities all over the state. More and more people lived in houses built with boards, and fewer people lived in log cabins. Pipes beneath streets carried water and gas to homes and businesses. Illinois had left behind its frontier days.

REVIEW How did the population of Illinois change between 1850 and 1860? **Main Idea and Details**

Summarize the Lesson

1837 John Deere designed a new steel plow.

1848 Illinois and Michigan Canal was completed.

1856 Illinois Central Railroad was completed.

▶ By 1860 Chicago was becoming one of the largest cities in the Midwest.

LESSON 2 REVIEW

Check Facts and Main Ideas

1. **Sequence** On a separate sheet of paper, list in sequence three events that helped improve transportation in Illinois during the 1800s.

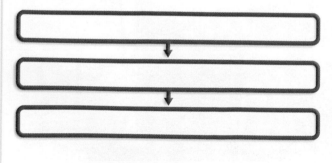

2. How did the work of McCormick and Deere improve the lives of farmers?

3. Which railroad line connected Galena and Cairo?

4. What region of Illinois experienced the most population growth?

5. **Critical Thinking:** *Predict* How do you think the state's transportation system will shape the future of Illinois?

Link to Mathematics

Make a Graph Using your textbook and other reference books, find out how the population of Illinois changed every ten years between 1820 and 1860. Then make a bar graph that shows the state's growth.

Changes in Transportation

As the United States grew, new forms of transportation developed. These were needed to move people and goods throughout the nation. Many people used these new ways of traveling to move to Illinois and to settle on the frontier.

1786
Steamboat
Inventor John Fitch used steam power to drive riverboats. One of his early experimental boats had 12 oars that were moved back and forth by the steam engine.

1825
Erie Canal
The 360-mile (580-km) Erie Canal opened in the United States in 1825. It enabled boats to travel from the Atlantic Ocean to the Great Lakes.

1840
Prairie Schooner
Families moving to the West often made the journey in rugged, canvas-covered wagons pulled by teams of horses, mules, or oxen. These white-topped wagons looked like sailing ships as they crossed the wide prairies, so they were called prairie schooners.

1843
Locomotive
As railroads grew rapidly, new companies were formed to supply them with locomotives. Those built by William Norris's company in Philadelphia had their main driving wheels at the back. The front rested on a four-wheeled "bogie" that could swivel as the locomotive turned around sharp bends.

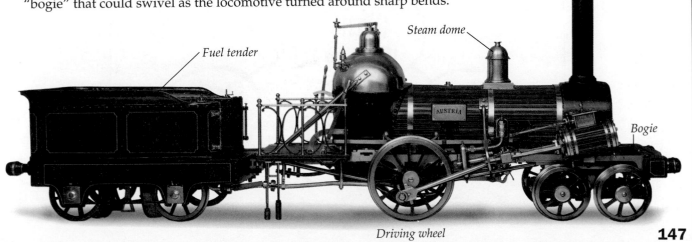

Chimney

Steam dome

Fuel tender

Bogie

Driving wheel

Research and Writing Skills

Take Notes and Write Outlines

What? Taking notes means writing down the main ideas about a topic you are studying. Later you can use your notes to review the most important ideas. An **outline** is a plan that shows information in an orderly way. Outlining helps you review the main points you have learned. Notes and outlines are study tools. They can help you remember what you hear in class and read in books.

Why? Taking notes and outlining help you study faster and better. When you prepare for a test, for example, you can study your notes or your outline. You do not need to reread all the pages in your book.

How? After you read a lesson, think about the main idea. Write it on notepaper. Do not copy sentences from the book. Use your own words. Then add the details that you think are important. Use abbreviations in your notes. For example, you might write IL for Illinois. Use words or phrases instead of sentences.

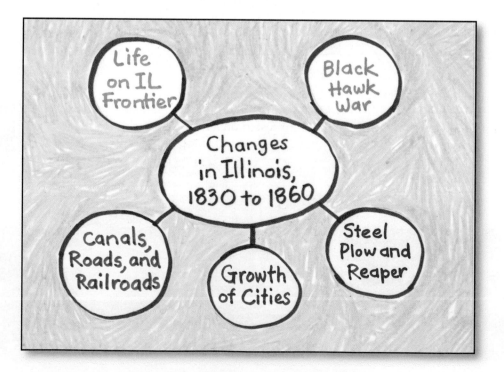

Growth and Change in Illinois

I. The People and the Land
   A. Daily Life on the Illinois Frontier
   B. Building a Society
   C. Taking More Land
   D. The War Ends

II. Growth and Technology
   A. New Methods for Farmers
   B. New Ways to Travel
   C. Changing Cities in Illinois
   D. Illinois in 1860

One quick way to take notes is to use a web. Write the main idea in the center circle. Then add details in the smaller circles around it. The web on page 148 shows details about the important changes that occurred in Illinois between 1830 and 1860.

Outlines follow a standard form. The outline on this page is of Chapter 6. The chapter title is at the top. The titles of the lessons are main headings. The headings in each lesson are written under the main headings. Notice that different kinds of numbering and lettering are used in the outline. Use Roman numerals for main headings. Use capital letters for the next level of detail.

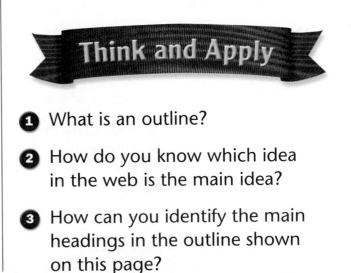

Think and Apply

1. What is an outline?

2. How do you know which idea in the web is the main idea?

3. How can you identify the main headings in the outline shown on this page?

1800   1810   1820

1804
The first land office opened at Kaskaskia.

Chapter Summary

 **Sequence**

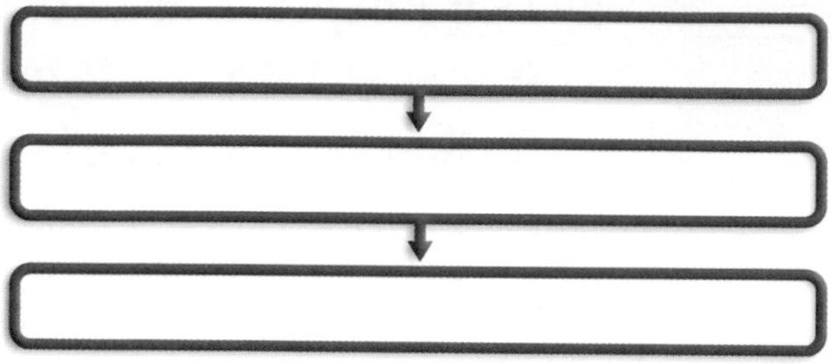

On a separate sheet of paper, draw the chart. Write one of these events in each box in the correct sequence.

- Native Americans sign the Treaty of Chicago.
- Illinois and Michigan Canal is completed.
- A land office opens in Kaskaskia.

[_____]
↓
[_____]
↓
[_____]

Vocabulary

Match each word with the correct definition or description.

① **institution** (p. 136)

② **reaper** (p. 143)

③ **canal** (p. 144)

④ **immigrant** (p. 145)

a. a place or an organization that serves the public

b. a person who travels to another country to live

c. a waterway dug to connect two bodies of water

d. a machine that cuts and gathers grain

People and Terms

Write a sentence explaining why each of the following people and terms were important in Illinois. You may use two or more in a single sentence.

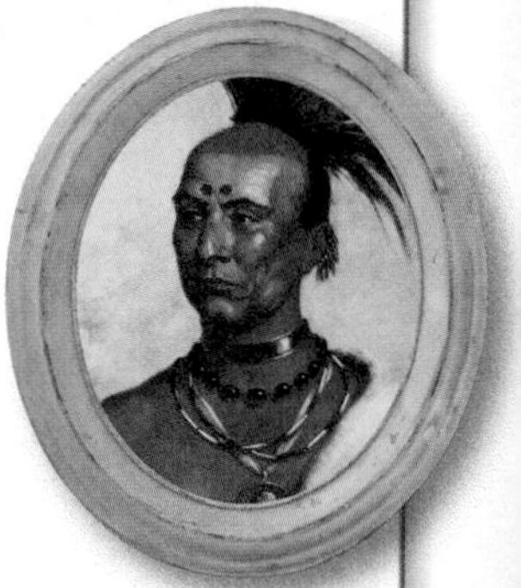

① **John Mason Peck** (p. 136)

② **Keokuk** (p. 137)

③ **Black Hawk** (p. 137)

④ **National Road** (p. 139)

⑤ **Cyrus McCormick** (p. 143)

⑥ **John Deere** (p. 143)

⑦ **Illinois and Michigan Canal** (p. 144)

⑧ **Illinois Central Railroad** (p. 144)

1830   1840   1850   1860

1832
Sauk and Fox forces were defeated by U.S. military in Black Hawk War.

1837
John Deere designed a new steel plow.

1848
Illinois and Michigan Canal was completed.

1856
Construction was completed on the Illinois Central Railroad.

Facts and Main Ideas

1. How did early settlers get along with their neighbors?

2. What two groups fought against the Native Americans in the Black Hawk War?

3. Which two men helped Illinois farmers increase their harvests?

4. How did people transport goods in Illinois in 1860?

5. **Time Line** How many years passed between the opening of the first land office in Kaskaskia and the end of the Black Hawk War?

6. **Main Idea** What institutions helped early settlers develop their communities?

7. **Main Idea** How was life in Illinois improved in the early to mid-1800s?

8. **Critical Thinking:** *Analyze* How did railroads and canals contribute to population growth in Illinois?

Apply Skills

Take Notes and Write Outlines

Copy the web below. Add details from Lesson 2 of this chapter to give more information about the topic in the center of the web.

Growth and Technology

Write About History

1. **Write a journal entry** about a day in the life of a ten-year-old child moving to Illinois in the early 1800s.

2. **Write a paragraph** telling how the lives of Illinois farmers changed during the early to mid-1800s.

3. **Write a news report** about the Black Hawk War. Use library resources to find additional information about the war. Include information that tells who, what, when, where, and why.

Internet Activity

To get help with vocabulary, people, and terms, select the dictionary or encyclopedia from *Social Studies Library* at www.sfsocialstudies.com.

The Flower-Fed Buffaloes

by Vachel Lindsay

Vachel Lindsay felt that poetry was a form of beauty. He believed that beauty could change people and make their lives better. During much of his life, Lindsay walked from state to state, chanting poetry for people in exchange for food and a place to spend the night.

Lindsay was born and died in Springfield. He loved Illinois, and some of his poems give a picture of the state in "the days of long ago." In "The Flower-Fed Buffaloes," Lindsay imagines a time before trains rolled through the countryside. In those days, buffaloes roamed the prairie, and Native Americans made their homes there.

The flower-fed buffaloes of the spring
In the days of long ago,
Ranged where the locomotives sing
And the prairie flowers lie low;
The tossing, blooming, perfumed grass
Is swept away by wheat,
Wheels and wheels and wheels spin by
In the spring that still is sweet.
But the flower-fed buffaloes of the spring
Left us long ago.
They gore no more, they bellow no more,
They trundle around the hills no more:—
With the Blackfeet, lying low,
With the Pawnees, lying low,
Lying low.

Review

Test Talk

Narrow the answer choices. Rule out answers you know are wrong.

Main Ideas and Vocabulary

TEST PREP

Read the passage below, and use it to answer the questions that follow.

After the American Revolution the land we call Illinois became part of the unnamed territory west of the United States. Then Congress passed the Northwest Ordinance in 1787. This <u>ordinance</u> created the Northwest Territory and laid out rules for governing the area. The Northwest Ordinance also banned slavery in these western lands. In 1800 the Indiana Territory, including present-day Illinois, was formed. Nine years later the U.S. government created the Illinois Territory.

In 1818 Illinois joined the Union as the twenty-first state. The Illinois constitution set the state's first capital at Kaskaskia. When Edward Coles became governor in 1822, he fought attempts to legalize slavery.

In 1833 Native American leaders met in Chicago with U.S. officials. By signing the Treaty of Chicago, these leaders sold the United States their remaining land in Illinois. A large area of the state was now open to <u>immigrants</u>. People from Sweden, Germany, and Ireland came to live and work in Illinois.

Beginning in the 1830s, the state experienced tremendous growth. When Illinois was granted statehood in 1818, it had a population of just over 40,000. By the time the United States census was taken in 1830, the population had more than tripled. By 1860 the population of Illinois reached over one and a half million people.

1 In this passage, <u>ordinance</u> means
  A government.
  B army.
  C territory.
  D law.

2 According to this passage, how many years passed between the Northwest Ordinance and Illinois statehood?
  A 13 years
  B 31 years
  C 21 years
  D 30 years

3 In this passage, <u>immigrants</u> means
  A pioneer families.
  B people who come to another country to live.
  C people who farm.
  D lawmakers.

4 By when was the population of Illinois higher than one and a half million?
  A 1830
  B 1840
  C 1850
  D 1860

People and Places

Match each person or place to its definition.

1 **Arthur St. Clair** (p. 119)

2 **Daniel Pope Cook** (p. 126)

3 **Rock Spring Seminary** (p. 136)

4 **Vandalia** (p. 136)

5 **John Deere** (p. 143)

a. proposed that Illinois join the Union as the twenty-first state

b. inventor of a new steel plow blade

c. the ending point of the National Road

d. first governor of the Northwest Territory

e. first college in Illinois

Write and Share

Make a Newspaper With three or four classmates, put together a newspaper that the members of a pioneer family might have enjoyed. One group member might write an article about new inventions. Another might draw and label a map of new railroad lines. Remember to include some advertisements and to address settlers who are your age.

Apply Skills

Take Notes and Write an Outline Using this textbook or another book, take notes on facts about the three capital cities of Illinois—Kaskaskia, Vandalia, and Springfield. Jot down when the capital was located in each place as well as other details about each capital. Then write an outline that organizes your information.

Read on Your Own

Look for these books in the library.

This Just In

Report breaking news in Illinois's history.

1 Choose an important event in the history of our state.

2 Choose roles to play for a press conference about the event: government officials or experts, news reporters, eyewitnesses, and other participants.

3 Research the event, focusing on one or two important details of the event. Work together to write questions and answers about the event.

4 Create a poster that a TV news station might use to announce breaking news about an event.

5 Hold your press conference as a class activity.

Internet Activity

For more information and activities, go to **www.sfsocialstudies.com.**

A Country in Conflict

What happens when people are divided by conflicting beliefs?

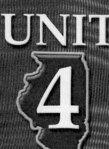

UNIT 4

Begin with a Primary Source

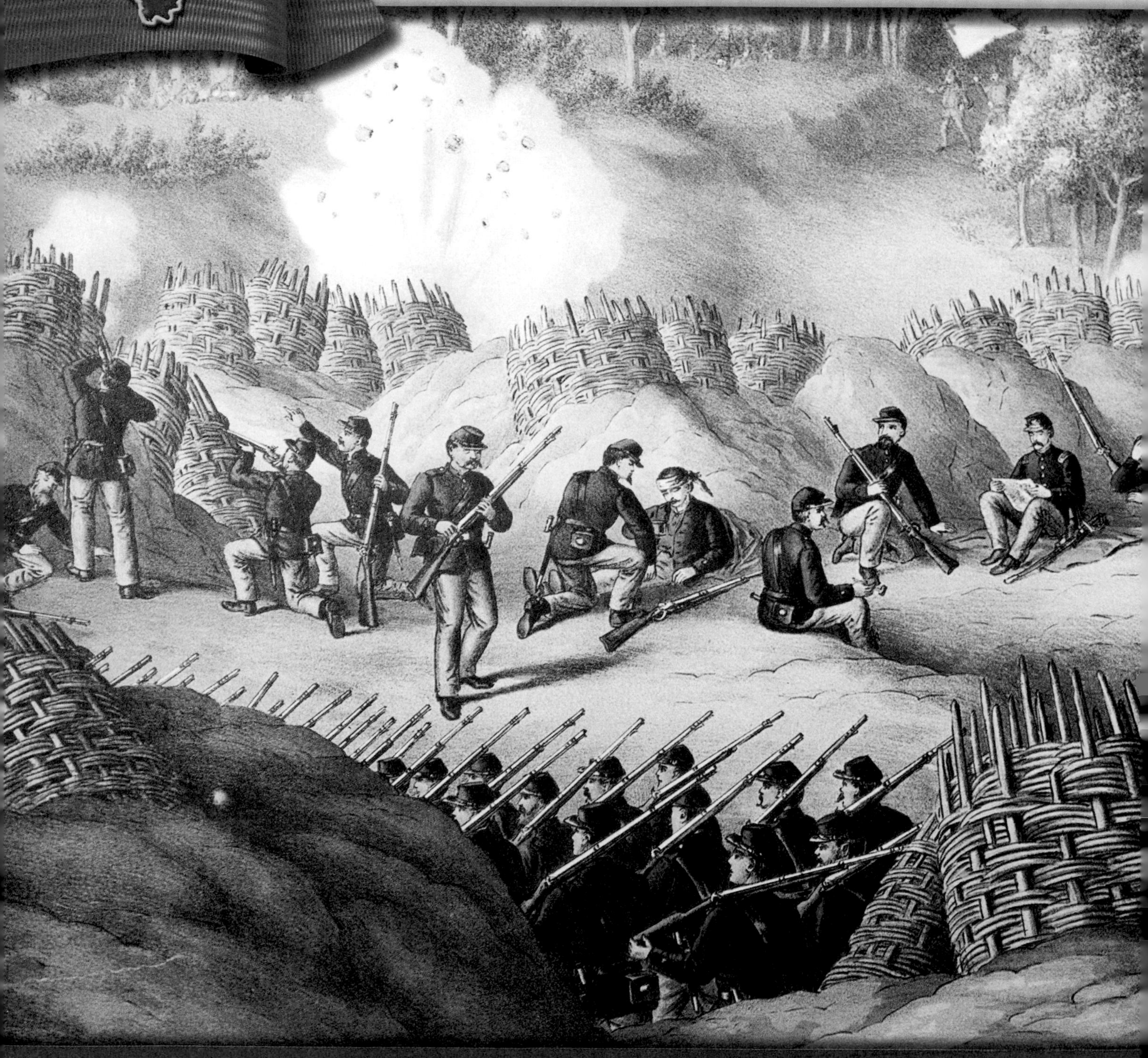

1855

1860

1856
Illinois abolitionist Owen Lovejoy is elected to Congress.

1858
U.S. Senate candidates Abraham Lincoln and Stephen A. Douglas participate in 7 debates.

1860
Lincoln is elected President of the United States.

> "With malice toward none, with charity for all, with firmness in the right . . . to do all which may achieve and cherish a just and lasting peace . . ."
>
> —Abraham Lincoln, March 4, 1865

This illustration was likely done by a group of artists shortly after the Confederate defeat at Vicksburg.

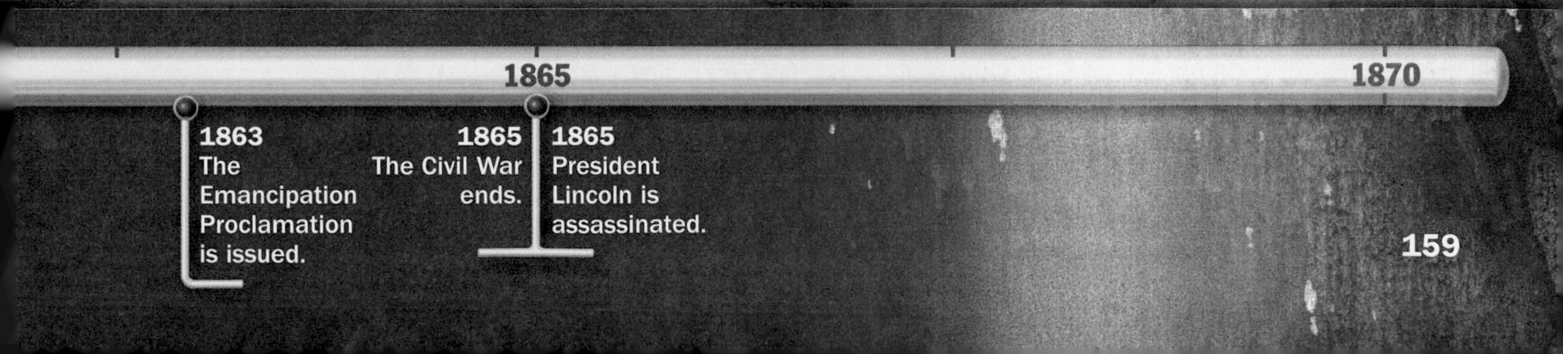

1865

1870

1863
The Emancipation Proclamation is issued.

1865
The Civil War ends.

1865
President Lincoln is assassinated.

Meet the People

Dred Scott

1795–1858

Birthplace: Virginia

Enslaved African American

- Was an enslaved African American from Missouri owned by an army surgeon
- For several years, lived in free territories with his owner
- Sued for freedom in U.S. Supreme Court but lost

Abraham Lincoln

1809–1865

Birthplace: Hodgenville, Kentucky

Lawyer, politician, U.S. President

- Lost Senate race to Stephen A. Douglas in 1858
- Was the sixteenth President of the United States (1861–1865)
- Issued the Emancipation Proclamation, which freed many slaves

Owen Lovejoy

1811–1864

Birthplace: Albion, Maine

Minister, abolitionist, politician

- Believed slavery could be ended through political action
- Was a conductor on the Underground Railroad
- Was elected to the U.S. House of Representatives in 1856

Stephen A. Douglas

1813–1861

Birthplace: Brandon, Vermont

Lawyer, politician

- Called the "Little Giant" because he was influential in Congress
- Defeated Republican candidate Abraham Lincoln in Senate race in 1858
- Lost presidential race to Abraham Lincoln in 1860

1790	1815	1840

1795 • Dred Scott

1809 • Abraham Lincoln

1811 • Owen Lovejoy

1813 • Stephen A. Douglas

1817 • Lizzie Aiken

1817 • Mary Ann Bickerdyke

1822 • Ulysses S. Grant

Lizzie Aiken

1817–1906

Birthplace: Auburn, New York

Union nurse, missionary

- Volunteered as a nurse, caring for troops in Illinois, Kentucky, and Tennessee
- Was known as "Aunt Lizzie" to the soldiers she treated
- Worked as a missionary in Chicago after the Civil War

Mary Ann Bickerdyke

1817–1901

Birthplace: Knox County, Ohio

Union nurse

- During the Civil War, was a member of the Corps of Union Nurses
- Moved from Galesburg to Cairo, Illinois, to treat wounded soldiers
- Helped get pensions for veterans and Civil War nurses after the war

Ulysses S. Grant

1822–1885

Birthplace: Point Pleasant, Ohio

Civil War general, U.S. President

- Attended the U.S. Military Academy at West Point, New York
- During the Civil War, commanded Union forces mostly in the West
- Served as the eighteenth President of the United States (1869–1877)

1865   1890   1915

1858

1865

1864

1861

1906

1901

1885

161

Reading Social Studies

A Country in Conflict

Cause and Effect

Recognizing cause and effect will help you understand your reading.

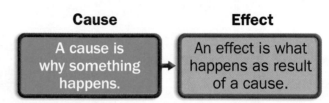

Cause	Effect
A cause is why something happens.	An effect is what happens as result of a cause.

- Writers sometimes, but not always, signal cause and effect by using clue words. These include *because, so, since,* and *therefore.*

- A cause can have more than one effect. An effect can have more than one cause. Sometimes an effect can become the cause of another effect.

- Sometimes a cause is not stated in the text. In that case, ask yourself, "Why did this probably happen?" Then back up your answer with information from the text or with facts that you already know.

Read the paragraph at the right. **Cause** and **effect** have been highlighted.

In Chapter 4 you read about the American Revolution. What caused this war? After the French and Indian War, Britain tried to raise money by taxing its American colonists. The colonists protested against the new taxes. Before long, the colonists' protests turned into rebellion.

Causes and Effects of the Civil War

In 1850 the government of the United States passed laws to reduce tensions between the slave-owning states in the South and the free states in the North. One of these laws was the Fugitive Slave Act. This law said that Northern citizens had to capture escaped African Americans and return them to the South. Some people in the North were angry about the cruelty of the law. They decided to work to abolish, or end, slavery. Many helped enslaved people escape to Canada. Relations between slave states and free states worsened.

In 1860 Abraham Lincoln was elected President of the United States. Soon after his election, several Southern states seceded, or broke away, from the Union. One of the reasons was that they feared the new President would work to outlaw slavery. A large part of the Southern culture and economy depended on slavery. Soon the nation was divided between the free states of the North, which wanted to save the Union, and the states of the South, which wanted to preserve slavery as a way of life.

Apply it!

Use the reading strategy of understanding cause and effect to answer these questions.

1 Why did the United States government pass the Fugitive Slave Act?

2 What effect did the Fugitive Slave Act have on some people in the North?

3 What caused Southern states to break away from the Union?

CHAPTER 7

A Divided Country

Lesson 1

**1840s–1850s
Princeton
Lovejoy Homestead**
Owen Lovejoy's home was used to hide escaped slaves.

1

Lesson 2

**1858
Galesburg
The Lincoln-Douglas Debates**
Before the 1858 election, Lincoln and Douglas debated in seven Illinois cities.

2

Why We Remember

As citizens of the United States, we often take for granted the right to speak freely and to choose where we live and work. But from the 1600s to the 1860s, hundreds of thousands of African Americans in the United States had to do what other people told them to do all the time. They were denied the most basic rights guaranteed by the Constitution. You will read about African Americans who risked everything to gain freedom. You will also read about people in Illinois who worked to end slavery and took great risks to help enslaved people.

1830   1840   1850   1860

1830s
The Underground Railroad is active in every free state, including Illinois.

1850
The Compromise of 1850, which includes the Fugitive Slave Act, is passed.

1856
Illinois abolitionist Owen Lovejoy is elected to the U.S. House of Representatives.

•Princeton

PREVIEW

Focus on the Main Idea
In 1850 the United States government passed the Compromise of 1850 and the Fugitive Slave Act, making it harder for escaped slaves to find safety in the North.

PLACE
Princeton

PEOPLE
Henry Clay
Owen Lovejoy

VOCABULARY
slavery
abolitionist

TERMS
Compromise of 1850
Fugitive Slave Act
Underground Railroad

▶ **Enslaved people who fled the South often had shackles such as these on their legs or arms.**

Illinois: A Free State

You Are There It is dark except for slits of light coming through the cracks between the floorboards overhead. Your mother whispers that you should be very quiet. From upstairs you hear footsteps and angry voices. Dust falls through the cracks with every footstep. You need to sneeze, but you are afraid to.

After what seems like a very long time, a hole opens in the floor over your head. Some people help you and your mother up into the light. A woman says, "Don't worry. The slave owners are gone. Tonight we will take you to the next station on the Underground Railroad."

Stop the Runaway!
$100 Reward!

Runaway from the subscriber, living in Clay county, Mo., 3 miles south of Haynesville and 15 miles north of Liberty, a negro boy named SANDY, about 35 years of age, about 5 feet 6 inches high, rather copper color, whiskers on his lip, quick when spoken to, had black plush cap, and coarse boots. If apprehended a reward of $25 will be given if taken in Clay county; $50 if out of the county, and $100 if taken out of the State, and delivered to me or confined in jail so that I can get him.
April 3, 1860.   ROBT. THOMPSON.

Cause and Effect As you read, think about why the events of the 1850s caused people who were opposed to slavery to start working even harder against it.

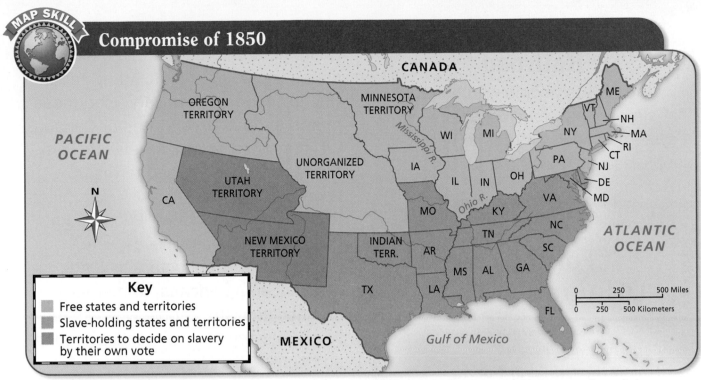

Compromise of 1850

CANADA

OREGON TERRITORY

MINNESOTA TERRITORY

PACIFIC OCEAN

ME

VT

NH

MA

RI

CT

NJ

DE

MD

NY

PA

OH

UTAH TERRITORY

CA

UNORGANIZED TERRITORY

WI

MI

IA

IL

IN

Mississippi R.

Ohio R.

VA

MO

KY

NEW MEXICO TERRITORY

INDIAN TERR.

AR

TN

NC

SC

ATLANTIC OCEAN

MS

AL

GA

TX

LA

FL

MEXICO

Gulf of Mexico

Key

Free states and territories

Slave-holding states and territories

Territories to decide on slavery by their own vote

0   250   500 Miles

0   250   500 Kilometers

▶ **An important part of the Compromise of 1850 was California's entry into the Union as a free state.**

MAP SKILL Movement *From which states would escaped slaves most likely come into Illinois?*

The Compromise of 1850 and the Fugitive Slave Act

In the 1800s Americans were sharply divided over the issue of **slavery,** which means owning a human being as property. In Southern states many landowners had crops that required a lot of work. Using slaves as workers allowed these people to sell their products more cheaply than products produced in other places. Slave owners eventually became dependent on slavery to support their way of life.

However, people in sixteen other states, including Illinois, believed that slavery was wrong. These states were called "free states" because they outlawed slavery. Many people who escaped from slavery thought they would be safe in Illinois. Then

Henry Clay, a senator from Kentucky, presented a set of laws known as the **Compromise of 1850.** Clay wanted to keep peace between the North and the South. One of the laws was the **Fugitive Slave Act,** which required all citizens, even people in free states, to help capture escaped slaves.

African Americans accused of being runaways were not allowed to speak in their own defense or have a jury trial. Instead, government officials decided what to do with them. Sometimes free African Americans were falsely accused of being runaways. They could be sent south into slavery, even if they were free men and women.

REVIEW What effect did the Fugitive Slave Act have on African Americans in free states? ➲ **Cause and Effect**

167

The Underground Railroad

By the 1830s people who believed that slavery was wrong began organizing a system of secret routes to help people escape from slavery. This system was called the **Underground Railroad**, and it ran through most free states, including Illinois. Many people who escaped from slavery used these routes to reach free states or Canada.

Different parts of the network were described using railroad terms. A secret route was a "line." A safe place to stop was a "station." People who helped the escaped slaves were "conductors." Conductors included free African Americans, former slaves, and **abolitionists**, people who worked to end slavery through politics, writing, and public speaking.

Many people escaping slavery found their way north by looking for the North Star, which was near the Big Dipper, or the "drinking gourd." They also passed messages about routes and secret signs in songs such as "Follow the Drinking Gourd."

> ## Literature and Social Studies
>
> ## "Follow the Drinking Gourd"
>
> When the sun comes back and
>   the first quail calls,
> Follow the Drinking Gourd.
> For the old man is waiting for to
>   carry you to freedom,
> If you follow the Drinking Gourd.
>
> The riverbank makes a very
>   good road,
> The dead trees show you the way,
> Left foot, peg foot, traveling on,
> Follow the Drinking Gourd.
>
> The river ends between two hills,
> Follow the Drinking Gourd.
> There's another river on the other
>   side,
> Follow the Drinking Gourd.
>
> Where the great big river meets
>   the little river,
> Follow the Drinking Gourd.
> For the old man is a-waiting for to
>   carry you to freedom,
> If you follow the Drinking Gourd.

REVIEW What effect did the North Star have on people escaping slavery?
◉ **Cause and Effect**

▶ **The Underground Railroad was a network of secret routes that were used to help African American slaves escape to freedom.**

The Lovejoy Homestead

Owen Lovejoy was a famous abolitionist in Princeton, Illinois. He was a minister who preached in his church against slavery. In 1856 he was elected to the United States House of Representatives. In Congress he became known for his powerful speeches against slavery.

Lovejoy served as a conductor on the Underground Railroad. Escaped African American slaves who passed through Princeton rode the "Lovejoy Line," using Lovejoy's home as a "station."

REVIEW How did Owen Lovejoy's beliefs about slavery affect his activities? ⟳ **Cause and Effect**

▶ Today Owen Lovejoy's house is a National Historic Landmark.

Summarize the Lesson

1830s The "Underground Railroad" was active in every free state, including Illinois.

1850 The Compromise of 1850, which included the Fugitive Slave Act, was passed.

1856 Illinois abolitionist Owen Lovejoy was elected to the U.S. House of Representatives.

LESSON 1   REVIEW

Check Facts and Main Ideas

1. ⟳ **Cause and Effect** On a sheet of paper, write an effect for each cause shown.

Cause		Effect
Many people believed that slavery was wrong.	→	
Clay wanted to ease tensions over slavery.	→	
Lovejoy wanted to help escaping slaves.	→	

2. How did the Fugitive Slave Act help slave owners?

3. How did the Underground Railroad help enslaved people escape?

4. Why was the song "Follow the Drinking Gourd" important to escaping slaves?

5. **Critical Thinking:** *Draw Conclusions* Were the activities of the abolitionists successful? Explain.

Link to 🔗 Science

Research the Big Dipper When slaves referred to the Drinking Gourd, they were talking about the Big Dipper, which is part of the constellation Ursa Major. Find out some facts about this constellation. Explain how the people who followed the Underground Railroad used the stars to guide them.

Fighting for Freedom

Dred Scott, an enslaved African American, became the center of attention in 1857 when his fight for freedom led him all the way to the United States Supreme Court.

Dred Scott was born on a Virginia plantation. As a young man, he traveled with his owner through parts of the slave-holding South. In the 1830s Scott's owner took him from Missouri into free territories such as Illinois and Wisconsin Territory. They lived outside slave states for several years before returning to Missouri. When Scott's owner died, Scott sued for his freedom. Because he had lived in free territories, he hoped a court would grant him his freedom. Beginning in 1846 Scott fought for his freedom in several different trials. In 1850 one Missouri court said that he was a free man. Two years later, however, the Missouri Supreme Court determined that he was still a slave and refused to give Scott his freedom.

Scott and his supporters felt this ruling was unfair. In 1856 they decided to take the case before the United States Supreme Court. One year later the highest court in the nation determined that Scott was a slave. The justices reasoned that since he was a slave, he did not have the rights of a citizen. Therefore, he was not able to bring the suit before the court.

BUILDING
CITIZENSHIP
Caring
Respect
Responsibility
Fairness
Honesty
Courage

Chief Justice Roger B. Taney said,

> "... it is the opinion of the Court. ...
> that neither Dred Scott himself nor any
> of his family, were made free by being
> carried into this territory. ..."

The Dred Scott decision made many Northerners afraid that slavery would soon spread all over the nation. Although Scott did not win his freedom, Justice Taney's ruling made people who were against slavery become more determined to work for fair treatment for all people. The court's decision influenced the Republican party to nominate Abraham Lincoln, who opposed the spread of slavery, as its candidate for President in 1860.

Fairness in Action

Taking turns to answer questions or express ideas in class is a good example of fairness in action.

171

1855

1860

1858
Lincoln and Douglas participate in seven debates.

1860
Abraham Lincoln is elected President.

Galesburg

PREVIEW

Focus on the Main Idea
In 1858 Lincoln and Douglas debated important issues that were dividing Americans.

PLACES
Freeport
Ottawa
Galesburg

PEOPLE
Stephen A. Douglas
Abraham Lincoln

VOCABULARY
candidate
debate
campaign
orator

TERM
Freeport Doctrine

EVENT
Presidential Election of 1860

▶ Abraham Lincoln debates Stephen A. Douglas at Galesburg.

The Great Debates

You Are There

October 7, 1858
    I am one of many newspaper reporters who have gathered here in Galesburg. People in the crowd are arguing and bumping each other as they eagerly await the latest debate between Abraham Lincoln and Stephen A. Douglas. I hear people arguing about the candidates. Some say that Douglas is a good man and Lincoln is going to cause trouble. Other people say that it's time to elect somebody who will take a stand against slavery instead of going along with the slave owners. As I peer through the crowd, I can see Lincoln and Douglas stepping up on to the platform. A hush falls over the audience. As the men debate the issues, I frantically scribble notes. I don't want to miss a single word!

Sequence As you read, note the sequence of events that led to Abraham Lincoln's election as President of the United States.

The Lincoln-Douglas Debates

Stephen A. Douglas, a Democrat from Chicago, had been a United States senator representing the state of Illinois since 1847. When he ran for reelection in 1858, the other candidate, or person running for political office, was Republican Abraham Lincoln from Springfield. Before the election, Lincoln challenged Douglas to debate, or publicly discuss, the issues.

One of the main topics during this campaign was slavery. A campaign is a competition by rival candidates leading up to an election. Lincoln did not want slavery to spread to the free states and territories. However, Douglas believed that each state and territory should make its own decisions about such issues. Douglas's belief became known as the Freeport Doctrine because he first explained it fully in Freeport, Illinois. The men debated before large crowds in seven Illinois cities: Ottawa, Freeport, Jonesboro, Charleston, Galesburg, Quincy, and Alton.

Unlike elections today, candidates for the Senate in the 1850s were not elected directly by voters. Instead, they were elected by representatives of the state government. Douglas won the support of most state officials, and was declared the winner of the election for the U.S. Senate seat.

Map Adventure

The Lincoln-Douglas Debates of 1858

Imagine that you are one of the newspaper reporters assigned to write about the Lincoln-Douglas debates.

1. Where and when is your first stop?
2. The longest trip to a debate was between which two cities?
3. About how much time passed between the first and last debates?
4. Why do you think the debates were held in so many cities across the state?

Freeport
August 27

Ottawa
August 21

Galesburg
October 7

Quincy
October 13

Charleston
September 18

Alton
October 15

Jonesboro
September 15

N
W   E
S

0   25   50   75   100 miles

0 25 50 75 100 kilometers

REVIEW Contrast how Lincoln and Douglas felt about slavery.
Compare and Contrast

The Election of 1860

Although Abraham Lincoln lost the 1858 race to become a senator, he won the respect of many people. He was a great **orator,** or public speaker, and many people liked his honest manner.

In May 1860 Lincoln was chosen to be the Republican party's presidential candidate. Later that year he defeated Stephen A. Douglas, John C. Breckinridge, and John Bell in the

▷ **Abraham Lincoln was the first Illinoisan to be President of the United States.**

Presidental Election of 1860 and became the sixteenth President of the United States in 1861. Many people were happy, but many Southern slave owners saw Lincoln's election as a threat to their way of life. To these people, Lincoln's election was a sign that it was time to act.

REVIEW How did the debates of 1858 help Lincoln win the 1860 Republican presidential nomination?
⟳ Cause and Effect

Summarize the Lesson

1858 Lincoln and Douglas participated in seven debates.

1860 Abraham Lincoln was elected President of the United States.

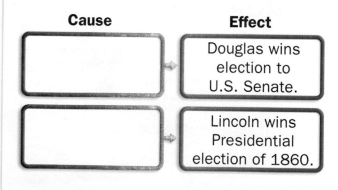

LESSON 2   REVIEW

Check Facts and Main Ideas

1. ⟳ Cause and Effect On a separate sheet of paper, fill in the cause for each effect listed below.

Cause	Effect
	Douglas wins election to U.S. Senate.
	Lincoln wins Presidential election of 1860.

2. Why was the topic of slavery one of the main issues debated by Lincoln and Douglas?

3. Why did debates in Illinois affect the way people around the country felt about Lincoln?

4. Why did some people dislike Lincoln's views on slavery?

5. Critical Thinking: *Compare and Contrast* How were Lincoln and Douglas alike, and how were they different?

Link to ⚭ Writing

Write a Speech Imagine that you are either Abraham Lincoln or Stephen A. Douglas. Write a speech that one of these orators might have delivered in 1860 to convince people that he was the better presidential candidate.

Abraham Lincoln 1809–1865

Abraham Lincoln came from Illinois to be our country's President during the Civil War.

Lincoln was born into a Kentucky farm family on February 12, 1809. He rarely went to school and had to work on the farm to help support his family. But he taught himself to read. His family moved to Indiana in 1816 and then to Illinois in 1830. While here, Lincoln became interested in politics. He was elected to the Illinois House of Representatives four times from 1834 to 1840.

BIOFACT *Abraham Lincoln is said to have carried important papers, such as letters and speeches, in his top hat.*

In 1836, after studying law on his own, Lincoln became a lawyer and moved to Springfield in 1837. As a lawyer, he became known for his honesty. He later went into national politics, believing that the government's role was

". . . to do for a community of people whatever they need to have done, but cannot do . . . for themselves."

Lincoln served in the U.S. Congress (1847–1849) and then returned home to his law career. He lost a campaign for the U.S. Senate in 1858. However, he was elected President in 1860—the first person born outside of the original thirteen states to hold the office.

Learn from Biographies

How do you think Lincoln's honesty served him as President?

Students can research the lives of significant people by clicking on *Meet the People* at **www.sfsocialstudies.com**.

Research and Writing Skills

Use Primary and Secondary Sources

What? A **primary source** is an eyewitness account or observation of an event. Primary sources are created by people who take part in or see an event. Diaries, speeches, letters, drawings, and photographs are all examples of primary sources.

Abraham Lincoln's "House Divided" speech to the Illinois State Republican convention in June, 1858, is also an example of a primary source.

> *. . . In my opinion, it [slavery] will not cease [stop] until a crisis shall have been reached and passed. "A house divided against itself cannot stand." I believe this government cannot endure [last], permanently, half slave and half free. I do not expect the Union to be dissolved [to be broken apart]; I do not expect the house to fall; but I do expect it will cease to be divided. It will become all one thing, or all the other. Either the opponents of slavery will arrest [stop] the further spread of it and place it where the public mind shall rest in the belief that it is in the course of ultimate extinction, or its advocates [those in favor of it] will push it forward till it shall become alike lawful in all the states, old as well as new, North as well as South.*

A **secondary source** is an account of an event written by someone who read or heard about it. This person did not take part in or see the event. An encyclopedia article or history book is an example of a secondary source.

> *Lincoln did not want slavery to spread to the free states and territories. However, Douglas believed that each state and territory should make its own decisions about such issues.*

Why? When you read a primary source, you get a firsthand account of the event and sometimes the writer's reactions to it. You can also learn about the writer. For example, the speech on page 176 was written by Abraham Lincoln in 1858. He was addressing his fellow Republicans at a state convention in Springfield, Illinois. The speech reveals Lincoln's concerns about what the issue of slavery was doing to the Union. Primary sources, such as the campaign poster of Abraham Lincoln on this page, can give you a clear picture of what Lincoln looked like before he became President. From an old poster you can learn general information about the period of history and personal information about the subject. Secondary sources provide more general information and often explain a primary source better.

How? You can often identify a primary source by the use of the pronouns *I* and *we.* Phrases such as "I saw," "we heard," and "I felt," can also help identify primary sources such as eyewitness accounts and reactions. A secondary source may use the pronouns *he, she,* and *they.* These pronouns signal that such an account was not written by an eyewitness. Secondary sources, such as history textbooks, may summarize historical events and explain why they are important.

Think and Apply

1. What important point was Abraham Lincoln trying to make when he gave this speech?

2. With a partner, list the different things that you can learn from the photo.

3. Compare and contrast the kinds of information you can get from primary and secondary sources of information.

1850

1850
The Compromise of 1850, including the Fugitive Slave Act, was passed.

Chapter Summary

Cause and Effect

On a separate sheet of paper, fill in an effect for each cause.

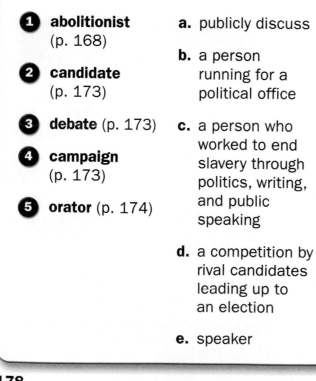

Cause	Effect
The Fugitive Slave Act was passed.	
Owen Lovejoy believed that slavery was wrong.	
Lincoln and Douglas debated slavery.	

Vocabulary

Match each word with the correct definition or description.

1. **abolitionist** (p. 168)

2. **candidate** (p. 173)

3. **debate** (p. 173)

4. **campaign** (p. 173)

5. **orator** (p. 174)

a. publicly discuss

b. a person running for a political office

c. a person who worked to end slavery through politics, writing, and public speaking

d. a competition by rival candidates leading up to an election

e. speaker

People

Write a sentence about each of the following people.

1. **Henry Clay** (p. 167)

2. **Owen Lovejoy** (p. 169)

3. **Dred Scott** (p. 170)

4. **Abraham Lincoln** (pp. 173, 175)

5. **Stephen A. Douglas** (p. 173)

1858
Stephen A. Douglas
defeated Abraham
Lincoln in the
U.S. Senate race.

1860
Lincoln was elected
President of the
United States.

Facts and Main Ideas

1 Why was Illinois considered a free state?

2 Why were songs such as "Follow the Drinking Gourd" important to people escaping slavery?

3 What was the purpose of the Compromise of 1850?

4 **Time Line** How long after the Compromise of 1850 was passed was Abraham Lincoln elected President of the United States?

5 **Main Idea** How did the Fugitive Slave Act change the lives of free African Americans in the North?

6 **Main Idea** Why was the topic of slavery one of the main issues debated by Lincoln and Douglas?

7 **Main Idea** How did Southern slave owners feel about Lincoln's election as President?

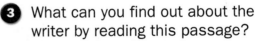

Internet Activity

To get help with vocabulary and people, select the dictionary or encyclopedia from *Social Studies Library* at **www.sfsocialstudies.com.**

Apply Skills

Use a Primary Source

Read the primary source below. Then answer the questions.

"He [Abraham Lincoln] tells you the Union cannot exist unless the States are all free or all slave; he tells you that he is opposed to making them all slave. . . . [Lincoln] is opposed to the admission of any more slave States under any circumstance."
Stephen A. Douglas
Freeport Doctrine 1858

1 Is this passage by Abraham Lincoln or is someone talking about Lincoln?

2 Why did Douglas write this part of his speech? To whom do you think Douglas is speaking?

3 What can you find out about the writer by reading this passage?

Write About History

1 **Write a letter** to a friend in Canada telling about your aunt's work on the Underground Railroad. Explain why she is willing to risk so much to help enslaved African Americans reach freedom.

2 **Write an editorial** for your local newspaper in 1860, explaining why you support Abraham Lincoln or Stephen A. Douglas in the presidential election.

CHAPTER 8

Illinois and the Civil War

Lesson 1

1861
Fort Sumter, South Carolina
Abraham Lincoln's inauguration helps trigger the Civil War.

1

Lesson 2

1863
Rock Island
Confederate prisoners of war are held at a camp on Rock Island.

2

Why We Remember

In 1860 the United States faced problems that threatened to destroy the nation. People had different opinions on the issues of slavery and the degree to which states should make decisions for themselves. The failure to solve these problems led to war. Almost 260,000 men from Illinois fought for the Union. Thousands never returned home. Those who did found that Illinois had been forever changed.

1860

1865

1861
The Confederate
States of America
is formed.

1863
Lincoln issues the
Emancipation Proclamation.

SOUTH
CAROLINA
Fort
Sumter

PREVIEW

Focus on the Main Idea
Disagreements over slavery
led to the outbreak of the Civil
War; Lincoln worked to restore
the Union and to free the
enslaved people of the South.

PLACE
Fort Sumter, South Carolina

PEOPLE
Jefferson Davis

VOCABULARY
secede
Confederacy

TERM
Emancipation
  Proclamation

EVENT
Civil War

Lincoln's Struggle

> **You Are There**
> You shift your weight from one leg to the other as you impatiently await your turn.
> News of the Emancipation Proclamation made it to Springfield a few days ago. From what you have heard, it seems clear that President Lincoln intends to free the enslaved people of the South. You have decided to join the Union Army. Your thoughts turn to what it will be like to be a soldier in the army and wear a uniform with brass buttons with an eagle on them.
> The officer at the table cries out "Next!" You are ready to become a soldier.

Cause and Effect As you read,
note how major events of the Civil War
period were caused by earlier events.

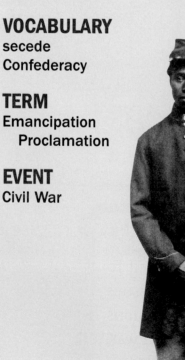

▶ **Many African Americans joined the Union forces as a result of the Emancipation Proclamation.**

▶ **The Confederates fired on the Union's Fort Sumter, starting the Civil War.**

The South Secedes

By 1860 growing differences divided the North and the South. Slavery was one of the biggest differences. By this time most Northern states had outlawed slavery. However, many people in the South were farmers who depended on slaves to care for and harvest their crops. Southerners argued for "states' rights," saying that the United States government should not tell them how to resolve issues like slavery. Tensions between the North and the South were so high that some states in the South threatened to **secede,** or formally withdraw, from the Union.

As you read in Chapter 7, Southerners were especially angry that Abraham Lincoln won the presidential election in 1860. By February 1861, seven Southern states—South Carolina, Mississippi, Florida, Alabama, Georgia, Louisiana, and Texas—seceded from the United States. They joined to form the Confederate States of America, also called the **Confederacy.** Mississippi's **Jefferson Davis** became president of the Confederacy. Davis's administration created its own constitution, which officially allowed slavery.

Fighting between the two sides did not start until April 12, 1861, about a month after Lincoln began his term in office. Confederate troops fired on **Fort Sumter,** a Union fort near the port city of Charleston, South Carolina. With this event the **Civil War** began. As Lincoln called for troops to end the rebellion, four more states joined the Confederacy: Virginia, Arkansas, Tennessee, and North Carolina.

REVIEW What event caused South Carolina to secede from the United States? ↺ **Cause and Effect**

▶ President Lincoln issued the Emancipation Proclamation to free slaves in the Confederate states.

Lincoln and Slavery

Abraham Lincoln had always made it clear that he thought slavery was wrong. He opposed the expansion of slavery into the western territories. At the same time, however, during the election of 1860 he promised to take no action to end slavery where it existed in the South. When the Civil War began, Lincoln was more concerned about restoring unity among the divided nation.

After several months of fighting, Lincoln's ideas about slavery slowly changed. By the summer of 1862, he believed that one of the Union's war aims should be the emancipation, or the freeing of enslaved people, in the South.

When Lincoln first became President, he tried to work out a plan for freeing the slaves gradually. However, Congress was not interested in this idea.

In September 1862, as the war raged on, Union forces defeated Confederate forces at Antietam, Maryland.

▶ This poster was used to encourage African American soldiers to join the Union forces.

Lincoln used this victory as an opportunity to warn the Confederate states that if they did not rejoin the Union, he would free all the slaves in the South. The Confederacy refused.

On January 1, 1863, after almost two years of war, President Lincoln issued the **Emancipation Proclamation.** With this document, Lincoln declared that all slaves in the Confederate states and territories were free. However, this freedom did not extend to slaves in states and territories that remained loyal to the Union, such as Kentucky, Missouri, and Maryland. Lincoln needed their support.

In addition to declaring freedom for enslaved people living in Confederate states, the Proclamation also stated that African Americans were free to enlist, or join the Union forces. Thousands of free African Americans and former slaves became Union soldiers.

Because of the Emancipation Proclamation, the Confederates knew that losing the war would mean they would have to give up slavery altogether.

REVIEW Why did Lincoln decide not to free the slaves as soon as he became President? Draw Conclusions

Summarize the Lesson

— **1861** The Confederate States of America was formed.

— **1863** Lincoln issued the Emancipation Proclamation.

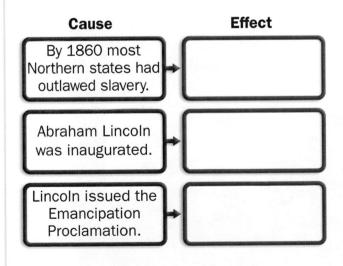

LESSON 1 REVIEW

1. **Cause and Effect** On a separate sheet of paper, write an effect for each cause shown.

Cause	Effect
By 1860 most Northern states had outlawed slavery.	
Abraham Lincoln was inaugurated.	
Lincoln issued the Emancipation Proclamation.	

2. What was the Confederate States of America? Was Illinois a member?

3. Why did the Confederate government draft its own constitution?

4. What event encouraged Lincoln to warn the Confederate states that he would free the slaves in the South if they did not rejoin the Union?

5. **Critical Thinking:** *Draw Conclusions* Why did President Lincoln not use the Emancipation Proclamation to free slaves in all states and territories?

Link to Mathematics

State Roll Call Before South Carolina seceded, 33 states, not including territories and West Virginia, made up the United States. If 11 states joined the Confederacy, how many states remained loyal to the Union? What percentage of states remained loyal?

Recognize Fact and Opinion

What? A **fact** is a statement that can be proved to be true. For example, if you say Illinois is west of Indiana, you can prove your statement by looking at a map of the United States. An **opinion** is the way a person thinks or feels about something. Opinions cannot be proved. Words such as *think, believe, feel, best,* and *worst* sometimes signal that a statement is an opinion.

Opinions on a thing or idea vary from person to person. Your opinion depends largely on your own experience and on what you have learned from other people. For example, the two pictures on this page show Abraham Lincoln. This is a fact. In which picture do you think Lincoln looks worried? The answer to that question is an opinion.

Why? Facts and opinions are often mixed together. Television, magazines, newspaper editorials, and Web sites often combine fact and opinion. In order to understand what you are reading or hearing, you must be able to tell the difference between a fact and an opinion.

▶ Abraham Lincoln before the Civil War, in 1860

▶ Lincoln near the end of the Civil War, in 1864

Illinois and Its Neighbors, 1850

WISCONSIN

Lake Michigan

MI

IOWA

Chicago

Rock Island

Peoria

Illinois River

ILLINOIS

INDIANA

Springfield

Mississippi River

Kaskaskia River

Wabash River

MISSOURI

Ohio River

KENTUCKY

Cairo

TENNESSEE

Key

Free state

Slave-holding state

N

0   50   100 Miles
0   50   100 Kilometers

▶ **Lincoln visits his troops during the Civil War.**

resources mentioned earlier? Yes, you can because it is a fact.

Look at the photograph. Think about this statement: "Abraham Lincoln was a good leader." Can you find proof of this statement? No, you cannot. It is an opinion.

Think and Apply

How? To decide whether a statement is a fact or an opinion, ask yourself whether you can prove the statement. Look for proof in resources such as an encyclopedia, a dictionary, an atlas, a textbook, or an almanac. If you can find proof in these sources that the statement is true, then it is a fact.

Look at the map. Think about the following statement: "Before the Civil War, Illinois was a free state." Is this statement a fact or an opinion? Can you find proof of this statement in the

Use the map to help you decide which of the following are facts and which are opinions. For each statement below, write **O** for opinion or **F** for fact.

1 The people of Illinois did not like having slave-holding states as neighbors.

2 Three of the states that neighbored Illinois did not allow slavery.

3 Slavery was allowed in Missouri and Kentucky.

187

1860   1865

1861
Illinois farm products and supplies support the Union.

1863
Ulysses S. Grant leads Union forces to victory at the Battle of Vicksburg.

1865
The Civil War ends.

1865
President Abraham Lincoln dies.

IOWA

Rock Island

ILLINOIS

PREVIEW

Focus on the Main Idea
During the Civil War, Illinois helped the effort to save the Union.

PLACES
Cairo
Galena
Vicksburg, Mississippi
Rock Island
Appomattox Court House, Virginia

PEOPLE
Ulysses S. Grant
Lizzie Aiken
Mary Ann Bickerdyke
Jennie Hodgers
Robert E. Lee
John Wilkes Booth

VOCABULARY
economy
regiment
surrender
assassination

Illinois Supports the Union

You Are There

April 8, 1862
Dear Father and Mother,
Yesterday, the Seventh Regiment of Illinois helped General Grant win the battle against the Confederates at Shiloh. We fought for two days. The fighting was fierce. Sometimes the smoke from the gunpowder was so thick that we could hardly see. And the roar of the gunfire never seemed to stop.

We have lost eighteen men of our regiment, and several more are badly wounded. But we are glad to be serving with a general who knows how to win. I hope the war is over soon.

Your son,
Robert

Main Idea and Details
As you read, note details that show how Illinois contributed to the war effort.

▶ Union forces battled Confederate troops at Shiloh in 1862.

The War and the Illinois Economy

When the Civil War began, it changed the Illinois **economy**, or the way people earn money and exchange it for things they need. Because farmers could no longer sell their crops in the South, they found new markets by selling their crops in the Northeast. The federal government needed a great deal of food for the Union troops. Therefore, after the first few months of the war, life for Illinois farmers greatly improved.

In addition to food, the Union needed supplies and military equipment. Illinois factories went to work manufacturing them. Railroads quickly moved goods from place to place. Trains brought Union soldiers everything from food and clothing to horses and weapons.

Because of its location where the Ohio and Mississippi Rivers meet, **Cairo** became an important military center for the Union. The Illinois Central Railroad transported soldiers and supplies to Cairo. A huge military camp was built in Cairo, and large amounts of military supplies were stored there. From Cairo, men and supplies were sent south to support General Grant's troops.

REVIEW How did the economy of Illinois change after the Civil War began?
Main Idea and Details

Rock Island

Rock Island is located in the Mississippi River. It is famous for being a Confederate prisoner of war camp, a national cemetery, and an arsenal.

▶ In 1863 a federal arsenal was created on Rock Island. Confederate prisoners of war were kept at the Rock Island prison camp. By the end of the war, more than 12,000 Confederates had been held prisoner at the camp.

▶ Today Rock Island is the site of a cemetery for Union and Confederate soldiers as well as an arsenal, a place where weapons are made, for the Department of Defense.

The War in the West

Almost 260,000 Illinois men joined the Union military forces. Many of them were volunteers. By the end of the war, there were 149 Illinois regiments. A **regiment** is a group of about 1,000 soldiers. Illinois regiments consisted of infantry, cavalry, and artillery units.

In 1862 **Ulysses S. Grant**, of **Galena**, Illinois, took charge of Union forces in the West, fighting for control of the Mississippi Valley. He led his troops into many battles, including those at Fort Donelson, Shiloh, and **Vicksburg**. Many Confederate prisoners captured in various battles were sent to a prisoner of war camp at **Rock Island**, beginning in 1863. Because of Grant's victories, President Lincoln appointed him General-in-Chief of the Union forces.

By April 1864, the first African American regiment from Illinois was formed. It was called the Twenty-Ninth Regiment Infantry. This regiment fought bravely and worked with other Union forces to defeat the Confederates.

REVIEW What happened to Grant as a result of his victories in the West?
Cause and Effect

FACT FILE

Key Battles in the West

▶ **A Union hat**

Map

ILLINOIS · INDIANA

Key
⚜ Union victory

Ohio River

KENTUCKY

MISSOURI

ARKANSAS

Mississippi River

⚜ Fort Donelson

TENNESSEE

⚜ Shiloh

Corinth ⚜

N

MISSISSIPPI · ALABAMA

0   50   100 Miles
0   50   100 Kilometers

LOUISIANA ⚜ Vicksburg

Date	Outcome
February 11–16, 1862	Union victory; made sure Kentucky would stay in Union; allowed Union troops to go into Tennessee
April 6–7, 1862	Union victory; Grant defeats Confederates; Confederates fall back
October 3–4, 1862	Union victory; Union controls railroads in the western Confederate states
May 18–July 4, 1863	Union victory; turning point in the war; Union forces separate Confederate forces in the East from those in the West

▶ Bugles such as this one were used in many Civil War battles.

▶ **A Civil War drum**

▶ Lizzie Aiken was one of many Illinois women to volunteer as a nurse for the Union forces.

Supporting the Troops

More and more men enlisted in the army and went off to fight. As a result, many Illinois women took on new and important responsibilities. Some women had to care for the farms so that there would be enough food. Others cared for sick and wounded soldiers.

Lizzie Aiken of Peoria and **Mary Ann Bickerdyke** of Galesburg were two such women who became nurses for the Union forces. Aiken volunteered as a nurse for the Sixth Illinois Cavalry. She was called "Aunt Lizzie" by the wounded soldiers. Mary Ann Bickerdyke volunteered as a nurse in Cairo. She set up hospitals along the Mississippi River and took care of wounded soldiers on 19 different battlefields.

During the Civil War, a few women served openly as women in the Union forces. It was more typical of such women to pose as men. For example, Illinoisan **Jennie Hodgers** wanted to join the Union forces so she dressed as a man and changed her name to Albert D. J. Cashier.

REVIEW In what ways did Illinois women help the Union during the Civil War? **Summarize**

The War Ends

The Civil War lasted four long years. In April 1865 Union troops surrounded and outnumbered General **Robert E. Lee** and his Confederate forces. Lee decided to stop fighting and **surrender,** or give up. Ulysses S. Grant, commander of the Union troops, accepted Lee's surrender at **Appomattox Court House** in Virginia. This surrender signaled the end of the war. It was time for the soldiers to go home.

Both the North and the South had lost many soldiers in battle. Of those who returned, many had permanent injuries.

In the North, the economy grew because farmers were growing and selling more crops, and factories were producing and selling more goods.

However, the South suffered great losses. Soldiers returning home found their farmland burned, factories destroyed, cities in ruins, and rail lines torn up. The South's entire way of life was forever changed.

REVIEW How were the effects of the Civil War on the North and the South the same, and how were they different? **Compare and Contrast**

▶ This picture shows Robert E. Lee surrendering to Ulysses S. Grant, but they actually sat at separate tables.

Death of the President

On the evening of April 14, 1865, President Lincoln was watching a play at Ford's Theater. **John Wilkes Booth,** who was angry that the South had lost the war, came up behind the President's box seat and shot him. Doctors desperately tried to save Lincoln, but he died the next morning. On April 26 Union forces cornered and shot Booth in a barn in northern Virginia. He died from his wounds.

Many Americans were deeply saddened by President Lincoln's **assassination,** or the murder of an important person. Lincoln's body was put on a funeral train to Illinois so that he could be buried in Springfield.

REVIEW Which event happened first—Lincoln's assassination or John Wilkes Booth's death? **Sequence**

▶ **Lincoln's funeral in Springfield**

THE LAST RITES AT OAKWOOD, NEAR SPRINGFIELD.

Summarize the Lesson

- **1860s** Illinois farm products and supplies supported the Union.
- **1863** Ulysses S. Grant led Union forces to victory at the Battle of Vicksburg.
- **1865** The Civil War ended.
- **1865** President Abraham Lincoln died.

LESSON 2 REVIEW

Check Facts and Main Ideas

1. **Main Idea and Details** On a separate sheet of paper, write at least three details to support the main idea below.

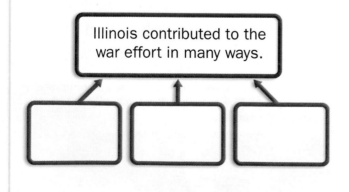

Illinois contributed to the war effort in many ways.

2. How did the Civil War change life in Illinois?

3. How were Lizzie Aiken and Mary Ann Bickerdyke alike?

4. What happened at Appomattox Court House?

5. **Critical Thinking: *Express Ideas*** Why do you think the Union won the Civil War?

Link to ➤ **Art**

Create a Poster Use words and drawings to design a recruitment poster encouraging people to volunteer their services to help win the Civil War.

Mary Ann Bickerdyke
1817–1901

Mary Ann Bickerdyke was born in Knox County, Ohio. As a young woman she attended Oberlin College and later studied nursing. When the Civil War began, Bickerdyke worked in a Union hospital in Cairo, Illinois. She cooked and cared for the sick and wounded soldiers.

In February 1862 after Fort Donelson fell, Bickerdyke followed Grant's army as the troops moved down the Mississippi River. Along the way, she set up hospitals to care for wounded soldiers. Dr. Benjamin Woodward, who was a Galeburg doctor and Union volunteer, described Bickerdyke as

BIOFACT

During the four years of the war, Mary Ann Bickerdyke was present at 19 battles and assisted in setting up 300 hospitals.

"a woman rough, uncultured . . . but a diamond in the rough."

Soldiers called her "Mother Bickerdyke" because she took such good care of them. She was greatly admired by many, including Union leaders such as General Ulysses S. Grant.

Learn from Biographies

Why do you think Mary Ann Bickerdyke was such a respected nurse?

Students can research the lives of significant people by clicking on *Meet the People* at **www.sfsocialstudies.com.**

Cairo, Illinois, and Vicksburg, Mississippi

Civil War Cities

Although no Civil War battles were fought in Illinois, many places in our state were important to the Union's war effort. Cairo became an important military center for the Union because it was located near railroads and ports. By the end of the war, Cairo contained many military camps, warehouses, and hospitals. Men and supplies from these facilities were sent to other states to assist with the war.

An important battle was fought at Vicksburg, Mississippi, from May 18 though July 4, 1863. Major General Ulysses S. Grant brought his Union forces, including many Illinois soldiers, to Vicksburg. The Confederate troops were trapped and finally surrendered. This Union victory separated Confederate forces in the West from those in the East and made it harder for the Confederate forces to work together.

▶ Many Illinois troops traveled through Cairo on their way to fight in the South.

▶ Grant's victory at Vicksburg, Mississippi, proved to be a turning point in the Civil War.

The Civil War

From April 1861 to April 1865, three million men joined the fighting forces of the Union and the Confederacy. More than 250,000 of the men in the Union forces were from Illinois. Soldiers fought in units of infantry—soldiers on foot, cavalry—soldiers on horseback, and artillery—soldiers using large weapons.

Infantry unit badge

Union Infantryman's Fatigue Cap
Union uniforms were made of heavy blue wool.

Confederate Knapsack
Soldiers often carried their personal belongings in a knapsack.

Wood frame

Cork stopper

Coffee

Lining

Back straps

Artillery insignia

Confederate Officer's Kepi
The red fabric of this cap indicates that it was worn by a Confederate artilleryman.

Soldier's Tin Camp Ware

Stamped tin plate

General Ulysses S. Grant and His Staff

General Grant

1860   **1861**

1861
The Confederate States of
America was formed.

Chapter Summary

Cause and Effect

On a separate sheet
of paper, fill in a
cause or an effect
for each statement.

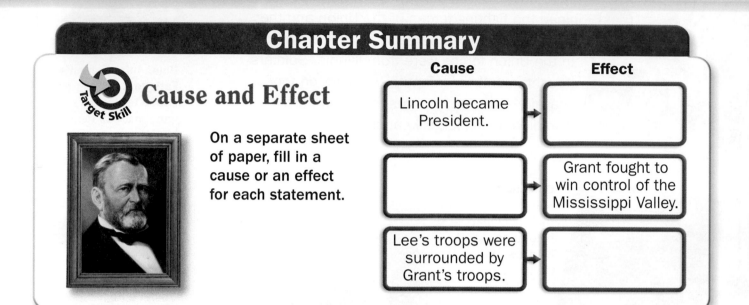

Cause	Effect
Lincoln became President.	
	Grant fought to win control of the Mississippi Valley.
Lee's troops were surrounded by Grant's troops.	

Vocabulary

Match each of the following words with the
correct meaning.

1 **secede** (p. 183)

2 **Confederacy** (p. 183)

3 **regiment** (p. 190)

4 **surrender** (p. 191)

5 **assassination** (p. 192)

a. a group of Southern states that joined together

b. to give up

c. a group of about 1,000 soldiers

d. murder of an important person

e. to formally withdraw

People and Places

List two important things about each of
the following places and people.

1 **Fort Sumter** (p. 183)

2 **Jefferson Davis** (p. 183)

3 **Cairo** (p. 189)

4 **Ulysses S. Grant** (p. 190)

5 **Mary Ann Bickerdyke** (p. 191, 193)

6 **Jennie Hodgers** (p. 191)

7 **Robert E. Lee** (p. 191)

8 **John Wilkes Booth** (p. 192)

1863
President Lincoln issued the Emancipation Proclamation.

1863
Ulysses S. Grant led Union forces to victory at the Battle of Vicksburg.

1865
Civil War ended.

1865
President Lincoln was assassinated.

Facts and Main Ideas

1 Why was slavery an issue that divided Americans in 1860?

2 How did the Civil War start?

3 During the presidential campaign, what was Lincoln's stand on slavery?

4 **Time Line** After Lincoln issued his Emancipation Proclamation, how many years did it take before the Civil War ended?

5 **Main Idea** What purpose did the Emancipation Proclamation serve?

6 **Main Idea** What did Ulysses S. Grant do when he took control of the Union forces in the West?

7 **Main Idea** How did the Civil War affect the Illinois economy?

8 **Critical Thinking:** *Draw Conclusions* Why did General Lee surrender to General Grant?

Internet Activity

To get help with vocabulary, people, and places, select the dictionary or encyclopedia from *Social Studies Library* at **www.sfsocialstudies.com**.

Apply Skills

Recognize Fact and Opinion

Use the photo to help you decide which of the following are facts and which are opinions. For each statement below, write *O* for opinion or *F* for fact.

1 Abraham Lincoln visited Union troops.

2 The soldiers were glad to see President Lincoln.

3 All the soldiers were worried about losing the war.

Write About History

1 **Write a speech** to convince Southern states that they should not secede. Explain why you think it is wrong for states to leave the Union.

2 **Write a diary entry** as if you are in an Illinois regiment. Tell whether you are in an infantry, a cavalry, or an artillery unit.

3 **Draw a mural** to show how the people of Illinois supported the Union during the Civil War. Include a paragraph describing the contributions made by both men and women.

Brother Jonathan's Lament for Sister Caroline

By Oliver Wendell Holmes
March 25, 1861

In this poem, the author makes South Carolina sound like a person rather than a state. It tells about South Carolina's secession from the Union. The poem was first published in The Atlantic Monthly *in May 1861.*

She has gone,—she has left us in passion and pride,—
Our stormy-browed sister, so long at our side!
She has torn her own star from our firmament's glow,
And turned on her brother the face of a foe!

Oh Caroline, Caroline, child of the sun,
We can never forget that our hearts have been one,—
Our foreheads both sprinkled in Liberty's name,
From the fountain of blood with the finger of flame!

You were always too ready to fire at a touch;
But we said, "She is hasty,—she does not mean much."
We have scowled, when you uttered some turbulent threat;
But Friendship still whispered, "Forgive and forget!"

Has our love all died out? Have its altars grown cold?
Has the curse come at last which the fathers foretold?
Then Nature must teach us the strength of the chain
That her petulant children would sever in vain.

They may fight till the buzzards are gorged with their spoil,
Till the harvest grows black as it rots in the soil,
Till the wolves and the catamounts troop from their caves,
And the shark tracks the pirate, the lord of the waves:

In vain is the strife! When its fury is past,
Their fortunes must flow in one channel at last,
As the torrents that rush from the mountains of snow
Roll mingled in peace through the valleys below.

Our Union is river, lake, ocean, and sky:
Man breaks not the medal, when God cuts the die!
Though darkened with sulphur, though cloven with steel,
The blue arch will brighten, the waters will heal!

Oh, Caroline, Caroline, child of the sun,
There are battles with Fate that can never be won!
The star-flowering banner must never be furled,
For its blossoms of light are the hope of the world!

Go, then, our rash sister! afar and aloof,
Run wild in the sunshine away from our roof;
But when your heart aches and your feet have grown sore,
Remember the pathway that leads to our door!

Review

Main Ideas and Vocabulary

TEST PREP

Read the passage below, and answer the questions that follow.

In 1850 the United States government passed the Compromise of 1850. The Fugitive Slave Act was one of the laws in the Compromise. This law said that African Americans who were escaped slaves in free states had to be returned to their owners. Abolitionists spoke out against slavery. Some risked their own freedom to become conductors on the Underground Railroad. This was a network of secret routes to help escaping people reach the North and Canada.

In 1860 Abraham Lincoln, who opposed the spread of slavery, was elected President. Several Southern states seceded from the Union. War began in 1861. Illinois men volunteered to fight to preserve the Union. Many women volunteered as nurses. After four years of fighting, the North won the war. However, life in Illinois and elsewhere was never the same.

1 Abolitionists are people who
   A live in the South and own slaves.
   B believe that war is wrong.
   C want to end slavery.
   D are running for public office.

2 In this passage, the Underground Railroad refers to
   A a subway that runs through Chicago.
   B a secret train that carries enslaved African Americans out of the South.
   C a newspaper that is written by abolitionists.
   D a network of secret routes leading to the North and Canada.

3 In this passage, seceded means
   A formally withdrew.
   B achieved a desired goal.
   C declared war.
   D protested.

4 According to this passage, what is one reason Illinois men fought in the Civil War?
   A They were forced to fight in the war.
   B They fought to preserve the Union.
   C They wanted adventure.
   D They fought to save Illinois.

Places and Vocabulary

Match each word or place to its description.

1 slavery (p. 167)

2 debate (p. 173)

3 Confederacy (p. 183)

4 Fort Sumter (p. 183)

5 Cairo (p. 189)

6 surrender (p. 191)

a. place where the Civil War began

b. a group of Southern states that joined together

c. owning another person as property

d. soldiers and supplies were shipped to and from this location

e. to give up

f. to publicly discuss issues

Write and Share

Write and perform a dramatic presentation of the Siege of Vicksburg. Your teacher will divide the class into groups. One group of students should research the details of the event. Another group should write the script for the dramatization. The third group should present the dramatization.

Apply Skills

Create a Scrapbook of Primary Sources Use primary sources, such as photos, diary and journal entries, and letters to create a scrapbook of one event or period in your life. When you have completed your scrapbook, write a journal entry explaining what you think historians in the future will be able to learn from your scrapbook about you and the time you lived in.

Read on Your Own

Look for these books in your library.

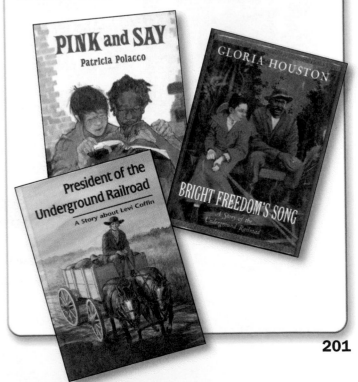

Discovery Channel School

UNIT 4 Project

Point of View

People often have different ideas about an issue. Take sides and discuss different points of view.

1. **Form** a group and choose an issue that was important to the history of Illinois. Write a sentence about your issue.

2. **Prepare** to debate the issue. Find two sides of the issue, and write sentences with facts that support each side. Write several questions and answers about the issue as well.

3. **Decide** who will argue each side.

4. **Debate** your issue for the class. You may want to set a time limit for each side's presentation before taking questions.

Internet Activity

For more information and activities, go to **www.sfsocialstudies.com.**

Illinois Grows

In what ways did Illinois become a modern place in which to live?

Begin with a Primary Source

1870

1871
The Chicago Fire destroys much of the city.

1895

1893
Chicago hosts the World's Columbian Exposition.

1920

1917
The United States enters World War I.

"... we are moving forward to greater freedom, to greater security for the average man than he has ever known before in the history of America."

—Franklin D. Roosevelt, from a "Fireside Chat," 1934

Chicago hosted the World's Columbian Exposition in 1893.

1945

1970

1995

1945
World War II
ends.

1979
Jane Byrne becomes
first woman elected
mayor of Chicago.

1992
Mae Carol Jemison
flies a mission on
the space shuttle

Meet the People

Daniel Hale Williams

1858–1931

Birthplace: Hollidaysburg, Pennsylvania

Physician

- Graduated from Northwestern University in 1883
- Founded Provident Hospital in Chicago in 1891
- Performed first open-heart surgery in 1893 at Provident Hospital

Ellen Gates Starr

1859–1940

Birthplace: Laona, Illinois

Reformer

- Opened Hull House in Chicago with Jane Addams
- Worked to change child labor laws and to improve wages and working conditions for factory workers
- Taught arts and crafts to poor residents for almost 30 years at Hull House

Jane Addams

1860–1935

Birthplace: Cedarville, Illinois

Reformer

- Co-founder of Hull House
- Helped make Hull House successful, offering many services in 13 buildings on Chicago's south side
- Won the Nobel Peace Prize in 1931

Frank O. Lowden

1861–1943

Birthplace: Sunrise City, Minnesota

Illinois state representative, governor of Illinois

- In Illinois House of Representatives, worked to support farmers
- As governor, led programs to develop agriculture and build roads and canals
- Managed a large farm using scientific principles

1850	1900

1858 • Daniel Hale Williams 1931

1859 • Ellen Gates Starr

1860 • Jane Addams 1935

1861 • Frank O. Lowden

1863 • Richard Sears 1914

1896 • Everett Dirksen

1911 • Ronald Reagan

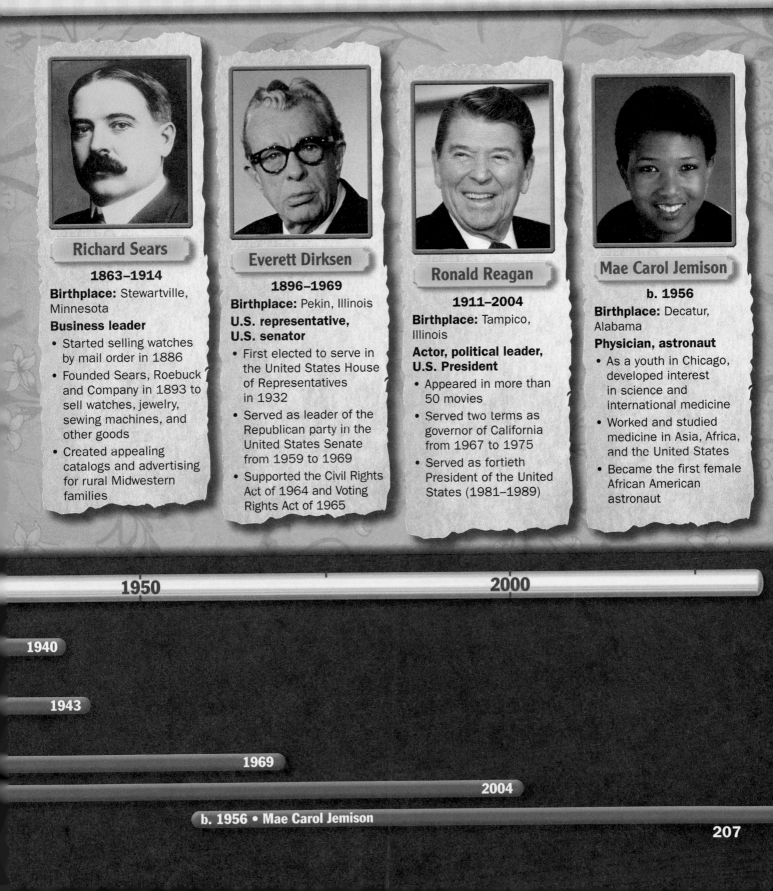

Richard Sears

1863–1914

Birthplace: Stewartville, Minnesota

Business leader

- Started selling watches by mail order in 1886
- Founded Sears, Roebuck and Company in 1893 to sell watches, jewelry, sewing machines, and other goods
- Created appealing catalogs and advertising for rural Midwestern families

Everett Dirksen

1896–1969

Birthplace: Pekin, Illinois

U.S. representative, U.S. senator

- First elected to serve in the United States House of Representatives in 1932
- Served as leader of the Republican party in the United States Senate from 1959 to 1969
- Supported the Civil Rights Act of 1964 and Voting Rights Act of 1965

Ronald Reagan

1911–2004

Birthplace: Tampico, Illinois

Actor, political leader, U.S. President

- Appeared in more than 50 movies
- Served two terms as governor of California from 1967 to 1975
- Served as fortieth President of the United States (1981–1989)

Mae Carol Jemison

b. 1956

Birthplace: Decatur, Alabama

Physician, astronaut

- As a youth in Chicago, developed interest in science and international medicine
- Worked and studied medicine in Asia, Africa, and the United States
- Became the first female African American astronaut

1950   2000

1940

1943

1969

2004

b. 1956 • Mae Carol Jemison

Illinois Grows

Summarize

A summary is a short statement that describes a longer piece of writing. A good summary presents all the important information briefly and clearly.

Main Facts and Information	Main Facts and Information	Main Facts and Information

Summary

- A summary should include only the main facts or information from the text.

- Learning to summarize can help you remember the most important parts of the material you read.

Read this summary of Chapter 8, Lesson 2. The **main facts and information** have been highlighted.

In Chapter 8 you learned about how the results of the Civil War changed the economic structure of Illinois, improving markets, manufacturing, and transportation. Farmers found new markets for their crops. Factories were built and improved. Shipping by waterway and by rail became even more important.

Growing and Changing

In the years after the Civil War, industry in Illinois cities became more and more important. Illinois became well known for machinery, food products, steel, and furniture.

As new factories opened, people began moving to Illinois to find work in these new industries. They moved from different parts of the United States as well as from other nations. Waves of immigrants came to Chicago, rapidly increasing the city's population.

As industry grew, some workplaces became unpleasant, unhealthy, and unsafe. Many employees were forced to work too long and too fast for too little money. Conflicts arose between workers and bosses in cities across the country. Workers organized themselves into groups to protest bad conditions.

As years passed, people worked to bring about changes in the industrial workplaces of the country. They won battles to end child labor, shorten work days, and raise wages. Some people worked to make changes in other areas, such as helping the poor and giving women the right to vote.

At the same time, Illinois became the home of many new hospitals, schools, and colleges. These promised to give the people of the state a better way of life.

Use the reading strategy of summarizing to answer these questions.

1 List three main ideas that are contained in the passage above.

2 List details that support the main ideas.

3 Rewrite your main ideas and supporting details to create a short, clear summary of the passage.

CHAPTER 9

Farm to Factory

Lesson 1

1890s
Chicago
Many immigrants came to live and work in Illinois.

1

Lesson 2

1857
Normal
Illinois State University was the first public university in the state.

2

Locating Time and Place

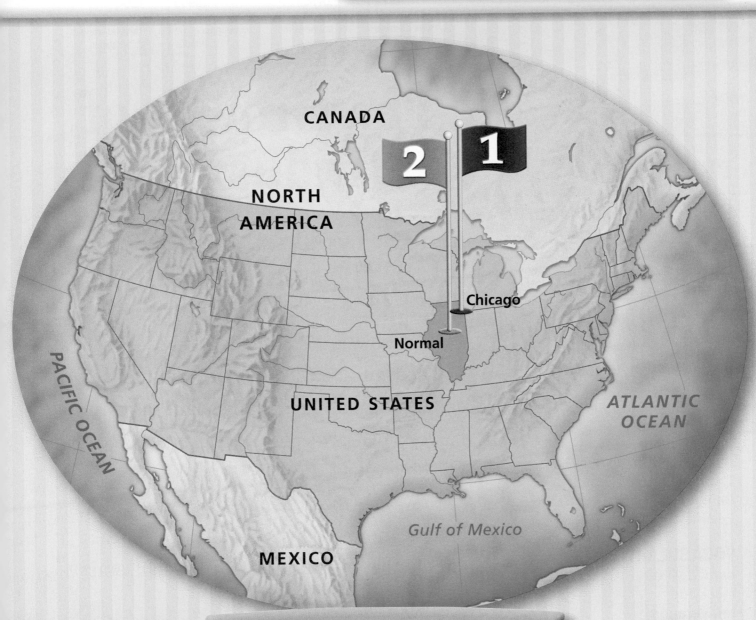

Why We Remember

When we think of cities today, we picture wide avenues lined with stores, hotels, businesses, and factories. These features began to appear in American cities in the years after the Civil War. Cities like Chicago grew at a rapid pace. Industry changed life for everybody—even those who lived far from the city streets. Along railroad lines, in mills and factories, on ships, among work crews digging canals and unloading sacks of grain—in all of these places, the modern world was taking shape.

1860   1880   1900

1871
The Great Chicago Fire destroys much of the city.

1874
Joseph Glidden improves the design of barbed wire.

1890s
Nearly one million immigrants come to Illinois.

1894
Pullman Railroad workers go on strike.

Chicago

PREVIEW

Focus on the Main Idea
After the Civil War, industry grew in importance in Illinois.

PLACE
Chicago

PEOPLE
George Washington Carver
Joseph Glidden
Daniel Burnham
Richard Sears
Philip Armour
Gustavus Swift
Thomas Edison
George M. Pullman
Eugene V. Debs

VOCABULARY
barbed wire
stockyard
refrigeration
labor union
strike

TERMS
Grange
Chicago Sanitary and
  Ship Canal

EVENTS
Haymarket Riot
Pullman Strike

The Growth of Industry

You Are There Tonight your parents have invited you to attend a Grange meeting with them.

You know almost everyone there. Your neighbors chat as they eat pie, drink coffee, and laugh. Many are talking about the corn harvest. Two farmers shake your hand and welcome you.

However, when the meeting starts, people become more serious. Several people speak angrily about how much railroad companies are charging farmers to ship grain. Your father says he will go to Springfield himself to speak against the high fees. The room fills with cheers.

Summarize As you read details about how industry grew after the Civil War, think about how you could summarize the information.

New Challenges and Opportunities for Farmers

At the end of the Civil War, Illinois farmers were selling their crops in markets around the country. Using the latest plows, mowers, and reapers, farmers produced more crops per acre than they had before.

Although Illinois was the nation's leading producer of corn and wheat from 1860 to 1890, Illinois farmers faced many economic problems. In some years farmers produced more grain than the country needed, and they had to cut back production. They also faced economic pressures from railroad companies that stored and transported grain. These companies were making more money from the grain than the farmers were. The farmers believed that the railroads were unfairly paying them less than they deserved.

Many farmers banded together in groups. One group, the Patrons of Husbandry, also known as the **Grange,** formed local chapters of this organization. Throughout the 1870s and 1880s, farmers met in Grange halls in Illinois and other states. Farmers shared ideas about farming and discussed ways to change laws to help people working in agriculture.

▶ **A Grange meeting in Winchester, Illinois**

Wheat Prices per Bushel for Illinois Farmers

Source: Illinois Agriculture Statistics 2000

▶ **Wheat prices declined for Illinois farmers in the late 1800s.**

During the 1890s farming methods improved further because of the work of **George Washington Carver.** Through his experiments Carver developed methods for farmers to refresh soil that had been "worn out" by too much farming. He learned that growing soybeans added minerals to "tired" soil. Today soybeans continue to be one of the state's largest crops.

At the same time farmers were facing these challenges, they also benefitted from new ideas. One such idea that helped farmers was **barbed wire,** a fencing material with little spikes to keep cattle from rubbing against it. In 1874 Illinoisan **Joseph Glidden** improved upon an earlier invention of barbed wire that would help farmers protect animals and crops.

REVIEW What improvements helped farmers after the Civil War?
🔁 **Summarize**

Industrial Growth in Illinois

During this same period, industries in Illinois were growing quickly. The state's location and resources contributed to this growth. Waterways and railroads brought raw materials such as iron ore into the state. They carried farm products and manufactured goods from Illinois all over the nation.

The industrial boom touched cities across the state. Rockford factories began producing machinery, cloth, and furniture. Workers in Moline made plows and other equipment. Peoria was known for farm tools and meatpacking. Steel mills thrived in Joliet. In East St. Louis, people produced flour and railroad equipment. Yet, the city of **Chicago** grew faster and bigger than all the others.

By 1870 Chicago's population and industries had made it the most important city in the Midwest. The lumber, grain, and meatpacking industries were supported by railroads, shipping facilities, and stockyards. A **stockyard** is an enclosed area where livestock are kept before they are shipped elsewhere or used for meat.

Then disaster struck. In 1871 a fire burned through the downtown area. Fortunately the fire never reached the stockyards, meatpacking plants, or major railroad facilities. But by the time it was put out, the fire had taken hundreds of lives and destroyed 18,000 buildings— nearly a third of the city's structures.

Out of these ashes grew a better, more modern city. **Daniel Burnham** and other architects designed department stores and office buildings. Soon the downtown business district was reborn.

▶ While the stockyards (below) were a part of "old" Chicago, the new Marshall Fields store (top right) and the Sanitary and Ship Canal (top left) were part of a new city.

214

Richard Sears and Retail

Starting in 1886, Richard Sears sold watches through the mail from a warehouse in Chicago. A few years later, Sears began publishing a catalog that showed a variety of goods for sale: jewelry, shoes, sewing machines, and bicycles. His catalogs were especially successful among families who lived far from city stores.

Although Sears still prints catalogs each year, it also does much of its business over the World Wide Web. Like the catalog that Sears published over a century ago, the Sears Web site offers shoppers the convenience of making purchases from anyplace in the country.

▶ In 1893 the Sears catalog contained 196 pages. The following year it grew to 507 pages. Nearly all of the descriptions were written by Richard Sears.

Chicago grew even faster than it had before. The Sears, Roebuck and Company, cofounded by **Richard Sears** in 1893, was one of many businesses to promote Chicago's growth.

Chicago's waterways were also improved. The **Chicago Sanitary and Ship Canal** was built in 1900. It improved sanitation, or the way waste water and sewage is treated to protect people's health.

Two other improvements helped the growth of industry. One was the addition of **refrigeration,** or the process of cooling, to railroad cars that carried food. This meant that meatpacking companies, like those of **Philip Armour** and **Gustavus Swift,** could send meat that was processed in Chicago almost anywhere in the country.

The other improvement was **Thomas Edison's** electric lamp and his circuits for sending electricity across great cities. In the late 1880s Chicago's first electric company begin to lay underground wires. Soon electricity was brought into many city homes and businesses.

REVIEW What events and technological advances helped industry grow? ↻ Summarize

Labor Troubles

As industries grew in Illinois, so did their problems. Many Illinoisans found themselves working long days in unsafe factories for little money. To improve working conditions, workers started **labor unions,** or organizations to help and protect workers. Sometimes labor unions called **strikes,** or protests during which they stopped working and shut down a factory until the owners would discuss the problems.

Some labor conflicts became violent. In 1886 Chicago police fired at the crowd of striking workers and killed one person. The next day, there was a protest meeting in Haymarket Square. Seven police officers were killed when someone threw a bomb. This became known as the **Haymarket Riot.**

▶ **Trouble at Haymarket Square happened after this meeting.**

In 1894 labor trouble in Chicago affected the entire nation. George M. Pullman's company made railroad sleeper cars. When Pullman cut workers' pay by 25 percent, the American Railway Union, led by **Eugene V. Debs,** called the **Pullman Strike.** It would be many years before workers' conditions improved.

REVIEW Over what kinds of issues did workers and owners disagree?
⟳ **Summarize**

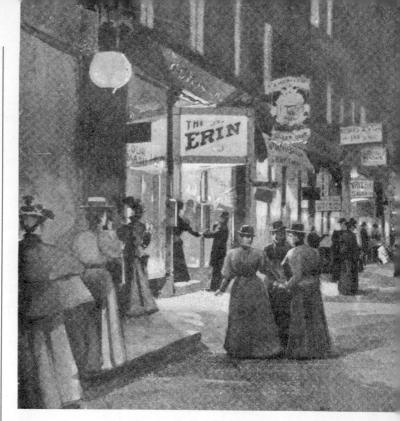

▶ **Chicago's Levee District was home to many immigrants.**

New Illinoisans

More and more immigrants came to the United States, and to Illinois, to find factory jobs. Between 1865 and 1890, 10 million people came to the United States from northern and western European countries such as Germany, England, and Ireland. Between 1890 and 1920, another 15 million immigrants came, mostly from countries in southern and eastern Europe such as Poland, Italy, Austria-Hungary, and Russia.

So many people moved to Illinois that by 1890 Illinois had passed Ohio in population and was nearly the size of New York and Pennsylvania. Chicago was the nation's second-largest city, with more than 1 million people.

During the 1890s, almost 1 million more people moved to Illinois. Nearly all of these newcomers moved to cities because few jobs were available in rural areas. Jobs in factories required no special skills and little knowledge of English. As a result, cities with factories grew quickly.

By 1900, Chicago's population was more than 1,600,000, making Chicago more than 10 times larger than the state's next-largest city, Peoria.

REVIEW Explain what caused Illinois's population to grow between 1865 and 1920. ⟳ Summarize

Summarize the Lesson

1871 The Great Fire destroyed much of Chicago.

1874 Joseph Glidden improved the design of barbed wire.

1890s Nearly one million immigrants came to Illinois.

1894 Pullman Railroad workers went on strike.

LESSON 1 REVIEW

Check Facts and Main Ideas

1. ⟳ Summarize On a separate sheet of paper, write the missing details that support the summary.

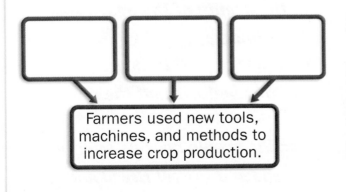

Farmers used new tools, machines, and methods to increase crop production.

2. What caused Illinois industries to grow between 1870 and 1900?

3. What caused the growth of labor unions?

4. What drew immigrants to Illinois in the late 1800s?

5. **Critical Thinking:** *Analyze* How did the Grange help improve the lives of Illinois farmers?

Link to 🔗 Science

Feeding the Soil Research why growing the same crop year after year can make soil "tired" and why rotating crops can make soil productive again. Use the names of specific crops and nutrients in your writing.

Labor Relations

Since the late 1700s, American workers have united for better pay and working conditions. Employers and politicians have not always favored the labor unions that worked for these changes.

As industry grew in the United States, work changed. In small shops and farms, workers knew the business owner. Often the owner and employees worked side by side. However, as factories grew larger, few workers ever met the owners. Employees had to work long hours, often in dirty and unsafe conditions. So workers began forming labor unions to ask for better conditions and higher wages. Unions were illegal at first, and strikers were jailed.

One of the most important strikes in the United States was organized by women who worked in the textile mills in Lawrence, Massachusetts. Labor leader Mary K. O'Sullivan went to Lawrence to see the strike firsthand. A famous song written in 1912, "Bread and Roses," celebrates the women strikers.

Unions were opposed by many business leaders. Among unions' opponents was David M. Parry, a manufacturer. Eugene V. Debs was a labor leader who organized the Pullman Strike in Chicago in 1894.

▶ **Union members found strength in numbers.**

As we come marching, marching in the beauty of the day,

A million darkened kitchens, and a thousand mill lofts gray

Are touched with all the radiance that a sudden sun discloses

For the people hear us singing "Bread and Roses! Bread and Roses!"

James Oppenheim, 1912

© Collection of Immigrant City Archives, Lawrence, Massachusetts / Immigrant City Archives

"It will be hard to find any fair minded person who went to Lawrence during the strike and examined the conditions there who is not fully in accord [agreement] with the object [goal] of the strikers."

Mary K. O'Sullivan, *recalling the Lawrence strike, 1912*

"There is that old battle cry of unionism that labor produces all. If labor had to produce all, mankind would today be next door to starvation. . . ."
[The union movement is] a standing mob engaged in acts of open rebellion against the government. . . ."

David M. Parry, *owner of Parry Auto Company and business leader, about 1900*

"When you unite and act together, the world is yours."

"Stand up and see how long a shadow you cast in the sunlight!"

Eugene V. Debs

Issues and You

Today union membership is legal in the United States, and people from many professions belong to unions. Find out about one of the unions representing people in your community, such as teachers, factory workers, or government employees. What are the advantages of union membership? What are the disadvantages? What has the union done for its members throughout its history?

Compare Line Graphs and Bar Graphs

What? A graph is a special kind of picture. It shows and compares information. Two common kinds of graphs are line graphs and bar graphs.

- A **line graph** often shows how something has changed over time. For example, the line graph here shows how the population of Illinois changed from 1860 to 1910.

- A **bar graph** often compares things by showing their sizes or their amounts.

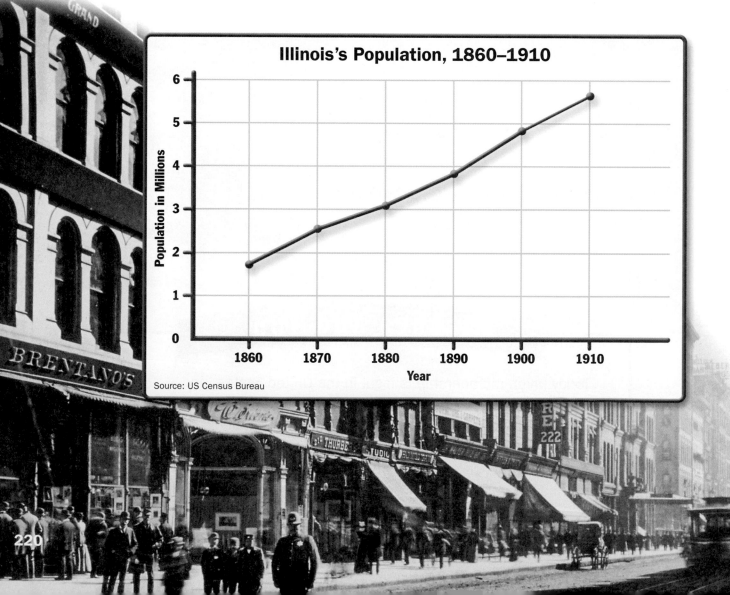

Illinois's Population, 1860–1910

Source: US Census Bureau

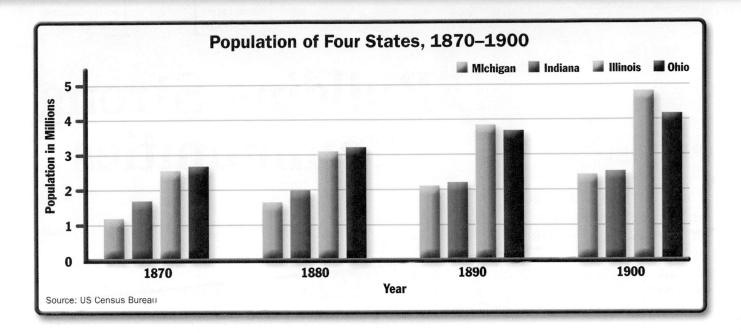

Population of Four States, 1870–1900

Legend: Michigan Indiana Illinois Ohio

Y-axis: Population in Millions (0, 1, 2, 3, 4, 5)

X-axis: Year (1870, 1880, 1890, 1900)

Source: US Census Bureau

Why? Graphs help you understand and show information at a glance. Understanding the purpose of a graph helps you use it correctly. Choose the correct graph for the kind of information you want to learn or show.

How? Start with the title. It tells what the graph is about. What is the title of the graph on page 220? What is the title of the graph on page 221?

Now look at the parts of each graph. Where are years shown on the line graph? What do the numbers along the left side of the chart represent?

Notice that each state is indicated by a different color on the bar graph. At the bottom of the chart, the years are labeled. Which state had the most people in 1880? Which state had the fewest?

Think and Apply

1. Would you choose a bar graph or a line graph to show changes in your height each year since your birth?

2. Suppose that you wanted to show the number of workers in several industries in Illinois. Which kind of graph would show that information better?

3. Look at the line graph. In which ten-year period did the population of Illinois grow the fastest? How did you find your answer?

1885   1890   1895

1889
Hull House
opens.

1891
Provident
Hospital opens
in Chicago.

1893
Chicago hosts the
World's Columbian
Exposition.

Normal

PREVIEW

Focus on the Main Idea
Many people worked hard
to build strong communities
in Illinois.

PLACES
Hull House
Evanston
Illinois State University
Normal
University of Illinois
Provident Hospital

PEOPLE
Florence Kelley
John P. Altgeld
Upton Sinclair
Jane Addams
Ellen Gates Starr
Frances Willard
Daniel Hale Williams

VOCABULARY
sweatshop
reform
skyscraper

TERMS
settlement house
Women's Christian
    Temperance Union

EVENT
World's Columbian Exposition

Building Strong Communities

You Are There You lie in bed listening to your parents talk in the next room. Your dad is very excited about the new governor, John P. Altgeld. The views of this governor are very different from those of the previous men who have held that position. Altgeld supports factory workers and farmers and is concerned about the poor. He has appointed Florence Kelley as the Chief Factory Inspector of Illinois. It's her job to make sure that the factories are following the new laws against sweatshops. Your dad hopes that she will help make changes at his factory. He also hopes that changes will come to all the laborers in Illinois.

Summarize As you read, look for details that help summarize the ways that Illinois communities became strong.

Workplace Reforms

In the late 1800s, men, women, and even children worked in factories that were crowded, unhealthy, and unsafe. Factories where people worked long hours in poor conditions for low pay were called **sweatshops.**

Florence Kelley studied the working conditions in Illinois factories. Kelley's findings convinced Illinois legislators to pass laws limiting child labor and requiring safety inspections in factories.

▶ **John P. Altgeld (top left) led many workplace reforms.**

In 1893 factory workers and farmers banded together to help elect **John P. Altgeld** governor. During his term Altgeld led many workplace reforms in Illinois. A **reform** is a change made to something to improve it. Company officials realized that they must make workplaces safer and healthier. Illinois companies made factories safer and built lunchrooms and washrooms. They also installed windows and fans to improve air quality. And they became prepared to give emergency medical care.

Some of Chicago's stockyards and meatpacking plants needed special attention. Working conditions there were especially dangerous.

Upton Sinclair, a newspaper writer, looked into conditions of Chicago's meatpacking industry. Then he wrote about his findings in the book *The Jungle.* Sinclair's book made people angry about the hard lives of immigrant workers. But people were even more shocked to learn details of how food was prepared. Political leaders passed laws forcing the food industry to improve the way that food was prepared.

REVIEW What caused companies to make working conditions safer and healthier? **Cause and Effect**

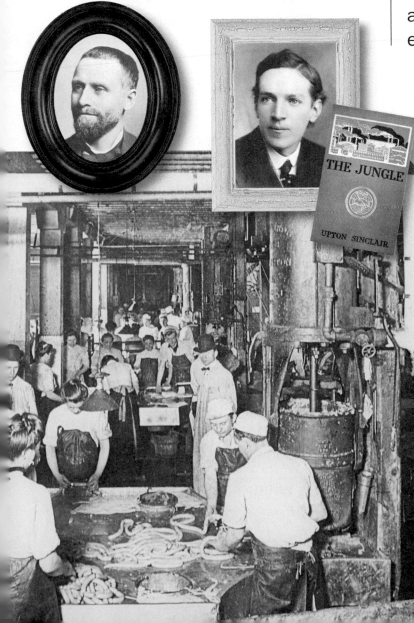

THE JUNGLE

UPTON SINCLAIR

▶ **Upton Sinclair (top right) captured the attention of the nation when he published *The Jungle*, a book about Chicago's meatpacking industry.**

223

Social Reforms

In 1889 two young women wanted to help poor people in Chicago. **Jane Addams** and **Ellen Gates Starr,** opened a settlement house called **Hull House.** A **settlement house** is a place that provides help for poor people in a community. People who came to Hull House for help found a nursery, a kitchen, a playground, a theater, and a gymnasium. They could get training in music, art, and crafts, and they also learned how to help other people.

The Hull House staff helped solve social problems in Chicago. Addams pressured city officials into making sure children were in school through the passage of child labor laws. She also worked with the Board of Health to improve people's health. As a result, Chicago became a cleaner place with fewer diseases.

Frances Willard of **Evanston** led a powerful group called the **Woman's Christian Temperance Union.** The group believed that women had the right to vote and that people should not use alcohol. They also worked to change labor laws and improve prisons.

▶ **Frances Willard**

REVIEW What services did Hull House offer? ⊙ **Summarize**

▶ **Illinois State University, in Normal**

Building Toward the Future

As the population of Illinois grew, many colleges and universities opened their doors to new students. In 1857 **Illinois State University,** in **Normal,** became the state's first public university. Illinois State University was formed to train teachers but soon added other types of courses. In 1867 Illinois Industrial University was founded in Champaign-Urbana. It was renamed the **University of Illinois** in 1885. This school offered classes in farming, machinery, and other trades and skills.

An African American doctor, **Daniel Hale Williams,** founded **Provident Hospital** in Chicago in 1891. Unlike other hospitals across the nation, Provident hired African American doctors and nurses. It also trained nurses and doctors.

REVIEW What made Provident Hospital different from other hospitals? **Compare and Contrast**

Chicago in the Spotlight

In the 1890s Chicago was growing in importance as its buildings rose higher into the sky. Tall buildings, called **skyscrapers,** seemed to touch the clouds. In 1892 riders could take an elevator to the top of the 21-story

Masonic Temple. The city also boasted an art museum and a symphony orchestra.

Chicago was honored to be chosen over St. Louis, Washington, D.C., and New York City to host a huge fair. The fair was named the

World's Columbian Exposition, in honor of the four-hundredth anniversary of Columbus's arrival in North America. In 1893 the dazzling fair introduced millions of visitors to a "city" of palaces, fountains, pools, and modern wonders such as electricity.

REVIEW Why was Chicago pleased to host the World's Columbian Exposition? **Draw Conclusions**

Summarize the Lesson

- **1889** Hull House opened.
- **1891** Provident Hospital opened in Chicago.
- **1893** Chicago hosted the World's Columbian Exposition.

▶ **Many new buildings were constructed for the Columbian Exposition.**

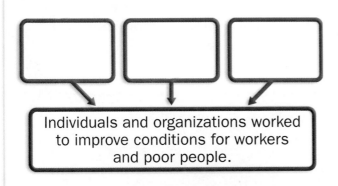

LESSON 2 REVIEW

Check Facts and Main Ideas

1. 🕥 **Summarize** On a separate sheet of paper, write the missing details that support the summary.

Individuals and organizations worked to improve conditions for workers and poor people.

2. How did conditions improve for many children in the early 1890s?

3. Which two universities opened in Illinois in the years after the Civil War?

4. What event in 1893 showed Chicago's growing importance as a U.S. city?

5. **Critical Thinking:** *Point of View* There were many people who wanted workplace reform. However, there were others who were against it. Why would some people be against reform?

Link to ⚭ **Art**

Make a Model Study an illustration of one of the 17 buildings built on the fairgrounds of the World's Columbian Exposition. Then, use clay or another material to make a model of the building.

Chicago, Illinois, and New York City, New York
Two World's Fairs

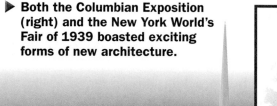

World's fairs became popular when London hosted one in 1851. Chicago had its turn in the spotlight when it hosted the World's Columbian Exposition in 1893. It took the city of Chicago three years to prepare for the event.

The Columbian Exposition was built on 686 acres of land beside Lake Michigan near the University of Chicago. (One of its buildings is now part of the Museum of Science and Industry.) Visitors could walk through exhibits and enjoy carnival rides. One of the most popular rides was G. W. G. Ferris's newly invented Ferris wheel.

Nearly 50 years later, the United States opened another world's fair in New York City. The 1939 New York World's Fair was organized around the theme "Building the World of Tomorrow." It showed examples of new inventions and new ideas.

▶ Both the Columbian Exposition (right) and the New York World's Fair of 1939 boasted exciting forms of new architecture.

Daniel Hale Williams

1858–1931

Daniel Hale Williams lived in Pennsylvania until he was eleven, when his father died. A few years later he moved to Janesville, Wisconsin, to live with his sister. There he became a barber, like his father, and worked part-time while he went to high school. While working as a barber, Williams met a doctor who told him about being a surgeon. Williams became interested in becoming a surgeon and entered Chicago Medical College in 1880.

After graduating, Williams became one of only a few African American doctors in Chicago. In 1891 he founded the Provident Hospital and Nursing Training Schools. Williams said

BIOFACT

Dr. Williams performed the first open-heart surgery, to repair stab wounds. The patient, James Cornish, lived for 20 more years.

". . . talk and success are widely different. Men may talk what they can and will do, but it takes knowledge and experience to accomplish much."

Williams went on to great success as a doctor, teacher, and leader. He encouraged African Americans to open hospitals in their own communities.

Learn from Biographies

How did being a doctor allow Daniel Hale Williams to help other African Americans?

Students can research the lives of significant people by clicking on *Meet the People* at **www.sfsocialstudies.com.**

Telling the Truth

Jane Addams spent her adult life taking a clear, honest look at the world's problems—and then working hard to help people overcome them.

After graduating from Rockford Female Seminary, Jane Addams and her friend Ellen Gates Starr visited a London settlement house called Toynbee Hall. The people who lived there wanted to help other people in the community. Addams and Starr decided to start a settlement house in Chicago.

In 1889 the two women moved into a building on South Halsted Street on Chicago's west side. This neighborhood was home to many people who had low-paying jobs and were struggling to feed their families. Many of the people who lived near the new settlement house, called Hull House, seen in the photo below, had recently come to the United States.

▶ **Hull House in the 1920s**

BUILDING
CITIZENSHIP
Caring
Respect
Responsibility
Fairness
Honesty
Courage

Jane Addams also took a special interest in education. She said,

> "America's future will be determined by the home and the school. The child becomes largely what he is taught; hence we must watch what we teach, and how we live."

Addams's belief in honest public service took her around the nation and around the world. She served as president of the Women's International League for Peace and Freedom and helped provide food to the women and children of nations that had fought against the United States in World War I. Jane Addams's honesty helped her win the Nobel Peace Prize in 1931.

Honesty in Action

Link to Current Events Find out about a person or group working to help the community where you live. How does this work show that taking an honest look at problems is the first step to finding solutions?

1870 **1875**

1871
The Chicago fire destroyed much of the city.

1874
Joseph Glidden improved the design of barbed wire.

Chapter Summary

Summarize

On a separate sheet of paper, write the missing details that support the summary shown here.

By 1900 Chicago had become a modern city.

Vocabulary

Match each word with the correct definition or description.

1. **refrigeration** (p. 215)

2. **labor union** (p. 216)

3. **strike** (p. 216)

4. **sweatshop** (p. 223)

5. **reform** (p. 223)

6. **skyscraper** (p. 225)

a. an organization set up to help protect workers

b. the process of cooling

c. a change made to something to improve it

d. a tall building

e. a protest in which a group of workers stops working

f. factory where people work long hours in poor conditions for low pay

People and Events

Write a sentence about each of the following people and events. You may use two or more in a single sentence.

1. **Joseph Glidden** (p. 213)

2. **Richard Sears** (p. 215)

3. **Haymarket Riot** (p. 216)

4. **Pullman Strike** (p. 216)

5. **Florence Kelley** (p. 223)

6. **Jane Addams** (pp. 224, 228–229)

7. **Frances Willard** (p. 224)

8. **World's Columbian Exposition** (p. 225)

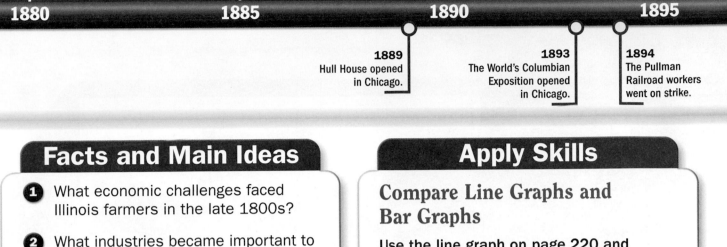

1880	1885	1890	1895

1889
Hull House opened
in Chicago.

1893
The World's Columbian
Exposition opened
in Chicago.

1894
The Pullman
Railroad workers
went on strike.

Facts and Main Ideas

1 What economic challenges faced Illinois farmers in the late 1800s?

2 What industries became important to Illinois after the Civil War?

3 How did Florence Kelley improve life for the people of Illinois?

4 Why were new schools, universities, and hospitals necessary in Illinois in the late 1800s?

5 **Time Line** Which event came first, the Chicago Fire or the World's Columbian Exposition?

6 **Main Idea** How did life change for Illinois workers in the decades after the Civil War?

7 **Main Idea** How were the goals of Jane Addams, Daniel Hale Williams, and Upton Sinclair similar?

8 **Critical Thinking:** *Express Ideas* Who do you think was the most important reformer in Illinois in the late 1800s? Why?

Internet Activity

To get help with vocabulary, people, and events, select the dictionary or encyclopedia from *Social Studies Library* at **www.sfsocialstudies.com.**

Apply Skills

Compare Line Graphs and Bar Graphs

Use the line graph on page 220 and bar graph on page 221 to answer these questions.

1 Which graph shows how the population of Illinois changed between 1860 and 1910?

2 According to the bar graph, which state had the largest increase in population between 1870 and 1880?

3 Compare the information in the two graphs. During which decade did the population of Illinois increase the least?

Write About History

1 **Write a postcard** in which you describe some of the attractions of the World's Columbian Exposition.

2 **Write a paragraph** describing the qualities and achievements of an Illinois reformer of the late 1800s.

3 **Write a news report** about a labor conflict such as the Pullman Strike or the Haymarket Riot. Include information that tells who, what, when, where, and why.

CHAPTER 10

The Modern Century

Lesson 1

1917
Coles County
Over 300,000 Illinoisans fight in World War I.

1

Lesson 2

1996
Springfield
The Illinois Korean War Memorial honors the more than 1,700 Illinoisans who died in that war.

2

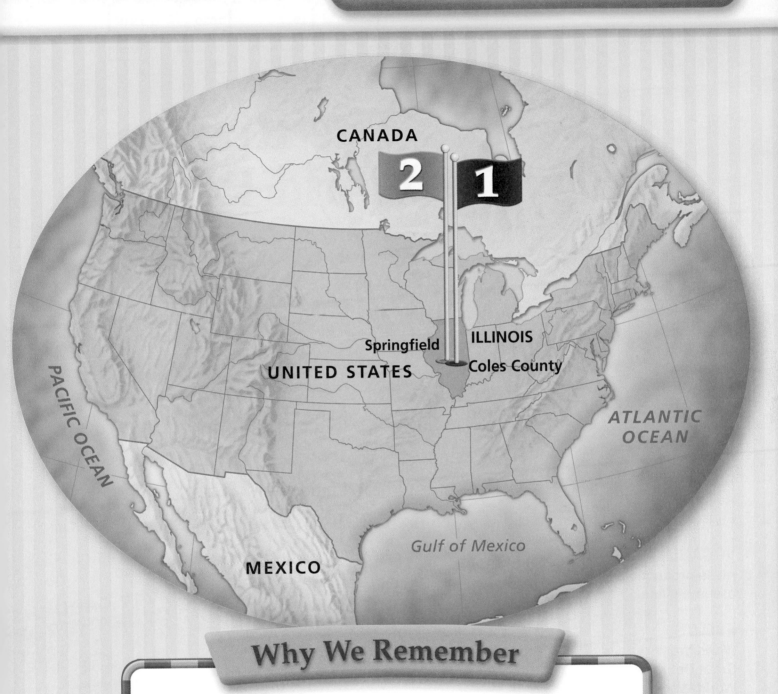

CANADA

2 1

Springfield | ILLINOIS

UNITED STATES   Coles County

PACIFIC OCEAN

ATLANTIC OCEAN

Gulf of Mexico

MEXICO

Why We Remember

The twentieth century exploded with change. Advances in science and manufacturing brought electric power, instant communication, and new ways of travel. Our country earned a place among the world's most powerful nations. Yet the twentieth century also saw two terrible wars and other hardships. You are living today in a world shaped by the people, events, and ideas of "the modern century."

1900   1925   1950

1908
Henry Ford uses mass production for automobile manufacturing.

1917
The United States enters World War I.

1929
The Great Depression begins.

1945
World War II ends.

Coles County

The Rise to World Power

PREVIEW

Focus on the Main Idea
The first half of the twentieth century was a time of dramatic changes and events.

PLACES
Coles County
Pearl Harbor

PEOPLE
Woodrow Wilson
Frank Lowden
Henry Ford
Franklin D. Roosevelt
Adolph Hitler
Enrico Fermi

VOCABULARY
mass production
assembly line

EVENTS
World War I
Great Depression
World War II

TERMS
Allies
New Deal
Works Progress Administration
Axis Powers

You Are There

Grandmother and I have come a long way with our victory garden. We started by plowing a small section of our backyard. Then we added fertilizer to the earth. Also, we got free seeds from a seed company downstate. We planted corn, onions, tomatoes, radishes, two kinds of beans, and a few flowers.

Since then, we've weeded and watered our garden every few days all summer. Now we are picking vegetables! We eat some fresh and can the rest in glass jars to eat this winter. I'm proud to be growing food for us and helping win the war at the same time!

 Summarize Look for details that summarize how society changed during the early 1900s.

▶ A victory garden poster from World War I

The Great War

Until the early part of the twentieth century, the United States was not very involved in events that happened in the rest of the world. In 1914, however, a war swept over most of Europe. At first called the Great War, we now call it **World War I.** Germany, Austria-Hungary, and Turkey were the Central Powers. Fighting against them were the **Allies:** Great Britain, France, Italy, Russia, and Japan.

At first the United States helped the Allies by sending food and supplies. Because German submarines had attacked American ships, and for other reasons, President **Woodrow Wilson** asked Congress to declare war on Germany in 1917.

Illinois Governor **Frank Lowden** urged citizens to sign up to fight in Europe. Illinoisans from all parts of the state

▶ **Illinoisans in Coles County board trains to go to war.**

Literature and Social Studies

Wilson's War Message

President Woodrow Wilson spoke these words to the members of the U.S. Congress on April 2, 1917.

We must put excited feeling away. Our motive will not be revenge or the victorious assertion [declaration] of the physical might of the nation, but only the vindication [confirmation] of right, of human right, of which we are only a single champion.

helped support the war. In **Coles County,** for example, people grew more food and ate less so that they could send more food to the soldiers.

As Illinois factories began making equipment for the war, they needed new workers to replace those who had left to fight. Many African Americans moved to Illinois from the South to fill these positions.

By the time the war ended in 1918, it had claimed the lives of more than 116,000 Americans. It also earned the United States a reputation as a world power.

REVIEW How did Illinoisans help with the war effort during World War I?
🔄 **Summarize**

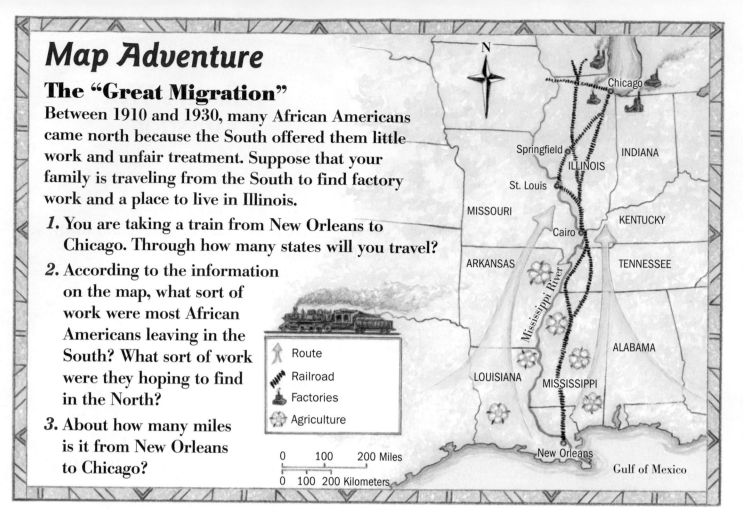

Map Adventure

The "Great Migration"

Between 1910 and 1930, many African Americans came north because the South offered them little work and unfair treatment. Suppose that your family is traveling from the South to find factory work and a place to live in Illinois.

1. You are taking a train from New Orleans to Chicago. Through how many states will you travel?

2. According to the information on the map, what sort of work were most African Americans leaving in the South? What sort of work were they hoping to find in the North?

3. About how many miles is it from New Orleans to Chicago?

Route
Railroad
Factories
Agriculture

0   100   200 Miles
0   100 200 Kilometers

The Machine Age

In addition to the end of the war, new inventions continued to change the lives of Illinoisans. By 1908 automobile manufacturer **Henry Ford** improved the process of **mass production,** a way to manufacture many identical items quickly. Ford's factory used an **assembly line,** or an arrangement of machines, tools, and workers in which a product is assembled. Ford's assembly line used a moving belt, along which the cars traveled as each worker put on a single part until the car was finished.

The use of assembly lines made the production of other new products faster and cheaper. As you will read on pages 240 and 241, many more new inventions of household products, such as vacuum cleaners and electric mixers, made people's lives easier. By the late 1920s many households in rural Illinois had a telephone.

As you will read on pages 240 and 241

REVIEW How did Henry Ford change the lives of many Illinoisans?
Main Idea and Details

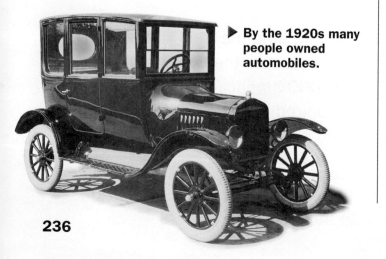

▶ **By the 1920s many people owned automobiles.**

236

Hard Times

For years the Illinois economy had been growing larger and more modern and successful. Then the United States was stunned by financial problems during the **Great Depression.** This was a time when companies had trouble staying in business, and many people lost their jobs. The Great Depression lasted from 1929 until the early 1940s. It spread from the United States to Europe and other parts of the world.

Illinoisans were hurt badly by the Great Depression. Some banks ran out of money and had to close, so many people lost their savings. Daily life was difficult during the Great Depression. People saved money by planting gardens, eating less meat, and canning food. They also learned to live with fewer new things and to make the clothing, shoes, cars, and appliances they owned last longer.

Like other states, Illinois turned to the U.S. government for help. President **Franklin D. Roosevelt** introduced a program called the **New Deal** to help companies and individuals survive. The government organized the Civilian Conservation Corps (CCC), which gave jobs to about 10,000 young men aged 18 to 25 in Illinois. They worked for $30 each month. CCC workers in about 50 camps in Illinois planted more than 60 million trees to prevent soil erosion. They also built nearly 400 bridges and created almost 1,200 miles of trails in state parks. Another New Deal program,

▶ **Many people in Illinois had to do different kinds of jobs during the Great Depression.**

the **Works Progress Administration,** gave work to many Illinoisans throughout the 1930s.

REVIEW How many years did the Great Depression last?
Main Idea and Details

237

Illinois and World War II

The Great Depression caused other countries to suffer too. Germany had harder challenges than the United States had. By promising to fix Germany's problems, **Adolf Hitler** was able to bring a political group called the Nazis (NAHT sees) to power in the early 1930s.

In 1939 the Nazis invaded Poland, a neighboring country. In response, Great Britain and France, and later the Soviet Union, declared war on Germany, marking the start of **World War II.** In 1940 Italy and Japan joined Germany's side; these nations became known as the **Axis Powers.**

The United States entered the war after Japanese planes attacked a United States Navy base at **Pearl Harbor** in Hawaii, on December 7, 1941. The U.S. joined Great Britain and the Soviet Union to form the Allies during the war.

President Franklin D. Roosevelt led the nation through most of World War II. In all, the United States sent 16 million soldiers to fight in the war between 1941 and 1945. About one million men and women from Illinois served as soldiers, sailors, and pilots.

At home, Illinois helped win the war by growing crops and making airplanes, weapons, and other heavy equipment. For example, Chicago's International Harvester Company, now Navistar, made torpedoes, or bombs used to sink ships. Many women entered the paid workforce for the first time in their lives. Illinois farmers helped feed Allied forces. The economy of Illinois thrived, along with that of the United States.

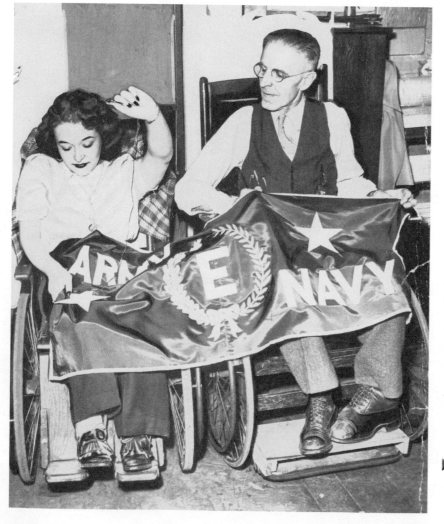

▶ *E* flags such as the one in this photo were awarded to factories that produced goods for the war. *E* was short for "excellent."

As the war raged, scientists such as **Enrico Fermi** at the University of Chicago were learning how to release the energy held inside atoms. This knowledge helped the United States develop atomic bombs. In 1943 Italy surrendered. But for two more years, the Allies fought German forces in Europe as well as Japanese forces in the Pacific Ocean. Finally, in May 1945, Germany surrendered.

Three months later the United States dropped atomic bombs on two Japanese cities. With Japan's surrender on August 14, 1945, World War II ended.

REVIEW What three nations formed the Axis nations? **Main Idea and Details**

▶ Happy crowds of people in Chicago celebrate the end of World War II.

Summarize the Lesson

1908 Henry Ford used mass production for automobile manufacturing.

1917 The United States entered World War I.

1929 The Great Depression began.

1945 World War II ended.

LESSON 1 REVIEW

Check Facts and Main Ideas

1. ⊙ **Summarize** On a separate sheet of paper, write the missing details that support the summary.

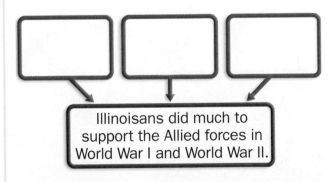

Illinoisans did much to support the Allied forces in World War I and World War II.

2. What event in the early 1940s caused the United States to enter World War II?

3. How did mass production change American industry?

4. How did the U.S. economy change from the 1930s to the 1940s?

5. **Critical Thinking:** *Cause and Effect* What factors caused African Americans to want to migrate to Chicago?

Link to ⦿─⦿ Writing

Write an Advertisement Use encyclopedias, history books, or the Internet to research the passenger trains linking Illinois to the South during the period from 1910 to 1930. Write an ad for a train offering one of these journeys. As you write your ad, think about the reasons people might be traveling north (or south) at that time.

Inventions Make Life Better

Television. Hair dryers. Crayons. Sound movies. It is hard to imagine life without many of the things that were invented in the early 1900s. Many of today's inventions are improvements on original ideas from the past and look much different from the originals. The first telephone, for example, was a metal tube. It did not have a ringer or buttons for numbers as telephones do today. Other products look almost identical to the way they did in the past. The stapler has kept the same basic design as earlier models. However, the first staplers were made to fasten together shoe parts, not paper! Look at the pictures of inventions from the early 1900s. How does each compare with its present-day version?

Cleaning Up

Early vacuum cleaners used hand pumps to suck up dirt. James Murray Spangler invented the first portable electric vacuum cleaner in 1907.

Zip Up

Gideon Sunback, a Swedish engineer living in the United States, developed the modern version of the zipper in 1912. The zipper began appearing on clothing for men and women in the late 1920s.

Easy Mixing

The 1918 food mixer had two blades driven by an electric motor. A hinge allowed the mixer to be turned to a horizontal position.

Electric motor

Keeping Cool

Electric refrigerators began to appear in the 1920s. Before then, people used large blocks of ice to keep food cold.

First Powered Flight

Brothers Wilbur and Orville Wright achieved the first powered flight in Kitty Hawk, North Carolina, in 1903. Their plane stayed in the air for 12 seconds.

1940　　　　1960　　　　1980　　　　2000

1947
The Cold War begins.

1965
Senator Everett Dirksen helps pass the Voting Rights Act.

1979
Jane Byrne becomes the first woman to be elected mayor of Chicago.

1980s
Service industries are an important part of Illinois's economy.

★Springfield

PREVIEW

Focus on the Main Idea
Life in Illinois and in the United States has changed dramatically since World War II.

PLACES
North Korea
South Korea
Springfield
North Vietnam
South Vietnam
Iraq
Kuwait

PEOPLE
Everett Dirksen
Mae Carol Jemison
Ronald Reagan

VOCABULARY
discrimination
communism
service

EVENTS
Civil Rights Movement
Cold War
Korean War
Vietnam War
Persian Gulf War

TERMS
Voting Rights Act of 1965
arms race
service industry

242

Post-War Challenges

> **You Are There** When we were downtown this morning, Mom and I saw a crowd of people on the sidewalk near a restaurant.
>
> When we could see through the restaurant window, we saw ten young African Americans sitting at the lunch counter. We could see the waitress asking them to leave. But the young people said they would not leave until they were served a meal.
>
> We asked someone in the crowd what was going on. He said that a group called the Congress of Racial Equality was holding a "sit-in."
>
> I felt excited and nervous. My mother held my hand tightly and said "It takes courage to demand justice peacefully in this world."

 Summarize As you read, look for details that help summarize the ways that society has changed since World War II.

Moving Toward Civil Rights

During and after World War II, more African Americans settled in Illinois. But even in the North, some people treated African Americans unfairly. Unfair treatment of a group of people is called **discrimination.**

The **Civil Rights Movement** was started by people who believed that all citizens deserve the rights that are guaranteed in the Constitution. In the 1950s and 1960s, Martin Luther King, Jr., was the nation's best-known African American leader.

After observing years of civil rights protests all over the country, Illinois Senator **Everett Dirksen** helped pass the **Voting Rights Act of 1965.** This law made it illegal to keep anyone from registering to vote because of his or her race.

The Civil Rights Movement has created new educational opportunities and better jobs for many African Americans. For example, **Mae Carol Jemison,** who grew up in Chicago, became the first female African American astronaut to go into space in 1992.

REVIEW In what decades was Martin Luther King, Jr. active as a civil rights leader? **Main Idea and Details**

FACT FILE

Civil Rights Leaders

▶ Martin Luther King, Jr. (center bottom) leads a civil rights march in Selma, Alabama.

▶ Chicago-based John Johnson founded the African American magazines *Ebony* and *Jet.* He helped fund the Civil Rights Movement up until his death in 2005.

▶ Jesse Jackson, who ran for President in 1984 and 1988, was the first major African American presidential candidate.

▶ Senator Everett Dirksen helped guide civil rights laws through the U.S. Congress.

Around the World

Even as World War II ended and more Americans received their rights, world peace was threatened again. After World War II, the Soviet Union (which included Russia) had forced several Eastern European nations to adopt their system of economics, called **communism.** In communist countries the government, rather than private citizens, owns factories and businesses. The United States thought that Soviet communism was dangerous and unfair. So American leaders were worried when the Soviet Union started to make other countries communist.

In 1947 disagreements between the United States and the Soviet Union grew stronger. For the next four decades, both countries kept building more and bigger weapons in an **arms race.** Because no direct fighting ever broke out between the two nations, this conflict is called a **Cold War.**

Communism also affected nations in Asia. In 1950 communist forces from **North Korea** invaded **South Korea,** starting the **Korean War.** The United States sided with South Korea to keep communism from spreading. The war ended in 1953. Later, in 1996 the Illinois state government opened the Illinois Korean War Memorial in **Springfield,** to honor those Illinoisans who served in that war.

In the mid-1950s the communist government in **North Vietnam** sent armies into **South Vietnam.** In the mid-1960s the United States began to send large numbers of troops to South Vietnam to fight the spread of communism. The **Vietnam War** was longer and more fierce than the Korean War. Many Americans opposed the war. In 1973 American forces finally withdrew from South Vietnam and the war ended in 1975. Shortly after American forces left, North Vietnam took over South Vietnam. The unified country is now called Vietnam.

Between 1981 and 1989, **Ronald Reagan,** the fortieth U.S. President, worked to end the Cold War. Because the Soviet Union was suffering from financial problems, it could not afford to continue an arms race.

► The Korean War Veterans' Memorial in Springfield

ILLINOIS KOREAN WAR MEMORIAL

Operation Iraqi Freedom: 2003

Korean War: 1950–1953

Operation Desert Storm: 1991

Vietnam War: 1964–1973

▶ The United States has been involved in several major conflicts since the end of World War II.

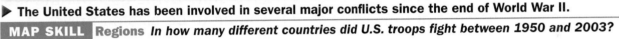

MAP SKILL Regions *In how many different countries did U.S. troops fight between 1950 and 2003?*

In 1991 the Soviet Union broke into separate countries with their own governments that began giving people more rights. Finally, the Cold War was over.

Unfortunately, U.S. forces were soon active in the Middle East, the part of the world where the continents of Europe, Africa, and Asia meet. The nation of **Iraq** invaded the nation of **Kuwait** in August 1990. Aided by forces from several European nations as well as Egypt and Saudi Arabia, U.S. forces drove Iraqi forces from Kuwait. The **Persian Gulf War,** also known as Operation Desert Storm, ended after a few weeks. In 2003 U.S. forces fought in Iraq in Operation Iraqi Freedom.

REVIEW What events led to the end of the Cold War? **Summarize**

New Faces in Politics

During the twentieth century, Illinois saw more women and African Americans active in government. In 1979 Jane Byrne became the first female mayor of Chicago. In 1983 Harold Washington became the first African American mayor of Chicago.

In 1992 Carol Moseley Braun of Illinois became the first African American woman elected to the United States Senate. When he took office in 2005, Barack Obama became only the fifth African American U.S. senator ever.

REVIEW How were the achievements of Jane Byrne and Carol Moseley Braun similar? **Compare and Contrast**

Economic Changes

The twentieth century also brought changes in the economy of Illinois. Economic activity can be divided into two groups—goods and services. Goods are usually things you can see, pay for, and take with you. Tools and grain are examples of important Illinois goods. A **service** is work someone does for you, such as mowing your lawn or maintaining your telephone line.

As societies develop, they need more **service industries**, or businesses dedicated to providing services to people and other businesses.

In 1929 only 54 percent of the U.S. economy was devoted to services. Fifty years later, service industries such as banks, telephone companies, and hospitals made up 66 percent of the economy.

Since the 1980s computers have helped service industries grow even faster. You can expect services to become an even more important part of the economy in the years to come.

REVIEW What is a service industry?
Main Idea and Details

Summarize the Lesson

1947 The Cold War began.

1965 Senator Everett Dirksen helped pass the Voting Rights Act.

1979 Jane Byrne became the first woman to be elected mayor of Chicago.

1980s Service industries became an important part of Illinois's economy.

LESSON 2 REVIEW

Check Facts and Main Ideas

1. **Summarize** On a separate sheet of paper, write the summary that supports the details.

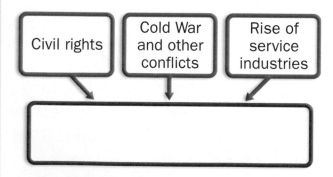

| Civil rights | Cold War and other conflicts | Rise of service industries |

2. How did Illinois Senator Everett Dirksen support civil rights for African Americans?

3. How did the Cold War differ from the wars in Korea, Vietnam, and the Persian Gulf?

4. How has technology helped the U.S. economy shift toward a service economy?

5. **Critical Thinking:** *Identify Opinions* Explain why the following statement is an opinion: A service economy is better than an economy based on manufactured goods.

Link to ⎯∞⎯ Art

Make a Mural With your classmates, make a mural that shows the differences between goods and services. On one side of the mural, illustrate several types of goods produced on Illinois's farms and in its factories. Then show several types of services that are provided by Illinois people working in today's service economy.

Mae Carol Jemison

b. 1956

The youngest of three children, Mae Carol Jemison attended public school in Chicago. While growing up, she developed a strong interest in science. She enjoyed studying stars and planets (astronomy) and cultures of different people around the world (anthropology). At age 16 Jemison entered Stanford University to study chemistry.

After graduating from college, Jemison studied to become a doctor. She worked as a medical volunteer in Thailand, Kenya, and West Africa. In 1986 Jemison was one of 2,000 people who applied to be an astronaut for the National Aeronautics and Space Administration (NASA). With 14 other people, she was accepted into the program. In 1992 she became the first female African American to go into space aboard the space shuttle *Endeavour*.

BIOFACT

Known first as a scientist, Jemison is also a trained dancer.

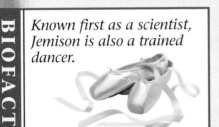

Today she encourages all people—especially girls and people of different backgrounds—to strive for careers in science. Girls, she says,

". . . should understand they have as much right and talent and responsibility to be in those fields as anyone else. They don't have to ask anyone's permission."

Learn from Biographies

What subjects did Jemison study that probably helped her become an astronaut?

Students can research the lives of significant people by clicking on *Meet the People* at **www.sfsocialstudies.com**.

Use Information Resources

What? **Information resources** include printed materials such as books and newspapers. Information resources also include electronic media such as the Internet and community resources such as people and organizations.

The **Internet** is a huge network of computers. It contains many **Web sites,** or sites on the World Wide Web. A Web site may be run by a government department, an organization, a university, a business, or a private citizen.

Why? Different information resources provide different kinds of information. For example, newspapers present the news of the day. Old newspapers offer a look at daily life in the past.

The Internet gives you quick access to thousands of sources of information. In fact, major newspapers now publish some of their sections online.

How? How you search for information depends on what resource you are using. For example, newspapers are usually printed in sections:

- News articles appear in one section.
- Other sections may include stories on the arts, sports, and other topics.

- Most newspapers contain an **editorial** section in which people express their opinions.

- Look for a table of contents to tell you where to find articles.

- Look at **headlines,** or phrases or sentences printed in large type, to tell you about the subject of an article.

To find information on the Internet, you can search in two basic ways.

- Each Internet location has an address, or **URL.** If you know the URL you wish to use, enter it in the strip at the top of your screen marked *location* or *address.*

- Another way to find information about a topic is to use a **search engine.** A search engine searches the Internet for pages that contain the topics or words you are looking for. A teacher or librarian can help you choose a search engine.

- Next type in a **key word** or two. A key word is a word or a phrase related to your topic, such as "Illinois history." Then click on "Search." You may have to experiment with different words or phrases. If you need help, click on *Help* or *Search Tips.*

- The search engine will create a list of Web sites that may contain the information you need.

- Look first for government and educational sites. Their URLs end in *.gov* or *.edu.* They usually have dependable information.

- Click on one of the sites. The information should appear on your screen.

- If your search brings no results, try another key word, or ask for help from someone with more Internet experience.

- Check the information you find on the Internet with another source, such as an encyclopedia. Also, use what you have learned about telling fact from opinion to judge how dependable a Web site is.

Think and Apply

1. What is the name of the newspaper shown on page 248?

2. What key words might you type to find information about Illinois history?

3. How would you choose the most reliable sites from a list created by a search engine?

1900	1910	1920	1930

1917 The United States entered World War I.

1929 The Great Depression began.

Chapter Summary

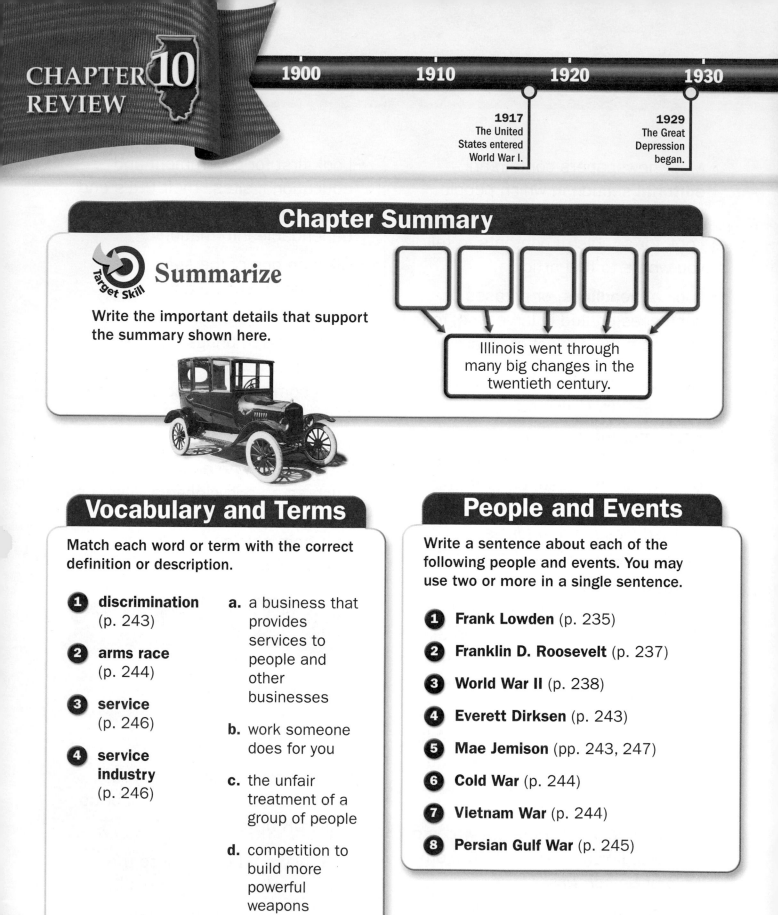

Summarize

Write the important details that support the summary shown here.

Illinois went through many big changes in the twentieth century.

Vocabulary and Terms

Match each word or term with the correct definition or description.

① **discrimination** (p. 243)

② **arms race** (p. 244)

③ **service** (p. 246)

④ **service industry** (p. 246)

a. a business that provides services to people and other businesses

b. work someone does for you

c. the unfair treatment of a group of people

d. competition to build more powerful weapons

People and Events

Write a sentence about each of the following people and events. You may use two or more in a single sentence.

① **Frank Lowden** (p. 235)

② **Franklin D. Roosevelt** (p. 237)

③ **World War II** (p. 238)

④ **Everett Dirksen** (p. 243)

⑤ **Mae Jemison** (pp. 243, 247)

⑥ **Cold War** (p. 244)

⑦ **Vietnam War** (p. 244)

⑧ **Persian Gulf War** (p. 245)

| 1940 | 1950 | 1960 | 1970 | 1980 |

1945
World War II ended.

1947
The Cold War between the Soviet Union and the United States began.

1965
Senator Everett Dirksen helped pass the Voting Rights Act.

1979
Jane Byrne became the first woman elected mayor of Chicago.

Facts and Main Ideas

1. What is the purpose of mass production?

2. How did the U.S. government help people during the Great Depression?

3. How did Illinois farms and factories contribute to the effort to win World War II?

4. How has new technology changed the economy of Illinois and of the United States as a whole?

5. **Time Line** What dramatic event happened between the world wars?

6. **Main Idea** What three events during the first half of the twentieth century challenged people around the world?

7. **Main Idea** How did the Civil Rights Movement change life in Illinois and around the nation?

8. **Critical Thinking:** *Compare and Contrast* How were the Korean and Vietnam wars similar?

Internet Activity

To get help with vocabulary, people, and events, select the dictionary or encyclopedia from *Social Studies Library* at **www.sfsocialstudies.com**.

Apply Skills

Use Information Resources

Find a local newspaper from the past week. Use it to answer these questions.

1. Find a news article in the newspaper. What is the headline? Summarize the story that follows it.

2. Find an editorial in the same newspaper. Summarize what it is about.

3. Look through the newspaper. Does it post some or all of its news on a Web site? If so, write down the URL. Then go to the Web site and find the table of contents.

Write About History

1. **Write a list** of ten tools, devices, machines, or other examples of new technology since World War I that have changed the way people live.

2. **Write a paragraph** in which you explain why the Civil Rights Movement was so important to Illinois and to the whole nation.

3. **Write a poem** in which you describe someone who you think is one of the heroes of the twentieth century.

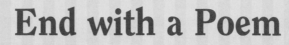
End with a Poem

As a child, Langston Hughes lived in several cities with his mother and grandmother, finally settling in the industrial city of Cleveland, Ohio. As a young man, Hughes traveled to Africa and Europe and then lived in the Harlem neighborhood of New York City. He published books of poetry from 1926 until the end of his life in 1967. Hughes's poems contain direct, honest expressions of the thoughts, feelings, and experiences of African Americans.

Starting in 1942, Langston Hughes wrote a weekly column for the *Chicago Defender,* a newspaper owned and edited by African Americans. The newspaper was popular around the country, and its writers and editors urged African Americans to leave the South and come to the industrial cities of the North. The *Defender* was largely responsible for the Great Migration of African Americans to the North beginning in 1910.

Hughes published a book called *One-Way Ticket* in 1949. The title poem is spoken by an African American who is leaving the South because he is tired of living under "Jim Crow laws." These laws were passed by state legislatures in the South from the 1870s until the

ONE-WAY TICKET

by Langston Hughes

I pick up my life
And take it with me
And I put it down in
Chicago, Detroit,
Buffalo, Scranton,
Any place that is
North and East—
And not Dixie.

I pick up my life
And take it on the train
To Los Angeles, Bakersfield,
Seattle, Oakland, Salt Lake,
Any place that is
North and West—
And not South.

I am fed up
With Jim Crow laws,
People who are cruel
And afraid,
Who lynch and run,
Who are scared of me
And me of them.

I pick up my life
And take it away
On a one-way ticket—
Gone up North,
Gone out West,
Gone!

beginning of the Civil Rights Movement
in the 1950s. Jim Crow laws required
that black people be separated from white
people on buses and trains and in schools,
parks, and restaurants. Hughes's speaker
is set on finding a place where he can live
in justice and with trust.

253

Main Ideas and Vocabulary

TEST PREP

Read the passage below, and use it to answer the questions that follow.

After the Civil War, Illinois farm production continued to increase, but manufacturing industries in Illinois grew much faster. Illinois became a noted producer of machinery, farm equipment, railroad equipment, cloth, and furniture. Chicago became the most important city in the Midwest.

Many people in factories found themselves working long hours in poor working conditions for low pay. Reformers began trying to improve the lives of working people. Workers also started unions to force factory owners to treat them fairly. Reforms were made in the workplace, in city sanitation, and in many other areas.

Early in the twentieth century, new technology changed the lives of Americans. More Illinois households had telephones and electricity as well as products such as cars from factories that used mass production.

During the 1950s and 1960s the Civil Rights Movement expanded opportunities for African Americans. Civil Rights leaders such as Senator Everett Dirksen helped pass the Voting Rights Act of 1965.

After two world wars came a time of distrust, called the "Cold War," between the United States and the Soviet Union. The Cold War ended in the early 1990s when the Soviet Union broke up into different countries that had their own governments.

1 According to this passage, manufacturing industries in Illinois
  A grew slowly after the Civil War.
  B were built primarily in the southern part of the state.
  C grew even faster than farming.
  D were unimportant to the average citizen.

2 In this passage, reform means
  A a bad judgment.
  B a new boss.
  C a governor who is willing to take action.
  D a change made to something to improve it.

3 In this passage, mass production means
  A the growing importance of labor unions.
  B a system for manufacturing products more quickly and easily.
  C custom-made products.
  D a shift toward a service economy.

4 According to this passage, the Cold War ended
  A between the world wars.
  B when the Soviet Union broke apart into new governments.
  C when Illinois's economy became a "service economy."
  D when the Civil Rights Movement began.

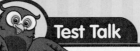
People and Places

Match each word with the correct definition or description.

1 **Hull House** (p. 224)

2 **University of Illinois** (p. 224)

3 **Daniel Hale Williams** (pp. 224, 227)

4 **Ronald Reagan** (p. 244)

a. fortieth President of the United States

b. offered classes in trades and skills

c. founder of Provident Hospital

d. Chicago settlement house established by Jane Addams

Apply Skills

Update a Population Graph Use information resources such as books, magazines, and the Internet to research recent population changes in your community, your county, and the state of Illinois as a whole. Then use this information to create a line graph or a bar graph that displays this information clearly. You might include population information from 1945 to the present day. According to your graph, which period had the greatest amount of change? Did population increase or decrease during this time?

Read on Your Own

Look for these books in the library.

Write and Share

Make a Scrapbook With several classmates, create a scrapbook that shows important people, places, and events from the twentieth century. You might include original drawings, as well as copies of photographs. For each image, write a short description that explains why the subject is important.

UNIT 5 Project

Ad Sales

Healthy businesses are good for the Illinois economy. Make your own infomercial about a product or a business.

1 Form a group. Choose a product or a business.

2 Research the product or business, and write a list of facts about it.

3 Write a script for an infomercial about the product or business. Include the value and cost, as well as the history of the product or business. Give examples of its successes. Tell how it contributes to our state's economy.

4 Make an advertisement on a poster or banner to use in your infomercial.

5 Present your infomercial to the class.

Internet Activity

For more information and activities, go to **www.sfsocialstudies.com**.

Into the Twenty-first Century

How do you think Illinois will change in the twenty-first century?

Begin with a Primary Source

Who Are the People of Illinois Today?

Today Illinoisans come from many backgrounds. They are working together in many ways to build a better state and to make stronger communities.

We work together to make our government better by learning about our laws and constitution, by voting for representatives, and by volunteering to help people in our communities.

The government in Illinois today is similar to the federal government in Washington, D.C. They both consist of three branches of government. The governor heads the executive branch of Illinois. The chief justice helps run the judicial branch. Senators and representatives make up the legislative branch.

Illinoisans have many choices of how to earn a living. Some people work on farms. Others work in factories. In the past few decades, more and more people have been finding work in many service industries and high-tech industries. The field of telecommunications, which includes computers, televisions, and Internet services, is an example of both a service and a high-tech industry.

Use the reading strategy of drawing conclusions to answer these questions.

1 Consider the following facts: People in Illinois learn about the laws and the constitution, they vote, and they volunteer to help other people where they live. What sort of conclusion could you form on the basis of these facts about the people who live in your state?

2 A governor, a chief justice, and state senators and representatives make up a large part of the Illinois state government. Draw a conclusion that answers this question: "Why did the Illinois Constitution create three branches of government?"

3 People from Illinois work on farms and in factories, as well as in service and high-tech industries. What conclusion can you make about the economy in Illinois?

CHAPTER 11

Citizenship in Illinois

Lesson 1

Springfield
Springfield is the capital of Illinois.

1

Lesson 2

Illinois
The people of Illinois are serious about their responsibilities as citizens.

2

CANADA

1 2

Springfield

ILLINOIS

UNITED STATES

PACIFIC OCEAN

ATLANTIC OCEAN

Gulf of Mexico

MEXICO

Why We Remember

As a citizen of the United States and of Illinois, you will someday be able to vote for the people whom you want to serve in government. You will be able to vote for the President of the United States, for the governor of your state, for your town or city council representatives, and for other officeholders. In this chapter you will learn how the actions of government representatives in the nation's capital, in your state capital, and in your community affect your life. You will also learn that when you vote, you become part of Illinois's proud political tradition.

★Springfield

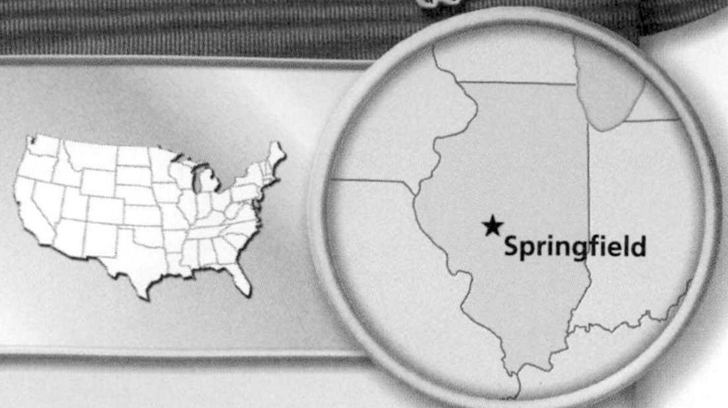

Government in Illinois

You Are There

Dear Grandma and Grandpa,
My class and I have flown all the way from Illinois to Washington, D.C., for a field trip! Today we are visiting the United States Congress. The room is huge, and we are sitting in a balcony. I hear different leaders discussing a new law. There's a long argument, with many people talking. Some of them want the law passed. Others are angry because they think the law is unfair. I listen carefully to both sides, and I'm not sure who will win.

Love,
Nicky

Draw Conclusions As you read, use information to draw conclusions about the ways in which the national, state, and local governments work for you.

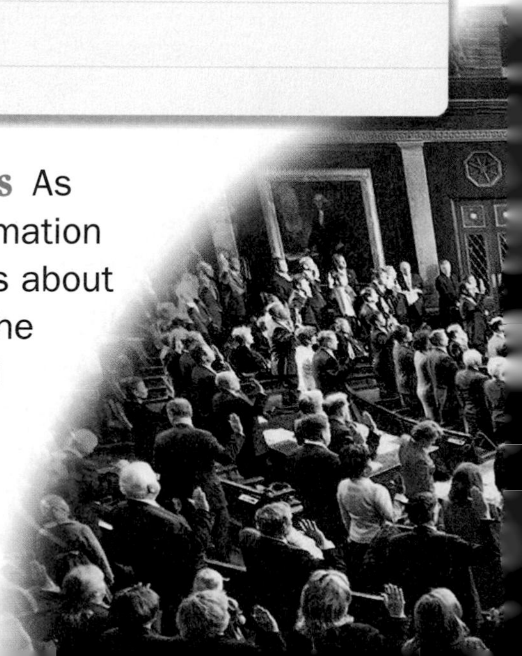

Illinoisans in Federal Service

In the United States, three main levels of government serve the people: the national or federal government, the state government, and the local government. Our national government is located in **Washington, D.C.** Even though the United States capital is far from Illinois, many of the things that happen there directly affect our state.

The Constitution of the United States, Article IV, Section 4, guarantees all states a republican form of government. In a **republic,** citizens of a state elect people to represent them and to pass laws for them.

The writers of the United States Constitution wanted to make sure that no part of the government has too much power. These founders divided the national government into three branches—executive, legislative, and judicial—which allows for **checks and balances.** This means that each branch

▶ Senator Richard Durbin began serving Illinois in the United States Senate in 1996.

▶ Senator Barack Obama began serving in the United States Senate in 2005.

▶ J. Dennis Hastert began serving Illinois's fourteenth congressional district in the U.S. House of Representatives in 1986. In 1999 he was elected Speaker of the House.

of government has the power to check, or limit, the power of the other branches.

Many Illinoisans have served in the federal government in the past. For example, Abraham Lincoln was the sixteenth President, Ulysses S. Grant served as the eighteenth President, and Ronald Reagan was the fortieth President. Recently, Illinoisans serving in the U.S. Senate and House of Representatives have included **Richard Durbin, Barack Obama,** and **J. Dennis Hastert.** Other Illinoisans who have worked for the federal government include **Donald Rumsfeld.** He began serving as Secretary of Defense under President George W. Bush in 2001.

REVIEW Why did the writers of the United States Constitution form a republic? ⟳ **Draw Conclusions**

▶ The U.S. Capitol is where the legislative branch of the federal government works.

How the Federal Government Helps Illinois

Many of the goods and services that you buy and use are provided by private businesses. However, some goods and services are provided by the government. How does the government pay for these? The government uses tax dollars, such as income tax, collected from citizens to provide goods and services to the public. The amount of **income tax** a person pays is based on how much money that individual earns each year. The federal government spends money on many **public goods and services,** such as education, health care, national parks, and national defense. The entire country benefits from these public goods and services.

Another example of public goods and services is the interstate highway system. The federal government pays for highways that link our states together. The federal government also spends tax dollars in Illinois and other states to help protect the environment.

REVIEW What do federally-sponsored programs such as education, health care, and national defense have in common? 🔄 **Draw Conclusions**

Our State Government

Springfield is Illinois's capital, the center of our state's government. Like the federal government, the state government provides public goods and services, such as schools, libraries, and state roads. These are paid for with tax dollars, such as a state income tax and sales tax. **Sales tax** is a tax on many goods and services that you buy.

Like the federal government, the government of Illinois is divided into three branches: executive, legislative, and judicial, with the same systems of checks and balances.

The governor is the head of the executive branch and watches over most areas of the state government. He or she may serve any number of four-year terms. **Adlai E. Stevenson** served one term as Illinois's thirty-third governor between 1949 and 1953.

Literature and Social Studies

Preamble of the Illinois State Constitution, 1970

We, the People of the State of Illinois . . . provide for the health, safety and welfare of the people; maintain a representative and orderly government; eliminate [end] poverty and inequality; assure legal, social and economic justice . . . and secure the blessings of freedom and liberty to ourselves. . . .

FACT FILE

Three Branches of Illinois Government

Branch of Government	Leader	Responsibilities
Executive	Governor of Illinois	▪ Oversees state government ▪ Reports on how the state is doing
Legislative	President, Illinois State Senate; Leader of the General Assembly	▪ Makes laws for the state ▪ Represents views of citizens of Illinois
Judicial	Chief Justice of the Illinois Supreme Court	▪ Determines the meaning of the Illinois constitution and Illinois laws ▪ Determines whether laws have been broken ▪ Decides what the punishment for breaking laws should be

▶ The State Seal of Illinois

▶ Rod R. Blagojevich became governor of Illinois in 2003.

▶ The state capitol building is a familiar symbol of our state government.

He was popular with many different groups, including business and labor organizations. **Rod Blagojevich** became Illinois's fortieth governor in 2003. Each year the governor presents the state budget to propose a plan for how tax money will be spent. A **budget** is a written plan that shows how money will be spent. Another important responsibility of the governor is to review legislative bills before they become laws. He has the power to **veto**, or reject a bill.

The legislative branch, also known as the **General Assembly**, is made up of the House of Representatives and the Senate. The 118 house members serve two-year terms. The 59 state senators serve four-year terms.

The judicial branch consists of more than 400 judges. Seven judges are elected to the Supreme Court, the state's highest court, for 10-year terms. The judges are responsible for understanding the constitution and laws of Illinois. The judges also must decide whether laws have been broken.

REVIEW Why is the governor allowed to veto legislation? ⟳ **Draw Conclusions**

269

Local Government in Illinois

Each county, city, town, and township in Illinois has its own local government and elected officials. Unlike the federal and state governments, local governments do not have a constitution.

County governments are the largest type of local government. If you look at the map, you will see that Illinois is divided into 102 counties. The counties vary in size. Some have large populations. Others have fewer residents. Most counties are governed by a county board that makes laws for the county.

Residents of Illinois counties pay taxes. In turn, the county governments provide services for the people. They build and repair roads, run hospitals and libraries, and keep records of births, marriages, and deaths.

In Illinois each county is divided into smaller sections called **townships.** The number of townships varies from county to county. Within the townships are cities and towns. Residents of the cities, towns, and townships pay taxes to these governments. These taxes help pay for services such as police and fire departments. City and town governments also provide safe drinking water, maintain parks, run transportation services, help build and repair roads and streets, and maintain schools. Many also provide trash collection and run recycling programs.

MAP SKILL · **Illinois Counties**

ILLINOIS COUNTIES	23 Will	50 Vermilion	77 Marion
	24 Kankakee	51 Pike	78 Clay
	25 Henderson	52 Scott	79 Richland
	26 Warren	53 Morgan	80 Lawrence
1 Jo Daviess	27 Knox	54 Sangamon	81 Monroe
2 Stephenson	28 Stark	55 Christian	82 Washington
3 Winnebago	29 Peoria	56 Macon	83 Jefferson
4 Boone	30 Marshall	57 Moultrie	84 Wayne
5 McHenry	31 Woodford	58 Douglas	85 Edwards
6 Lake	32 Livingston	59 Edgar	86 Wabash
7 Carroll	33 Ford	60 Calhoun	87 Randolph
8 Ogle	34 Iroquois	61 Greene	88 Perry
9 Whiteside	35 Hancock	62 Jersey	89 Franklin
10 Lee	36 McDonough	63 Macoupin	90 Hamilton
11 DeKalb	37 Fulton	64 Montgomery	91 White
12 Kane	38 Tazewell	65 Shelby	92 Jackson
13 Cook	39 McLean	66 Coles	93 Williamson
14 DuPage	40 Adams	67 Cumberland	94 Saline
15 Rock Island	41 Schuyler	68 Clark	95 Gallatin
16 Mercer	42 Brown	69 Madison	96 Union
17 Henry	43 Cass	70 Bond	97 Johnson
18 Bureau	44 Mason	71 Fayette	98 Pope
19 Putnam	45 Menard	72 Effingham	99 Hardin
20 La Salle	46 Logan	73 Jasper	100 Alexander
21 Kendall	47 DeWitt	74 Crawford	101 Pulaski
22 Grundy	48 Piatt	75 St. Clair	102 Massac
	49 Champaign	76 Clinton	

▶ When Illinois became a territory in 1809, St. Clair and Randolph Counties were the only two counties.

MAP SKILL Understand Borders *How many Illinois counties share a border with Missouri?*

Most cities are governed by a mayor and a city council. These elected officials work together to run the city. A town council is usually the governing body in a town.

Many Illinoisans get involved in local government. They do so because the decisions made by local governments affect people's everyday lives.

▶ Local taxes pay for fire and police departments.

REVIEW How are a county's elected government officials important to its residents? ☉ Draw Conclusions

Summarize the Lesson

- **Many Illinoisans serve in the federal government.**
- **The federal government provides important goods and services that affect the daily lives of people in Illinois.**
- **The Illinois state government is divided into three branches: executive, legislative, and judicial.**
- **Illinois counties, townships, cities, and towns have their own local governments.**

LESSON 1 REVIEW

Check Facts and Main Ideas

1. ☉ **Draw Conclusions** On a separate sheet of paper, write three details from the lesson that support the conclusion shown.

Details

Conclusion

Elected government officials at the national, state, and local level represent the views of citizens.

2. Compare the ways that the federal and state governments are organized.

3. What types of organizations supported Adlai Stevenson when he was Illinois's governor?

4. How do the citizens of Illinois benefit from paying taxes?

5. **Critical Thinking:** *Analyze* Describe how the federal government affects the daily lives of people in your community.

Link to ⬤⬤ Mathematics

Throw a Party Your class wants to invite the governor, state senators and representatives, and justices of the state supreme court to a party at your school. If all of these people attend the party, how many government officials will be at the party?

Donald Rumsfeld
b. 1932

Donald Rumsfeld grew up in Chicago, Illinois. As a young boy, he dreamed of becoming a navy pilot. He graduated from Princeton University and then served in the United States Navy as a pilot and as a flight instructor.

Rumsfeld has played an important part in the federal government for many years. In 1962 he was elected to represent Illinois in the U.S. House of Representatives. He was reelected for three more terms.

Rumsfeld served as Secretary of Defense twice. In 1975 he was appointed the thirteenth Secretary of Defense under President Gerald Ford. On January 20, 2001, he was sworn in as the twenty-first Secretary of Defense under President George W. Bush.

On June 7, 2001, in a speech about the threat of terrorism, Secretary Rumsfeld said,

"We must prepare together for the new and quite different challenges we will face in the new century."

When terrorists attacked the United States on September 11, 2001, Secretary Rumsfeld helped develop a new defense strategy to protect Americans.

BIOFACT *In 1977 Donald Rumsfeld was awarded the nation's highest civilian award, the Presidential Medal of Freedom.*

Learn from Biographies
Which position did Donald Rumsfeld hold under two different Presidents?

Students can research the lives of significant people by clicking on *Meet the People* at **www.sfsocialstudies.com**.

HERE AND THERE

Springfield and Washington, D.C.

Capital Cities

The President is the head of the executive branch of the United States government. The President lives in the White House, which is located in Washington, D.C. The governor of Illinois is the head of the executive branch of the state government. The Governor's Mansion, normally where the governor lives, is located in Springfield.

ILLINOIS
Springfield
Washington, D.C.

▶ The Governor's Mansion is located in Springfield. Joel A. Matteson, the first governor to live there, moved into the house in 1855.

▶ Sixteen rooms in the Governor's Mansion are open to public viewing. One of them, the Lincoln bedroom, sometimes hosts official overnight guests. It is furnished with a carved bed given to Lincoln before he left for Washington.

▶ This overhead view of the Oval Office shows the room in the White House where the President often works, has meetings, and delivers televised speeches to the American people.

▶ Construction of the White House began in 1792. President John Adams and his wife Abigail were the first people to live there.

273

Map and Globe Skills

Use a Street Map

What? A **street map** of a city or town shows its streets and avenues. It also shows important buildings, historic sites, parks, railway lines, and other places of interest.

Below is a map of Chicago in 1917. Look at the wider map on the next page to see a few ways that Chicago has changed.

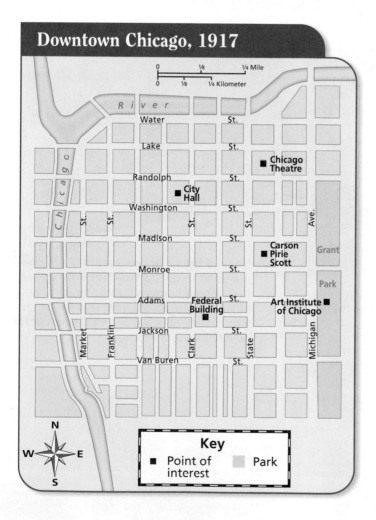

Downtown Chicago, 1917

Key
- Point of interest
- Park

Why? You need to know how to use a street map so that when you travel, you can figure out where you are and how to get to other places.

How? Read the title of the map first. The title will tell you what kind of information is included on the map. Then look for a **key.** On some maps, the key explains the symbols that are used on the map. Most maps also include a scale. A **scale** will help you figure out how far it is in miles or kilometers from one point on a map to another. A compass rose, included on most maps, tells you the directions: north, south, east, and west.

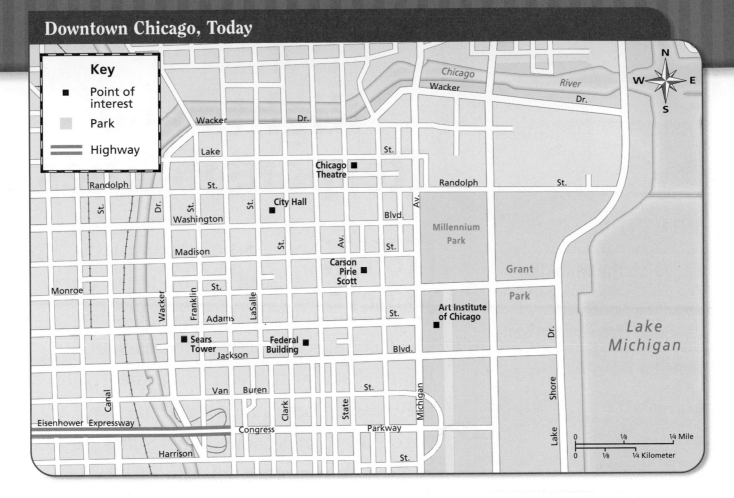

Downtown Chicago, Today

Key
- Point of interest
- Park
- Highway

When you use a street map, it is important to find your current location. The easiest way to do this is to look at the intersections at either end of the block on which you are standing. **Intersections** are places where roads meet or cross. For example, look on the map above. If you are standing at the intersection of LaSalle Street and Jackson Boulevard and you want to go to City Hall, you can walk toward the intersection of LaSalle Street and Washington Boulevard. When you have found this intersection, you know that you are going in the right direction.

For more information, go online to *Atlas* at **www.sfsocialstudies.com**.

Think and Apply

1. You are visiting Chicago in 1917. You leave the Federal Building and travel to the Art Institute. In which direction are you going?

2. If you are walking down Clark Street from City Hall to the Federal Building, how many streets will you cross between Washington and Adams?

3. On which map would you find Market Street? What is this street named on the other map?

ILLINOIS

Rights and Responsibilities

You Are There Six years ago your parents decided to come to live and work in the United States. They took special classes to learn about United States history and government. After they passed a test, a judge said that they were allowed to become United States citizens. Your mother tells you that day was one of the most exciting days of their lives. Father adds that today is just as important. He has come home early from work. Today your parents are registering to vote in their very first election!

Summarize As you read the lesson, summarize the rights and responsibilities of the citizens of Illinois.

► Citizens in Chicago register to vote.

Rights and Responsibilities of Citizenship

How do people become citizens? You have to be born in the United States, be born to a parent who is a United States citizen, or pass a citizenship test. As American citizens we have both rights and responsibilities. Our rights are freedoms that are protected by law. When the United States Constitution was approved in 1789, some people thought that it did not go far enough to protect the rights of citizens. Consequently, in 1791 ten **amendments,** or formal additions to a legal document, were added. These amendments make up the **Bill of Rights.** They protect a variety of freedoms, including freedom of religion, freedom to meet as a group, and freedom of speech. Although the government protects rights of Americans, each citizen must also accept the responsibilities of citizenship. Citizens have the responsibility of being active in our society. This includes voting.

You might be surprised to learn that for almost 75 years after the signing of the Constitution, only white males could vote. After the Civil War, many people thought that African Americans should have the right to vote. As a result, the Fifteenth Amendment was passed. The **Fifteenth Amendment** says that all men, regardless of race, can vote. **Illinois** voted to accept that amendment in 1869.

▶ Through the efforts of Mary Livermore, above left, and others, Illinois women gained the right to vote in state elections in 1913.

But what about women? Women had to wait another fifty years to win **suffrage,** or the right to vote. **Mary Livermore** was one woman who worked tirelessly to persuade the people of Illinois to allow woman suffrage. She helped start the **Illinois Woman Suffrage Association,** which began asking for women's voting rights in 1870. **Ida B. Wells** was another woman who fought for woman's rights. She founded the first African American woman suffrage organization.

In 1913 the Illinois legislature in Springfield passed a bill giving women the right to vote. Women in Illinois could vote for state and local issues, but they could not vote in national elections until 1920, when the **Nineteenth Amendment** was passed. Today the National **League of Women Voters** is a group that encourages citizens across the United States to vote.

REVIEW How was suffrage different before and after the Civil War? **Compare and Contrast**

Being a Good Citizen

Being a good citizen means that you act responsibly so that other Americans can enjoy the same freedoms that you enjoy. It is important to follow the rules at your school and to obey the laws of your community, state, and nation. Because you have the right to make choices for yourself, you are responsible for your actions and must accept the consequences of those actions.

What else do good citizens do? Good citizens respect the rights and property of others. They do not pass judgment because of a person's gender, race, or religion.

Good citizens have responsibilities to their government. Adults are expected to pay income tax and other taxes. The government may also ask citizens to serve on a jury. The members of a jury listen to a court case and decide whether someone is guilty of a crime. Sometimes they decide what a criminal's punishment will be.

Good citizens stay informed about issues that affect their communities.

FACT FILE

How to Contact Government Officials

To contact your representative in the U.S. House of Representatives:
www.house.gov/writerep

To contact the President of the United States:
The White House
1600 Pennsylvania Ave.
Washington, D.C. 20500
E mail: president@whitehouse.gov

To contact your U.S. senator:
www.senate.gov

To contact the Governor of Illinois:
Office of the Governor
207 State House
Springfield, IL 62706
888-261-3336
E mail: governor@state.il.us

▶ Organizations such as Access Living train volunteers to make their communities stronger.

They let elected officials know what they think about these issues by voting and through letters, e-mails, and phone calls. They work together to improve their communities by getting involved in such projects as cleaning up the environment.

Good citizens also volunteer to help others. **Marca Bristo** is one Illinois citizen who was determined to make a difference in the lives of people with disabilities. In 1979 she created an organization in **Chicago** called Access Living. This organization helps people with disabilities learn to live on their own. Marca Bristo is one of many Illinoisans who acts as a good citizen by helping others in her community.

REVIEW Summarize the responsibilities of a United States citizen. **Summarize**

Summarize the Lesson

- **The Nineteenth Amendment gave women the right to vote in all elections.**
- **Illinois citizens have many responsibilities.**

LESSON 2 · REVIEW

Check Facts and Main Ideas

1. **Summarize** On a separate sheet of paper, write a summary of the details shown below.

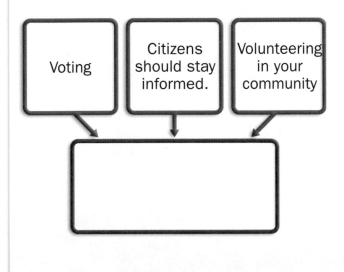

2. How are Mary Livermore and Ida B. Wells alike?
3. What rights do the Fifteenth and Nineteenth Amendments guarantee?
4. Why is it important for citizens to vote?
5. **Critical Thinking:** *Express Ideas* How is voting both a right and a responsibility for citizens in the United States and Illinois?

| Link to | Art |

Create a Campaign Poster Work in pairs. Create a campaign poster for your partner, who is running for president of a club. Draw pictures of the candidate in action to persuade members of the club to vote for your candidate. Display the posters around the classroom.

Winning the Right to Vote

Women did not have the right to vote throughout the United States until 1920. For many years, people had worked long and hard for women's suffrage—the right for women to vote. Here are some of the ways they tried to persuade others to join their fight.

Parades and Parties
Suffrage groups held parades and parties to gain publicity. This woman played patriotic songs on her cornet to cheer on the crowd.

Association Banner
The National American Woman Suffrage Association was one group of women who worked hard for suffrage. This group helped convince President Woodrow Wilson to support woman suffrage. In 1920 he signed the Nineteenth Amendment to the Constitution, giving women the right to vote.

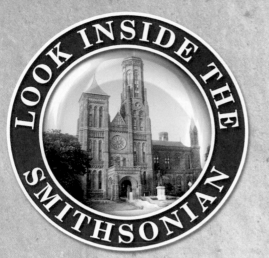

Newspapers and Magazines
The Suffragist was the name of one magazine that women sold on street corners. A person who worked for suffrage was also called a suffragist.

"I go for all sharing the privileges of Government who assist in bearing its burdens, not excluding Women." Abraham Lincoln

Banner
This banner used words spoken by Abraham Lincoln. President Lincoln was in favor of women having the right to vote.

VOTES FOR WOMEN

HOUSEWIVES LEAGUE

VOTES FOR WOMEN on Nov. 5, 1912

DISTRICT OF COLUMBIA SUFFRAGE ASSOCIATION I WANT TO VOTE

PLANKS
To Be Presented By The
NATIONAL LEAGUE OF WOMEN VOTERS
To The
Democratic Platform Committee

I Child Welfare.
Prohibition of Child Labor
Infancy and Maternity Care
Adequate Appropriation for Children's Bureau

II Education.
Federal Department of Education
Increased Teachers' Salaries and Removal of Illiteracy
Citizenship Instruction

III Home and High Prices.
Increased Training in Home Economics
Federal Regulation of Marketing and Distribution of Food

IV Women In Gainful Occupation.
Representation of Women on all Commissions
Having to do with Women's Occupations
Civil Service Re-classified on Merit Basis
and freed from Sex Discrimination

V Public Health and Morals.
Continued Appropriation for Public Education
and Hygiene

VI Independent Citizenship for Married Women.
To forfeiture of citizenship through marriage to foreigner
or American born women who continue to reside in the
U.S. acquiring of Citizenship by foreign born women
except through individual naturalization

Women Voters
After women won the right to vote, the National American Woman Suffrage Association became the National League of Women Voters. The group worked to register people to vote, to protect the health of women and children, and for education for all.

Buttons
Members of women's clubs made and wore buttons as publicity for their cause. They were trying to gain approval and support.

Artifacts are from the Smithsonian Institution.

281

Speaking Out for Others

Many people in Illinois and other places across the United States are caring citizens who work to help others in their communities. Marca Bristo is one of those caring individuals.

Marca Bristo is a recognized leader in the area of rights for people with disabilities. On January 20, 2000, she wrote a report to President Bill Clinton. In it she said,

". . . People with . . . disabilities are, first and foremost, citizens who have the right to expect that they will be treated according to the principles of law that apply to all other citizens."

In 1979 Bristo created an organization called Access Living. Located in Chicago, Access Living offers a program that allows people with disabilities to live independently. The mission of this organization is to teach people with disabilities to live on their own and to educate the public about people with disabilities.

Bristo was appointed by President Clinton as the chairperson of the National Council on Disability.

Caring
Respect
Responsibility
Fairness
Honesty
Courage

This council makes sure that people are obeying laws that protect the rights of people with disabilities. In addition, this council advises Congress and the President about policies regarding Americans with disabilities. She was the first person with a disability to hold this position.

Marca Bristo is considered to be a caring citizen by her community, state, and nation. She has received many awards and has been recognized by different groups and individuals for her work in disability rights. She helped write the Americans with Disabilities Act of 1990 and worked to persuade Congress to make it a law. As a result, she won the Americans with Disabilities Act Award. In 1993 she received the Henry B. Betts Laureate, an important award in her field.

Caring in Action

Link to Current Events Research to find a person or group that is helping an Illinois community. What does the person or group do? How does that person or group care for others?

Chapter Summary

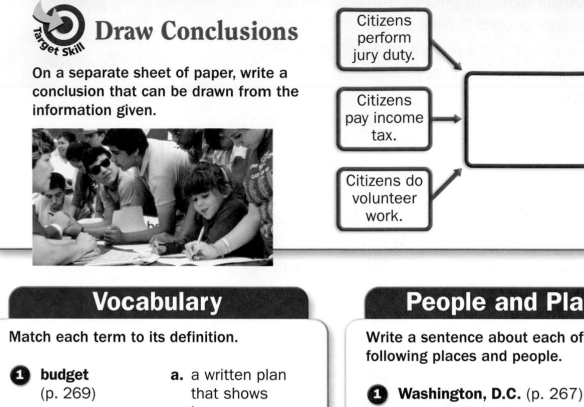

Draw Conclusions

On a separate sheet of paper, write a conclusion that can be drawn from the information given.

Citizens perform jury duty. →

Citizens pay income tax. →

Citizens do volunteer work. →

Vocabulary

Match each term to its definition.

1 budget (p. 269)

2 veto (p. 269)

3 amendment (p. 277)

4 suffrage (p. 277)

a. a written plan that shows how money will be spent

b. the right to vote

c. a formal change to a legal document

d. to reject

People and Places

Write a sentence about each of the following places and people.

1 Washington, D.C. (p. 267)

2 Donald Rumsfeld (pp. 267, 272)

3 Springfield (p. 268)

4 Mary Livermore (p. 277)

5 Ida B. Wells (p. 277)

6 Marca Bristo (pp. 279, 282–283)

Facts and Main Ideas

1. What are the three levels of government in the United States?

2. What are the three branches of both the national and Illinois state governments?

3. Which amendment to the U.S. Constitution allowed women to vote in all elections?

4. **Main Idea** Why do governments collect taxes?

5. **Main Idea** What role does the governor play in government?

6. **Main Idea** What are two ways in which you can be a responsible citizen?

7. **Critical Thinking:** *Make Inferences* Both the United States Constitution and the Illinois Constitution can be changed by adding amendments. How has history shown that making changes to the constitutions is important?

Internet Activity

To get help with vocabulary, people, and places, select the dictionary or encyclopedia from *Social Studies Library* at **www.sfsocialstudies.com**.

Apply Skills

Use a Street Map

Look at the street map on page 275 to answer the following questions.

1. Name two points of interest that are located near Jackson Blvd.

2. Which direction would you travel to go from the Chicago Theatre to Carson Pirie Scott?

3. Which point of interest is closest to the intersection of Adams St. and Franklin St.?

Write About Citizenship

1. **Write a speech** urging your fellow students to vote in a school election. Explain why every one of their votes is important to the outcome of the election.

2. **Write a report** on the League of Women Voters. Use reference materials and the Internet to find out how this organization encourages citizens to register to vote.

3. **Write a letter** to your state representative, describing a problem you have identified in your community. Explain the problem, and suggest ways that the representative might be able to help solve the problem.

Living in Illinois Today

Lesson 1

Champaign-Urbana
College students learn about new forms of technology, such as this virtual reality simulator, that will help prepare them for the future.

1

Lesson 2

Springfield
The Springfield Highland Games and Celtic Festival is just one of many cultural events in Illinois.

2

CANADA

2 1

Springfield

Champaign-Urbana

UNITED STATES

PACIFIC OCEAN

ATLANTIC OCEAN

MEXICO

Gulf of Mexico

Why We Remember

People in Illinois today make a living in a variety of ways. The agricultural, mining, and manufacturing industries that once made Illinois great in the twentieth century are still strong. New technology and service industries are growing even faster, and hold out new opportunities for the people in this state. Illinoisans can choose careers and products that did not exist even a few years ago. We also celebrate who we are through the art, music, and literature of the different cultures in our state.

Champaign-
Urbana

Focus on the Main Idea
Agriculture, service, and technology industries are important to the Illinois economy.

PLACES
Des Plaines
Champaign-Urbana

PEOPLE
Ray Kroc

VOCABULARY
supply
demand
export
import
consumer
telecommunication

TERMS
service industry
high-tech industry

New Opportunities in Illinois

You Are There

Dear Mom and Dad,

I am having a great time at Uncle Frank and Aunt Susan's farm in Illinois. Today I got to ride with Uncle Frank in his tractor. Wow! What a machine! I had no idea what a modern tractor was like until now. The cab is as comfortable as a car. It has heat and air conditioning and a CD player so that we can listen to music while we work. The tractor even has a computer that helps Uncle Frank use just the right amount of fertilizer for his crops. Uncle Frank says that all of this new technology in tractors makes farming easier. It would be fun to be a farmer and drive a tractor like Uncle Frank's.

Draw Conclusions As you read, draw conclusions about how the products we buy and produce affect our state's economy.

More Choices for Illinois Consumers

Like the rest of the United States, Illinois has a free enterprise system. This means that most businesses choose what to sell and what to charge for their products. The prices that people pay depend largely on supply and demand. **Supply** refers to the amount of a product that is available for sale. **Demand** refers to the amount of a product that people need or want. If businesses produce more than people want or need, the supply is greater than the demand. That makes the price go down. When popular goods or services are in short supply, however, their cost increases, or goes up.

Many Illinois businesses sell their products to people who live within the state, in other states, and even in other countries. Products that are shipped to other countries are called **exports.** Illinois exports billions of dollars of machinery, computers, electrical equipment, and agricultural goods. The chart on this page shows those countries that are the biggest consumers of Illinois products. Illinois's economy also depends on **imports**, or products that are made in other countries. In the long run, competition from other countries gives Illinois **consumers,** or people who buy and use products and services, more and better choices.

When you are thinking about buying a product, first think about whether it would be better to save the money for something else. What will you be giving up if you make this purchase? Do research to learn about the product. When you have decided on a product, find out what different stores charge for the same product.

REVIEW Based on what you know about Illinois, what types of product do you think the state would most likely import? ⦿ **Draw Conclusions**

Illinois Exports, 2001

Amount Purchased (in billions)

$9 —
$6 —
$3 —
$0 —

Canada Mexico Japan United Kingdom Germany

Country

Source: Illinois Department of Commerce

▶ The above chart shows the five leading countries with whom Illinois trades.

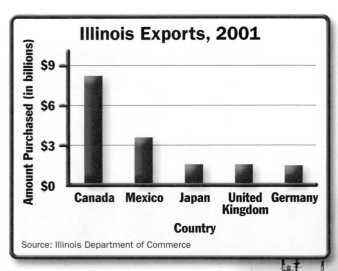

▶ Freighters such as this one carry goods from Illinois to countries around the world.

Agriculture and Mining in Illinois

The fertile soil and natural resources that helped Illinois become great still support much of our state's economy today. Agriculture remains the largest industry in Illinois. Our state is a leading producer of corn, wheat, soybeans, oats, hay, poultry, hogs, and cattle.

While rural areas benefit from growing crops and livestock, Illinois cities also benefit from making farm machinery and making items from farm products, such as ink, paper, soap, and clothing. Illinois's location and excellent transportation network allow our state to sell its agricultural products throughout the country.

Mining has changed in Illinois, but it is still very important. The lead mines that brought many people to Galena more than a century ago have closed. Even fluorspar (FLOOR spahr), which was once so important that it became our state's official mineral, is no longer mined in Illinois. However, we still mine and process coal, oil, tripoli, stone, and industrial sand. Each year mining companies sell almost two billion dollars' worth of these materials from Illinois. The mining companies provide jobs for thousands of Illinoisans. They also work closely with the Illinois government to protect the environment during mining operations.

REVIEW How do Illinois cities benefit from our farming industry?
🟢 **Draw Conclusions**

▶ **Illinois rock is mined for construction projects.**

Changes in Telecommunications

Television sets first became popular in the late 1940s. Television shows kept people informed and entertained. Today the field of telecommunications continues to grow. People can get news, other information, and entertainment from a variety of sources, including high-definition television (HDTV). Many of these televisions are made in Illinois.

▶ A 1955 television set

▶ HDTV is a type of television that produces realistic images, such as this Chicago Bears football game. It makes viewers feel as if they are present during events, rather than watching them on a screen.

Changes in the Illinois Economy

Service industries are businesses that provide services to consumers, an important part of Illinois's economy. Retail businesses, tourism, and banking are examples of service industries. Fast food is also a service industry. In 1955 **Ray Kroc** took a chance when he spent money to create a new kind of restaurant. The McDonald's™ restaurant chain that Kroc started in **Des Plaines** soon spread to other states around the country and the world.

High-tech industries are also important to Illinois. A **high-tech industry** is one that uses the latest forms of technology to make new goods and services. The field of **telecommunications,** which deals with sending messages by radio, telephone, and television, is a good example of a high-tech industry. Telecommunication companies use the latest technology to make products such as cellular phones.

REVIEW Why are high-tech industries important to Illinois?
↻ **Draw Conclusions**

Map Adventure

What We Make and Grow

Look at the map to see different types of products and services that can be found in Illinois.

1. What important industry is found in the southern part of Illinois?

2. What types of jobs are common around Chicago?

3. What kinds of jobs do Peoria and East St. Louis have in common?

4. According to this map, which cities are large manufacturing centers?

5. What is the main industry in Quincy?

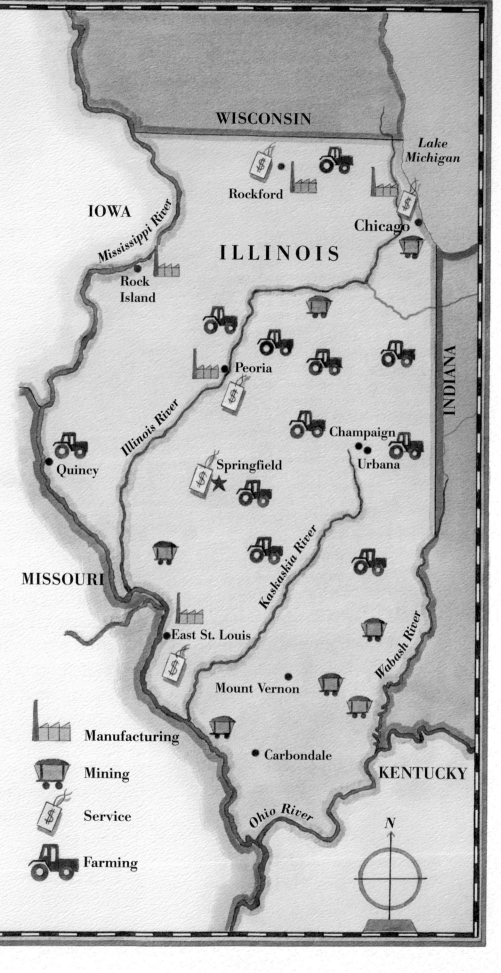

Manufacturing

Mining

Service

Farming

Jobs for the Future

New technology has had an effect on many of the industries in Illinois. Changes in machinery have helped the farming, mining, and manufacturing industries. However, some manufacturing jobs no longer exist, and more and more people are being employed by service industries.

As high-tech industries continue to grow, they will need raw materials, money to invest in growth, and trained workers. Colleges and universities, such as the University of Illinois at **Champaign-Urbana,** expect to train more people who want to learn about high-tech careers. A college education can lead to more opportunities in Illinois's workplace.

REVIEW Why is Illinois interested in helping high-tech industries?
⊙ **Draw Conclusions**

▶ **This college student learns new types of technology.**

Summarize the Lesson

• **Supply and demand affect the price of goods and what products are sold.**

• **Agriculture and mining are important industries in Illinois.**

• **Service and high-tech industries will help provide jobs in our state's future.**

LESSON 1 REVIEW

Check Facts and Main Ideas

1. ⊙ **Draw Conclusions** On a separate sheet of paper, write details that support the conclusion below.

Details

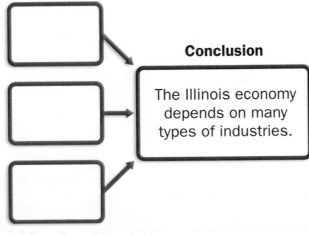

Conclusion

The Illinois economy depends on many types of industries.

2. How does a company's supply of goods affect the price it can charge consumers?

3. How has technology changed the telecommunications industry?

4. Why does Illinois import goods from other countries?

5. **Critical Thinking:** *Evaluate* In your opinion, which industry is most important to the Illinois economy? Why?

Link to ⚭ Writing

Interview an Industry Worker Interview a person who works in an agricultural, mining, service, or high-tech industry. Write a summary of the interview to present to your class.

Use a Time Zone Map

What? A **time zone** is a region in which one standard time is used. The world is divided into twenty-four time zones. A time zone map shows the boundaries of different time zones. The map on this page shows the time zones in the United States. Illinois is in the Central Time Zone, as are most of our neighboring states. Parts of Indiana and Kentucky, however, are in the Eastern Time Zone.

Hawaii-Aleutian

Alaska

Pacific

Mountain

Central

Eastern

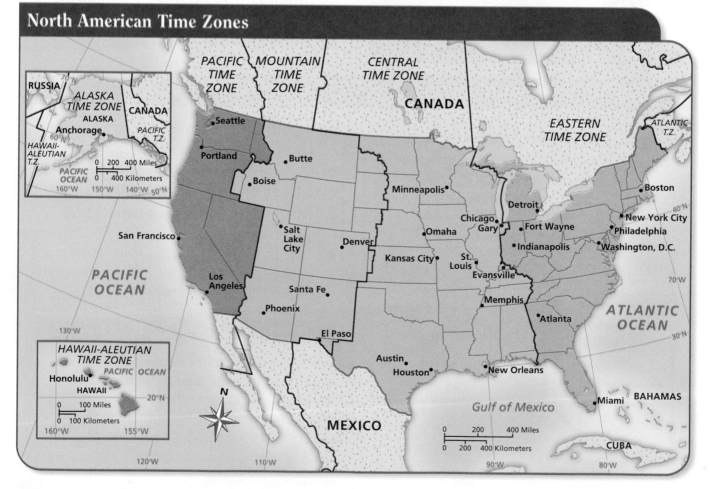

North American Time Zones

Why? Suppose you work for a company in Chicago. You want to call a company in Detroit, Michigan, to order some supplies. The time in Chicago is 4:00 P.M. What time is it in Detroit? You can use a time zone map to find out. Because Chicago is in the Central Time Zone and Detroit is in the Eastern Time Zone, it is one hour later in Detroit than in Chicago. If the business you are calling closes at 5:00 P.M., you may be too late to reach anyone there.

You can also use a time zone map when you travel. Will your trip take you to a city in a different time zone? What time will it be when you arrive?

Nationally broadcast television programs are also affected by time zones. A program that is shown at 9:00 P.M. in Detroit airs at 8:00 P.M. in Chicago.

How? To read and understand a time zone map, follow these steps.

• Notice that each time zone on the map is shown in a different color. You can see that some states are in more than one time zone. Is Gary, Indiana, in the same time zone as Indianapolis, Indiana?

• Next, look at the clock face above each time zone. What time does each face show? When it is 10:00 A.M. in San Francisco, what time is it in Chicago?

• Compare the times on all of the clock faces shown on the map on page 294, beginning with the Eastern Time Zone. What do you notice as you move from east to west across the map? What is the time difference between Boston, Massachusetts, and Salt Lake City, Utah?

Think and Apply

❶ It is 10:00 A.M. in Illinois. You want to phone a friend in San Francisco. What time is it there?

❷ You live in East St. Louis. You are going to Washington, D.C. What is the time difference between the two cities?

❸ If you drive from Chicago to Seattle, in which time zone will you be?

For more information, go online to *Atlas* at **www.sfsocialstudies.com.**

★Springfield

Celebrating Diversity

PREVIEW

Focus on the Main Idea
Illinois has a rich cultural tradition.

PLACES
Chicago
Springfield
Oak Park

PEOPLE
Gwendolyn Brooks
Ernest Hemingway
Walt Disney
Theresa Gutierrez

VOCABULARY
cultural diversity

EVENTS
Chicago Blues Festival
Chicago Jazz Festival
World Music Festival

You Are There You are with your parents at the Chicago Blues Festival. Your parents have been looking forward to this event for several weeks. You are excited, but you don't know what to expect. People have come from all over the state and even different parts of the country to see the performers. You notice that many of the people have brought lawn chairs and blankets. Your parents also packed some food for the outing.

Since you arrived early, you and your family are close to the stage. When the music starts, you notice how the bass guitar keeps time with the drummer. You find yourself really enjoying the music. You can't wait to hear the next group.

▶ **The Chicago Blues Festival**

Draw Conclusions As you read, use facts to draw conclusions about how different cultures have affected Illinois.

The Diverse People of Illinois

Many people who live in Illinois today have come from other countries. Years ago many immigrants settled in cities where they found jobs in mines or factories. Many of today's immigrants work as professionals in universities, hospitals, and high-tech companies.

Almost anywhere you go in Illinois, you will see people who look different from you and your family, and who may speak different languages. Illinois has cultural diversity, which means that people from different cultures are living, learning, and working together.

Today Illinoisans are proud to share their different cultures through celebrations and festivals. Many of these take place in Chicago, one of the world's most culturally diverse cities. Chicago shows off its cultural diversity through large outdoor music festivals. For example, the Chicago Blues Festival offers three days of free blues concerts on three stages. The Chicago Jazz Festival is the world's largest free outdoor jazz festival. The World Music Festival offers concertgoers the opportunity to hear music as it is performed in every continent around the world.

Springfield hosts the Highland Games and Celtic Festival each year. Festivals such as this one help Illinoisans keep their cultural heritage alive through music and dance.

REVIEW What facts support the statement that Chicago is a center of cultural diversity? Summarize

▶ The Cinco de Mayo parade (below), in Chicago, and Springfield's Highland Games and Celtic Festival (top left) are examples of Illinois's diverse cultures.

297

Cultural and Historical Traditions

Illinoisans have shaped our state and our nation. Many creative people were born in Illinois or have made Illinois their home. **Gwendolyn Brooks,** an author and poet who grew up in Chicago, was the first African American to win the Pulitzer Prize. **Ernest Hemingway,** a former **Oak Park** resident, wrote many books that are still printed and read around the world today. **Walt Disney,** a Chicago native, created animated cartoons, movies, and parks such as Disneyland™ that

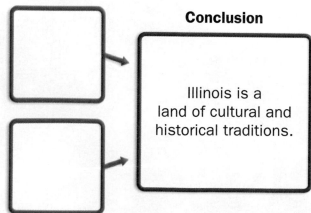

▶ In 1968 Gwendolyn Brooks was named the poet laureate of Illinois.

have entertained millions of people. **Theresa Gutierrez,** a resident of Chicago, became one of the first Latina television reporters.

As you live and learn in Illinois, remember the people, places, and events that make our state important and unique. From being the "Land of Lincoln," to the home of Ulysses S. Grant, and the birthplace of Ronald Reagan, Illinois has something for everyone.

REVIEW What are some of the ways that the creative people of Illinois have shared their ideas with the rest of the world? Summarize

Summarize the Lesson

- Illinois is a land of cultural diversity.
- Illinois is a land of cultural and historical traditions.

LESSON 2 ▸ REVIEW

Check Facts and Main Ideas

1. **Draw Conclusions** On a separate sheet of paper, write details that support the conclusion below.

Details

Conclusion

Illinois is a land of cultural and historical traditions.

2. How is Illinois a land of cultural diversity?

3. How are the Chicago Blues Festival and the Chicago Jazz Festival alike?

4. Who are some of the famous creative people who lived in Illinois?

5. **Critical Thinking: *Evaluate*** Why were so many immigrants drawn to Chicago?

Link to ⬡ Music

Write a Song Write a song that tells about your cultural heritage. Set your lyrics to the music of your choice. Hold an Illinois Music Festival in your class. Share your song during the festival.

Theresa Gutierrez

During the early 1970s, Theresa Gutierrez began producing television shows, but she did not start out in front of the camera. She was one of the first Latinas to work in television journalism. She also hosted two radio shows. One of these shows addressed issues affecting women; the other discussed issues affecting Chicago's Latino community.

Gutierrez later hosted television specials that show famous Latinos who are working to improve the community.

Since 1986 Gutierrez has been a news reporter for ABC7 News in Chicago.

Over the years Theresa Gutierrez has earned many honors and awards for her achievements. She serves the Chicago community in a variety of ways. She is a board member for several organizations and helps raise funds for many worthwhile causes.

Theresa Gutierrez has this advice for people who are trying to make their dreams come true:

"Prepare yourself, balance your life, and set priorities and goals."

Learn from Biographies

How has Gutierrez helped preserve the cultural heritage of Chicago?

Students can research the lives of significant people by clicking on *Meet the People* at **www.sfsocialstudies.com**.

Review

Chapter Summary

 Draw Conclusions

On a separate sheet of paper, write details that support the conclusion.

Details

Conclusion

In the twenty-first century, Illinoisians have more economic choices and opportunities.

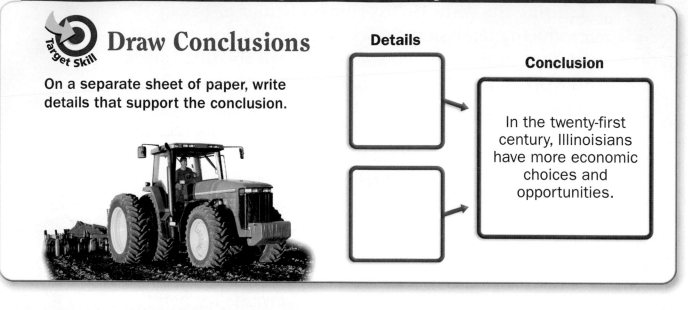

Vocabulary

Match each of the following words with its definition.

1. **supply** (p. 289)

2. **demand** (p. 289)

3. **export** (p. 289)

4. **import** (p. 289)

5. **cultural diversity** (p. 297)

a. a product from another country

b. a product sent to another country

c. the amount of a product that people need or want

d. people from different cultures living, learning, and working together

e. the amount of a product that is available

People and Places

List one important fact about each of the following places and people.

1. **Ray Kroc** (p. 291)

2. **Champaign-Urbana** (p. 293)

3. **Springfield** (p. 297)

4. **Gwendolyn Brooks** (p. 298)

5. **Ernest Hemingway** (p. 298)

6. **Oak Park** (p. 298)

7. **Walt Disney** (p. 298)

8. **Theresa Gutierrez** (pp. 298, 299)

Facts and Main Ideas

1. In what ways is agriculture still important to Illinois?

2. What are some examples of minerals that are mined or processed in Illinois?

3. How do imports help Illinois's economy?

4. What is the difference between a high-tech industry and a service industry?

5. **Main Idea** What industries are growing faster in Illinois than farming, mining, and manufacturing?

6. **Main Idea** How does trade with other countries help Illinois consumers?

7. **Main Idea** Why is Illinois considered a land of cultural diversity?

8. **Critical Thinking:** *Express Ideas* One goal of technology is to make people's lives easier. Do you agree with this statement? Explain.

Internet Activity

To get help with vocabulary, people, and places, select the dictionary or encyclopedia from *Social Studies Library* at **www.sfsocialstudies.com.**

Apply Skills

Use a Time Zone Map

Refer to the time zone map on page 294 to answer the following questions.

1. You want to have a three-way chat with your friend in New York and your friend in Oregon. If it is 11:00 A.M. in Illinois, what time is it in New York? What time is it in Portland?

2. You are visiting Colorado. You tell your mother that you will call her tomorrow at noon, Colorado time. What time will it be in Illinois?

3. You just landed in Hawaii. Your watch is still set for Illinois time. If your watch says that it is 2:00 P.M., what time is it in Hawaii?

Write About Economics

1. **Write a newspaper ad** for a job opening in Illinois in 2025. Use information from the chapter to help you predict what sorts of jobs will be available in that year.

2. **Write a description** of a high-tech product that you would like to invent. Give detailed information about how the product will be made and what purpose it will serve.

3. **Write an essay** explaining what you would like and dislike about being a farmer or miner in Illinois.

End with a Song

My Kind of Town (Chicago)

Many songs have been written about Chicago. One of the most famous was written by Sammy Cahn and James Van Heusen. In 1964 "My Kind of Town" was used for a movie that was set in Chicago. Here are a few verses of the song, which singer Frank Sinatra made very popular.

Don't ever, ever ask me what Chicago is,
Unless you've got an hour or two or three.
'Cause I need time to tell you what Chicago is,
All the things Chicago is to me.

Gee! It's my kind of town Chicago is,
My kind of town, Chicago is
My kind of people, too,
People who smile at you.

And each time I roam, Chicago is
Calling me home, Chicago is
One town that won't let you down.
It's my kind of town.

Main Ideas and Vocabulary

TEST PREP

Read the passage below, and answer the questions that follow.

The people of Illinois govern themselves by voting for their leaders. Our state's constitution and its amendments, or changes that have been made to the constitution, describe how the government works. The United States has a Constitution too. Many of the amendments to the U.S. Constitution guarantee citizens their rights, such as the right to vote.

Illinois citizens receive services from their government. The citizens pay taxes, such as income tax on their earnings, to help pay for these services. Citizens also help the government run smoothly by electing the people they think will do the best job. Many citizens also volunteer their time to help their communities.

Every Illinoisan has a choice of how to earn a living. Farming and mining are still main industries in Illinois. Service and high-tech industries are growing even more important. Our state's resources and location help us provide goods and services to people all over the world.

Today's Illinoisans come from many backgrounds. The people of Illinois celebrate the cultures of their families through parades and festivals. People also keep cultural traditions alive in the music they play and listen to. Our writers, poets, and other artists have affected the culture of Illinois and of the United States.

1 Amendments are
   A services that the government provides.
   B the people elected to serve in a government.
   C changes to a legal document.
   D the things a person must do to become an American citizen.

2 In this passage, income tax means a tax paid on
   A what you spend.
   B what you earn.
   C the value of your home.
   D the amount of savings you have.

3 According to the passage, an industry growing in importance is
   A farming.
   B mining.
   C service.
   D manufacturing.

4 According to the passage, today's Illinoisans celebrate the cultures of their families by
   A holding parades and festivals and enjoying music.
   B voting and paying taxes.
   C farming and mining.
   D working in service and high-tech industries.

Places and Vocabulary

Match each word or place to its description or definition.

1 **Washington, D.C.** (p. 267)

2 **sales tax** (p. 268)

3 **suffrage** (p. 277)

4 **import** (p. 289)

5 **Des Plaines** (p. 291)

a. the city where Ray Kroc built his first McDonald's™ restaurant

b. a product we buy from another country

c. the right to vote

d. the capital of the United States

e. helps pay for public goods and services

Apply Skills

Plan Your Calls You and a friend are riding a train across the country. You will stop in Atlanta, Georgia; Denver, Colorado; and San Francisco, California. You have to phone your mother every day at 1:00 P.M. *her time*. She lives in Illinois. At what time do you need to phone her from each city? Use the time zone map on page 294 to create a schedule of phone calls.

Write and Share

Present a skit that shows why Illinois is considered a land of cultural diversity. First, do background research to find out how different cultures are celebrated in Illinois. Outline the important facts that you want to include in your skit. Next, write the script for your skit. Rehearse your skit before you present it to the class.

Read on Your Own

Look for these books in your library.

UNIT 6 Project

Great State

Create a booklet that shows what is great about Illinois today—and what will be great in the future.

1 Form a group. Choose a current news story about something that might make news in the future too.

2 Write a paragraph about the event. Predict what will happen in the future and write several sentences.

3 Draw or find pictures that illustrate the event today and what might occur in the future.

4 Put your group's paragraphs and pictures together in a booklet. Share it with the class.

Internet Activity

For more information and activities, go to **www.sfsocialstudies.com.**

Reference Guide

Table of Contents

Atlas
Map of the World: Political

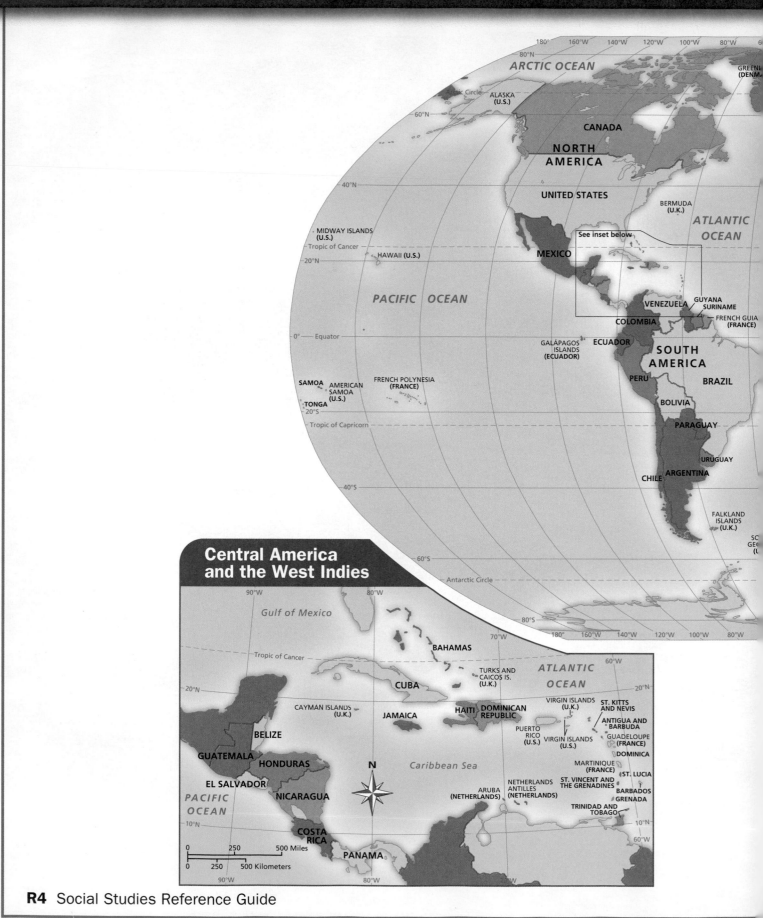

180° 160°W 140°W 120°W 100°W 80°W 6

80°N

ARCTIC OCEAN

GREENL
(DENM

Arctic Circle   ALASKA
(U.S.)

60°N

CANADA

**NORTH
AMERICA**

40°N

UNITED STATES

BERMUDA
(U.K.)

*ATLANTIC
OCEAN*

MIDWAY ISLANDS
(U.S.)
Tropic of Cancer

See inset below

20°N   HAWAII (U.S.)

MEXICO

PACIFIC   OCEAN

VENEZUELA   GUYANA
SURINAME

FRENCH GUIA
(FRANCE)

COLOMBIA

0° Equator

GALÁPAGOS
ISLANDS
(ECUADOR)

ECUADOR

**SOUTH
AMERICA**

SAMOA
AMERICAN
SAMOA
(U.S.)

FRENCH POLYNESIA
(FRANCE)

PERU   **BRAZIL**

TONGA
20°S

BOLIVIA

Tropic of Capricorn

PARAGUAY

URUGUAY

CHILE   **ARGENTINA**

40°S

FALKLAND
ISLANDS
(U.K.)

SC
GE
(U

Antarctic Circle

80°S

180° 160°W 140°W 120°W 100°W 80°W

Central America
and the West Indies

90°W   80°W

Gulf of Mexico

70°W   *ATLANTIC
OCEAN*

60°W

Tropic of Cancer   **BAHAMAS**

20°N

TURKS AND
CAICOS IS.
(U.K.)

20°N

CUBA

CAYMAN ISLANDS
(U.K.)

VIRGIN ISLANDS
(U.K.)

ST. KITTS
AND NEVIS

JAMAICA   **HAITI** **DOMINICAN
REPUBLIC**

ANTIGUA AND
BARBUDA

BELIZE

PUERTO
RICO
(U.S.)

VIRGIN ISLANDS
(U.S.)

GUADELOUPE
(FRANCE)

DOMINICA

GUATEMALA

N

Caribbean Sea

MARTINIQUE
(FRANCE)

ST. LUCIA

HONDURAS

EL SALVADOR

*PACIFIC
OCEAN*

NICARAGUA

ARUBA
(NETHERLANDS)

NETHERLANDS
ANTILLES
(NETHERLANDS)

ST. VINCENT AND
THE GRENADINES

BARBADOS
GRENADA

TRINIDAD AND
TOBAGO

10°N

10°N

60°W

0   250   500 Miles

**COSTA
RICA**

0   250   500 Kilometers

PANAMA

90°W   80°W

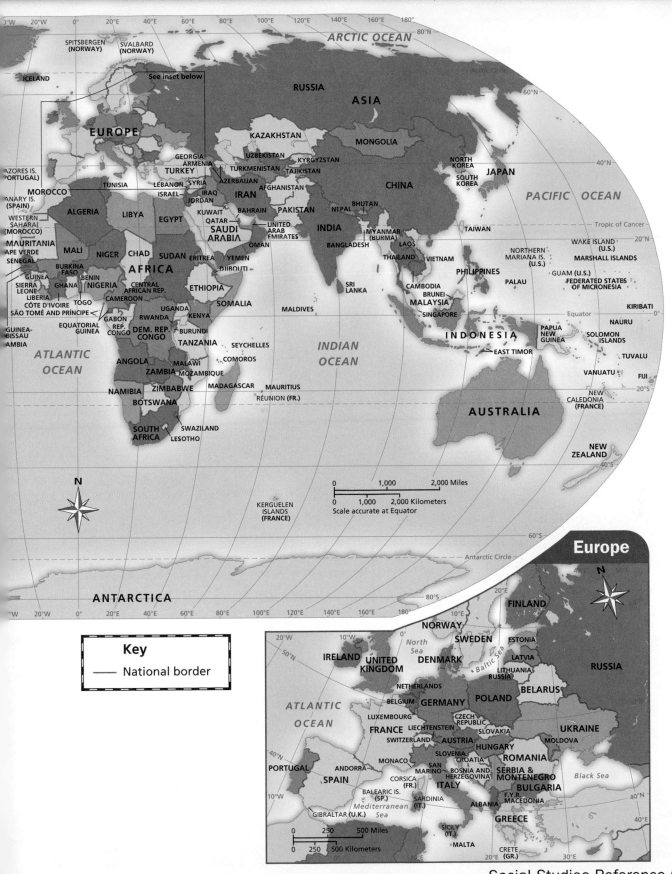

ARCTIC OCEAN

SPITSBERGEN (NORWAY) SVALBARD (NORWAY)

ICELAND

See inset below

RUSSIA

ASIA

EUROPE

KAZAKHSTAN

MONGOLIA

AZORES IS. (PORTUGAL)

GEORGIA
ARMENIA
TURKEY

UZBEKISTAN KYRGYZSTAN

TURKMENISTAN TAJIKISTAN

NORTH KOREA

JAPAN

PACIFIC OCEAN

CANARY IS. (SPAIN)

MOROCCO

TUNISIA

LEBANON SYRIA

ISRAEL

AZERBAIJAN

AFGHANISTAN

SOUTH KOREA

CHINA

WESTERN SAHARA (MOROCCO)

ALGERIA

LIBYA

EGYPT

IRAQ
JORDAN

IRAN

PAKISTAN

NEPAL BHUTAN

TAIWAN

Tropic of Cancer

KUWAIT
QATAR

BAHRAIN

INDIA

MYANMAR (BURMA)

WAKE ISLAND (U.S.)

MAURITANIA

CAPE VERDE

SENEGAL

MALI

NIGER CHAD

UNITED ARAB EMIRATES

OMAN

BANGLADESH

LAOS

THAILAND VIETNAM

NORTHERN MARIANA IS. (U.S.)

MARSHALL ISLANDS

GUAM (U.S.)

FEDERATED STATES OF MICRONESIA

GUINEA

SIERRA LEONE

LIBERIA

CÔTE D'IVOIRE

SÃO TOMÉ AND PRÍNCIPE

BURKINA FASO

GHANA

BENIN

TOGO

NIGERIA

AFRICA

SUDAN

ERITREA

YEMEN

DJIBOUTI

ETHIOPIA

SOMALIA

CENTRAL AFRICAN REP.

CAMEROON

SAUDI ARABIA

SRI LANKA

MALDIVES

CAMBODIA
BRUNEI
MALAYSIA

SINGAPORE

PHILIPPINES

PALAU

KIRIBATI

Equator

NAURU

GUINEA-BISSAU

GAMBIA

EQUATORIAL GUINEA

GABON

RWANDA

DEM. REP. CONGO

REP. CONGO

BURUNDI

UGANDA

KENYA

TANZANIA

SEYCHELLES

INDIAN OCEAN

INDONESIA

PAPUA NEW GUINEA

EAST TIMOR

SOLOMON ISLANDS

TUVALU

ATLANTIC OCEAN

ANGOLA

ZAMBIA

MALAWI

MOZAMBIQUE

COMOROS

MADAGASCAR MAURITIUS

RÉUNION (FR.)

VANUATU

NEW CALEDONIA (FRANCE)

FIJI

NAMIBIA

ZIMBABWE

BOTSWANA

SOUTH AFRICA

SWAZILAND

LESOTHO

AUSTRALIA

N

NEW ZEALAND

0   1,000   2,000 Miles

0   1,000   2,000 Kilometers

Scale accurate at Equator

KERGUELEN ISLANDS (FRANCE)

Antarctic Circle

ANTARCTICA

Key

— National border

Europe

N

FINLAND

NORWAY

North Sea

SWEDEN

ESTONIA

IRELAND

UNITED KINGDOM

DENMARK

Baltic Sea

LATVIA

LITHUANIA

RUSSIA

RUSSIA

ATLANTIC OCEAN

NETHERLANDS

BELGIUM

GERMANY

POLAND

BELARUS

LUXEMBOURG

CZECH REPUBLIC

UKRAINE

FRANCE

LIECHTENSTEIN

SLOVAKIA

MOLDOVA

SWITZERLAND

AUSTRIA

HUNGARY

MONACO

SLOVENIA

CROATIA

ROMANIA

PORTUGAL

ANDORRA

SAN MARINO

BOSNIA AND HERZEGOVINA

SERBIA & MONTENEGRO

Black Sea

SPAIN

CORSICA (FR.)

ITALY

BULGARIA

F.Y.R. MACEDONIA

BALEARIC IS. (SP.)

SARDINIA (IT.)

ALBANIA

GIBRALTAR (U.K.)

Mediterranean Sea

GREECE

SICILY (IT.)

0   250   500 Miles

0   250   500 Kilometers

MALTA

CRETE (GR.)

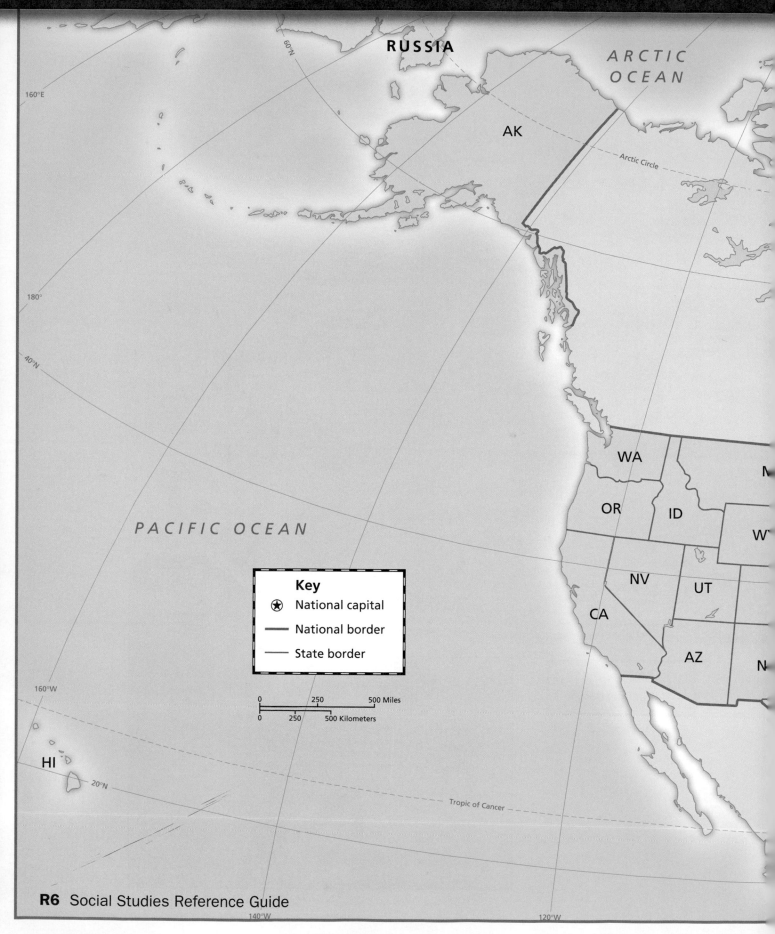

RUSSIA

ARCTIC OCEAN

60°N

160°E

AK

Arctic Circle

180°

40°N

PACIFIC OCEAN

WA

M

OR

ID

W

NV

UT

CA

AZ

N

160°W

Key

⊛ National capital

━━ National border

── State border

0   250   500 Miles

0   250   500 Kilometers

HI

20°N

Tropic of Cancer

140°W

120°W

Greenland
(DENMARK)

CANADA

ND

MN

SD

WI

NE

IA

MI

ME

VT

NH

NY

MA

CT

RI

PA

NJ

IL

IN

OH

DE

MD

DC

KS

MO

WV

VA

OK

KY

AR

TN

NC

SC

MS

AL

GA

TX

LA

ATLANTIC

OCEAN

FL

EXICO

Gulf of Mexico

N

BAHAMAS

CUBA

HAITI

DOM.
REP.

P.R.

JAMAICA

100°W

80°W

60°N

40°W

40°N

60°W

20°N

State or area	Abbreviation
Alabama	AL
Alaska	AK
Arizona	AZ
Arkansas	AR
California	CA
Colorado	CO
Connecticut	CT
Delaware	DE
District of Columbia	DC
Florida	FL
Georgia	GA
Hawaii	HI
Idaho	ID
Illinois	IL
Indiana	IN
Iowa	IA
Kansas	KS
Kentucky	KY
Louisiana	LA
Maine	ME
Maryland	MD
Massachusetts	MA
Michigan	MI
Minnesota	MN
Mississippi	MS
Missouri	MO
Montana	MT
Nebraska	NE
Nevada	NV
New Hampshire	NH
New Jersey	NJ
New Mexico	NM
New York	NY
North Carolina	NC
North Dakota	ND
Ohio	OH
Oklahoma	OK
Oregon	OR
Pennsylvania	PA
Puerto Rico	PR
Rhode Island	RI
South Carolina	SC
South Dakota	SD
Tennessee	TN
Texas	TX
Utah	UT
Vermont	VT
Virginia	VA
Washington	WA
West Virginia	WV
Wisconsin	WI
Wyoming	WY

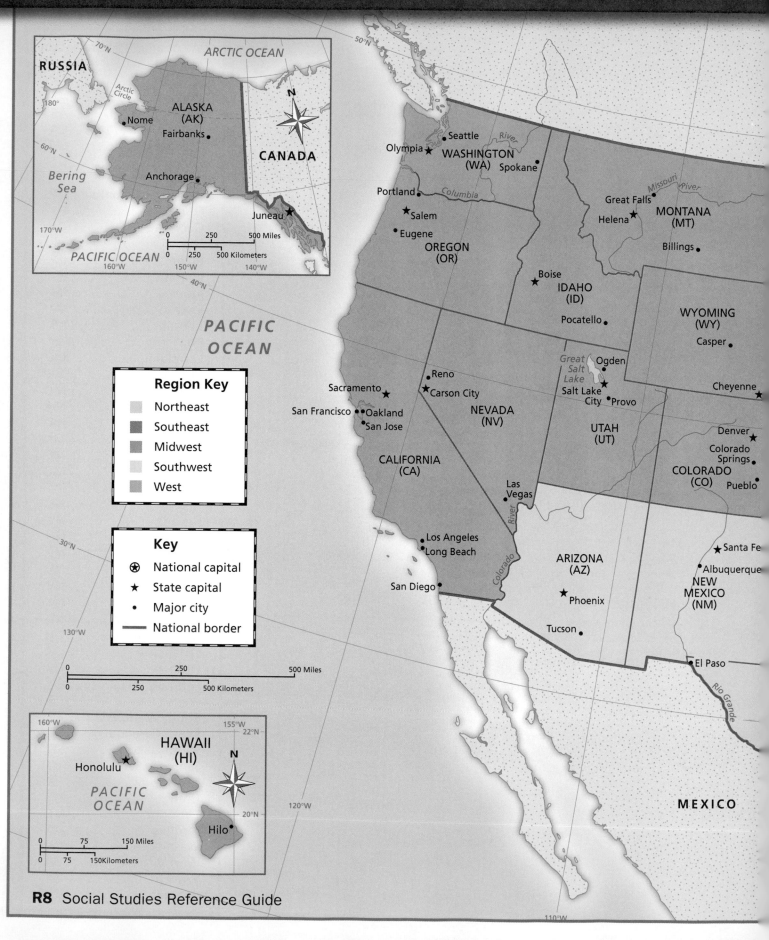

RUSSIA

ARCTIC OCEAN

ALASKA
(AK)

Nome

Fairbanks

CANADA

N

Bering
Sea

Anchorage

Juneau

PACIFIC OCEAN

0   250   500 Miles

0   250   500 Kilometers

PACIFIC
OCEAN

Region Key

Northeast
Southeast
Midwest
Southwest
West

Key

⊛ National capital
★ State capital
• Major city
— National border

0   250   500 Miles

0   250   500 Kilometers

HAWAII
(HI)

Honolulu

N

PACIFIC
OCEAN

Hilo

Seattle

Olympia ★   WASHINGTON
(WA)   Spokane

Portland   Columbia

Salem   OREGON
(OR)

Eugene

Boise

IDAHO
(ID)

Pocatello

Great Falls   MONTANA
(MT)
Helena ★

Billings

WYOMING
(WY)

Casper

Missouri River

Great
Salt
Lake   Ogden

Salt Lake
City   Provo

Cheyenne

Reno

Sacramento ★   Carson City

San Francisco   Oakland
San Jose

NEVADA
(NV)

UTAH
(UT)

Denver

Colorado
Springs

COLORADO
(CO)   Pueblo

CALIFORNIA
(CA)

Las
Vegas

Los Angeles
Long Beach

San Diego

Colorado River

ARIZONA
(AZ)

Phoenix

Tucson

★ Santa Fe

Albuquerque

NEW
MEXICO
(NM)

El Paso

Rio Grande

MEXICO

CANADA

NORTH DAKOTA
(ND)
★ Bismarck
Grand
Forks •
• Fargo

SOUTH DAKOTA
(SD)
★ Pierre

Sioux
Falls •

Missouri
River

NEBRASKA
(NE)
Omaha •
Lincoln ★

MINNESOTA
(MN)
Minneapolis • ★ St. Paul

Duluth •

Lake Superior

WISCONSIN
(WI)
Madison ★
Milwaukee •
Rockford •

Green
Bay

Lake Michigan

IOWA
(IA)
Cedar
Rapids •
Davenport •
Des
Moines
Peoria •

MICHIGAN
(MI)
Lansing •
Grand
Rapids •
Detroit •

Lake Huron

Lake Ontario

Lake Erie

NEW HAMPSHIRE (NH)
VERMONT (VT)

MAINE
(ME)
★ Augusta

Burlington •
Montpelier ★
★ Concord
• Portland

Albany ★
Buffalo •

NEW YORK
(NY)

MASSACHUSETTS
(MA)
Boston ★
Providence ★

Hartford ★
RHODE ISLAND
(RI)

CONNECTICUT
(CT)

KANSAS
City
Topeka ★
KANSAS
(KS)
Wichita •

Kansas
City •

Jefferson •
City

MISSOURI
(MO)

St.
Louis •

ILLINOIS
(IL)
Springfield ★

Chicago •
Gary •

INDIANA
(IN)
Indianapolis ★

Evansville •

Fort
Wayne •

OHIO
(OH)
Columbus ★
Cincinnati •

Toledo •
Cleveland •

Wheeling •

Pittsburgh •

PENNSYLVANIA
(PA)
Harrisburg ★

Newark •
New York •

Trenton ★

Philadelphia •
Baltimore •
Dover ★

NEW JERSEY (NJ)

DELAWARE (DE)

MARYLAND (MD)

Annapolis ★⊗
Washington, D.C.

WEST
VIRGINIA
(WV)
Charleston ★

Frankfort ★

Ohio River
Louisville •

KENTUCKY
(KY)

Richmond ★

VIRGINIA
(VA)

Norfolk •

OKLAHOMA
(OK)
Oklahoma ★
City
Tulsa •

Fort
Smith •

ARKANSAS
(AR)
Little
Rock ★

Memphis •

TENNESSEE
(TN)
Nashville ★
Knoxville •
Charlotte •

Raleigh ★

NORTH CAROLINA
(NC)

TEXAS
(TX)

Fort
Worth • • Dallas

Shreveport •

LOUISIANA
(LA)

MISSISSIPPI
(MS)
Jackson ★

Birmingham •

ALABAMA
(AL)
Montgomery ★

GEORGIA
(GA)
Atlanta ★
Columbus •

Columbia ★

SOUTH
CAROLINA
(SC)
Charleston •

Savannah •

ATLANTIC
OCEAN

Austin ★
San
Antonio •
Laredo •
Corpus
Christi •
Houston •

Baton Rouge ★
New Orleans •

Biloxi •

Mobile •

Tallahassee ★

Jacksonville •

FLORIDA
(FL)
Tampa •

Miami •

N

Gulf of Mexico

BAHAMAS

50°N
40°N
70°W
30°N
80°W
90°W
100°W

Atlas
Map of the United States: Physical

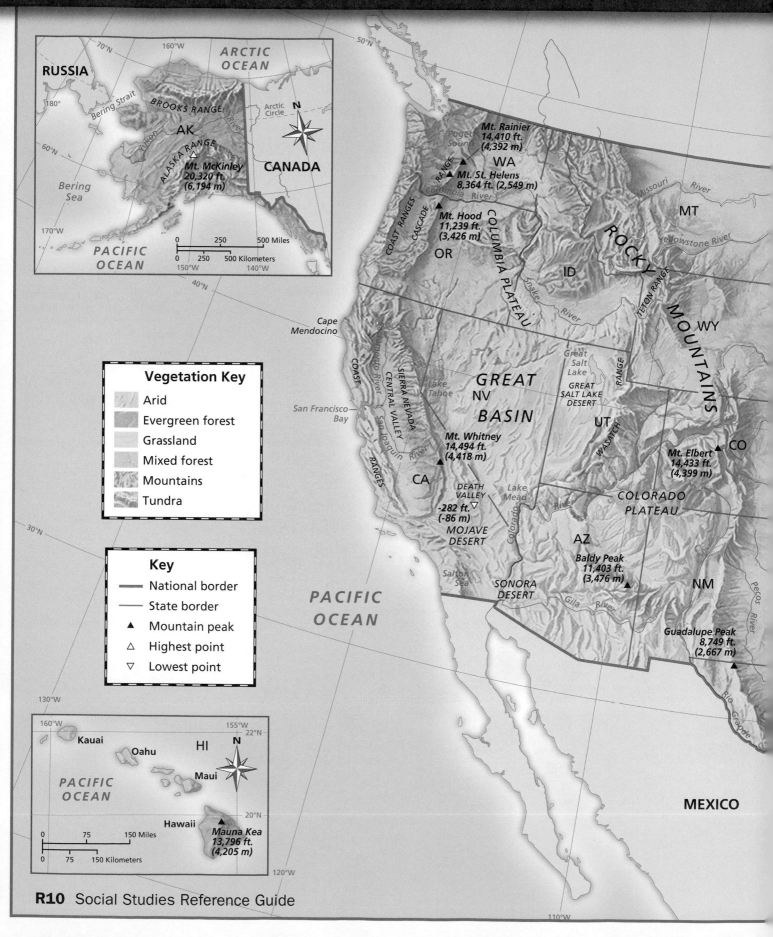

Vegetation Key
- Arid
- Evergreen forest
- Grassland
- Mixed forest
- Mountains
- Tundra

Key
- National border
- State border
- ▲ Mountain peak
- △ Highest point
- ▽ Lowest point

RUSSIA

ARCTIC OCEAN

BROOKS RANGE

AK

ALASKA RANGE

Mt. McKinley 20,320 ft. (6,194 m)

Bering Strait

Yukon River

Arctic Circle

N

CANADA

Bering Sea

PACIFIC OCEAN

0 250 500 Miles
0 250 500 Kilometers

Mt. Rainier 14,410 ft. (4,392 m)

Puget Sound

WA

RANGE

Mt. St. Helens 8,364 ft. (2,549 m)

Columbia River

COAST RANGES

CASCADE

Mt. Hood 11,239 ft. (3,426 m)

OR

COLUMBIA PLATEAU

ID

Snake River

MT

ROCKY

Missouri River

Yellowstone River

TETON RANGE

MOUNTAINS

WY

Cape Mendocino

COAST

Sacramento River

SIERRA NEVADA

CENTRAL VALLEY

Lake Tahoe

GREAT

NV

BASIN

Great Salt Lake

GREAT SALT LAKE DESERT

RANGE

WASATCH

UT

San Francisco Bay

San Joaquin River

Mt. Whitney 14,494 ft. (4,418 m)

CA

DEATH VALLEY -282 ft. (-86 m) ▽

MOJAVE DESERT

Lake Mead

Colorado River

COLORADO PLATEAU

Mt. Elbert 14,433 ft. (4,399 m)

CO

RANGES

Salton Sea

SONORA DESERT

AZ

Baldy Peak 11,403 ft. (3,476 m)

Gila River

NM

PACIFIC OCEAN

Guadalupe Peak 8,749 ft. (2,667 m)

Pecos River

Rio Grande

Kauai

Oahu

HI

N

Maui

PACIFIC OCEAN

Hawaii

Mauna Kea 13,796 ft. (4,205 m)

0 75 150 Miles
0 75 150 Kilometers

MEXICO

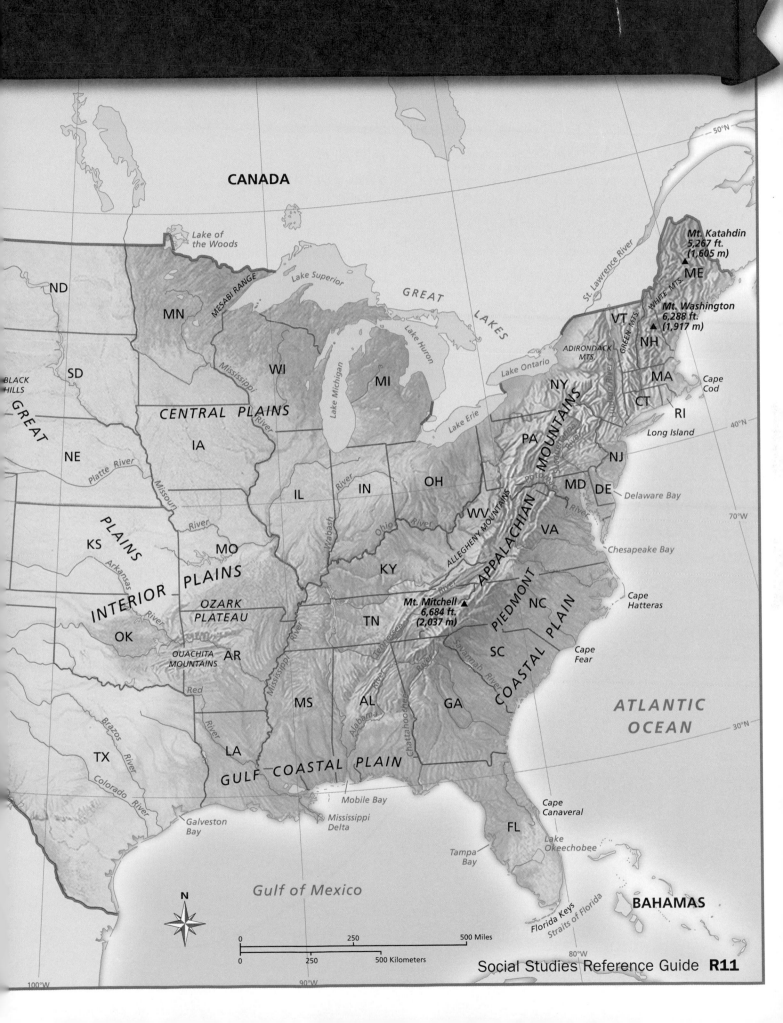

CANADA

Lake of the Woods

ND

Lake Superior

GREAT LAKES

MESABI RANGE

MN

Lake Huron

BLACK HILLS

SD

WI

MI

GREAT

NE

IA

Mississippi River

CENTRAL PLAINS

Lake Michigan

Lake Ontario

ADIRONDACK MTS.

St. Lawrence River

Mt. Katahdin 5,267 ft. (1,605 m) ▲

ME

WHITE MTS.

Mt. Washington 6,288 ft. (1,917 m) ▲

VT

GREEN MTS.

NH

MA

Cape Cod

NY

CT

RI

Lake Erie

Long Island

PA

Hudson River

Susquehanna River

Platte River

Missouri River

PLAINS

KS

Arkansas River

MO

INTERIOR PLAINS

OZARK PLATEAU

OK

OUACHITA MOUNTAINS

AR

Red River

IL

Wabash River

IN

Ohio River

OH

WV

ALLEGHENY MOUNTAINS

KY

TN

Tennessee River

Mt. Mitchell 6,684 ft. (2,037 m) ▲

APPALACHIAN MOUNTAINS

VA

MD

Potomac River

NJ

DE

Delaware Bay

70°W

James River

Chesapeake Bay

Cape Hatteras

PIEDMONT

NC

SC

Savannah River

COASTAL PLAIN

Cape Fear

TX

Colorado River

Brazos River

Red River

LA

Mississippi River

MS

Alabama River

AL

Chattahoochee River

GA

GULF COASTAL PLAIN

Mobile Bay

Mississippi Delta

ATLANTIC OCEAN

30°N

Cape Canaveral

FL

Lake Okeechobee

Galveston Bay

Gulf of Mexico

Tampa Bay

Florida Keys

Straits of Florida

BAHAMAS

N

50°N

40°N

0   250   500 Miles

0   250   500 Kilometers

100°W

90°W

80°W

Geography Terms

basin bowl-shaped area of land surrounded by higher land

bay narrower part of an ocean or lake that cuts into land

canal narrow waterway dug across land mainly for ship travel

canyon steep, narrow valley with high sides

cliff steep wall of rock or earth, sometimes called a bluff

coast land at the edge of a large body of water such as an ocean

coastal plain area of flat land along an ocean or sea

delta triangle-shaped area of land at the mouth of a river

desert very dry land

fall line area along which rivers form waterfalls or rapids as the rivers drop to lower land

forest large area of land where many trees grow

glacier giant sheet of ice that moves very slowly across land

gulf body of water, larger than most bays

harbor sheltered body of water where ships safely tie up to land

hill rounded land higher than the land around it

island land with water all around it

lake large body of water with land all or nearly all around it

mesa hard-to-climb flat-topped hill, with steep sides

mountain a very high hill; highest land on Earth

mountain range long row of mountains

mouth place where a river empties into another body of water

ocean any of four largest bodies of water on Earth

peak pointed top of a mountain

peninsula land with water on three sides

plain very large area of flat land

plateau high, wide area of flat land, with steep sides

port place, usually in a harbor, where ships safely load and unload goods and people

prairie large area of flat land, with few or no trees, similar to a plain

river large stream of water leading to a lake, other river, or ocean

riverbank land at a river's edge

sea large body of water somewhat smaller than an ocean

sea level an ocean's surface, compared to which land can be measured either above or below

slope side of a mountain or hill

source place where a river begins

swamp very shallow water covering low land filled with trees and other plants

tributary stream or river that runs into a larger river

valley low land between mountains or hills

volcano mountain with opening at the top formed by violent bursts of steam and hot rock

waterfall steep falling of water from a high to a lower place

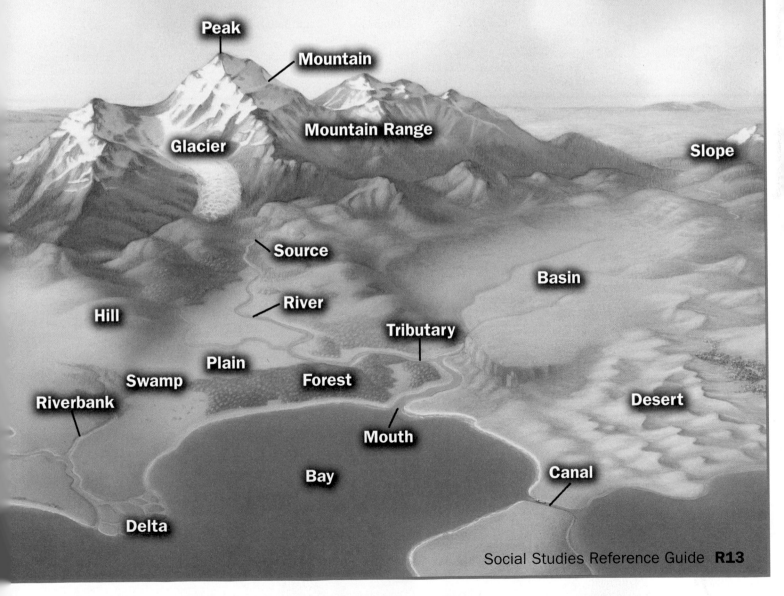

Facts About Our Fifty States

	AL Alabama	AK Alaska	AZ Arizona	AR Arkansas	CA California	CO Colorado
Capital	Montgomery	Juneau	Phoenix	Little Rock	Sacramento	Denver
Date and order of statehood	1819 (22)	1959 (49)	1912 (48)	1836 (25)	1850 (31)	1876 (38)
Nickname	Heart of Dixie	The Last Frontier	Grand Canyon State	Land of Opportunity	Golden State	Centennial State
Population	4,447,100	626,932	5,130,632	2,673,400	33,871,648	4,301,261
Square miles and rank in area	50,750 (28)	570,374 (1)	113,642 (6)	52,075 (27)	155,973 (3)	103,730 (8)
Region	Southeast	West	Southwest	Southeast	West	West

	IN Indiana	IA Iowa	KS Kansas	KY Kentucky	LA Louisiana	ME Maine
Capital	Indianapolis	Des Moines	Topeka	Frankfort	Baton Rouge	Augusta
Date and order of statehood	1816 (19)	1846 (29)	1861 (34)	1792 (15)	1812 (18)	1820 (23)
Nickname	Hoosier State	Hawkeye State	Sunflower State	Bluegrass State	Pelican State	Pine Tree State
Population	6,080,485	2,926,324	2,688,418	4,041,769	4,468,976	1,274,923
Square miles and rank in area	35,870 (38)	55,875 (23)	81,823 (13)	39,732 (36)	43,566 (33)	30,865 (39)
Region	Midwest	Midwest	Midwest	Southeast	Southeast	Northeast

	CT	DE	FL	GA	HI	ID	IL
	Connecticut	Delaware	Florida	Georgia	Hawaii	Idaho	Illinois
Capital	Hartford	Dover	Tallahassee	Atlanta	Honolulu	Boise	Springfield
Statehood	1788 (5)	1787 (1)	1845 (27)	1788 (4)	1959 (50)	1890 (43)	1818 (21)
Nickname	Constitution State	Diamond State or First State	Sunshine State	Peach State	Aloha State	Gem State	Land of Lincoln
Population	3,405,565	783,600	15,982,378	8,186,453	1,211,537	1,293,953	12,419,293
Area	4,845 (48)	1,955 (49)	53,997 (26)	57,919 (21)	6,423 (47)	82,751 (11)	55,593 (24)
Region	Northeast	Northeast	Southeast	Southeast	West	West	Midwest

	MD	MA	MI	MN	MS	MO	MT
	Maryland	Massachusetts	Michigan	Minnesota	Mississippi	Missouri	Montana
Capital	Annapolis	Boston	Lansing	St. Paul	Jackson	Jefferson City	Helena
Statehood	1788 (7)	1788 (6)	1837 (26)	1858 (32)	1817 (20)	1821 (24)	1889 (41)
Nickname	Free State	Bay State	Wolverine State	North Star State	Magnolia State	Show Me State	Treasure State
Population	5,296,486	6,349,097	9,938,444	4,919,479	2,844,658	5,595,211	902,195
Area	9,775 (42)	7,838 (45)	56,809 (22)	79,617 (14)	46,914 (31)	68,898 (18)	145,556 (4)
Region	Northeast	Northeast	Midwest	Midwest	Southeast	Midwest	West

Facts About Our Fifty States

	NE Nebraska	NV Nevada	NH New Hampshire	NJ New Jersey	NM New Mexico	NY New York
Capital	Lincoln	Carson City	Concord	Trenton	Santa Fe	Albany
Date and order of statehood	1867 (37)	1864 (36)	1788 (9)	1787 (3)	1912 (47)	1788 (11)
Nickname	Cornhusker State	Silver State	Granite State	Garden State	Land of Enchantment	Empire State
Population	1,711,263	1,998,257	1,235,786	8,414,350	1,819,046	18,976,457
Square miles and rank in area	76,644 (15)	109,806 (7)	8,969 (44)	7,419 (46)	121,365 (5)	47,224 (30)
Region	Midwest	West	Northeast	Northeast	Southwest	Northeast

	SC South Carolina	SD South Dakota	TN Tennessee	TX Texas	UT Utah	VT Vermont
Capital	Columbia	Pierre	Nashville	Austin	Salt Lake City	Montpeller
Date and order of statehood	1788 (8)	1889 (40)	1796 (16)	1845 (28)	1896 (45)	1791 (14)
Nickname	Palmetto State	Mount Rushmore State	Volunteer State	Lone Star State	Beehive State	Green Mountain State
Population	4,012,012	754,844	5,689,283	20,851,820	2,233,169	608,827
Square miles and rank in area	30,111 (40)	75,898 (16)	41,220 (34)	261,914 (2)	82,168 (12)	9,249 (43)
Region	Southeast	Midwest	Southeast	Southwest	West	Northeast

NC	ND	OH	OK	OR	PA	RI
North Carolina	**North Dakota**	**Ohio**	**Oklahoma**	**Oregon**	**Pennsylvania**	**Rhode Island**
Raleigh	Bismarck	Columbus	Oklahoma City	Salem	Harrisburg	Providence
1789 (12)	1889 (39)	1803 (17)	1907 (46)	1859 (33)	1787 (2)	1790 (13)
Tar Heel State	Sioux State	Buckeye State	Sooner State	Beaver State	Keystone State	Ocean State
8,049,313	642,200	11,353,140	3,450,654	3,421,399	12,281,054	1,048,319
48,718 (29)	68,994 (17)	40,953 (35)	68,679 (19)	96,003 (10)	44,820 (32)	1,045 (50)
Southeast	Midwest	Midwest	Southwest	West	Northeast	Northeast

VA	WA	WV	WI	WY
Virginia	**Washington**	**West Virginia**	**Wisconsin**	**Wyoming**
Richmond	Olympia	Charleston	Madison	Cheyenne
1788 (10)	1889 (42)	1863 (35)	1848 (30)	1890 (44)
Old Dominion	Evergreen State	Mountain State	Badger State	Equality State
7,078,515	5,894,121	1,808,344	5,363,675	493,782
39,598 (37)	66,582 (20)	24,087 (41)	54,314 (25)	97,105 (9)
Southeast	West	Southeast	Midwest	West

Flag Etiquette

Our National Flag

The flag of the United States of America is an important symbol for our country. The flag should be shown respect at all times. When we say the Pledge of Allegiance to the flag, we are saying that we will be good citizens of the United States of America.

When saying the Pledge of Allegiance, stand, face the flag, and place your right hand over your heart.

The Pledge of Allegiance

I pledge allegiance to the Flag
of the United States of America,
and to the Republic for which it stands,
one Nation under God, indivisible,
with liberty and justice for all.

Displaying the Flag

- Display the flag only from sunrise to sunset, except when it is properly illuminated. Do not display the flag when bad weather might damage it.

- No other flag or pennant should be placed above the U.S. flag. If another flag is displayed at the same level, it should be to the right of the flag of the United States of America.

- When the flag passes in a parade, stand and put your right hand over your heart.

- When singing the National Anthem, everyone should rise and stand at attention with the right hand placed over the heart. Men should remove their hats.

Flag Holidays

The flag of the United States may be flown on any day, but especially on these holidays:

New Year's Day	January 1
Inauguration Day	January 20
Dr. Martin Luther King, Jr., Day	third Monday in January
Lincoln's Birthday	February 12
Presidents' Day (Washington's Birthday)	third Monday in February
Mother's Day	second Sunday in May
Armed Forces Day	third Saturday in May
Memorial Day	last Monday in May (half-staff until noon)
Flag Day	June 14
Independence Day	July 4
Labor Day	first Monday in September
Constitution Day	September 17
Columbus Day	second Monday in October
Navy Day	October 27
Veterans Day	November 11
Thanksgiving Day	fourth Thursday in November

By Public Law or Executive Order, the flag flies 24 hours a day at the following locations:

The White House,
Washington, D.C.

The United States Capitol, Washington, D.C.

Iwo Jima Memorial to U.S. Marines,
Arlington, Virginia

Battleground in Lexington, MA (site of the first shots in the Revolutionary War)

Winter Encampment Cabins,
Valley Forge, Pennsylvania

Fort McHenry,
Baltimore, Maryland (A flag flying over Fort McHenry after a battle during the War of 1812 provided the inspiration for "The Star-Spangled Banner.")

The Star-Spangled Banner Flag House,
Baltimore, Maryland (This is the site where the famous flag over Fort McHenry was sewn.)

Washington Monument,
Washington, D.C.

Many other places fly the flag at night as a patriotic gesture by custom.

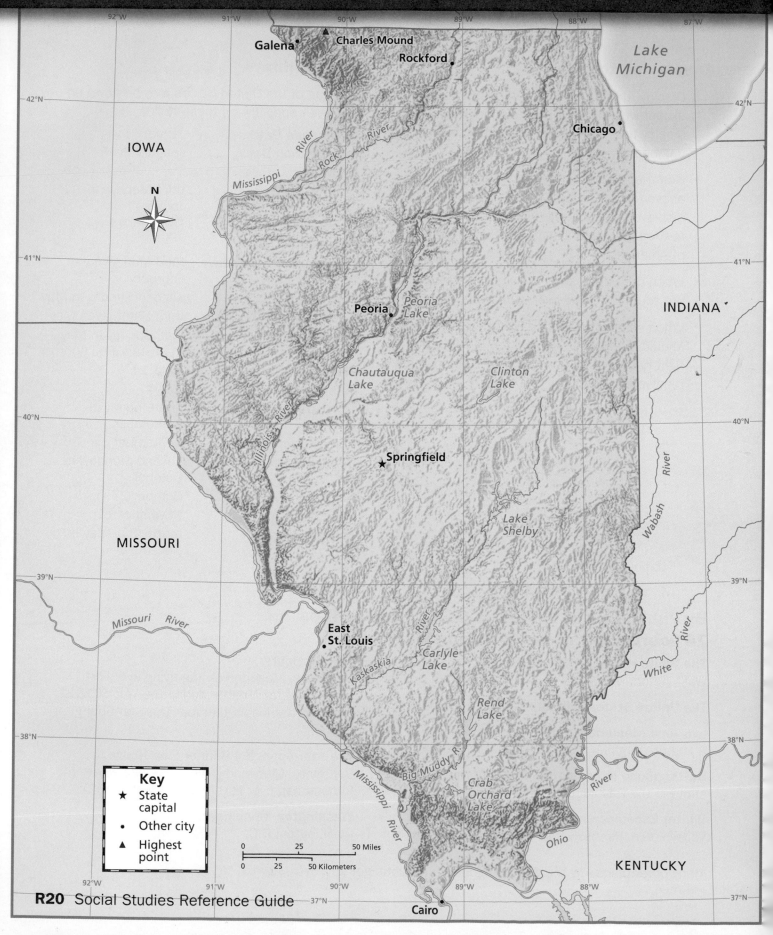

Lake Michigan

Galena

Charles Mound

Rockford

Chicago

IOWA

N

Mississippi River

Rock River

Peoria

Peoria Lake

INDIANA

Chautauqua Lake

Clinton Lake

Illinois River

Springfield

MISSOURI

Lake Shelby

Wabash River

Missouri River

East St. Louis

River

Carlyle Lake

Kaskaskia

White River

Rend Lake

Big Muddy R.

Crab Orchard Lake

Mississippi River

Ohio River

KENTUCKY

Key
★ State capital
● Other city
▲ Highest point

0   25   50 Miles
0   25   50 Kilometers

Cairo

Illinois Road Map

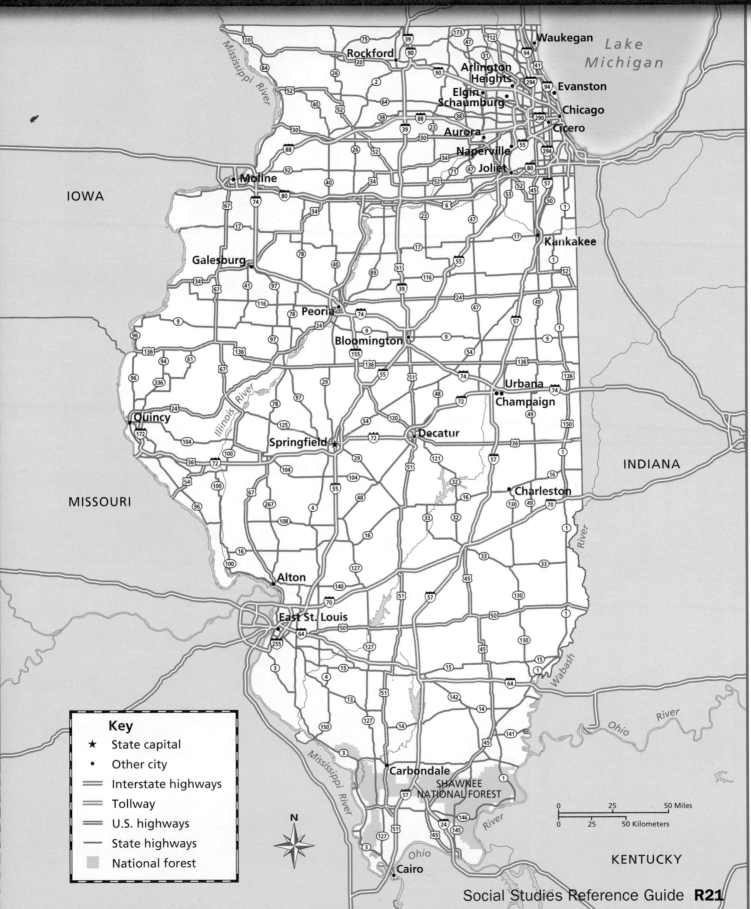

IOWA

MISSOURI

INDIANA

KENTUCKY

Lake Michigan

Mississippi River

Illinois River

Wabash River

Ohio River

Waukegan
Rockford
Arlington Heights
Elgin
Schaumburg
Evanston
Chicago
Cicero
Aurora
Naperville
Joliet
Moline
Kankakee
Galesburg
Peoria
Bloomington
Urbana
Champaign
Quincy
Decatur
Springfield ★
Charleston
Alton
East St. Louis
Carbondale
SHAWNEE NATIONAL FOREST
Cairo

Key

- ★ State capital
- • Other city
- Interstate highways
- Tollway
- U.S. highways
- State highways
- National forest

N

0   25   50 Miles
0   25   50 Kilometers

Atlas
Illinois Counties

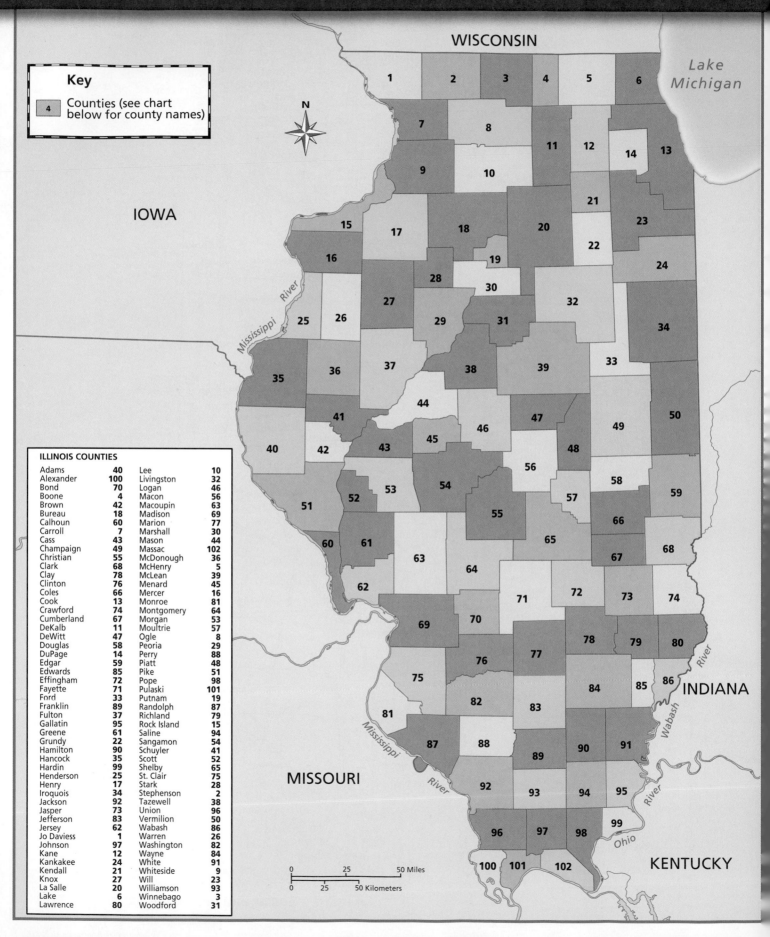

Key

4 Counties (see chart below for county names)

ILLINOIS COUNTIES

County	No.	County	No.
Adams	40	Lee	10
Alexander	100	Livingston	32
Bond	70	Logan	46
Boone	4	Macon	56
Brown	42	Macoupin	63
Bureau	18	Madison	69
Calhoun	60	Marion	77
Carroll	7	Marshall	30
Cass	43	Mason	44
Champaign	49	Massac	102
Christian	55	McDonough	36
Clark	68	McHenry	5
Clay	78	McLean	39
Clinton	76	Menard	45
Coles	66	Mercer	16
Cook	13	Monroe	81
Crawford	74	Montgomery	64
Cumberland	67	Morgan	53
DeKalb	11	Moultrie	57
DeWitt	47	Ogle	8
Douglas	58	Peoria	29
DuPage	14	Perry	88
Edgar	59	Piatt	48
Edwards	85	Pike	51
Effingham	72	Pope	98
Fayette	71	Pulaski	101
Ford	33	Putnam	19
Franklin	89	Randolph	87
Fulton	37	Richland	79
Gallatin	95	Rock Island	15
Greene	61	Saline	94
Grundy	22	Sangamon	54
Hamilton	90	Schuyler	41
Hancock	35	Scott	52
Hardin	99	Shelby	65
Henderson	25	St. Clair	75
Henry	17	Stark	28
Iroquois	34	Stephenson	2
Jackson	92	Tazewell	38
Jasper	73	Union	96
Jefferson	83	Vermilion	50
Jersey	62	Wabash	86
Jo Daviess	1	Warren	26
Johnson	97	Washington	82
Kane	12	Wayne	84
Kankakee	24	White	91
Kendall	21	Whiteside	9
Knox	27	Will	23
La Salle	20	Williamson	93
Lake	6	Winnebago	3
Lawrence	80	Woodford	31

WISCONSIN

IOWA

Lake Michigan

INDIANA

MISSOURI

KENTUCKY

Mississippi River

Wabash River

Ohio River

N

| 0 | 25 | 50 Miles |
| 0 | 25 | 50 Kilometers |

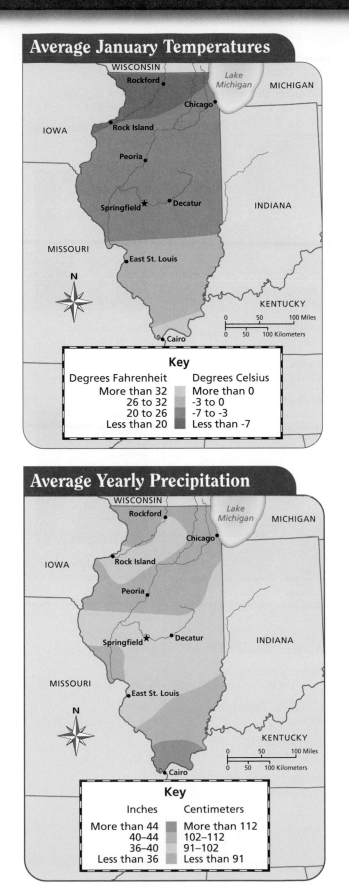

Average January Temperatures

Key

Degrees Fahrenheit	Degrees Celsius
More than 32	More than 0
26 to 32	-3 to 0
20 to 26	-7 to -3
Less than 20	Less than -7

Average Yearly Precipitation

Key

Inches	Centimeters
More than 44	More than 112
40–44	102–112
36–40	91–102
Less than 36	Less than 91

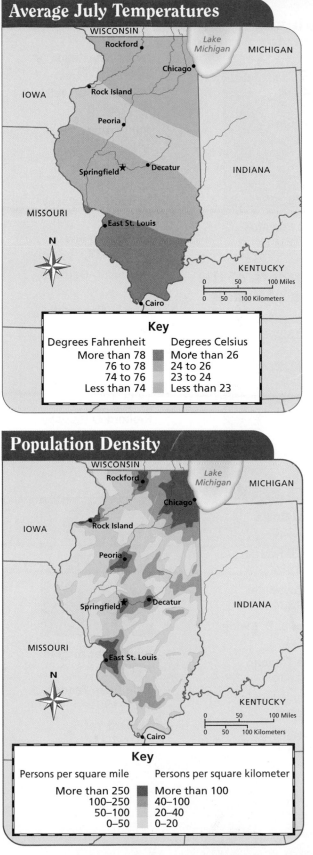

Average July Temperatures

Key

Degrees Fahrenheit	Degrees Celsius
More than 78	More than 26
76 to 78	24 to 26
74 to 76	23 to 24
Less than 74	Less than 23

Population Density

Key

Persons per square mile	Persons per square kilometer
More than 250	More than 100
100–250	40–100
50–100	20–40
0–50	0–20

Illinois Governors

Territorial Governor

Ninian Edwards
1809–1818

Governors of the State of Illinois

Shadrach Bond
1818–1822

Edward Coles
1822–1826

Ninian Edwards
1826–1830

John Reynolds
1830–1834

William L. D. Ewing
1834

Joseph Duncan
1834–1838

Thomas Carlin
1838–1842

Thomas Ford
1842–1846

Augustus C. French
1846–1853

Joel A. Matteson
1853–1857

William H. Bissell
1857–1860

John Wood
1860–1861

Richard Yates
1861–1865

Richard J. Oglesby
1865–1869

John M. Palmer
1869–1873

Richard J. Oglesby
1873

John L. Beveridge
1873–1877

Shelby M. Cullom
1877–1883

John M. Hamilton
1883–1885

Richard J. Oglesby
1885–1889

Joseph W. Fifer
1889–1893

John Peter Altgeld
1893–1897

John Riley Tanner
1897–1901

Richard Yates
1901–1905

Charles S. Deneen
1905–1913

Edward F. Dunne
1913–1917

Frank O. Lowden
1917–1921

Lennington Small
1921–1929

Louis L. Emmerson
1929–1933

Henry Horner
1933–1940

John Stelle
1940–1941

Dwight H. Green
1941–1949

Adlai E. Stevenson
1949–1953

William G. Stratton
1953–1961

Otto Kerner, Jr.
1961–1968

Samuel H. Shapiro
1968–1969

Richard B. Ogilvie
1969–1973

Daniel Walker
1973–1977

James R. Thompson
1977–1991

James Edgar
1991–1999

George H. Ryan
1999–2003

Rod Blagojevich
2003–Present

Famous Illinoisans

Franklin Pierce Adams,
author, Chicago

Jane Addams,
social worker, Cedarville

Mary Astor,
actress, Quincy

Jack Benny,
comedian, Chicago

Black Hawk,
Sauk chief, near Rock Island

Harry A. Blackmun,
jurist, Nashville

Ray Bradbury,
author, Waukegan

William Jennings Bryan,
politician, Salem

Dick Butkus,
athlete, actor, Chicago

John Chancellor,
TV commentator, Chicago

Raymond Chandler,
writer, Chicago

Jimmy Connors,
tennis player,
East St. Louis

James Gould Cozzens,
author, Chicago

Cindy Crawford,
model, DeKalb

Michael Crichton,
author, Chicago

Miles Davis,
musician, Alton

Walt Disney,
entertainment pioneer,
Chicago

Wyatt Earp,
sheriff, Monmouth

James T. Farrell,
author, Chicago

George Ferris,
inventor of the Ferris wheel,
Galesburg

Harrison Ford,
actor, Chicago

Betty Friedan,
author, Peoria

Benny Goodman,
musician, Chicago

Dorothy Hamill,
ice skater, Chicago

Ernest Hemingway,
author, Oak Park

Charlton Heston,
actor, Evanston

Wild Bill Hickok,
frontiersman, showman,
Troy Grove

William Holden,
actor, O'Fallon

Rock Hudson,
actor, Winnetka

Burl Ives,
singer, actor, Hunt City

James Jones,
author, Robinson

Quincy Jones,
composer, Chicago

Walter Kerr,
drama critic, Evanston

Ray Kroc,
restaurateur, Oak Park

Archibald MacLeish,
poet, Glencoe

David Mamet,
playwright, Chicago

Marlee Matlin,
actress, Morton Grove

Homer Z. Martin,
inventor, Chicago

Stanley Mazor,
inventor, Chicago

Robert A. Millikan,
physicist, Morrison

Bill Murray,
actor, Wilmette

Bob Newhart,
actor, comedian, Chicago

Frank Norris,
author, Chicago

Ronald Reagan,
U.S. President, actor,
Tampico

Carl Sandburg,
poet, Galesburg

Sam Shepard,
playwright, Fort Sheridan

William L. Shirer,
author, historian, Chicago

Shel Silverstein,
author, poet, Chicago

Al Spalding,
pitcher, sporting goods
manufacturer, Byron

McLean Stevenson,
actor, Bloomington

Preston Sturges,
director, Chicago

Gloria Swanson,
actress, Chicago

Carl Van Doren,
writer, educator, Hope

Melvin Van Peebles,
playwright, Chicago

Irving Wallace,
author, Chicago

Alfred Wallenstein,
conductor, Chicago

Raquel Welch,
actress, Chicago

Robin Williams,
comedian, actor, Chicago

Florenz Ziegfield,
theatrical producer, Chicago

1,000 years ago
Mississippians build cities and mounds.

2,000–3,000 years ago
People in Illinois begin to grow their own food.

1600s
Illiniwek peoples settle in this area.

1673
Marquette and Jolliet explore the Mississippi.

1600	1620	1640	1660	1680

10,000–20,000 years ago
The first people arrive in Illinois.

1682
La Salle claims Mississippi Valley for France.

1858
Lincoln debates Douglas in seven Illinois cities.

1857
The Dred Scott Decision makes people fear the spread of slavery.

1850
The Compromise of 1850 is passed, including the Fugitive Slave Act.

1837
John Deere designs a new steel plow.

1754
French and British begin to fight the French and Indian War.

1787
Northwest Ordinance is passed.

1812
War of 1812 begins.

| 1700 | 1720 | 1740 | 1760 | 1780 | 1800 | 1820 | 1840 | 1860 |

1776
Declaration of Independence is signed.

1809
Illinois Territory is created.

1860
Lincoln is elected President of the United States.

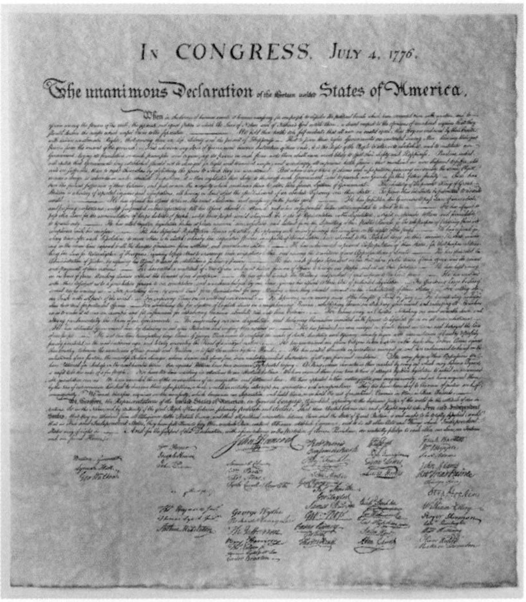

1818
Illinois becomes the twenty-first state.

IN CONGRESS, JULY 4, 1776.

The unanimous Declaration of the thirteen united States of America.

1832
Black Hawk War.

Illinois Time Line

1861
The Civil War begins.

1863
Lincoln issues the Emancipation Proclamation.

1871
The Great Chicago Fire destroys much of the city.

1889
Jane Addams opens Hull House.

1893
Chicago hosts the World's Columbian Exposition.

1920
The Nineteenth Amendment gives women the right to vote in all states.

1929
The Great Depression begins.

1973
U.S. role in Vietnam War ends.

1979
Jane Byrne becomes the first woman to be elected mayor of Chicago.

1880   1900   1920   1940   1960   1980   2000

1867
Patrons of Husbandry is established.

1865
The Civil War ends.

1917
The United States enters World War I.

1894
The Pullman Railroad Strike ends when federal troops intervene.

1945
World War II ends.

1947
Cold War between the Soviet Union and the United States begins.

1965
Senator Everett Dirksen helps pass the Voting Rights Act.

1983
Harold Washington becomes the first African American mayor of Chicago.

1992
Carol Moseley Braun becomes the U.S. Senate's first African American woman.

2005
The Abraham Lincoln Presidential Library and Museum completes its grand opening in Springfield.

This gazetteer is a geographic dictionary that will help you locate and pronounce places in this book. It also gives latitude and longitude for many places. The page numbers tell you where each place appears on a map (m.) or in the text (t.).

Apple River Canyon State Park (ap′ əl riv′ ər kan′ yən stāt pärk) state park in northern Illinois that features hills and canyons. 42°N, 90°W. (t. 33)

Appomattox Court House (ap′ ə mat′ əks kôrt hous) small town in northern Virginia. Site of Robert E. Lee's surrender to Ulysses S. Grant in 1865. 37°N, 78°W. (t. 191)

Bad Axe River (bad aks riv′ ər) site of Black Hawk's defeat in the Michigan territory. (t. 137)

Bering Strait (ber′ ing strāt) narrow body of water that separates the continents of Asia and North America. (m. 63, t. 63)

Cahokia (ka hō′ kē ə) site of a Mississippian settlement on the Mississippi River, later a British fort that was captured in 1778 by George Rogers Clark. 39°N, 98°W. (t. 66)

Cairo (kā′ rō) small city at the southernmost tip of Illinois, where the Ohio and Mississippi Rivers meet. 37°N, 89°W. (m. 14, t. 44)

Carbondale (kär′ bən dāl) small city at the northern edge of the Shawnee National Forest. 37°N, 89°W. (m. 292, t. 44)

Central Mississippi River valley (sen′ trəl mis′ ə sip′ ē riv′ ər val′ ē) part of North America surrounding the Mississippi River between Wisconsin and Louisiana. (t. 71)

Central Plains (sen′ trəl plānz) central region of Illinois, originally mostly prairie, now mostly farmland. (m. 30, t. 32)

Champaign-Urbana (sham pān′ ėr ba′ nə) Dual city location of the University of Illinois. 40°N, 88°W. (t. 224, m. 292)

Charles Mound (chärlz mound) hilly field that is the highest point in Illinois. 42°N, 90°W. (m. 25, t. 33)

Chicago (shə kȯ′ gō) third largest city in the United States, in northeastern Illinois on Lake Michigan. Chicago is an important cultural center and transportation hub. 42°N, 88°W. (m. 9, t. 12)

Coles County (kōlz koun′ tē) rural county in Eastern Illinois. (m. 233, t. 235)

Concord (kong′ kərd) Massachusetts town west of Boston where British soldiers fought American colonists in April 1775. 42°N, 71°W. (t. 98)

Cumberland (kum′ bər lənd) Maryland city where the National Road began. 39°N, 78°W. (t. 139)

Des Plaines (des plānz′) Illinois city that was the site of Ray Kroc's first McDonald's™ restaurant. 42°N, 88°W. (t. 291)

Gazetteer

East St. Louis (ēst sānt lü′ is) small city across the Mississippi River from St. Louis, Missouri. 38°N, 90°W. (m. 292, t. 44)

Erie Canal (i′ rē kə nal′) canal in New York state that connects the Hudson River with Lake Erie. (t. 139)

Evanston (e′ vən stən) city in northeastern Illinois that was the home of Frances Willard. 42°N, 87°W. (t. 224)

Fort de Chartres (fôrt də shärt) French fort built by La Salle and flooded by the Mississippi River. (m. 87, t. 87)

Fort de Crèvecour (fôrt də krev kür) French fort built by La Salle near present-day Peoria. 40°N, 89°W. (m. 87, t. 87)

Fort Dearborn (fôrt dēr′ bôrn) fort that once stood where Chicago is today; the Potawatomi destroyed it during the War of 1812. 42°N, 88°W. (m. 117, t. 125)

Fort Detroit (fôrt di troit′) site of attack by Pontiac, in what is now Michigan. (m. 83, t. 93)

Fort St. Louis (fôrt sānt lü′ is) French fort built by La Salle and used by the French and Kaskaskia people. (m. 87, t. 87)

Fort Sumter (fôrt sum′ tər) island fort near Charleston, South Carolina. Firing on this fort in 1861 began the Civil War. 32°N, 79°W. (m. 181, t. 183)

Freeport (frē pôrt) Illinois city in which Stephen A. Douglas explained his view of slavery and states' rights during the Lincoln-Douglas debates. 42°N, 89°W. (m. 173, t. 173)

Galena (gə lē nə) city in Northwest Illinois, a home of Ulysses S. Grant. 42°N, 90°W. (t. 190)

Galesburg (gālz′ bėrg) Illinois city in which Lincoln debated Douglas. 40°N, 90°W. (m. 173, t. 173)

Grand Village of the Kaskaskia (grand vil′ ij ov ᴛʜə kas kas′ kē ə) large Illini settlement on the Illinois River. (m. 61, t. 71)

Hull House (hul hous) settlement house started in Chicago in 1889. (t. 224)

Illinois (il′ ə noi′) state in the Midwest region of the United States, bordered partially by Lake Michigan and the Mississippi, Ohio, and Wabash Rivers. (m. 11, t. 11)

Illinois Beach State Park (il′ ə noi′ bēch stāt pärk) state park along the shores of Lake Michigan. 42°N, 87°W. (t. 33)

Illinois River (il′ ə noi′ riv′ ər) tributary of the Mississippi River that crosses almost the entire state of Illinois. (m. 14, t. 14)

Illinois State University (il′ ə noi′ stāt′ yü′ nə vėr′ sə tē) the first public university in Illinois. (t. 224)

Illinois Territory (il′ ə noi′ ter′ ə tôr′ ē) division of the Indiana Territory created in 1809. (m. 120, t. 120)

Indiana Territory (in′ dē an′ ə ter′ ə tôr′ ē) division of the Northwest Territory in 1800; it included the area that is now Illinois. (m. 120, t. 120)

Iraq (i rak′) Middle Eastern nation entered by U.S. troops in 2003 at beginning of Operation Iraqi Freedom. (m. 245, t. 245)

Jamestown (jāmz′ toun) first permanent English settlement in North America, built in 1607 on Virginia's James River. 37°N, 76°W. (m. 91, t. 91)

★ K ★

Kaskaskia (kas kas′ kē ə) British fort on the Mississippi River in southwestern Illinois, captured by George Rogers Clark in 1778. 37°N, 89°W. (m. 87, t. 100)

Kuwait (kü wāt′) Middle Eastern nation and ally of the United States that was invaded by Iraq in 1990. (m. 245, t. 245)

Lake Michigan (lāk mish′ ə gən) Great Lake that provides a waterway for Illinois shippers through Canada to the Atlantic Ocean. (m. 11, t. 11)

Lexington (lek′ sing tən) Massachusetts town west of Boston where the first shots of the Revolutionary War were fired in April 1775. 42°N, 71°W. (t. 98)

Little Egypt (lit′ l ē′ jipt) southern tip of Illinois, so called because it looks like Egypt's Nile River valley. (t. 41)

Michigan Territory (mish′ ə gən ter′ ə tôr′ ē) division of territory that was separated from the Indiana Territory, containing parts of what are now the states of Michigan and Wisconsin. (m. 133, t. 137)

Midwest (mid′ west′) region of the United States that includes Illinois, Indiana, Ohio, Wisconsin, Iowa, Missouri, Michigan, Minnesota, North Dakota, South Dakota, Nebraska, and Kansas. (m. 11, t. 11)

Mississippi River (mis′ ə sip′ ē riv′ ər) river that drains most of the central North American continent and forms the western border of Illinois. (m. 14, t. 14)

Monks Mound (mungks mound) large mound at Cahokia, apparently built by the Mississippian culture. (m. 61, t. 66)

New France (nü frans) early French settlements in North America on the St. Lawrence River in what is now Canada. (m. 83, t. 85)

Normal (nôr′ məl) site of Illinois State University. (t. 244)

North Korea (nôrth kô rē′ ə) East Asian communist nation against which the United States defended South Korea during the Korean War. (m. 245, t. 244)

North Vietnam (nôrth vē et′ näm′) Southeast Asian communist nation against which the United States attempted to defend South Vietnam in the late 1960s and early 1970s. (m. 245, t. 244)

Northern Plains (nôr′ ᴛʜərn plānz) northern region of Illinois, originally mostly prairie, now mostly farmland and urban areas. (m. 30, t. 32)

Northwest Territory (nôrth west ter′ ə tôr′ ē) land stretching north from the Ohio River to Canada and west from Pennsylvania to the Mississippi River. Ohio, Michigan, Indiana, Illinois, and parts of Wisconsin and Minnesota were created from this territory. (m. 117, t. 119)

Oak Park (ōk′ pärk′) former residence of Ernest Hemingway. (t. 298)

Ohio River (ō hī′ ō riv′ ər) tributary of the Mississippi that forms part of the southeast border of Illinois. (m. 14, t. 14)

Ottawa (ot′ ə wə) Illinois city in which Lincoln debated Douglas. 41°N, 88°W. (m. 173, t. 173)

Pearl (pėrl) Illinois village on the Illinois River. 39°N, 91°W. (m. 9, t. 19)

Pearl Harbor (pėrl här′ bər) U.S. Navy port in Hawaii that was bombed by Japan in 1941. 21°N, 157°W. (t. 238)

Peoria (pē ôr′ ē ə) city in north central Illinois on the Illinois River. 40°N, 98°W. (m. 14, t. 87)

Philadelphia (fil′ ə del′ fē ə) eastern Pennsylvania city where the Declaration of Independence was signed in 1776. 39°N, 75°W. (t. 98)

Pronunciation Key

a	in hat	ō	in open	sh	in she
ā	in age	ȯ	in all	th	in thin
â	in care	ô	in order	ᴛʜ	in then
ä	in far	oi	in oil	zh	in measure
e	in let	ou	in out	ə	= a in about
ē	in equal	u	in cup	ə	= e in taken
ėr	in term	u̇	in put	ə	= i in pencil
i	in it	ü	in rule	ə	= o in lemon
ī	in ice	ch	in child	ə	= u in circus
o	in hot	ng	in long		

Gazetteer

Princeton (prin′ stən) Illinois town where Owen Lovejoy operated a station on the Underground Railroad. 41°N, 89°W. (m. 166, t. 169)

Provident Hospital (prov′ ə dənt hos′ pi təl) hospital that hired and accepted patients of all races. (t. 224)

Roanoke Island (rō′ ə nōk′ ī′ lənd) North Carolina island located between Pamlico Sound and Albemarle Sound. Site of first English colony in America. 35°N, 75°W. (m. 91, t. 91)

Rock Island (rok ī′ lənd) Illinois city named after an island in the Mississippi River. Site of a Civil War prisoner of war camp. 41°N, 90°W. (m. 181, t. 190)

Rock Spring Seminary (rok spring sem′ ə ner′ ē) first college in Illinois. (t. 136)

Shawnee National Forest (shȯ nē′ nash′ ə nal fôr′ ist) national forest in southern Illinois, featuring wilderness areas and unique landscapes. 37°N, 88°W. (m. 42, t. 42)

Shawneetown (shȯ′ nē toun) village on the Wabash River where an early land office opened. 37°N, 88°W. (t. 136)

Southern Forests and Hills (suᴛʜ′ ərn fôr′ ists and hilz) region of Illinois that has rolling hills, valleys, and canyons. (m. 40, t. 41)

South Korea (south kô rē′ ə) East Asian nation the United States defended from communist aggression during the Korean War. (m. 245, t. 244)

South Vietnam (south vē et′ näm′) Southeast Asian nation the United States attempted to defend from communist aggression in the late 1960s and early 1970s. (m. 245, t. 244)

Springfield (spring′ fēld) capital of Illinois, located near the center of the state. 39°N, 89°W. (m. 14, t. 135)

Starved Rock State Park (stärvd rok stāt pärk) state park in north central Illinois that features forests and sandstone canyons. 41°N, 88°W. (t. 33)

University of Illinois (yü′ nə vėr′ sə tē ov il′ ə noi′) state university in the Urbana-Champaign area. (t. 224)

Vandalia (van dāl′ yə) city in south central Illinois that was a destination on the National Road and an early capital of Illinois. 38°N, 89°W. (t. 136)

Vicksburg (viks′ bėrg′) Mississippi city that was the site of a significant Union victory during the Civil War. 32°N, 90°W. (m. 190, t. 190)

Wabash River (wȯ′ bash riv′ ər) tributary of the Ohio River that forms part of the border between Illinois and Indiana. (m. 14, t. 14)

Washington, D.C. (wäsh′ ing tən dē sē) capital of the United States, located on the Potomac River between Maryland and Virginia. 38°N, 77°W. (t. 267)

Winchester (win′ ches′ tər) rural community in western Illinois. 39°N, 90°W. (t. 213)

Yorktown (yôrk′ toun′) Virginia city where British troops surrendered to George Washington, ending major fighting in American Revolution. 37°N, 76°W. (t. 100)

Biographical Dictionary

This biographical dictionary tells you about the people in this book and how to pronounce their names. The page numbers tell you where the person first appears in the text.

A

Adams, John (ad′ əmz) (1735–1826) Political leader and second President of the United States. (p. 99)

Addams, Jane (ad′ əmz) (1860–1935) U.S. social worker and writer. She founded the Hull House in Chicago to help poor people. (p. 224)

Aiken, Lizzie (ā′ kən) (1817–1906) Nurse and missionary. She aided Union troops during the Civil War. (p. 191)

Altgeld, John P. (ȯlt′ geld) (1847–1902) Reformer and governor of Illinois from 1892 to 1896. (p. 223)

Armour, Philip (är′ mər) (1832–1901) Meatpacking industrialist. (p. 215)

B

Bickerdyke, Mary Ann (bik′ ėr dik) (1817–1901) Union nurse in the U.S. Civil War, called "Mother Bickerdyke." (p. 191)

Black Hawk (blak′ hȯk) (1767–1838) Native American chief. Led Sauk and Fox warriors against the Illinois militia. (p. 137)

Blagojevich, Rod (blə goi′ ə vich) (1956–) Governor of Illinois, 2003– . (p. 269)

Bohrer, Florence Fifer (bôr′ ər) (1877–1960) Illinois state senator. She supported laws to protect the poor. (p. 13)

Bond, Shadrach (bond) (1773–1832) The first governor of the state of Illinois, from 1818 to 1822. (p. 126)

Booth, John Wilkes (büth) (1838–1865) Actor who assassinated Abraham Lincoln. (p. 192)

Bristo, Marca (bris′ tō) (?–) Activist for the disabled. (p. 279)

Brooks, Gwendolyn (brüks) (1917–2000) U.S. poet and novelist. She was the first African American to win the Pulitzer Prize. (p. 298)

Burnham, Daniel (bėrn′ əm) (1846–1912) Architect and city planner. (p. 214)

Byrne, Jane (bėrn) (1934–) Chicago's first woman mayor. (p. 243)

C

Carver, George Washington (kär′ vər) (1861?–1943) Botanist and chemist who helped develop uses for soybean products. (p. 213)

Clark, George Rogers (klärk) (1752–1818) Military leader during the Revolution. In 1778 Clark's troops captured British forts in the Northwest Territory. His victories helped the United States claim the region. (p. 100)

Clark, William (klärk) (1770–1838) U.S. soldier who explored the North American West with Meriwether Lewis from 1804 to 1806. (p. 121)

Clay, Henry (klā) (1777–1852) Statesman and orator. (p. 167)

Coles, Edward (kōlz) (1786–1865) Second governor of Illinois, from 1822 to 1830. He worked to keep slavery illegal. (p. 126)

Cook, Daniel Pope (kůk) (1794–1827) U.S. congressman. He helped Illinois enter the Union as a free state. (p. 126)

D

Davis, Jefferson (dā′ vis) (1808–1889) Only President of the Confederate States of America. (p. 183)

Pronunciation Key

a	in hat	ō	in open	sh	in she
ā	in age	ȯ	in all	th	in thin
â	in care	ô	in order	ᴛʜ	in then
ä	in far	oi	in oil	zh	in measure
e	in let	ou	in out	ə	= a in about
ē	in equal	u	in cup	ə	= e in taken
ėr	in term	ů	in put	ə	= i in pencil
i	in it	ü	in rule	ə	= o in lemon
ī	in ice	ch	in child	ə	= u in circus
o	in hot	ng	in long		

Biographical Dictionary

Debs, Eugene V. (debz) (1855–1926) Labor leader. (p. 216)

Deere, John (dēr) (1804–1886) Blacksmith who invented a plow that made farming on the Illinois prairie easier. (p. 32)

Dirksen, Everett (dėrk′ sən) (1896–1969) U.S. senator from Illinois who helped pass the Civil Rights Bill and the Voting Rights Act. (p. 243)

Disney, Walt (diz′ nē) (1901–1966) Filmmaker who pioneered many kinds of entertainment, including full-length animated movies and theme parks. (p. 298)

Douglas, Stephen A. (dug′ ləs) (1813–1861) U.S. senator for Illinois. He debated Abraham Lincoln on the subject of slavery. (p. 173)

Durbin, Richard (dûr′ bən) (1944–) U.S. senator for Illinois. (p. 267)

du Sable, Jean-Baptiste-Point (dü sa′ bəl) (1745–1818) Pioneer, trader, and early settler of Chicago. (p. 86)

★ E ★

Edgar, James, "Jim" (ed′ gər) (1946–) Governor of Illinois (1991–1999). He signed legislation creating the Illinois Conservation Foundation. (p. 22)

Edison, Thomas (ed′ ə sən) (1847–1931) Inventor who improved the electric light bulb. (p. 215)

Edwards, Ninian (ed′ wėrdz) (1775–1833) Sole governor of the Illinois Territory and third governor of the state (1826–1830). (p. 120)

★ F ★

Fermi, Enrico (fer′ mē) (1901–1954) Physicist. He created the first self-sustaining chain reaction in uranium at Chicago in 1942. (p. 239)

Ford, Henry (fôrd) (1863–1947) Entrepreneur. He applied mass production to automobile manufacturing. (p. 236)

Franklin, Benjamin (frang′ klən) (1706–1790) Statesman, diplomat, author, scientist, and inventor. (p. 99)

Froman, John (frō′ mən) (1961–) Chief of the Peoria people. (p. 75)

★ G ★

Glidden, Joseph (glid′ ən) (1813–1906) Illinoisian who improved barbed wire. (p. 213)

Grant, Ulysses S. (grant) (1822–1885) Commander of the Union armies in the Civil War. He was the eighteenth U.S. President. (p. 190)

Gutierrez, Theresa (gü tē e′ rez) (?–) News reporter and news program host for ABC7 Chicago. (p. 298)

★ H ★

Harrison, William Henry (har′ ə sən) (1773–1841) Governor of the Indiana Territory and ninth president of the United States. (p. 125)

Hastert, J. Dennis (has′ tėrt) (1942–) U.S. congressman, Speaker of the U.S. House (1999–). (p. 267)

Hemingway, Ernest (hem′ ing wā) (1899–1961) Novelist, short-story writer, and journalist. (p. 298)

Hennepin, Louis (hen′ ə pin) (1626?–1701?) Roman Catholic missionary and explorer of the Mississippi River valley. (p. 86)

Hitler, Adolph (hit′ lər) (1889–1945) Nazi dictator of Germany before and during WWII. (p. 238)

Hodgers, Jennie (hä′ jərz) (1843–1915) Illinois woman who dressed as a man and fought for the Union. (p. 191)

★ J ★

Jackson, Jesse (jak′ sən) (1941–) Political activist. (p. 243)

Jefferson, Thomas (jef′ ər sən) (1743–1826) Third President of the United States. He was also a diplomat, author, scientist, and inventor. (p. 99)

Jemison, Mae Carol (je′ mi sən) (1956–) First African American woman in space. She has worked to improve health care in developing nations. (p. 243)

Jolliet, Louis (jō′ lē et) (1645–1700) Explorer and mapmaker. In 1673 he traveled down the Mississippi River with Jacques Marquette. (p. 86)

Johnson, John (jon′ sən) (1918–2005) Magazine publisher and civil rights funder. (p. 243)

ette, Jacques (mär ket′) (1637–1675) French
issionary who explored the Mississippi with Louis
liet in 1673. (p. 86)

mick, Cyrus (mə kôr′ mik) (1809–1884) He began
ufacturing the reaper in the 1830s. (p. 143)

Joy (môr′ tən) (1855–1934) Conservationist who
ted Morton Arboretum. (p. 22)

Braun, Carol (mōz′ lē) (1947–) First African
ican woman in the U.S. Senate. (p. 245)

Muir, John (yür) (1838–1914) Conservationist. He
argued for protection of national wilderness areas.
(p. 42)

★ O ★

Obama, Barack (o bom′ ə) (1961–) U.S. senator from
Illinois.

Outelas, Françoise (ü tə lä′) (c.1730–1801) Early French
colonial settler and businesswoman. (p. 86)

★ P ★

Peck, John Mason (pek) (1789–1858) Professor,
newspaper editor, and Baptist minister. He opened the
first college in Illinois. (p. 136)

Piggott, James (pig′ ət) (1735?–1799) Pioneer and
entrepreneur. He operated a ferry from what is today
East St. Louis, Illinois to St. Louis, Missouri. (p. 44)

291)

le (lä säl′)
aimed the
e. (p. 86)

nfederate general
ppomattox Court House.

4–1809) U.S. explorer. He
red the North American
p. 121)

(1809–1865) Sixteenth U.S.
the Union during the Civil
in 1865. (p. 135)

9–1931) Illinois poet.

) (1820–1905) Reformer. She
oman Suffrage Association in

11–1864) Abolitionist, pastor,
ctor on the Underground

861–1943) Governor of
ar I. (p. 235)

Pronunciation Key

a in hat	ō in open	sh in she
ā in age	o in all	th in thin
â in care	ô in order	TH in then
ä in far	oi in oil	zh in measure
e in let	ou in out	ə = a in about
ē in equal	u in cup	ə = e in taken
ėr in term	u̇ in put	ə = i in pencil
i in it	ü in rule	ə = o in lemon
ī in ice	ch in child	ə = u in circus
o in hot	ng in long	

Pontiac (pon'tē ak) (1720–1769) Leader who organized Native Americans against British forces in 1763. (p. 93)

Pope, Nathaniel (pōp) (1784–1850) Statesman. He h pass the bill that made Illinois a state. (p. 126)

Pullman, George M. (pul' mən) (1831–1897) Devel of the railroad sleeping car. A town he built for workers was the site of a famous labor strike. (p

★ R ★

Reagan, Ronald (rā' gən) (1911–2004) Fortieth President of the United States, from 1981 to 1989 (p. 244)

Roosevelt, Franklin Delano (rōz' ə velt) (1882–1945) Thirty-second President of the United States, from 1933 to 1945. (p. 237)

Rumsfeld, Donald (rumz' feld) (1932–) Secretary of Defense for Presidents Gerald Ford and George W. Bush. (p. 267)

★ S ★

Sandburg, Carl (sand' bėrg´) (1878–1967) U.S. poet and biographer. (p. 48)

Scott, Dred (skot) (1795–1858) Enslaved African American who sued for freedom before the U.S. Supreme Court. (p. 170)

Sears, Richard (sērz) (1863–1914) Mail-order retailer who popularized the mail-order catalog. (p. 215)

Sinclair, Upton (sin kler') (1878–1968) Novelist and reformer. He exposed unsafe practices at meatpacking plants. (p. 223)

Skilling, Tom (skil' ing) (1952–) Illinois meteorologist and broadcaster. (p. 19)

Starr, Ellen Gates (stär) (1859–1940) Reformer. With Jane Addams, she co-founded Hull House. (p. 224)

St. Clair, Arthur (sānt kler) (1736–1818) Governor of the Northwest Territory. (p. 119)

Stevenson, Adlai (stē' vən sən) (1900–1965) U.S. statesman and diplomat. He was governor of Illinois from 1949 to 1953 and ambassador to the UN from 1960 to 1965. (p. 268)

Williams, who orga States. (p.

Wilson, Woodrow United States d

This glossary will help you understand and pronounce the terms and vocabulary words in this book. The page number tells you where the word first appears.

abolitionist (ab′ ə lish′ ə nist) person who worked to end slavery (p. 168)

adapt (ə dapt′) to change or adjust ways of life to fit different conditions (p. 63)

Allies (al′ īz) Great Britain, France, Russia, the United States, and the other countries that joined the fight against the Central Powers in World War I or against the Axis Powers in World War II (p. 235)

ally (al′ ī) partner or supporter who pledges help (p. 92)

amendment (ə mend′ mənt) alteration of or addition to a motion, bill, or constitution (p. 277)

arboretum (är′ bə rē′ təm) land set aside to grow many different trees or shrubs for study or display (p. 22)

archaeologist (är′ kē ol′ ə jist) person who studies ancient peoples and their cultures (p. 63)

arms race (ärmz rās) competition between countries to obtain more and better weapons (p. 244)

artifact (är′ tə fakt) object made by humans, discovered by archaeologists (p. 63)

assassination (ə sas′ n ā′ shən) murder of an important person (p. 192)

assembly line (ə sem′ blē lin) type of manufacturing in which workers perform the same task repeatedly on a line of products that moves steadily along (p. 236)

Axis Powers (ak′ sis pou′ ərz) alliance mainly of Germany, Italy, and Japan during World War II (p. 238)

barbed wire (bärbd wīr) fencing material with small, sharp spikes, used to enclose cattle (p. 213)

bar graph (bär′ graf) a special kind of picture that compares things by showing their sizes or their amounts (p. 220)

Bill of Rights (bil ov rīts) formal statement of the fundamental rights of the people of the United States, incorporated in the Constitution as Amendments 1–10 (p. 277)

budget (buj′ it) estimate of expected income and expense for a given period in the future (p. 269)

campaign (kam pān′) competition by rival political candidates and organizations for public office (p. 173)

canal (kə nal′) human-made waterway meant to carry small boats or ships (p. 144)

candidate (kan′ də dāt) person who seeks an office or other honor (p. 173)

checks and balances (cheks and bal′ ens iz) system for dividing the powers of government among the different branches to keep one branch from having too much power (p. 267)

climate (klī′ mit) type of weather an area has over a long period of time (p. 19)

colony (kol′ ə nē) settlement of people in a new land or territory who remain loyal to their home nation (p. 85)

communism (kom′ yə niz′ əm) political system in which all economic and social activity is controlled by the government (p. 244)

Pronunciation Key

a in hat	ō in open	sh in she
ā in age	ȯ in all	th in thin
â in care	ô in order	ŦH in then
ä in far	oi in oil	zh in measure
e in let	ou in out	ə = a in about
ē in equal	u in cup	ə = e in taken
ėr in term	ù in put	ə = i in pencil
i in it	ü in rule	ə = o in lemon
ī in ice	ch in child	ə = u in circus
o in hot	ng in long	

Glossary

Compromise of 1850 (kom′ prə mīz) series of laws passed to ease tensions between slave and free states (p. 167)

Confederacy (kən fed′ ər ə sē) government established by the Southern states of the United States after their secession from the Union (p. 183)

conservation (kon′ sər vā′ shən) carefully using, protecting, and preserving a natural resource or treasured possession (p. 22)

constitution (kon′ stə tü′ shən) system of principles according to which a nation, state, or organization is governed (p. 119)

consumer (kən sü′ mər) person who buys and uses products and services (p. 289)

continent (kon′ tə nənt) one of the seven great land masses on Earth (p. 11)

cultivate (kul′ tə vāt) to prepare and work on land in order to raise crops (p. 74)

cultural diversity (kul′ chər əl də vėr′ sə tē) variety of different cultures living, learning, and working in a region (p. 297)

cultural group (kul′ chər əl grüp) group of people who share similar cultural aspects (p. 65)

culture (kul′ chər) ways of living, social customs, arts, and religions of a nation, a people, or a community (p. 63)

debate (di bāt′) to publicly discuss the reasons for or against an issue (p. 173)

Declaration of Independence (dek′ lə rā′ shən ov in′ di pen′ dəns) document officially declaring that the American colonies were breaking away from Great Britain to form a new nation (p. 99)

degree (di grē′) unit of measurement, for latitude, longitude, temperature, or angle (p. 122)

delta (del′ tə) flat plain made up of deposits at the mouth of a river (p. 43)

demand (di mand′) amount of a product that consumers need or want (p. 289)

discrimination (dis krim′ ə nā′ shən) unfair treatment of people because of their race, gender, or beliefs (p. 243)

district (dis′ trikt) division of a territory, marked off for governing purposes (p. 119)

economy (i kon′ ə mē) business affairs of a country or region (p. 189)

ecosystem (ē′ kō sis′ təm) system formed by the interaction of living things with their environment (p. 20)

editorial (ed′ ə tôr′ ē əl) section of an information resource, such as a newspaper, in which people state their opinions (p. 249)

elevation map (el′ ə vā′ shən map) map that shows how high land is (p. 24)

Emancipation Proclamation (i man′ sə pā′ shən prok′ lə mā′ shən) declaration that granted freedom to slaves held in the Confederate states in 1863 (p. 185)

environment (en vī′ rən mənt) air, water, objects, and living things surrounding a person or other living thing (p. 22)

equator (ē quā′ tər) latitude line that circles the globe at its widest point, halfway between the North and South Poles (p. 122)

erosion (i rō′ zhən) process by which Earth's surface is worn away by the action of water, glaciers, wind, and waves (p. 33)

executive branch (eg zek′ yə tiv branch) branch of government in charge of carrying out laws (p. 126)

expedition (ek′ spə dish′ ən) journey made for exploration or for some other purpose (p. 121)

export (ek′ spôrt) product that is sent out of one country or state for sale in another (p. 289)

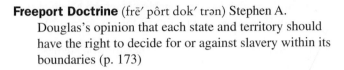

Freeport Doctrine (frē′ pôrt dok′ trən) Stephen A. Douglas's opinion that each state and territory should have the right to decide for or against slavery within its boundaries (p. 173)

Fifteenth Amendment (fif′ tēnth ə mend′ mənt) amendment to the U.S. Constitution that gave all male U.S. citizens the right to vote (p. 277)

Fugitive Slave Act (fyü′ jə tiv slāv akt) 1850 law requiring that all escaping slaves be captured and returned to their owners (p. 167)

General Assembly (jen′ ər əl ə sem′ blē) Illinois's state legislature (p. 269)

generalization (jen′ ər ə lə zā′ shən) broad statement that applies to many examples (p. 68)

glacier (glā′ shər) huge mass of ice and packed snow that moves very slowly across a land surface (p. 12)

government (guv′ ərn mənt) organized system of leaders, delegates, or assemblies that controls a community or country (p. 65)

growing season (grō′ ing sē′ zn) period when it is warm enough to grow most crops (p. 19)

headline (hed′ līn′) phrase in large type that describes the subject of an article (p. 249)

high-tech industry (hī′ tek′ in′ də strē) an industry that uses the latest forms of technology to make new goods and services (p. 291)

hub (hub) center of activity, or a crossroads for transportation routes (p. 14)

hunter-gatherer (hun′ tər gaᴛʜ′ ər ər) person who survives by hunting or fishing in the wild (p. 63)

Illinois and Michigan Canal (il′ ə noi′ and mish′ ə gən kə nal′) canal that linked the Chicago and Illinois Rivers in 1848, making it easier to transport goods from Lake Michigan to the Mississippi River (p. 144)

Illinois Central Railroad (il′ ə noi′ sen′ trəl rāl′ rōd′) railroad that linked Chicago to Cairo in 1856 (p. 144)

Illinois Woman Suffrage Association (il′ ə noi′ wüm′ ən suf′ rij ə sō′ sē ā′ shən) organization formed in 1868 to work toward giving women the right to vote (p. 277)

immigrant (im′ ə grənt) person who settles in a new or different country (p. 145)

import (im′ pôrt) a product that is brought into one country or state from another (p. 289)

income tax (in′ kum taks) tax placed on the money a person or business earns (p. 268)

information resource (in′ fər mā′ shən rē′ sôrs) places and resources, such as books and the Internet, to search for information (p. 248)

institution (in′ stə tü′ shən) establishment or organization that provides services (p. 136)

Internet (in′ tər net′) international network of computers for publicly sharing information (p. 248)

intersection (in′ tər sek′ shən) place where roads meet or cross (p. 275)

Pronunciation Key

a in hat	ō in open	sh in she
ā in age	ȯ in all	th in thin
â in care	ô in order	ᴛʜ in then
ä in far	oi in oil	zh in measure
e in let	ou in out	ə = a in about
ē in equal	u in cup	ə = e in taken
ėr in term	u̇ in put	ə = i in pencil
i in it	ü in rule	ə = o in lemon
ī in ice	ch in child	ə = u in circus
o in hot	ng in long	

Glossary

judicial branch (jü dish′ əl branch) branch of government that interprets laws of the land (p. 126)

★ K ★

key (kē) box on a map that explains the symbols that are used (p. 274)

keyword (kē wėrd) word or phrase related to a topic being researched on a computer (p. 249)

★ L ★

labor union (lā′ bər yü′ nyən) organization to help and protect workers (p. 216)

landform (land′ fôrm′) hill, plain, mountain, or other physical feature of Earth's surface (p. 12)

latitude (lat′ ə tüd) imaginary line that circles the globe from east to west, used to measure location (p. 122)

League of Women Voters (lēg ov wim′ ən vō′ tərz) group that encourages U.S. citizens to vote (p. 277)

legislative branch (lej′ ə slā′ tiv branch) branch of government that makes laws (p. 126)

line graph (līn graf) a special kind of graph that shows how something has changed over time (p. 220)

longhouse (lòng′ hous) large, rectangular dwelling used by North American natives (p. 72)

longitude (lon′ jə tüd) imaginary line that runs from north to south between the poles, used to measure location (p. 122)

Louisiana Purchase (lü ē′ zē an′ ə pėr′ chəs) treaty signed with France in 1803 by which the United States purchased French holdings between the Mississippi River and the Rocky Mountains (p. 121)

★ M ★

maize (māz) kind of corn being grown by Native Americans when Europeans arrived in North America (p. 72)

mass production (mas prə duk′ shən) manufacturing products in large numbers to reduce costs (p. 236)

meridian (mə rid′ ē ən) line reaching from the North to the South Pole, also called a line of longitude (p. 122)

meteorologist (mē′ tē ə rol′ ə jist) person who studies weather (p. 19)

metropolitan area (met′ rə pol′ ə tan âr′ ē ə) area consisting of or dominated by cities (p. 35)

Michigan Territory (mish′ ə gən ter′ ə tôr′ ē) early name for unsettled land in what is now Michigan and Wisconsin (p. 137)

migrate (mī′ grāt) to move from one region to settle in another (p. 63)

missionary (mish′ ə nār′ ē) person who travels to tell others about his or her religion (p. 86)

moraine (mə rān′) mass of dirt and rocks scraped up by a glacier that remains after the glacier melts or retreats (p. 32)

mound (mound) pile of earth, sand, and stone shaped to form a hill (p. 64)

★ N ★

National Road (nash′ ə nəl rōd) early roadway that allowed settlers to move more easily from Maryland to the middle of Illinois (p. 139)

natural hazard (nach′ ər əl haz′ ərd) danger from a natural phenomenon, such as an earthquake, hailstorm, flood, or tornado (p. 19)

New Deal (nü dēl) domestic jobs program of the Franklin D. Roosevelt administration to help people survive the Great Depression (p. 237)

Nineteenth Amendment (nīn′ tēnth′ ə mend′ mənt) amendment to the U.S. Constitution, ratified in 1920, that gave women the right to vote (p. 277)

Northern Cross Railroad (nôr′ ŦHərn krȯs rāl′ rōd) in 1838, the first railroad in Illinois (p. 144)

Northwest Ordinance (north west′ ord′ n əns) law directing how the Northwest Territory would be divided into states. It outlawed slavery in the region and gave settlers religious freedom and civil rights (p. 119)

orator (ôr′ ə tər) person who is eloquent and persuasive when speaking publicly (p. 174)

ordinance (ord′ n əns) rule or law made by an authority (p. 119)

parallel (par′ ə lel) another name for a line of latitude (p. 122)

prairie (prâr′ ē) level or rolling plain with fertile soil, growing mostly coarse grass (p. 12)

precipitation (pri sip′ ə tā′ shən) water that falls as rain, hail, sleet, or snow (p. 19)

prehistoric (prē′ hi stôr′ ik) of a time before history was written or recorded (p. 63)

prime meridian (prīm mə rid′ ē ən) line of longitude that measures zero degrees (p. 122)

proclamation (prok′ lə mā′ shən) official public announcement made in a speech or document (p. 93)

public goods and services (pub′ lik güdz and sėr′ vis iz) products and work provided by government (p. 268)

Quartering Act (kwôr′ tər ing akt) 1765 law requiring colonists to provide British troops with shelter, food, and supplies (p. 97)

reaper (rē′ pər) person or machine that cuts and harvests grain or other crops (p. 143)

rebellion (ri bel′ yən) uprising or fight against a ruling government (p. 93)

reform (ri fôrm′) taking political, legislative, or legal action to improve a situation or solve a problem (p. 223)

refrigeration (ri frij′ ə rā′ shən) science of keeping objects cool (p. 215)

regiment (rej′ ə mənt) military unit containing two or more battalions and about 1,000 people (p. 190)

repeal (ri pēl′) to withdraw or cancel a law or tax (p. 97)

republic (ri pub′ lək) political system in which people elect representatives to make decisions (p. 267)

revolution (rev′ ə lü′ shən) overthrow and replacement of an existing government by the people governed (p. 99)

sales tax (sālz taks) money added to the cost of an item and paid to a government (p. 268)

scale (skāl) part of a map that helps to figure out how far it is in miles or kilometers from one point on a map to another (p. 274)

search engine (sėrch en′ jən) Internet program for finding topics by keyword (p. 249)

secede (si sēd′) to formally leave an organization or group (p. 183)

service (sėr′ vis) useful work that is done for others (p. 246)

service industry (sėr′ vis in′ də strē) business that provides services for customers, such as a utility company, hotel, or airline (p. 246)

settlement house (set′ l mənt hous) place that helps poor people in the community (p. 224)

skyscraper (skī′ skrā′ pər) an iron- or steel-framed building that is many stories high (p. 225)

Pronunciation Key

a in hat	ō in open	sh in she
ā in age	ȯ in all	th in thin
â in care	ô in order	ᴛʜ in then
ä in far	oi in oil	zh in measure
e in let	ou in out	ə = a in about
ē in equal	u in cup	ə = e in taken
ėr in term	ụ in put	ə = i in pencil
i in it	ü in rule	ə = o in lemon
ī in ice	ch in child	ə = u in circus
o in hot	ng in long	

Glossary

slavery (slāv′ ər ē) keeping other people as though they were possessions and forcing them to work (p. 167)

Stamp Act (stamp akt) 1765 law designed to raise money in the American colonies by requiring government stamps to be used on important documents (p. 97)

stockyard (stok′ yärd′) an enclosed area where livestock are kept temporarily (p. 214)

street map (strēt map) map of a city or town showing all of its streets and avenues (p. 274)

strike (strīk) an action by workers in which they stop working and shut down a factory to put pressure on owners (p. 216)

suffrage (suf′ rij) right to vote (p. 277)

supply (sə plī′) amount of a product that is available for sale (p. 289)

surrender (sə ren′ dər) to give up to another, such as to an opponent in a battle (p. 191)

sweatshop (swet′ shop′) factory in which people work long hours in poor conditions for low pay (p. 223)

telecommunications (tel′ ə kə myü′ nə kā′ shənz) the sending of messages by radio, telephone, and television (p. 291)

temperate climate (tem′ pər it klī′ mit) climate in which the seasons are neither very hot nor very cold (p. 19)

time zone (tīm zōn) region in which one standard time is used (p. 294)

Townshend Acts (toun′ zənd akts) British laws passed in 1767 that taxed imports to the American colonies and made other changes that the colonists resented (p. 97)

township (toun′ ship) part of a county that has governmental powers (p. 270)

trade (trād) voluntary exchange of goods or services (p. 64)

tributary (trib′ yə ter′ ē) river or stream that flows into another river (p. 32)

Underground Railroad (un′ dər ground rāl′ rōd) network of escape routes and hiding places that helped enslaved people reach freedom before the Civil War (p. 168)

urban (ėr′ bən) located in or belonging to a city (p. 32)

URL (yü är el) Universal Resource Locator, the name for a location on the Internet (p. 249)

veto (vē′ tō) right, as by a President or governor, to reject a law that has been passed by the legislative branch (p. 269)

Voting Rights Act of 1965 (vō′ ting rīts akt) law that removed barriers that had prevented African Americans in the South from voting (p. 243)

voyageur (vwä yä zhėr′) French Canadian who traveled into North America to trade for furs with Native Americans (p. 88)

War of 1812 (wôr) war between the United States and Great Britain from 1812 to 1815 (p. 125)

waterway (wȯ′ tər wā′) lake, river, canal, or other body of water that provides a transportation route (p. 14)

Web site (web sīt) easily readable information displayed on the Internet (p. 248)

wigwam (wig′ wäm) hut made of bark, mats, or animal skins laid over a dome-shaped frame of bent poles (p. 72)

Works Progress Administration (wėrks prog′ res ad min′ ə strā′ shən) government program initiated during the Great Depression that provided unemployed people with paid work on useful projects (p. 237)

Index

Titles appear in *italic*. **Bold** page numbers indicate vocabulary definitions. An *m* before a page number indicates a map. The terms *See* and *See also* direct the reader to alternative entries.

Index

Index

Index

Credits

TEXT

DORLING KINDERSLEY (DK) is an international publishing company specializing in the creation of high quality reference content for books, CD-ROMs, online materials, and video. The hallmark of DK content is its unique combination of educational value and strong visual style. This combination allows DK to deliver appealing, accessible, and engaging educational content that delights children, parents, and teachers around the world. Scott Foresman is delighted to have been able to use selected extracts of DK content within this Scott Foresman Social Studies program.

16–17: from *Earth* by Susanna Van Rose, Copyright ©1994 by Dorling Kindersley Limited; 78–79: *Archaeology* by Dr. Jane McIntosh. Copyright ©2000 by Dorling Kindersley Limited; 147: *The Visual Timeline of Transportation* by Anthony Wilson. Copyright ©1995 by Dorling Kindersley Limited; 195: The *Visual Dictionary of the Civil War* by John Stanchak; Copyright ©2000 by Dorling Kindersley Limited; 240–241: *Inventions* by Lionel Bender. Copyright ©2000 by Dorling Kindersley Limited.

MAPS

MapQuest.com, Inc.

ILLUSTRATIONS

14 Gary Antonelli; 20, 21, 64, 65 James Kevin Torline; 43 Greg Harris; 57, 89 Eric Reese; 68 Christina Wald; 73, 80, 138 Derek Grinnell; 77 Hal Just; 87 Joe LeMonnier; 95, 201 Daniel DelValle; 104, 173 Guy Porfirio; 141 Peter Siu; 206 Ron Croci; 236 Drew-Brook Cormack; 292 Rodica Prato; R12 Leland Klanderman

PHOTOGRAPHS

Every effort has been made to secure permission and provide appropriate credit for photographic material. The publisher deeply regrets any omission and pledges to correct errors called to its attention in subsequent editions.

Unless otherwise acknowledged, all photographs are the property of Scott Foresman, a division of Pearson Education.

Photo locators denoted as follows: Top (T), Center (C), Bottom (B), Left (L), Right (R), Background (Bkgd)

Cover: (C) Corbis, (B) ©Gary W. Carter/Corbis, (Bkgd) ©Roy Ooms/Masterfile Corporation; **Endsheets:** ©2001 USPS. All Trademarks and copyrights used herein are properties of the United States Postal Service and are used under license to Scott Foresman. All rights reserved. **Front Matter:** iii Robert Marshall Root/Illinois Historical Art Project; ix Terry Farmer Photography, Inc.; v Chase Studio, Inc.; vi Jeffrey Grant/Illinois Historical Art Project; vii The Granger Collection; viii ©Hulton Archive/Getty Images; x (CR) ©Julie Habel/Corbis, (TL) ©Earth Imaging/Getty Images; xii Grant Heilman/Grant Heilman Photography; H4 (TR) David Young-Wolff/PhotoEdit, (TL) Chris Sheridan, (TC) ©Jeff Cadge/Getty Images, (BC) Jeff Greenberg/Unicorn Stock Photos, (BR) ©Peter Cade/Getty Images, (BL) Jeff Greenberg/Index Stock Imagery; H5 (TR) ©Stephen Wilkes/Getty Images, (TL) Bill Aron/PhotoEdit; H6 Jason Lindsey/Perceptive Visions; H7 (BL) AP/Wide World Photos, (BR) ©David Muench/Corbis; H8 ©Earth Imaging/Getty Images; H17 ©David Young-Wolff/Getty Images; **Unit 1:** 1 Robert Marshall Root/Illinois Historical Art Project; 2 Robert Marshall Root/Illinois Historical Art Project; 3 ©David Muench/Corbis; 4 (CR) Photo courtesy Morton Salt, A Rohm and Haas Company/Morton Salt, (CL) Corbis, (R) Illinois State Historical Society, (TL) "Detail image" of John Deere Carries New Plow to Test Site by Walter Haskell Hinton, oil on canvas, 11x16 inches/Courtesy of the John Deere Art Collection; 5 (L) Office of the Governor, State of Illinois, (R) WGN TV; 7 Robert Marshall Root/Illinois Historical Art Project; 8 (T) ©AFP/Corbis, (B) Jim Wark/Lonely Planet Images; 10 ©AFP/Corbis; 12 J. Lighter/Photo Researchers, Inc.; 13 ©David Muench/Corbis; 16 Bryan and Cherry Alexander Photography; 17 (TL, C, TR) ©Dorling Kindersley, (BL) Colin Keates/Natural History Museum/©Dorling Kindersley, (BR) Clive Streeter/©Dorling Kindersley; 18 ©Layne Kennedy/Corbis; 19 Jim Wark/Lonely Planet Images; 20 Getty Images; 21 (C) Getty Images, (BC) ©Dorling Kindersley; 22 Getty Images; 23 (Bkgd) ©Richard Corey/Getty Images, (BR) WGN TV, (C) Corbis; 24 David Ulmer/Stock Boston; 27 Getty

Images; 28 (T) Churchill and Klehr, (B) ©Richard Hamilton Smith/Corbis; 30 Jason Lindsey/Perceptive Visions; 32 Churchill and Klehr; 33 (TR) Jason Lindsey/Perceptive Visions, (BL) Robert Shaw Photography/Perceptive Visions; 34 (CR) David R. Frazier/Folio Inc., (TR) Vic Bider/PhotoEdit, (TL) Nels Akerlund Collection/Tinker Swiss Cottage Museum/Getty Images, (TC) ©Jerry Driendl/Getty Images; 35 Churchill and Klehr; 36 (TL) ©Wallace Kirkland/Getty Images, (Bkgd) Getty Images, (BR) "Detail image" of John Deere Carries New Plow to Test Site by Walter Haskell Hinton, oil on canvas, 11x16 inches/Courtesy of the John Deere Art Collection; 37 (CR) ©Layne Kennedy/Corbis, (B) ©Yann Layma/Getty Images; 38 Jim Strawser/Grant Heilman Photography; 40 ©Gunter Marx Photography/Corbis; 41 ©David Muench/Corbis; 42 ©Richard Hamilton/Corbis; 44 Metropolis Chamber of Commerce; 45 Corbis; 46 ©Gunter Marx Photography/Corbis; 47 Jim Strawser/Grant Heilman Photography; 48 ©Layne Kennedy/Corbis; 49 Joe McDonald/Visuals Unlimited; **Unit 2:** 53 Chase Studio, Inc.; 56 (CL) North Wind Picture Archives, (CR) The Granger Collection, (L) Corbis; 57 (TC) The Granger Collection, (TR) 2001 Shyers Photography/Peoria Tribe of Indians of Oklahoma; 59 Chase Studio, Inc.; 60 William Iseminger/Cahokia Mounds Historic Site; 64 Illinois State Museum; 66 (BL) William Iseminger/Cahokia Mounds Historic Site, (Inset) Cahokia Mounds Historic Site; 70 Illinois State Museum; 71 Carnegie Museum of Art, Pittsburgh; 74 George Catlin/Mary Evans Picture Library; 75 (Bkgd, C) Peoria Tribe of Indians of Oklahoma, (BR) 2001 Shyers Photography/Peoria Tribe of Indians of Oklahoma; 76 Corbis; 77 Peoria Tribe of Indians of Oklahoma; 78 British Museum/©Dorling Kindersley; 79 (BR, CR, BL) British Museum/©Dorling Kindersley, (TR) British Museum Copyright - Permission of Jonathan Tubb/©Dorling Kindersley; 82 (T) Réunion des Musées Nationaux/Art Resource, (C) Frederic Remington/The Granger Collection, (B) Corbis; 84 Phil Martin Photography; 85 Réunion des Musées Nationaux/Art Resource; 86 (BR, Inset, L) ©Texas Historical Commission, (C) The Granger Collection; 89 Stock Montage Inc.; 90 ©Photodisc/Getty Images; 91 The Granger Collection; 92 Jean Leon Gerome Ferris/SuperStock; 94 (BL) Jean Leon Gerome Ferris/SuperStock, (BR) Frederic Remington/The Granger Collection; 95 (TR) Laura Dwight, (TL) Michael Newman/PhotoEdit, (CR) Laura Dwight, (BL) Myrleen Ferguson Cate/PhotoEdit; 96 ©Hulton Archives/Getty Images; 97 (CL) ©Dorling Kindersley, (C) Courtesy of The Boston Society/Old State House, (CR) The Granger Collection; 98 (B) Jean Leone Gerome Ferris/SuperStock, (R) SuperStock; 99 Gallery of the Republic; 100 Illinois State Historical Society; 101 (CR) The Granger Collection, (BR) George Rogers Clark National Historic Park; 102 North Wind Picture Archives; 103 George Rogers Clark National Historic Park; **Unit 3:** 109 Jeffrey Grant/Illinois Historical Art Project; 110 Jeffrey Grant/Illinois Historical Art Project; 112 (R) Charles Bird King/The Granger Collection, (CR, CL, L) Illinois State Historical Society; 113 (CL) Illinois State Historical Society, (C) Wisconsin Historical Society, (CR) The Granger Collection; 115 Jeffrey Grant/Illinois Historical Art Project; 116 (TC) Illinois State Historical Society, (B) Stock Montage Inc.; 118 ©Hulton Archive/Getty Images; 119 University of Illinois at Chicago; 120 Getty Images; 121 American President Thomas Jefferson in an oil painting by nineteenth century painter Rembrandt Peale./The Granger Collection; 124 David Weintraub/Stock Boston; 125 (BC) Stock Montage Inc., (CR) ©Russell Ingram//Corbis; 127 Illinois State Historical Society; 128 (TL) Illinois State Historical Society, (CL) Terry Farmer Photography, Inc.; 129 James Shaffer/PhotoEdit; 130 David Weintraub/Stock Boston; 132 (T) North Wind Picture Archives, (B) ©The Bridgeman Art Library/Getty Images; 134 The Granger Collection; 136 (CR, BL) ©Dorling Kindersley, (BR) Runk/Schoenberger/Grant Heilman Photography; 137 (B) George Catlin/Smithsonian American Art Museum, Washington DC/Art Resource, NY, (T) North Wind Picture Archives; 139 North Wind Picture Archives; 140 (Bkgd) North Wind Picture Archives, (L, CL) Wisconsin Historical Society; 141 (CL) Michael Rutherford/SuperStock, (B) Robert Frerck/Woodfin Camp & Associates, (BR) Richard Cummins/Viesti Collection, Inc., (CR) Dennis MacDonald/PhotoEdit; 142 Corbis; 143 (T) The Granger Collection, (Inset) North Wind Picture Archives; 144 The Granger Collection; 146 ©The Bridgeman Art Library/Getty Images; 147 (CL) Corbis, (CR) Science Museum/©Dorling Kindersley, (B) ©Dorling Kindersley, (TR) ©Bettmann/Corbis; 150 Charles Bird King/The Granger Collection; 152 The New York Public Library/Art Resource; **Unit 4:** 157 The Granger

Credits

Collection; 158 The Granger Collection; 160 (L, R) The Granger Collection, (CL) Tom McHugh/Photo Researchers, Inc., (CR) Illinois State Historical Society; 161 (R) The Granger Collection, (C) Chicago Historical Society, (L) Peoria Public Library; 163 The Granger Collection; 164 (T) Illinois State Historical Society, (B) Robert Marshal Root/Illinois State Historical Society; 166 (BL) ©Adam Woolfitt/Corbis, (CR) Bridgeman Art Library; 168 Loren Drummond; 169 Illinois State Historical Society; 170 The Granger Collection; 171 ©Charles Gupton/Corbis; 172 Robert Marshal Root/Illinois State Historical Society; 174 Corbis; 175 (Inset) ©Kelly-Mooney Photography/Corbis, (BR) The Granger Collection, (C) Matt Hucke; 177 PictureHistory; 178 (CL) Robert Marshal Root/Illinois State Historical Society, (BR) The Granger Collection; 180 (T) The Granger Collection, (B) Illinois State Historical Society; 182 Chicago Historical Society; 183 The Granger Collection; 184 (T) The Granger Collection, (B) E. Sachse and Company/Chicago Historical Society; 186 National Portrait Gallery, Smithsonian Institution/Art Resource, NY; 187 Getty Images; 188 Kurz & Allison/The Granger Collection; 189 (CR) Illinois State Historical Society, (B) Rock Island Arsenal; 190 (BR) Flesh Public Library and Museum, (CR) Corbis, (BL) Robert W. Parvin; 191 (BR) Appomattox Court House/The National Park Service, (BL) Peoria Public Library; 192 PictureHistory; 193 (Bkgd) Corbis, (CR) Chicago Historical Society, (CL) Knox College Special Collections; 194 (B) The Granger Collection, (TR) Corbis; 195 (TR, CR, CL, C) Confederate Memorial Hall/©Dorling Kindersley, (B) Corbis; 196 The Granger Collection; 197 Getty Images; 198 The Granger Collection; 201 (TR) Illinois State Historical Society, (TL) Mark C. Burnett/Stock Boston; **Unit 5:** 203 ©Hulton Archive/Getty Images; 204 ©Hulton Archive/Getty Images; 206 (L) Corbis, (CR) The Granger Collection, (R) Illinois State Historical Library; 207 (L) Brown Brothers, (CL, CR) Corbis, (R) NASA; 209 ©Hulton Archive/Getty Images; 210 (T) North Wind Picture Archives, (B) Illinois State University Archives; 212 The Granger Collection; 214 (BR, BL) North Wind Picture Archives, (B) Corbis; 215 (TL) The Granger Collection, (R) Michael Newman/PhotoEdit; 216 The Granger Collection; 217 North Wind Picture Archives; 218 (Bkgd) ©Hulton Archive/Getty Images, (B) Collection of Immigrant City Archives, Lawrence, Massachusetts; 219 (C) Indiana State Library, (T) Schlesinger Library, Radcliffe Institute, Harvard University, (B) Brown Brothers; 220 North Wind Picture Archives; 223 (B) Illinois State Historical Society, (C) ©Hulton Archive/Getty Images, (CL, CR) Corbis; 224 (BL) The Granger Collection, (T) Illinois State University Archives; 225 Chicago Historical Society; 226 ©Hulton Archive/Getty Images; 227 (Bkgd, BR) Corbis, (C) Gilai Collectibles; 228 ©Bettmann/Corbis; 229 Aaron Haupt/Stock Boston; 230 The Granger Collection; 232 (T) Coles County Historical Society, (B) Terry Farmer Photography, Inc.; 234 ©Swim Ink/Corbis; 235 (BL) Coles County Historical Society, (CR) The Granger Collection; 236 Corbis; 237 (T) ©Underwood & Underwood/Corbis, (B) Corbis; 238 Chicago Historical Society; 239 Chicago Historical Society; 240 (B) Wright State University Library, (TR) Science Museum/©Dorling Kindersley; 241 (TL, C) Science Museum, London/©Dorling Kindersley, (TR) Gaslight Ad

Archives, Commack NY; 243 (Bkgd) Corbis, (BL) Bob Adelma/©Magnum Photos, (BC) Corbis, (TR) Eli Reed Dist./©Magnum Photos ; 244 Terry Farmer Photography, Inc.; 247 (Bkgd) ©Nasa/Roger Ressmeyer/Corbis, (R) NASA, (C) Getty Images; 248 (C) Bell & Howell Company, (B) David Young-Wolff/PhotoEdit; 250 Corbis; 252 Jacob Lawrence, "The Migration of the Negro Panel No. 23," 1940-1941. Acquired 1942/The Phillips Collection, Washington, D.C.; 255 (B) Terry Farmer Photography, Inc., (TR) ©Underwood & Underwood/Corbis, (L) Chicago Historical Society, (Bkgd) Corbis; **Unit 6:** 257 Terry Farmer Photography, Inc.; 258 ©Richard Cummins/Corbis; 259 Terry Farmer Photography, Inc.; 260 (L) The Granger Collection, (CL) Getty Images, (CR) Corbis, (R) Library of Congress; 261 (CR) AP/Wide World Photos, (L) U.S. Department of Defense, (CL) AP/Wide World Photos, (R) Theresa Gutierrez/ABC Channel 7 Chicago; 263 ©Richard Cummins/Corbis; 264 (T) Paul Conklin/PhotoEdit, (B) Access Living; 266 Paul Conklin/PhotoEdit; 267 AP/Wide World Photos; 269 (C) ©Doris De Witt/Getty Images, (CR) Steve Gorton/©Dorling Kindersley, (CL) AP/Wide World Photos, (TR) One Mile Up, Inc.; 271 AP/Wide World Photos; 272 (Bkgd) Dennis Brack/Black Star, (BL) U.S. Department of Defense, (C) Corbis; 273 (BR) Getty Images, (CL) Terry Farmer Photography, Inc., (BL) AP/Wide World Photos, (CR) Charles Rex Arbogast/AP/Wide World Photos; 276 ©Marc PoKempner/Getty Images; 277 (TC) Illinois State Historical Society, (TR) Chicago Historical Society; 278 Getty Images; 279 Access Living; 280 Smithsonian Institution; 281 Smithsonian Institution282 Access Living283 Myrleen Ferguson/PhotoEdit; 284 (BR) The Granger Collection, (CL) ©Marc PoKempner/Getty Images; 286 (B) AP/Wide World Photos, (T) ©2001 Bob Sacha; 288 Courtesy of Deere & Company; 289 digitalvisiononline.com; 290 ©Dave G. Houser/Corbis; 291 (T) ©Bettmann/Corbis, (C) Hitachi America, Ltd., (Inset) Greg Fiume/IPN/Aurora & Quanta Productions; 293 ©2001 Bob Sacha; 296 ©Kelly-Mooney Photography/Corbis; 297 (CL) AP/Wide World Photos, (B) Cathy Melloan/PhotoEdit; 298 Corbis; 299 (Bkgd) Neal Slavin/SuperStock, (BR) Theresa Gutierrez/ABC Channel 7 Chicago, (C) Getty Images; 300 (TR) Courtesy of Deere & Company, (CR) Corbis; 302 ©Harald Sund/Getty Images; 305 Jonathan Nourok/PhotoEdit; **Back Matter:** R1 ©Earth Imaging/Getty Images; R2 ©Earth Imaging/Getty Images; R18 Bob Daemmrich/Daemmrich Photography; R24 (BL) Corbis, (TC) Illinois State Historical Library, (BR) AP/Wide World Photos, (TR) Office of the Governor, State of Illinois, (TL, BL) Illinois State Historical Society, (BR) ©Bettmann/Corbis; R25 (B) Getty Images, (TL) The Granger Collection, (TR, TC) Corbis, (BL) Charles Bird King/The Granger Collection; R26 (TR) Chase Studio, Inc., (TL) Cahokia Mounds Historic Site, (BR) The Granger Collection, New York, (BL) Illinois State Museum; R27 (BC) Charles Bird King/The Granger Collection, (TL) Frederic Remington/The Granger Collection, (BL) SuperStock, (TR) North Wind Picture Archives, (BR) National Portrait Gallery, Smithsonian Institution/Art Resource, NY; R28 (TL) The Granger Collection, (BR, TC) Corbis, (BL) The Granger Collection, (TR) ©Bettmann/Corbis

MICHIGAN

THE SPIRIT OF THE LAND

Text by KATHY-JO WARGIN

Photographs by ED WARGIN

VOYAGEUR PRESS

page one
Au Sable Lighthouse on Lake
Superior

pages two-three
A misty morning on the Sturgeon
River

Edited by Danielle J. Ibister and Michael Dregni
Designed by Kristy Tucker
Printed in Hong Kong

99   00   01   02   03   5   4   3   2   1

Library of Congress Cataloging-in-Publication Data

Wargin, Kathy-jo.
    Michigan : the spirit of the land / text by Kathy-jo Wargin ; photography by
Ed Wargin.
        p.   cm.
    ISBN 0-89658-381-3
    1. Michigan—Pictorial works. 2. Michigan—Description and travel.
    I. Wargin, Ed. II. Title.
    F567.W37 1999
    977.4—dc21   98-45251
                                                               CIP

ISBN 0-89658-381-3

Distributed in Canada by Raincoast Books,
8680 Cambie Street, Vancouver, B.C. V6P 6M9

Published by Voyageur Press, Inc.
123 North Second Street, P.O. Box 338, Stillwater, MN 55082 U.S.A.
651-430-2210, fax 651-430-2211

Educators, fundraisers, premium and gift buyers, publicists, and marketing managers:
Looking for creative products and new sales ideas? Voyageur Press books are available
at special discounts when purchased in quantities, and special editions can be created
to your specifications. For details contact the marketing department at 800-888-9653.

Sunrise over Presque Isle Harbor

ACKNOWLEDGMENTS

We would like to express sincere appreciation to Danielle Ibister and Michael Dregni, as well as the rest of the staff at Voyageur Press, for their creative suggestions and assistance in editing this book; Mike Lussier of AGX Imaging Labs in Sault Ste. Marie, Michigan; Michigan State Parks; and to all of the wonderful, helpful people we met along the way. In addition, we would like to thank the Wallins and Bill Altier for watching over the homestead as we came and went—you are the best neighbors! And special thanks to the David Harwood and Jim Kelly families for all of their help and support in the coordination of this project. A final thank you to Rodney Rascona.
—Ed and Kathy-jo Wargin

DEDICATIONS

To Randy Bowen, Tom White, Bob King, and Richard Hamilton Smith, on behalf of their dedication and mentoring, which allowed me to follow my dreams. —Ed Wargin

To Carol Nelson Kelly, superb mother and friend. You are spirit in every sense of the word. And always, to our son Jake Peter Wargin, the happy traveler. You are our spirit. —Ed and Kathy-jo Wargin

above
Holland Lighthouse on Lake Michigan during February

overleaf
A beachhead on Lake Michigan's north shore

CONTENTS

INTRODUCTION

the

SPIRIT

of the LAND

Munising Creek waterfall in the Pictured Rocks
National Lakeshore

"IF YOU SEEK a pleasant peninsula, look about you." The phrase is the motto of the state of Michigan—*Si quaeris peninsulam amoenam circumspice*—and the words ring true. Look about you at the wild celebration of shores and the sweet communion of rivers. Look about you at the unpredictable mountains and riotous dunes. Look about you at the lakes that beckon with historical, haunting beauty. Look about you at the rivers and streams that baptize the earth with warmth and grace.

As you look, be prepared to discover the soul of the Great Lakes unfolding before you. Embedded within the shores of the world's largest freshwater system, Michigan is a state defined by water and governed by nature. Indeed, the state's name is derived from the Native American name *michi gama*, which means "big lake." Look about you and be touched by a land that brings forth abundant and generous pleasures.

This book is for those who seek Michigan and the spirit of the land.

It is in this place of freshwater seas that discovery and regeneration unfold in harmony. The thick, rich forests of the Upper Peninsula come alive with stories of indigenous tribes, adventurous explorers, and colorful voyageurs. The vigorous, rocky outcroppings of the Keweenaw tell tales about precious ore that waits beneath the ground, and the brilliantly hued cliffs of Pictured Rocks National Lakeshore arouse echoes of disbelief from those who see them for the first time.

right, top
Ice slabs lay along Cozy Point on
Lake Michigan

right, bottom
Ice patterns on a window of a home
along Lake Michigan's north shore

opposite
A lone tree in the clutches of winter
near Petoskey

Dew-laden autumn bulrushes near
Crystal Lake

It is a place that steals your heart while soothing your mind. More than three thousand miles of shore line the state, and the interior of the Lower Peninsula is laced by waterways that have inspired commerce and trade for hundreds of years. The rivers flowing into Saginaw Bay carried the lumber that built our nation's homes and factories. On the west coast, the ever loyal Sleeping Bear rests peacefully upon the high dunes, calling her cubs to shore as the wind blows and blows.

The history of this place is about the truth of exploration, the brutality of loss, the magic of legends, and the innocence of joy. It is more than a story about the impact of nature upon itself and the splendor one state can bestow. Michigan is a story that fills the soul with the smell of pine and the sweetness of water—and it is yours if you look about you.

Horsetail grass paints the sky north
of Pontiac

Wild iris along the wet shores of
Gros Cap on Lake Michigan

CHAPTER 1

the NORTHWEST COAST

Waugoshance Point in Wilderness State Park

WITH PINK LADY'S slippers peeking out of deep forests and Petoskey stones clattering to the crash of high waves, the northwestern coast of Michigan's Lower Peninsula is filled with delights. This jagged line of bays and peninsulas is alive with memories of Michigan's past and the ghosts of Native Americans, British explorers, cherry farmers, and weathered fishermen.

The spirit of this land is like a soul liberated, left to drift affably upon the breeze, fly madly about in forests where alluring lady's slippers tread, or roll through orchards where cherry blossoms ripple. This spirit surges with the swells of Lake Michigan, resonates in the beat of the wind, and echoes in the hearts of its guests forever.

above
Sunrays breaking through at
Fisherman's Island State Park

right
Fisherman's Island State Park

There is an enchanting story about the origin of the lady's slipper.

Long, long ago, a young Indian woman left her village in the depths of winter in the hope of saving her people, who were besieged by a devastating illness. The woman set out for a far-off village that had medicine to cure them. She ran through the frozen forest, desperate and exhausted, until she finally reached the camp and secured the magic tonic.

She returned through the same forest, her body tiring and her mind growing feverish. She came at last to her village, and the medicine saved her people.

It was too late for the young woman, however. The journey had weakened her, and the illness raged through her body.

As she lay dying, her family and friends gathered around her. They decorated her moccasins with the most beautiful bead- and quillwork ever seen, to ensure that her journey into the afterlife would be filled with honor and dignity. Then, as her spirit slowly slipped from her body, the moccasins she wore became glorious, delicate flowers . . . lady's slippers.

There are three varieties of lady's slippers—pink, yellow, and showy—in the thirty-acre Thorne Swift Nature Preserve. The showy lady's slipper, *Cypripedium reginae*, is the most stunning of the species, displaying the true glory of the orchid family. Its leafy stalk bears large flowers with pouchlike petals, often tinted with deep pink or purple veins. As the tallest of northern native orchids—growing up to three feet tall—it thrives in cool, moist forest conditions, such as the lowlands of Thorne Swift along the Lake Michigan shore, where it blooms from May until August.

above
Pink Lady's Slipper

below, left
Yellow Lady's Slipper

opposite
Showy Lady's Slipper

21

If British trader and adventurer Alexander Henry were still alive, he would undoubtedly remember Fox Point.

The name "Fox Point" is a derivative of the Anishinaabe Ojibwe word *waugoshance* or *waugosh*, which means "fox." This area, once known as Fox Point and now called Waugoshance, is a quiet, marshy extension of land reaching into Lake Michigan and the spot where Henry barely escaped with his life.

Henry had been taken prisoner by the Ojibwe after they overran Fort Michilimackinac in 1763. Henry, along with three other English prisoners, was being transported by canoe from Mackinac to Beaver Island. Traveling westward, the Ojibwe stayed near the shore to avoid a thick fog that enveloped the straits for miles. As they glided through the waters, the ecstatic Ojibwe let out war whoops, and near Fox Point, they suddenly heard a war whoop returned from shore. When the Ojibwe and their captives neared the shore to speak with the Ottawa Indian who had called to them, a clutch of Ottawa leaped out of their hiding places and captured the British prisoners for themselves.

Things looked grim for Henry and the three others, but the Ottawa eventually took them to Montréal to set them free. Henry would live on to write and publish several narratives about his exploits as a trader during Michigan's lively fur era.

The area now known as Wilderness State Park was once home to Native Americans, who prized the area as hunting and fishing grounds. Here, the Ottawa and Ojibwe used their nets and spears to fish for the great Mackinaw trout.

The eight-thousand-acre park remains much as it once was, except for the addition of roads and facilities. It is still a place where fish school, where wild orchids bloom in early summer, where red fox haunt the icy shores in winter, and where the footprints of our ancestors seem to linger in the rushes.

Waugoshance Point in Wilderness State Park

Petoskey Stones prevail for those
who can spot them

The waves here create a unique sound as they push against the stone-laden shore. It's not the slap of the water striking the shore but the rattling sound that draws you in. It happens when a big wave rolls upon the beach, then quickly retreats back into the lake. It happens when the wind is high and the current is strong. That shivering, quaking, trembling rattle is the sound of millions of tiny, smooth, round stones rolling along the shoreline with every push of the waves.

When you hear it, you will be mesmerized by the sound and never forget it. You will hear it again and again in your mind. If you drop a button into a glass jar, or if you roll some marbles around in a tin cup, you will hear those stones, and you will smell the water once more.

Shorelines padded with such small, smooth stones are common and rather ordinary. But the delightful percussion the waves and the stones produce is far less common and in no way ordinary.

In 1965, Michigan became the first state to adopt a fossil as its state stone. The Petoskey Stone, *Hexagonaria percarinata*, is characterized by a honeycomb pattern that is distinguishable when the stone is wet. As a dry, unpolished stone, it is unremarkable in appearance, looking much like any typical round, gray stone that beds itself into shorelines and ditches.

Petoskey Stones were formed more than 350 million years ago when warm, shallow Devonian seas covered most of what is now Michigan. These warm waters gave birth to tropical formations such as coral. The Petoskey Stone is actually a fossilized colony coral. When it was alive, the corallite's soft tissue, called the polyp, secreted a limey substance that eventually hardened into a corallite skeleton that kept the polyp from being buried alive amidst the sea's bottom debris. Over time, many corallites would combine to form a coral "colony." Eventually, the movement of land and water compressed the coral colony and filled it with minerals. During the Pleistocene Age, some two million years ago, this stone was broken up and distributed through the Grand Traverse Bay region by slow-moving glaciers.

Although *Hexagonaria* fossils can be found in other sites around the world, this specific type of fossil, *percarinata*, can only be found in the Traverse Bay region.

above and opposite
Blooming cherry trees along Old
Mission Peninsula

A ceremonial breeze waltzes through a cherry orchard in bloom, inviting the blossoms to dance. In the wake of the wind, calico skirts and cotton blouses flutter, and dark woolen caps are left slightly askew.

It's May 1926, and the Reverend David Moore and his congregation are standing in prayer on the hillside of Old Mission Peninsula. These orchards provide them with their livelihood, but the days leading up to the harvest are always filled with uncertainty. The farmers gather on the hillside with their families, sweethearts, and friends to affirm their faith, hope, and friendship. With folded hands and lowered heads, they listen to the invocation, and the delicate blossoms of the orchard are blessed.

The Blessings of the Blossoms was a simple service that preceded the annual cherry harvest, and eventually lead to the creation of the National Cherry Festival.

The Old Mission Peninsula has long been fertile land for fruit such as cherries and grapes. The light soils of the long, narrow drumlin fields— fields made by glacial drift—are well drained. Its temperate zone and location on the forty-fifth parallel protect the peninsula from late frost. Its crops benefit from a long growing season that ranges from 110 days inland to 150 days closer to the Lake Michigan shore.

Presbyterian Reverend Peter Dougherty arrived at Old Mission in 1839 with fellow missionary Reverend John Fleming, both of whom had been sent from Mackinac to establish a mission. Upon his arrival, Reverend Dougherty found apple trees growing in the thin soil of the peninsula. He discovered that they were the remnants of trees planted by Native Americans. With his encouragement, more fruit trees were planted, and by 1905, cherry orchards were an integral part of the Traverse Bay farming community.

Today, Michigan leads the nation in cherry production. The state grows nearly 75 percent of the tart cherries that are canned and used for pies and preserves. Michigan's smaller production of sweet cherries, however, is its true source of fame.

The sweaty docks of Fishtown still carry the smell of fresh fish, even though the peak of the fishing era ended more than fifty years ago. In the late 1800s, as families began to settle in the cozy harbor town of Leland, the Carp River and its harbor were recognized for the excellent protection they provided from the bigger lake. Soon settlers began fishing the waters with their Mackinaw boats—small, single-mast sailboats that bounced along the waves. They fished for whitefish and trout, spreading their gillnets throughout the harbor before sunrise. The fish were used to feed their families and the growing community of Leland.

above
Drying fishnets in Leland's Fishtown

bottom, left
A Lake Michigan boatslip in Leland

opposite
Fish nets at rest in Leland's Fishtown

When the railroad was developed, the demand to ship fish became apparent, and soon dark, heavy barrels of salted whitefish and trout were making their way from Leland to Chicago and Detroit. During the heyday of the fishing era in the 1930s, there were eight fishing operations in Leland; the harbor also supported hoards of transient fishermen.

During the 1940s and 1950s, the sea lamprey invaded the area and eliminated most of the area's whitefish and trout, and commercial fishing operations dwindled.

Today, the worn shanties of the fishermen and their families reflect in the waters of Lake Michigan. Quiet and weathered, they are mirror images of the fishermen who left them behind.

GLEN HAVEN CANNERY

The Glen Haven cannery processed fruit in the early 1900s; today it is used to house historic boats. Within its walls are rowboats and lifeboats, as well as other artifacts that illustrate the maritime past of Sleeping Bear Bay.

During the late 1800s and early 1900s, steamboats making their way to Chicago frequently stopped at Glen Haven in Sleeping Bear Bay to replenish their wood supply. The area was known as a good place for passengers to eat a meal or find an overnight resting place while the ship's captain supervised the restocking of the vessel's supplies and food.

above and left
Glen Haven Canning Company Boat Museum

Jack-in-the-Pulpit

Wildflowers are miracles of color. The hues can be scientifically explained as combinations of nutrients and chlorophyll—but when you look closely, when you lose yourself in the velvet-soft skin of a petal or the intricate details of a stem, it is difficult to grasp their complexity.

The petals of the Indian Turnip hide beneath the plant's own large leaves, masking the plant amidst the damp woods where it grows in abundance. One of the many wildflowers of the Grand Traverse region, the Indian turnip (*Arisaema triphyllum*) is also known as the "Jack-in-the-Pulpit," because its bent hood envelops its spadix, or "Jack." The plant supports clusters of shiny red berries in late summer and fall.

above
Hairy Vetchs sway gently in the summer winds

opposite
Marsh marigold

CHAPTER 2

the DUNE COAST

Grasses sway atop Sleeping Bear Dunes
National Lakeshore

T HE SANDY DUNES that wrap Lake Michigan's eastern shore swirl in the wind, burying entire forests and giving rise to mythical stories. With Sleeping Bear Dune rising above the shoreline, the beckoning spires of the ghost forests, and marram grass fluttering in the wind, the coastal dunes are a place that inspires intense introspection. It is a place where raw energy cannot be governed or captured. As the wind continually shifts, footprints disappear and the sand is drawn and twisted into animate life forms.

Sleeping Bear Dunes National Lakeshore

Sometimes, the greatest discoveries are not found in the face of life, but rather, in its folds.

Crowning the ridges and swales of the southern Lake Michigan plain are the sands that revealed a scientific breakthrough.

Nearly a hundred years ago, University of Chicago Professor Henry Chandler Cowles set out to study the relationship between plants and their environment. He found the best laboratory for his studies to be the ecosystem formed by the southern rim of Lake Michigan. In this narrow band of sand dunes, created nearly 4,500 years ago in the Nipissing Age, he identified the concept of plant succession. In all its glory and resulting controversy, Cowles discovered a new area of scientific study, ecology.

In the late 1800s, dunes areas such as this were considered worthless. But a man named E. K. Warren of Three Oaks, Michigan, had the foresight to purchased 250 acres of lakeshore and donated it to the state. Now, these "barren" dunes are protected as Warren Dunes State Park, and generations to come will be able to enjoy the fascinating diversity of life that thrives along the lake plain.

Warren Dunes State Park

A ghost forest among the dunes at
Warren Dunes State Park

Sleeping Bear Dunes ghost forest

THE GHOST FORESTS

Brittle spires of beech trees beckon like bony fingers, luring you into the ghost forests that inhabit the shoreline of the Sleeping Bear Dunes National Lakeshore.

Along these sandy shores, vital, breathing ecosystems are transformed into ghost forests when tumbling mounds of sand migrate with the wind, burying every tree, shoot, wildflower, and shrub in their path. Suffocated by the heavy shroud of sand, the forest dies.

As time passes, the sand whirls away, leaving behind these stark remnants of its passage, reminders of the power of nature.

above
Sleeping Bear Dunes ghost forest

opposite
Pyramid Point ghost forest

"Big Red" was once a simple wood tower lighthouse that focused its light upon Lake Michigan during the late 1800s. Today, it is a stronger, more modern version of its original self, yet its function remains the same: to bring travelers home safely.

Holland Lighthouse

A lone tree lives on in Silver Lake
State Park's dune preserve area

A waxing moon fills Silver Lake with brilliant reflections. In the distance, eerie dunes recreate themselves beneath the moonlight.

These dunes are *alive*.

The bleak dunescape of Silver Lake State Park is an ecosystem in perpetual motion. The smaller, tumbling mounds are classified as "live" dunes, because they are constantly moving with the wind. Every breeze reshapes and redefines the topography, exhibiting the artistry of the regional air currents.

Looking out over this desert landscape, it is difficult to imagine Silver Lake as the abundant forest it once was. The Silver Lake region was ripe with woods, but like much of Michigan, the timber was logged in the late 1800s, leaving the area barren and vulnerable to erosion.

Fortunately, hardy grasses took root and stabilized the exposed ground. As the wind blew through the years, mounds of sand collected around the vegetation, creating dune after dune. Once stabilized, a sand dune can host several types of vegetation, such as bearberry and bluestem. Most common, however, are the fluttering wisps of marram grasses, which seem to thrive in this otherwise desolate environment.

The landscape of Silver Lake is intertwined in life, death, and rebirth.

above
Little Sable Point Lighthouse at
Silver Lake State Park

below, left
Silver Lake State Park

Lake Michigan is the only one of the Great Lakes that lies entirely within the boundaries of the United States. Connected to Lake Huron via the Straits of Mackinac, it is part of the St. Lawrence Seaway and is thus an integral link in international commerce. The third largest of the Great Lakes, it is 307 miles in length and about 900 feet at its deepest point.

above
A laker breaks through the morning light near Manitou Island

opposite
Light plays along Lake Michigan near Sleeping Bear Dunes

There is a legend that has been passed down through the ages about the sandy dark mound known as the Sleeping Bear Dune.

The legend tells us that long ago, in eastern Wisconsin, a mother bear and her two cubs were desperate to escape a raging forest fire. The mother urged her cubs to follow her into Lake Michigan, where she proceeded to swim across the mighty lake.

When they became tired and weak, the mother bear fiercely urged her cubs on. But the lake was large, and the peril was great. When Mother Bear reached the other side, she saw that her beloved cubs were not behind her.

In her sorrow, she climbed to the top of the highest dune so she could look out over the wide, deep waters. It was there on that dune, perched high above the water, that Mother Bear laid down sadly and slipped into eternal slumber. She sleeps there still, waiting for her cubs to reach the shore.

The actual Sleeping Bear Dune, a large, darkened area of sand and vegetation that rests high above the water's edge, is about two thousand years old. Classified as a perched dune—or a dune that rests upon a plateau above a lake—it stands 103 feet above the lakeshore.

At the dawn of the 1900s, the dune was estimated to be almost 235 feet high. Major wave action has since cut away at the base of the plateau, causing portions to tumble down the hill. Wind has also eroded the dune and destroyed its protective plant cover. Someday, the dune will disappear from the landscape. When it does, only its legends and descriptions from the Native Americans, voyageurs, fishermen, and merchant seamen who have passed this way will remain.

The Sleeping Bear Dunes National Lakeshore is a complex ecosystem of towering sand dunes, beech-and-maple forests, and small inland lakes. The park encompasses more than thirty-five miles of Lake Michigan shoreline, and includes the North and South Manitou Islands.

South Manitou Island, Sleeping Bear Dunes

CHAPTER 3

the HEARTLAND

Snow sparkles on tree tops at the Chippewa
Nature Center

Some 150 years ago, farmers drained southern Michigan's wetlands, converting them to farmland and leaving only scattered pockets of a once-lush ecosystem of prairies, savannas, and marshes. The remnants of this heartland prairie are akin to the pieces of an old patchwork quilt—every piece has its own story, every stitch has its own tale.

Black Ash Swamp, the Kalamazoo Interlobate, and the Grand Ledges are all portions of this patchwork of destruction and survival. These varied segments of tallgrass prairie, lowlands, valleys, and forested outcroppings define Michigan's heartland. They host youthful flowers emerging through sweet, limber grasses; narrow, lively streams embroidering gentle hills and valleys; and mature oaks lining the edges of open, sunlit grasslands.

above
A single daisy competes with the Hawkweed near Monroe

opposite
Maple leaves dance in the sky along the Huron River in Ann Arbor

When European settlers arrived in southern Michigan nearly two hundred years ago, they encountered a vast tallgrass prairie covered with undulating ribbons of bluestems and sunflowers. The wide open grasslands were choice building sites for the newcomers. Here, amidst the savannas and marshes, they built homesteads and began new lives. Some would fish, many more would begin to work the land.

The coming of these eager immigrants had a tremendous impact upon the rolling landscape. They drained the rich wet prairies and converted them to farmland. Their efforts were well rewarded. The soil was fertile, the growing season warm and long, and the business of agriculture blossomed beyond all boundaries. By the mid 1800s, long, straight rows of farm crops had redefined the land, virtually eliminating all but a few remnants of the original prairie.

Before agricultural conversion, there were more than 158,000 acres of rich tallgrass prairie. Today, only a little more than 1,000 acres remain, scattered throughout southern Michigan. These little pockets of history often go unnoticed by the casual observer, but as long as the sun penetrates the soil and forests do not close around them, these jewels of the earth will continue to shine.

above
Farm tools hang in a barn in Huron County

opposite
A June storm at sunset in Sanilac County

In a cathedral of stone, chickadees and robins attend vespers while whitetailed deer act as solitary ushers, greeting the dusk with silent footsteps and quiet breath. The Grand Ledges are proof that spirit takes root within all living creatures.

These 270-million-year-old outcroppings were formed by the Grand River. The glacial outwash channel created a till plain that rose nearly two hundred feet above the riverbed, inspiring awe in all who congregate here.

With ceremony provoked by nature, this has been a spiritual place throughout the ages. Native Americans, European settlers, and nineteenth century spiritualists were all drawn to the ledges to conduct their rituals and offer their prayers.

In a place where nature communes with spirit, thin streams of light break through the forest canopy, illuminating the lichens and liverworts. Here, there is no need for stained glass, velvet carpets, white-robed choirs, or dark, wooden pews. All that is needed is the immensity of nature and the music of the wind through the trees, striking accord within the church of the heart.

BLACK ASH SWAMP

A regional name on a Michigan map from the 1800s speaks across the decades about the history of the Black Ash Swamp, an area that covered most of Lenawee County in the southeast corner of Michigan. The same map designates areas of "lowlands and wet swales" throughout the state.

The potential of this great wetland tempted settlers, and farmers joined forces to dig ditches and drain the swamp for farmland. Despite their efforts, the Black Ash Swamp resisted.

Throughout the late 1800s, settlers returned to the Black Ash Swamp and again attempted to claim this wetland, but their labors met with continual disappointment, as the swamp constantly rejuvenated itself with pockets of water. However, the farmers were persistent, and in the early 1900s, they finally overcame the great Black Ash Swamp with the help of a newly introduced piece of machinery, the steam shovel. It changed the face of the wetlands forever.

The Grand Ledges near Lansing

Young lupines near the Kalamazoo
Nature Center

The area near Kalamazoo is part of an outwash of wet prairie and fen known as the Kalamazoo Interlobate. This interlobate—the area between lobes of projecting glacial drift—extends more than 150 miles northward, and is considered the northernmost portion of the prairie peninsula.

Prior to settlement, this was the only extensive region of tallgrass prairie in Michigan. The grasses spread over the flatlands where no natural fire barriers, such as streams or marshes, existed.

above
Wild geraniums bloom in the
Kalamazoo Nature Center

opposite
A blooming flower at Dowagiac
Woods

CHAPTER 4

the
HURON COAST

Moonrise over Lake Huron near
Besser Natural Area

WHEN FRENCH EXPLORERS first came upon the body of water that borders the east side of the Lower Peninsula, they believed it to be a lone sea, and named it *La Mer Douce*, which means "freshwater sea."

The trade carried by the rivers into the lake eventually required the building of trading posts and forts, sawmills and lighthouses. Over time, ships—symbolic vessels of travel and change—replaced birchbark canoes and cedar paddles.

It has been centuries since their passing, centuries since those first French explorers paddled along the coast of *La Mer Douce*. Today, the Lake Huron coast is a juxtaposition of dense wetland habitat and sophisticated port cities. The wetlands support waterfowl and diverse ecosystems, such as the deep sinkholes west of Presque Isle, sacred Ocqueoc Falls, and magical Iargo Springs, whereas the port cities support progress and change.

above
Dusk over Lake Huron

right
Sunset at Sturgeon Point Lighthouse
on Lake Huron

Hartwick Pines State Park

Hartwick Pines State Park

The timber cruiser tugged at his dusty blue cap and wiped his brow. In the approaching peak of autumn, he surveyed the deep forest. In a nearby white pine, an angry bluejay called, catching the woodsman's attention and snapping him out of his daze. He turned and muttered to the bird, and smiled as he dug the heel of his heavy black boot into the soft forest floor and marked it with an X.

He had found "green gold."

Winter fell upon the forest, and with it the arrival of the shanty boys, whistling all the way down the pike. They arrived with rucksacks and eagerness in tow. They were young and strong, and it was their job to harvest the virgin white pine. Soon, the aroma of pine filled their souls as deeply as it filled the crisp winter air. In the daylight, they pulled logs to the riverbanks along sled roads carved wide and flat, and piled up timber along the network of rivers that laced the interior. Back at the lumber camp, the tired and hungry men waited for the sound of the gabriel to cut though the night. Upon the horn's first note, they assembled at long tables to sup on pork and beans.

This was the logging boom of the 1800s. The Michigan interior was filled with tall, straight, virgin pine, and the rivers that crisscrossed the land provided easy transportation to the mills. By 1869, Michigan led the nation in timber production, and it continued to do so for the next three decades. The dollar value of the state's logging industry surpassed that of California's Gold Rush. Throughout the state, timber barons built mansions and towns sprang up near the mills.

One by one the trees fell, and one by one the forests were logged out. By the late 1800s, the boom was over. In 1899, the State Forestry Commission was created to reforest the land. As foresters planted new pine, new woods began to appear, new sentinels of "green gold."

Hartwick Pines State Park includes one of Michigan's last stands of true virgin white pine. The largest state park in the Lower Peninsula, the area includes more than 9,500 acres. The park was donated to the state in 1927 by Karen Hartwick in memory of her late husband, Edward E. Hartwick.

Ocqueoc Falls in Mackinaw State Forest

SACRED WATER

The name of the Ocqueoc River derives from the Anishinaabe Ojibwe word meaning "sacred water." The name rings true, for this river anoints the bedrock with the tumbling water of the Lower Peninsula's only waterfall.

SINKHOLES

Sinkholes lace the ground in the area west of Presque Isle. These examples of "karst" depressions occur when underground water erodes porous limestone and the ground collapses in on the cavity. Some of the sinkholes in this region dive down one hundred feet toward the center of the earth.

When you look down upon a sinkhole, and are eye to eye with the tops of the trees, you begin to realize just how complex life below your feet can be.

Red maple at the Sinkholes in the Pigeon River Country State Forest

Ocqueoc Falls in Mackinaw State Forest

Ice "kegs" float near the shore of Lake Huron, smashing about like tiny boats caught in the icy grip of a winter squall. In the blue shadows of the birch, they clank against each other time and time again.

Here, Lake Huron melts into Saginaw Bay, and there are many shallow areas along the shore. In 1857, a lighthouse, affectionately named Point Aux Barques was built to warn mariners of the potential trouble that waited at the mouth of the bay. Point Aux Barques means "point of the little boats," and refers to the canoes that journeyed into Saginaw Bay during the fur trade era.

Today, the lighthouse still casts its light upon the chilling waters, illuminating the ice packs as they bob up and down, marking the point of the little boats.

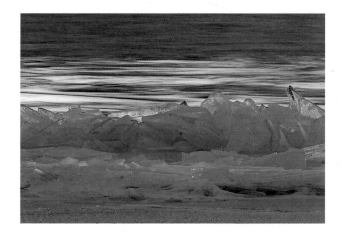

above
Ice stacks up along Lake Huron near Besser Natural Area

left
Point Aux Barques Lighthouse, Bald Eagle Point, Lake Huron

Dew drops cling to a web in the Iargo Springs

Bulrushes along Sturgeon Bay on Lake Huron

Fresh waters magically rise out of the earth at Iargo Springs. The springs are imbedded in a thick forest bottom amongst dewy pines and rocky bluffs blanketed with woolly mosses and lichens.

Iargo, which means "many waters" in Anishinaabe Ojibwe, was a popular gathering place for the Ojibwe for hundreds of years. Beckoned to this mystical resting place by the gentle trickle that feeds into the Au Sable River, they came here to wash, tell stories, repair canoes, and mend souls. With the footsteps of ancestors etched firmly in the ground, Iargo still hums the cadences of those who traveled the Saginaw-Mackinaw Trail.

This is a gentle place, where beads of water seem to cling indefinately to a spider's web, where a fern can uncurl beneath even the spottiest sunlight, and where dew assumes a constant state of being.

Diaphanous beads of dew cling intimately to the fresh strands of an orb weaver's web. The early morning sunlight catches the web and sets it aglow.

There are between five hundred and six hundred kinds of spiders in Michigan. Some, such as the funnel weaver, hang their threads in meadows and other open places. The most distinct webs are those of the orb weaver, *Araneidae*, which create delicate geometric designs cradled within long, silky grasses. In the low, wet areas around the Au Sable River, these talented creatures create layers of webs upon webs, providing a truly spectacular display of function and form.

AU SABLE RIVER

In 1876, the Au Sable River was stocked with wild and hatchery-raised steelhead trout from California and Oregon. By 1903, more than fifty Michigan counties were planting trout fry. Five years later, more than a million fish were being planted each year, and by 1911 that number had doubled. Today, those strains have evolved into the Michigan or Little Manistee trout.

CHAPTER 5

the STRAITS *of* MACKINAC

Mackinac Bridge rises over a grass bay at
Point La Barbe

MANY SOUNDS OF history have been heard in the strait that connects the eastern Great Lakes with Lake Michigan. The Straits of Mackinac have heard the smack of canoe paddles slicing the water in tandem, the heaves of men carrying armfuls of beaver and marten pelts, and the battle cries of Native Americans, French explorers, and British colonists fighting for control of the valuable waterway.

As a crucial passage during America's fur trade era, the Straits of Mackinac was integral to early commerce and settlement. For over two centuries, from the arrival of the French explorers in the 1600s to the mid-1800s when the beaver population dwindled, the struggle of natives versus foreigners resonated throughout this coveted passage.

A meandering stream in Mackinac Island State Park

Mackinac Bridge from Fort
Michilimackinac

Ten red paddles, dipping through the night,
Ten red paddles, slipping into sight.
Ten red paddles, pulling close to shore,
Ten red paddles, soon at rest once more.

The birchbark canoe hit the shore with a muffled scrape, and ten red-capped voyageurs paused their full-throated song as they began to unload bundles of wool blankets and cloth, bags of knives and bullets, and pouches of brilliant glass beads. The early spring air chilled them, and the water that slapped at their bare ankles was bitterly cold.

After unloading, they continued to sing the strains of their *chanson,* "La Claire Fontaine," as they broke into the tobacco pouches that hung from their sashes. The men carried their goods to the entrance of the fort, stopping twice along the way to smoke from their pipes.

The voyageurs had come to Fort Michilimackinac to trade with the natives, making an eager exchange of tools and gunpowder for beaver and marten pelts. If it was a good day and a fair trade, they enjoyed dancing to the fiddler's music, drinking spirits, and exchanging stories about their exploits. And when the firelight faded and the morning sun rose, they would don their deerskin leggings and pull on their shirts. After a quick, hearty breakfast, they would pack their canoe with their newly acquired furs and push off into the mighty lake, pressing onward into a new adventure. Stroke after stroke of their cedar paddles carried them quickly away.

Ten red paddles, slipping out of sight.

The Straits of Mackinac was critical to the development of the fur trade as all water traffic from the eastern Great Lakes had to pass through the channel to reach the Northwest. Of vital importance to the straits was the "great turtle," Mackinac Island, which slept lazily amidst the straits as the large canoes, called *canots du maître,* passed by.

The exchange of furs began in the 1600s with the arrival of the first French explorers. The demand for fur continued to grow, and in 1715, the French built Fort Michilimackinac on the shore of the Lower Peninsula. The fort was used as a meeting place for the Huron, Ottawa, and Ojibwe to trade their beaver pelts for the weapons and beads brought by the French.

By 1781, the fort was controlled by the British, who considered it vulnerable to invasion by Native Americans and the French. The British disassembled Fort Michilimackinac and burned all the remaining buildings. They rebuilt the fort on the bluffs of Mackinac Island. The new fort was strategically placed on one of the highest points of the island, allowing the

Wilderness surrounds Fort Michilimackinac

Duncan Bay at Cheboygan State Park

British greater visibility for monitoring the straits.

In 1796, the fort was claimed by the United States. The British gained control of it again during the War of 1812, but were forced to give it up three years later upon the signing of the Treaty of Ghent, the Treaty of Peace and Amity between His Britannic Majesty and the United States of America. Both parties wanted firm and universal peace, and they agreed that all places and possessions taken during the war would be returned.

The next thirty years saw the real boom in the fur trade on Mackinac Island, with the opening of John Jacob Astor's American Fur Company. The beaver supply soon dwindled, however, and along with it the profitability of the fur trade.

Fishermen had set up shop at Mackinac by the 1830s and were busy packing salted whitefish into barrels and shipping it to Canada and New York. Twenty years later, tourism began to supersede the dwindling fur trade's place on the island and by the mid-1800s, the fur traders were gone, and only stories of the voyageurs remained.

CHEBOYGAN STATE PARK

Coastal fens and marshes exist in shallow depressions near lakeshores, slow-moving ponds atop limestone mud. Brimming with life, these are the wetlands of the dune and swale complexes of northern Lake Huron.

Such wetlands and ponds are some of the world's most biologically productive ecosystems. Among the sedges, nesting waterfowl linger, muskrats slip through the shallows seeking food, and plants root themselves firmly in the muck, where they germinate and thrive.

Over time, some of these marshes may drain and dry out, eventually becoming young forests. Or, depending upon fluctuations in water levels, young vegetation may be overwhelmed by high water and new shorelines could emerge. An ecological system this rich will either evolve from abundance, or digress from the strain of over-productivity.

This raises the question: Is a marsh such as this an inkling of what is to be—or a remnant of what has already been?

Perhaps, like humanity, it is both.

Bulrushes are the ushers of morning. Their resilient stems discreetly capture dawn's first light.

Despite their name, bulrushes, or *Scirpus*, are not true rushes like the soft rush used for mat and basket weaving. They are sedge grasses that thrive in marshy shallows, such as those along the edge of Duncan Bay in Cheboygan State Park.

Fort Michilimackinac

CHAPTER 6

the WILDERNESS

Autumn birches in the Sturgeon
River Gorge

THE WESTERN HALF of Michigan's Upper Peninsula is a geological story of a paradise conceived in layers. The rocks and precipices of the Michigan wilderness are the relics of massive glaciers that carved mountainous gorges and craggy waterfalls, of prehistoric volcanic eruptions that left behind rugged hills and escarpments. It is a land so wild and intimidating that it has remained almost unspoiled in the face of progress and development. State parks, national forests, and designated wilderness areas abound in this place of breathtaking wildlife, virgin forests, and cliff-lined river gorges.

above
Laughing Whitefish Falls State Scenic Area

opposite
Blazing red autumn leaf

Presque Isle Park, Marquette

The Black Rocks at the northern end of Presque Isle are some of the oldest exposed rocks on the continent. The Precambrian bedrock exhibits a diverse array of shale, gneiss, quartzite, and other types of volcanic and sedimentary bedrock.

Thin soil tops most knobs of bedrock, providing a footing for white and red pine. Lower areas with richer soils are able to support northern hardwoods.

Shoreline along Presque Isle Park in Marquette

SYLVANIA WILDERNESS AREA

A tranquil morning on a cedar-lined lake in the Sylvania Wilderness Area at Ottawa National Forest speaks many truths, tells many tales. Canoe paddles slice through glassy waters, and common loons cry for their mates from shore.

The area is comprised of more than 18,000 acres of primitive wilderness. Nearly all the inland lakes that fill the area are landlocked, fed only by bogs, springs, or healthy rains. A virgin forest traversed by black bear and moose, it embraces hundreds of lakes that comprise Sylvania Wilderness Area and the nearby Cisco chain of lakes. This area possesses a network of more than 4,000 acres of water and twenty-five portages connecting twenty-nine lakes. Indeed, Sylvania is a place for listening, watching and believing.

Wild iris on Cloverleaf Lake in the Sylvania Recreation Area

PRESQUE ISLE RIVER

When the water of the wild and scenic Presque Isle River is high, it cascades through a series of falls and fissures located near its mouth, leading into Lake Superior. Named after Ojibwe spirit warriors such as Nawadaha, Manido, and Manabezho, the waters move with dauntless rhythm, as if performing a high-spirited dance for a deity of nature. And maybe they are.

The rocks in the riverbed cavort with the river, taunting and teasing the water until it roils up into a vicious lather. Only where the river feeds into the depths of Lake Superior does it become calm, joining other big waters in a common, inanimate way.

above
Manabezho Falls, Porcupine Mountain Wilderness State Park

overleaf
Scott Falls near Munising

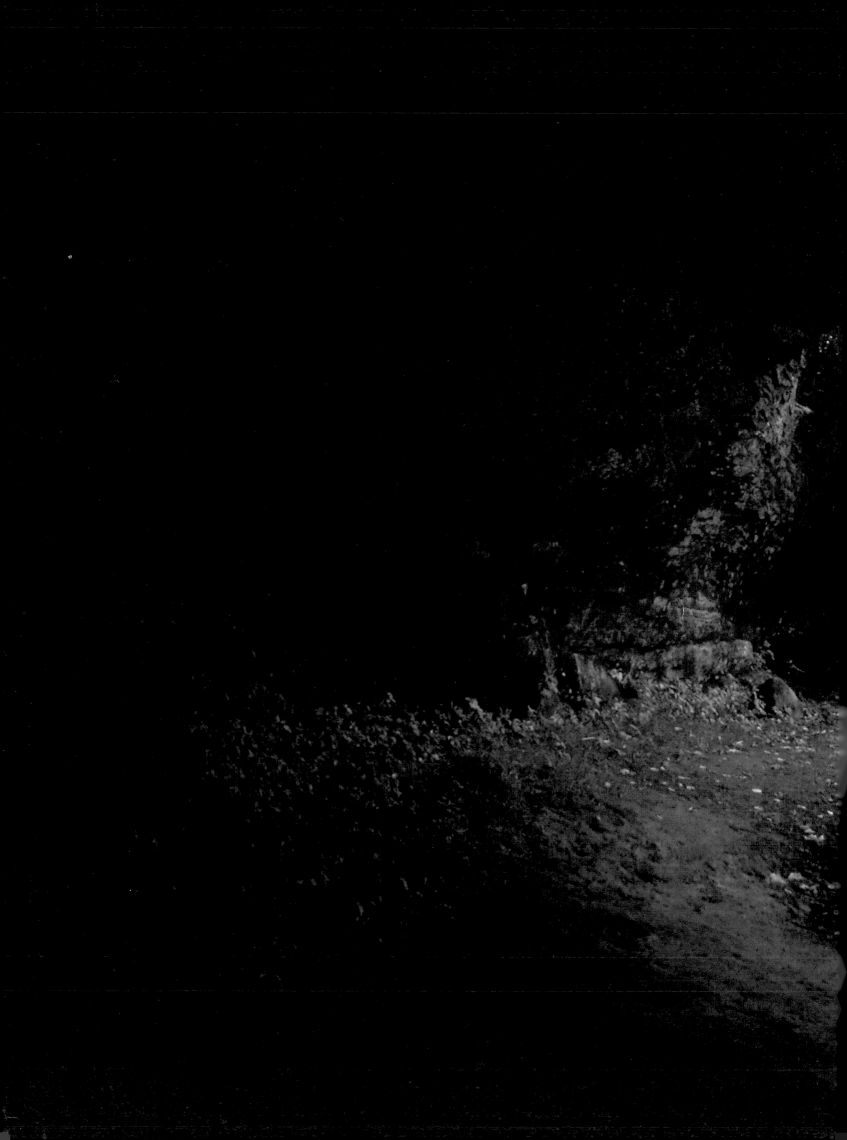

The Ojibwe called this place *Kaugabissing*, or "place of the porcupine," when they first described a vast wilderness area along the southern shore of Lake Superior.

The rugged terrain was massaged and developed over millions of years. Divergent rocks of the area—hard, erosion-resistant conglomerates and soft, erodable lavas—paired together to form a series of steep, hardened ridges and low wetland areas. In the Lake Superior region, most Keweenawan rock is sandstone, silstone, or shale, as well as some conglomerates and lava flows.

The ridges formed by Keweenawan basalt and other conglomerates appeared to resemble the spiny back of a porcupine—and they proved to act like one, too. In the 1800s, when most Michigan forests were logged, this region escaped the fall of the ax because the terrain was much too rugged for cutting and hauling.

In 1945, the Porcupine Mountain Wilderness State Park was established to protect the more than 60,000 acres of towering maple, pine, and hemlock trees tucked neatly into the interior of its bedrock ridges.

Lake of the Clouds, Porcupine
Mountain Wilderness State Park

The past is preserved in the smoothing of stones and the rounding of rocks. Through centuries of water passing over these shores and riverbanks or through the erosion of exposed beaches and cliffs, the story of time exists in the mad encounters of water upon land.

Nowhere is this story of water and stone more apparent than amidst the steep hillsides of sugar maple and pine in the Sturgeon River Gorge, where the waters of the Sturgeon River have left their ancient imprint. Gentle ponds and terraces give way to shale-lined oxbows and rushing falls, while the Sturgeon River weaves gingerly between them. In some places, the river has applied strength greater than modern machinery, cutting gorges hundreds of feet deep. In other areas, gentle trickles of water have delicately etched the stone with the precision of a fine jeweler. Throughout the river-bed, plates of shale and igneous rock are left stacked upon the tree-lined banks, leaving bold clues to the dramatic fluctuations of water and force.

The Sturgeon River and its main tributary, the Little Silver River, provide more than deep canyons and volcanic outcroppings. The hard-edged cliffs and perfectly smooth stones provide proof that we live in an ever-changing world, and will continue to do so as long as there is rock and as long as there is water.

A cedar and birch twisted together
along the Sturgeon River

A cedar tree clings to the edge of the
Sturgeon River Gorge

Sturgeon River

The Marquette Harbor Light was established in 1853, and it still brightens the dark waters of Lake Superior today. The lighthouse, made of the architectural design called "square" or "integral brick" construction, is now an active Coast Guard station.

The lake it illuminates is the deepest and coldest of the Great Lakes. It was once called *Le Lac Supérieur* by French explorers, which means "the upper lake."

ISLE ROYALE NATIONAL PARK

One frozen night in 1949, a small pack of gray wolves dared to cross a rare natural ice bridge leading out of Canada and spanning a channel of Lake Superior to enter the unspoiled wilderness area called Isle Royale National Park.

Before that night, no known wolf packs inhabited Isle Royale. This group may have crossed in search of lost pack mates or in pursuit of the island's thick supply of moose. Whatever the reason, amidst a dark boreal forest, the straying, immigrant pack established future packs, and their survival on the island has been the subject of intense study ever since.

An island wild and free, the area was created over millions of years. More than a billion years ago, there was a rift in the earth's crust that extended south to the Gulf of Mexico. Molten lava oozed from the cracks and the area nearest the rift zone dropped to form the Superior Basin. The telltale signs of volcanic rocks and sandstones form the island's bedrock to this day. A few thousand years ago, the last glacier retreated in an event known as the Wisconsinan, which carved hilly grooves and curves throughout the terrain.

A combination of lakes, bogs, and primitive forests, the island is burdened with balancing old and new forest growth. The relationship between the wolves and the island's other inhabitants, especially the moose, marks the balance of the island's food chain.

Beneath an icy winter sky, dusky wolf calls ring freely through the night in bone-chilling songs that give fodder to those who believe in the wolves of fables and fairy tales. These wolves are real, however, and they have marked their territory on an island that is accessible to humans only by boat or seaplane.

Marquette Lighthouse

Chapter 7

the KEWEENAW

Sandstone shores along the Keweenaw Peninsula

THE KEWEENAW PENINSULA, jutting out into Lake Superior from Michigan's Upper Peninsula, bespeaks a colorful past tinged with the cornucopia of autumn hues in virgin forests, the luster of copper extracted from the earth, and the delicate shades of rare orchids on mountaintops. The peninsula, surrounded on three sides by the coldest and deepest of the Great Lakes, is marked with pathways created by indigenous peoples and voyageurs hundreds of years ago, by mines dug by copper harvesters a century ago, and the road laid by workers on Brockway Mountain during the Great Depression. Within its watery boundaries, the Keweenaw Peninsula explodes in monumental beauty and peerless history.

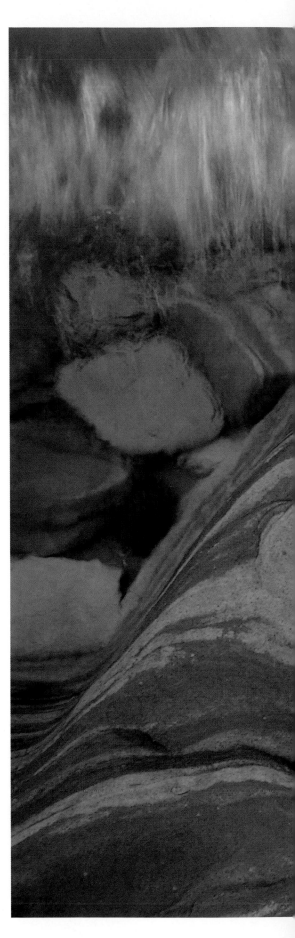

above
A stone rests along the Keweenaw's
Lake Superior shoreline

right
Lake Superior caresses the stones
along the Keweenaw Peninsula

Estivant Pines in autumn splendor

French explorer Pierre Esprit Radisson, a fur trader whose knowledge of the fur trade led to the creation of the Hudson Bay Company, traversed the Keweenaw Peninsula in the seventeenth century seeking an inland North-west Passage. He wrote in his journal of well-marked trails, and in his 1660s narrative, he described forests filled with the footsteps of "comers and goers." He based his stories on well-worn paths that he believed had been created by the earliest voyageurs and native peoples as they portaged the peninsula. Crossing the peninsula offered a shorter route, as well as a place to rest.

Traces of these paths can still be found in the deep forests of the peninsula—paths that wind between trees, paths that disappear beneath pine needles, and reappear by overturned tree trunks. Paths created by simple shoes with tightly puckered seams. Paths plodded upon by thick leather boots. Pathways through time made by the deliberate footsteps of "comers and goers."

Some trees in the Keweenaw Peninsula are more than five hundred years old. Only twenty-seven years ago, these two hundred acres of virgin white pine were threatened with logging. In response to these threats, the Michigan Nature Association claimed these acres as the Estivant Pines Sanctuary. With the help of people throughout the state, the logger's efforts were blocked. Today, this preserved congregation of white pine, red oak, tamarack, and spruce trees serves as a sentinel of Michigan's verdant past.

Pine needles and leaves in Estivant Pines

Lighthouses pepper the perimeter of the Keweenaw Peninsula. This outcropping of land and its rocky shoals posed an enormous threat to mariners during the peak of the Great Lakes shipping era. When the Soo Locks opened in 1855, congestion on Lake Superior was common as large vessels made their way west to port cities in Michigan, Wisconsin, and Minnesota. During that time, at least ten lighthouses were operating along the shore of the peninsula.

Some of the lighthouses have been deactivated and preserved as museums; others have been converted to private residences. Some, such as the Gull Rock Light or the Manitou Light, are still in use by the Coast Guard, although they have been automated. The Gull Rock Light, which consists of a brick tower with a schoolhouse-type building once used as the lightkeeper's residence, sits out on an island and is now run by solar power.

above
Copper Harbor lighthouse

right
Gull Island lighthouse

The miners were tunneling straight into the belly of mother earth. They labored in deep and narrow mine shafts—thin, dark passages cut through the soil and rock hundreds of feet below the surface and illuminated only by candlelight. These immigrants to the Keweenaw Peninsula were breaking open the crust of the earth in search of copper ore.

The miners had been drawn to the Keweenaw because the shore of Lake Superior was rumored to house a massive vein of native copper far below the sandstone and shale shields of its Precambrian crust. There were no roads on Keweenaw Peninsula when the copper rush began in the 1840s, and most of the men arrived by boat.

The rumors of copper were correct. The Keweenaw region was mineral rich—and remains so still. Native copper deposits are embedded in the volcanic and sedimentary rocks created during Late Precambrian era. The Portage Lake Lava Flow, which contains several important host rocks, is mostly comprised of basaltic lava flows, some of which are nearly 1,500 feet thick. These complex underground structures are filled with vast minefields of copper ore.

With callused hands and aching shoulders, the miners harvested the red ore, working decade after decade from dawn to dusk, deep beneath the ground where the sun never shined. Along the interior of the peninsula, they opened up one mine after another. They ate, they worked, they laughed. They slept in ramshackle bunkhouses with dirt floors, and washed their grit-covered faces in drafty bathhouses.

They also built communities and began families. Square saltbox houses replaced the first tarpaper shacks, towns emerged, ships came to transport the ore, and lighthouses were built to guide the ships. The population soared, as did the spirits of the people. From 1845 to 1929, the jagged outcropping of land known as the Keweenaw produced more than 8 billion pounds of copper, making Michigan the second largest copper producer in the world.

The boom of the copper mining era lasted from the 1840s to the 1960s. Eventually, some mines lost profits, while others suffered inhumane disasters. Mines shut down, families moved on, and merchants closed their doors. The hearts of the miners, much like the veins of red ore that once laced the earth, were left empty and scarred forever.

Today on the Keweenaw Peninsula, amidst the glistening shores, thick virgin forests, and music of waterfalls, more copper waits. It remains beneath the ground, dripping wet, deep within the belly of the earth.

The 1800s were not the first time that the mineral-stocked netherworlds of the peninsula revealed its richness. Between 5000 and 1200 BC, the Keweenaw was home to an ancient people whose existence and disappearance remain a great mystery. No burial grounds have been discovered, no tablets or cave drawings have been unearthed to provide details about their lives.

What stories can be pieced together about these people come from the remnants of ancient copper pits and hammering stones used to mine them. It has been suggested that these people worked the rock by alternating fire with cold water to break the copper ore into small pieces. They would then extract the copper with hand-held stones, and use the metal to make tools such as axes and knives.

Lake Bailey shrouded in fog near the Brockway Mountains

Geese flying across Brockway
Mountain

Autumn displays itself along
Brockway Mountain

Brockway Mountain is an ancient protrusion of rock that has somehow, with enduring patience, deliberately linked the earth to the sky.

Brockway is the highest point between the Alleghenies and the Rockies, and one of our nation's oldest mountains. It is the backbone of the Keweenaw Peninsula, which is a portion of a failed continental rift system nearly 1.2 billion years old. It crowns the Upper Peninsula, gazing out over ancient pines and hardwoods scattered across a vast hillside overlooking Lake Superior. During their autumn migration, hawks and eagles soar gallantly off the cliffs of the mountain, catching air currents that catapult them high into the sky.

Nearly 10,000 years ago, during the retreat of the last ice age, this mountain cut a migrating glacier in two. The mountain was taller than the glacier, and the glacier cracked around it, protecting the mountain's highest points from the enormous ice sheet's scouring, thereby saving rare and unusual plants from extinction. Today, among the forest's dark and lovely pathways, you can still find ancestors of those plants in the form of rare and elegant orchids.

The slender, curving road that winds over Brockway Mountain was constructed during a Great Depression–era "make-work" project. Jobless miners and loggers carved their way through the hillside, building a road and white guard posts to mark it.

Did these workers marvel at the birds overhead or the unusual flowers sprouting around them? Did they gasp with wonder as they reached the peak of the mountain and looked down upon the pristine wilderness?

One can only hope.

the NORTH COUNTRY

Wagner Falls near Munising

MICHIGAN'S NORTH COUNTRY sprawls across the rugged Lake Superior shore- line and the inner needleleaf forests of the eastern half of the Upper Penin- sula. Sailors have been shipwrecked at Whitefish Point, and native tribes have triumphed and been defeated at Iroquois Point. But it is also a place of pathways that lead to calm and shady places, rivers that shift between tu- mult and rest, and the madcap richness of colorful sandstone cliffs at Pic- tured Rocks National Lakeshore.

above
Agates at Whitefish Point on Lake Superior

opposite
Chapel Rock pillars, Pictured Rocks National Lakeshore

An Edmund Fitzgerald memorial for one of the many brave seaman

"We're holding our own."

    The words floated over the Coast Guard radio.

    Then silence.

    Those were the last words heard from Captain Ernest McSorley as he fought to save the *Edmund Fitzgerald* and the lives of his twenty-eight men.

    The *Edmund Fitzgerald* plunged to the depths of Lake Superior on a cold, gray day in November 1975. Bearing the title "The Pride of the American Flag," the ship was on course to Detroit when she fell into a violent storm and huge waves overtook her deck. The wreck was catastrophic, the fatalities gripping.

    For many years, the eighty-mile stretch of shoreline at Whitefish Point on Lake Superior has been known as the "Graveyard of the Great Lakes." Filled with shallow shoals and tumultuous waters, the area has been responsible for numerous shipwrecks. But even more feared than the rocky shoals are the murderous winds that roil up over two hundred miles of open water, blasting away at the lake's surface to create mammoth waves and blinding conditions.

    In remembrance of lost sailors, the shoreline at Whitefish Point is dotted with makeshift headstones of rocks and photographs—raw reminders that the lake has taken more than 320 known sailors and uncounted voyageurs, explorers, and Native Americans.

    The Ojibwe have a name for Lake Superior: *Gitche Gumee*, or "Big Sea." Standing on the shores of these waters, this *Gitche Gumee*, it is not hard to comprehend the imbalance of power between humans and Nature.

top
Whitefish Point Lighthouse

bottom
Storm clouds create a light show over Whitefish Bay

Waves crash along an old pier at Whitefish Point

Enormous icicles hang like crystal shards, decorating the gorge of Munising Falls. In spring, the area around Munising Bay explodes with the sound of water rushing through Wagner, Chapel, Laughing Whitefish, Miners, and Rock River Falls. In the hard, cold depths of winter, however, we can hear another sound—the low, quiet popping of ice as it expands and shrinks through the depths of winter.

Both of these seasonal sounds are the truest music of the waterfalls, separate movements in an ongoing symphony.

The moist, wet forests of the Munising area are healthy environments for hardwoods such as the Yellow Birch, which becomes silvery yellow as it ages. As it grows, its trunk expands, breaking the bark into narrow strips that curl at the edges. The older the birch, the more deeply and irregularly fissured its wrap becomes.

The Yellow Birch, or *Betulaceae*, thrives in mesic and mixed hardwood forests and poorly drained sites, where seedlings establish themselves in biologically healthy places like mineral soil, rotted logs, and decaying tree stumps.

Munising Creek's frozen waterfall

opposite
Wagner Falls

Pine roots reaching from Chapel
Rock, Pictured Rocks

Chapel River flowing into Lake
Superior, Pictured Rocks

The first travelers to make their way along the southern shore of Lake Superior must have been astonished when they caught sight of what is now called the Pictured Rocks National Lakeshore. They may have deemed this a place worthy of worship, or simply been stunned by this displace of nature's beauty.

This place of puzzling magnificence was created by fantastic forces. As the last glacier retreated 10,000 years ago, its weight lessened, and the land beneath it rose, exposing vulnerable bedrock to erosion. The newly created lake battered the bedrock, sculpting cliffs, ramparts, and precipices in every direction. The power of its onslaught enlarged the lake and magnified the disarray of the shoreline. Its arches, jagged profiles, and irregular caverns remain as evidence of this massive scouring.

The name "pictured rocks" alludes to the brilliant colors of the cliffs— the result of mineralized water oozing out between cracks in the stone, staining the faces of the cliffs with the casts of copper, manganese, and iron.

These cliffs are composed of sandstone that dates back at least 500 million years. It is part of the Munising Formation, a series of light gray to pink-gray rock that lies above the Jacobsville Formation, a mottled red sandstone that is nearest to lake level. The entire formation is protected by the Ordovician Au Train Formation, a hard, limy sandstone that acts as a cap, sheltering the softer, underlying sandstone from washing away amidst the continuous battering of waves.

In 1957 and 1958, the National Park Service surveyed more than 5,500 miles of Great Lakes shoreline for incorporation into the National Park system. The Pictured Rocks of Alger County, by the distinction of its unparalleled features, was named as a potential candidate.

Nearly ten years later, in 1966, Congress passed a law to establish the Pictured Rocks National Lakeshore, and when President Lyndon B. Johnson signed the law, these forty-three miles of Lake Superior shoreline became America's first National Lakeshore.

right, top
Grand Portal Point, Pictured Rocks

right, bottom
Chapel River, Pictured Rocks

Shoreline erosion at the mouth of
the Mosquito River

Spider webs at dawn, Seney National
Wildlife Refuge

Seney National Wildlife Refuge

During the late 1800s, nearly 95,000 acres of the Great Manistique Swamp in the middle of the Upper Peninsula was burned by loggers in an effort to clean up after "The Big Cut"—the term for the logging that destroyed most of Michigan's forests. Land speculators then sold off plots of this land sight unseen to farmers who were rarely able to cultivate a single crop from this thick, marshy swamp. Many of them had to forfeit their useless parcels to the government for nonpayment of taxes, and eventually, all the land reverted to the government.

In 1935, the area was named the Seney National Wildlife Refuge. That year, the Civilian Conservation Corporation built a series of manually controlled dikes and pools, creating permanent marshes filled with bulrushes and duckweed, an ideal habitat for nesting waterfowl. Today, the refuge is home to more than two hundred species of birds and more than fifty types of mammals.

Loons are common at Seney, and in the past ten years, they have begun nesting throughout the refuge. In early May, the male loon returns from winter migration along the Atlantic and Gulf coasts and awaits his female partner, who arrives shortly thereafter. They court, then build a nest near the water's edge. Both parents incubate the nest, waiting patiently for the chicks to hatch.

After the chicks arrive in mid-June or July, they are guided by their parents to a small, shallow, secluded spot of water near the shoreline, a loon's "nursery." In this calm, covert area, the parents teach their young how to swim and find food.

Sunrise and sunset is the best time for spotting winged residents such as loons, herons, and geese or for watching the shadows of the tamaracks as they melt into the cattail-edged bogs. In these quiet hours, as the wetland songbirds perch in the bulrushes, Seney becomes not only a haven for waterfowl, but for people, as well.

"In the solitary forest, By the rushing Taquamenaw"

Hush now, make no sound.

Hear his solid footsteps crush the forest floor. Listen to his thunderous hands rattle balsam and cedar. Slow your thoughts, hush your spirit. Blowing through the forest lush, Hiawatha is on the move.

In his 1855 epic poem *The Song of Hiawatha*, Henry Wadsworth Longfellow places the magical demi-god Hiawatha along the shores of the Tahquamenon River. Longfellow describes how the mythical character built his ghostly canoe from the birch, cedar, and tamarack found along the banks of the mighty river.

> *My canoe to bind together*
> *So to bind the ends together*
> *That the water may not enter*
> *That the river may not wet me*

Along those banks in a forest thick and soft, Hiawatha built his canoe with tears of balsam and the resin of firs.

> *all the toughness of the cedar*
> *all the larch's supple sinews*
> *and it floated on the river*
> *Like a yellow leaf in Autumn*
> *Like a yellow water-lily.*

As his canoe was bound and sealed, he readied himself for his journey. Hiawatha needed no paddle; he was certain his thoughts could glide him to the left or right as he wished. So he steadied himself and appealed to his friend Kwasind, who was the strongest man of all, asking him to use his magical strength to clear the river. And so the mighty Kwasind dove into the river and pulled away sunken logs and branches so Hiawatha could float swiftly upon the Taquamenaw.

Upper falls, Tahquamenon State Park

And thus sailed my Hiawatha
Down the rushing Taquamenaw
Sailed through all its bends and windings,
sailed through all its deeps and shallows

The Tahquamenon River has long been an attraction for the believers of mystical and magical events. Its tannin-stained waters gush over waterfalls as large as two hundred feet across and nearly fifty feet deep, draining a watershed of more than 820 square miles. As the ninety-four-mile-long river spills into Lake Superior's Whitefish Bay, it carries with it the dreams of the voyageurs who plied it, the sweat of the lumbermen who bathed in it, and the musings of Hiawatha, who sailed quickly and gently upon it.

Steps up to the light

This is the place of the Iroquois bones.

During the 1600s, rivers and waterways were invaluable trade routes, and the livelihood of many societies, indigenous and immigrant alike, were dependent upon them.

The Ojibwe lived near the Saint Mary's River. Here, they would hunt and fish and trade furs with the French. In 1662, the British, in an attempt to take control of the Saint Mary's River, allied with the Iroquois, who were trying to displace the Ojibwe tribes from these desirable hunting grounds.

High on the hill now known as Iroquois Mountain, a lone Ojibwe spotted the advancing Iroquois war party just hours away. He warned his village, rallied the support of neighboring villages, and the Ojibwe fled into the forest to prepare a surprise attack for the invading Iroquois. When the last war cry was heard, the Ojibwe were victorious, and the Iroquois dead lay scattered across the forest floor.

Iroquois Point lighthouse

WHITEFISH BAY

The sandy lake plain of Whitefish Bay forms a broad zone that is character-ized by pockets of drained sand soils. Near Whitefish Point and along the thirty-four-mile-wide bay, hundreds of complex swales and spits provide a contour atypical of most Lake Superior shoreline.

Autumn edges up to Whitefish Bay near Iroquois Point

127

top
Blowing dune grasses, Grand Sable Dunes

bottom
Grand Sable Dunes

Souffle, souffle, la vieille!

Blow, Old Woman, blow!

The red-capped voyageurs chanted heartily to the "Old Woman of the Wind" as they passed Au Sable Point.

Souffle, souffle, la vieille!

Au Sable Point was known for its dangerous reef, a Jacobsville Sandstone Formation that in some spots is only several feet below the water's surface. As early as the 1600s, stories about the perilous point were passed from one explorer to the next.

Along this waterway, voyageurs threw handfuls of glass beads and tobacco into the water to appease the Old Woman of the Wind. They would hoist simple sails in the middle of their canoes and call on the Old Woman to conjure up tremendous winds, in the hope of quickly and safely being blown past the treacherous Au Sable Point.

It wasn't an easy task.

When the warm air from the Grand Sable Dunes mixed with the cold Lake Superior wind, a thick shroud of fog engulfed the rocky shoreline. The voyageurs' light canoes often banged against the rocky outcroppings and precipices, lost amidst the blanket of gray.

Souffle, souffle, la vieille! they chanted, and handfuls of beads were scattered upon the water.

In 1872, more than two hundred years later, Congress appropriated funds to build Big Sable Light Station, now referred to as Au Sable Light. The area between Whitefish Point and Grand Island—the most dreaded stretch of shoreline on Lake Superior—was finally illuminated to ensure safe passage.

And perhaps, at the bottom of the lake sits the Old Woman of the Wind admiring her baskets of beads and tobacco smiling at the underbellies of the modern passersby.

Grand Sable Dunes, Pictured Rocks National Lakeshore

Chapter 9

the HISTORIC SOUTH COAST

Boulders along one of the Les Cheneaux
Islands' shorelines

T HE SOUTH COAST of Michigan's upper peninsula bears the imprint of the European explorers who made their way west through the straits from Lake Huron to Lake Michigan. The travelers who followed the south coast discovered quiet coves and peaceful resting stops. Lighthouses were built at key points to shine their far-reaching rays over the most treacherous waterways.

The Upper Peninsula's south coast is defined by a mellowness that comes from harboring a mostly navigable shoreline, a huge percolating spring in Palms Book State Park called Kitch-iti-kipi, and the quiet ghost town of a once-thriving iron company.

Point Peninsula, Little Bay De Noc, Lake Michigan

In the small town of Hessel, there is a Native American cemetery that is named for Father Jacques Marquette. The Father established a mission on Mackinac Island in 1669, but in 1671, he moved it to St. Ignace, not far from present-day Hessel.

Small white crosses dot the grass—tributes to deceased sisters, brothers, mothers, fathers, and loved ones. The cemetery was named after Marquette in honor of his work and dedication to the people of the area. The Father made the shore of Lake Huron his home for two years; the effects of his life and work will be apparent for much longer.

Father Marquette Indian Cemetery
near Hessel

Les Cheneaux Islands shoreline

Infinity is a concept easily grasped by children and old people, because youngsters have not yet found reason not to believe, and seasoned folks have every reason to believe.

But infinity is more than believing in forever. It is also believing in the power of the impossible. It can be found in a moment spent beneath towering pines and hemlocks, as you lay on your back and try to count the number of times the branches intersect, or wonder how huge boulders were scattered along a sandy shoreline thousands of years ago.

Huge limestone boulders line the beaches of northern Lake Huron. They are scattered randomly throughout the embayments that mark a set of thirty-six islands known as Les Cheneaux Islands. *Les Cheneaux* is French for "the channels"—an apt name for the maze of islands and narrow waterways created by the rocky outcroppings of limestone and sand.

The series of sheltered bays and coves within the narrow channels and shoreline gives excellent protection from harsh wave action, resulting in healthy marsh zones.

Looking across the bay to Fayette Village

On a cold, quiet day in February 1867, Fayette Brown, manager of the Jackson Iron Company, arrived at Snail Shell Harbor along the Garden Peninsula. Brown analyzed the deep, well-protected harbor that gave way to the exposed dolomite cliffs of the Niagaran Escarpment, a prominent ridge that arcs across the Great Lakes Region from the Niagara River to northern Michigan. He studied the dry, linear beach ridges that supported thick stands of maple and beech.

Brown liked what he saw. He knew that the success of the Jackson Iron Company's pig iron smelting operation would be dependent upon the natural resources of the area. The limestone cliffs offered quarry for flux, an ingredient needed for the furnace-blasting process; the hardwoods would produce fuel; and the deep, protected harbor would provide good docking for ships. And so, in the bosom of the shore, an early Midwest company town, known as Fayette Village, emerged.

Small, wood-frame homes were built to house the immigrant laborers and their families. Wives of Irishmen, Scandinavians, Belgians, and French Canadians bought calico and supplies at the company store and made dresses for special outings to the company Opera House. Men joined the company baseball team, and their children were taught at the company schoolhouse. Soon the town swelled to a population of five hundred, and amidst the choke of the beehive furnaces, they shared the common goal of ensuring that Fayette Village would become a leader in iron production.

As they harvested the earth, the nation's need for iron remained insatiable, inspiring competition. Better-quality coke iron and steel penetrated the market from the eastern states. Eventually, Fayette found its process becoming antiquated, its costs rising, and its profits shrinking. By the end of 1891, after producing nearly 230,000 tons of iron, the Jackson Iron Company closed its doors.

Today, a mere ghost of Fayette Village remains. But if you listen carefully, you may hear the voices of the workers echoing through the narrow halls of town buildings and the footsteps of their wives and children marking time upon the floorboards of the company store.

Fayette Village Historic Site State
Park

Limestone boulders on Lake Michigan's shore in Fayette State Park

The limestone shores of Sandy Lake Plain represent the northern shore of Lake Michigan. Over time, the lake has created rolling dunes and embayments that support a variety of hardwoods and rare plants. The Niagaran Escarpment, formed of dolomite and Silurian limestone, exposes itself as limestone cliffs along the shoreline.

Waves crash along Lake Michigan's limestone shores

Warm morning light melts into the iris of Kitch-iti-kipi, scattering brilliant green hues along the surface of the spring. The light is quickly absorbed by the pool reflecting downward to its depths—the bright, clear depths—which are marbled with brown, dusky trout.

Eerie and unflinching, the soft bottom of the pool percolates more than 10,000 gallons of temperate water per minute through the limestone fissures that underly Palms Book State Park. Meanwhile, the surface water remains motionless, flickering like a cat's eye caught in the light.

Kitch-iti-kipi is Anishinaabe for "big springs," and it is Michigan's largest natural spring. Located in the southwestern part of the Upper Peninsula, the water from the two hundred-foot-wide pool leads gently into Indian Lake, which eventually flows into the Manistique River.

However, the real underpinnings of activity occur far beneath the surface of the spring where trout play and mud spins feverishly, driven by the hydraulic pressure of the spring. Beautiful and mysterious, this is a perfect dance between motion and calm, a tango of sorts, and it is observed only by the damp, heavy pines and tamaracks that rest along the edges, nodding with approval.

HISTORIC SOUTH COAST

In 1634, Jean Nicolet and seven Huron braves passed westward through the Straits of Mackinac. Their quest—or so it seemed—was to find a northwest passage to the Pacific Ocean.

As an agent of the Company of New France, Nicolet had learned the native languages of the Algonquin and Huron people, and was engaged to travel west to find the "people of the sea."

As he passed through the straits, could he have guessed what new discoveries would unfold before him? As he plied the waters of the straits and discovered Lake Michigan, who—watching, listening—was standing upon the dense, wet ground that surrounds the straits? Who was crouching in the rushes and weeds of these northern wetlands?

We will never know, but we do know that voyage unveiled the ample supply of fur-bearing animals, and Nicolet reported back to New France of the animals' abundance, initiating decades of trade and exploration.

Nicolet and the seven Huron braves passed uneventfully through the straits and across Lake Michigan, but for the land that lay around them, urging them on as they passed, change was in the air.

Early winter Tamaracks, Kitch-iti-
kipi Spring

ABOUT THE AUTHOR AND PHOTOGRAPHER

Kathy-jo Wargin is the author of Michigan's Official State Children's Book, *The Legend of Sleeping Bear*, as well as *The Legend of Mackinac Island* and *Scenic Driving Michigan*.

Her love of the outdoors began amidst the forests and lakes of northern Minnesota, and has inspired her to share those experiences through vivid descriptions and poetic stories about nature.

With more than a decade of experience as a professional writer, she also conducts workshops, writing seminars, and educational programs for children and adults. She resides in the Great Lakes area with her husband Ed and son Jake.

Ed Wargin pursued a career in photography out of his love for being outdoors. As a location photographer, he has spent the past ten years shooting assignments for commercial clients such as GMC Trucks, Caterpillar, Anheuser-Busch Inc., Arctic Cat Inc., and OMC; for his photography stock agency Fresh Coast Images and other agencies such as Corbis Inc. and AgStock USA; and for book publishers and fine art print customers.

Born and raised in Duluth, Minnesota, he learned his craft by photographing the many moods of the Great Lakes, inspired continually by its ever-changing light. It was this experience that led him to capture the nuances and details of his surroundings, specializing in crafting his images with natural light.

Photos © Mike Burian

144